JENSEN INTERCEPTOR

Gold Portfolio

1966-1986

Compiled by
R.M. Clarke

ISBN 1 869826 035

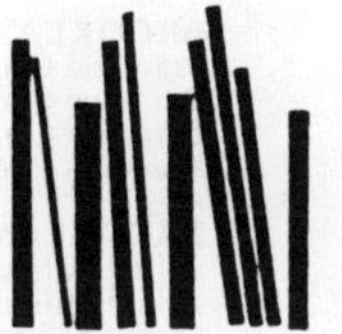

Distributed by
Brooklands Book Distribution Ltd.
'Holmerise', Seven Hills Road,
Cobham, Surrey, England

BROOKLANDS BOOKS SERIES
AC Ace & Aceca 1953-1983
AC Cobra 1962-1969
Alfa Romeo Giulia Coupés 1963-1976
Alfa Romeo Spider 1966-1981
Aston Martin Gold Portfolio 1972-1985
Austin Seven 1922-1982
Austin A30 & A35 1951-1962
Austin Healey 100 1952-1959
Austin Healey 3000 1959-1967
Austin Healey 100 & 3000 Collection No. 1
Austin Healey 'Frogeye' Sprite Collection No. 1
Austin Healey Sprite 1958-1971
Avanti 1962-1983
BMW Six Cylinder Coupés 1969-1975
BMW 1600 Collection No. 1
BMW 2002 1968-1976
Bristol Cars Gold Portfolio 1946-1985
Buick Riviera 1963-1978
Cadillac Eldorado 1967-1978
Cadillac in the Sixties No. 1
Camaro 1966-1970
Chevrolet Camaro Collection No. 1
Chevelle & SS 1964-1972
Chevy II Nova & SS 1962-1973
Chrysler 300 1955-1970
Citroen Traction Avant 1934-1957
Citroen 2CV 1949-1982
Cobras & Replicas 1969-1983
Cortina 1600E & GT 1967-1970
Corvair 1959-1968
Daimler Dart & V-8 250 1959-1969
Datsun 240z & 260z 1970-1977
De Tomaso Collection No. 1
Dodge Charger 1966-1974
Excalibur Collection No. 1
Ferrari Cars 1946-1956
Ferrari Cars 1962-1966
Ferrari Cars 1969-1973
Ferrari Dino 1965-1974
Ferrari Dino 308 1974-1979
Ferrari 308 & Mondial 1980-1984
Ferrari Collection No. 1
Fiat X1/9 1972-1980
Ford Falcon 1960-1970
Ford GT40 1964-1978
Ford Mustang 1964-1967
Ford Mustang 1967-1973
Ford RS Escort 1968-1980
High Performance Escorts MkI 1968-1974
High Performance Escorts MkII 1975-1980
Hudson & Railton Cars 1936-1940
Jaguar (& S.S) Cars 1931-1937
Jaguar Cars 1948-1951
Jaguar Cars 1957-1961
Jaguar Cars 1961-1964
Jaguar Cars 1964-1968
Jaguar E-Type 1961-1966
Jaguar E-Type 1966-1971
Jaguar E-Type 1971-1975
Jaguar XKE Collection No. 1
Jaguar XJ6 1968-1972
Jaguar XJ6 Series II 1973-1979
Jaguar XJ6 & XJ12 Series III 1979-1985
Jaguar XJ12 1972-1980
Jaguar XJS 1975-1980
Jensen Cars 1946-1967
Jensen Cars 1967-1979
Jensen Interceptor Gold Portfolio 1966-1986
Jensen-Healey 1972-1976
Lamborghini Cars 1964-1970
Lamborghini Cars 1970-1975
Lamborghini Countach Collection No. 1
Lamborghini Countach & Urraco 1974-1980
Lamborghini Countach & Jalpa 1980-1985
Lancia Stratos 1972-1985
Land Rover 1948-1973
Land Rover Series II & IIa 1958-1971
Land Rover Series III 1971-1985
Lotus Cortina 1963-1970
Lotus Elan 1962-1973
Lotus Elan Collection No. 1
Lotus Elan Collection No. 2
Lotus Elite 1957-1964
Lotus Elite & Eclat 1974-1981
Lotus Esprit 1974-1981
Lotus Europa 1966-1975
Lotus Europa Collection No. 1
Lotus Seven 1957-1980
Lotus Seven Collection No. 1
Maserati 1965-1970
Maserati 1970-1975
Mazda RX-7 Collection No. 1
Mercedes 230/250/280SL 1963-1971
Mercedes 350/450SL & SLC 1971-1980
Mercedes Benz Cars 1949-1954
Mercedes Benz Cars 1954-1957
Mercedes Benz Cars 1957-1961
Mercedes Benz Competition Cars 1950-1957
Metropolitan 1954-1962
MG Cars 1929-1934
MG Cars 1935-1940
MG TC 1945-1949
MG TD 1949-1953
MG TF 1953-1955
MG Cars 1957-1959
MG Cars 1959-1962
MG Midget 1961-1980
MG MGA 1955-1962
MGA Collection No. 1
MG MGB 1962-1970
MG MGB 1970-1980
MGB GT 1965-1980
Mini Cooper 1961-1971
Morgan Cars 1960-1970
Morgan Cars 1969-1979
Morris Minor Collection No. 1
Old's Cutlass & 4-4-2 1964-1972
Oldsmobile Toronado 1966-1978
Opel GT 1968-1973
Pantera 1970-1973
Pantera & Mangusta 1969-1974
Plymouth Barracuda 1964-1974
Pontiac GTO 1964-1970
Pontiac Firebird 1967-1973
Pontiac Tempest & GTO 1961-1965
Porsche Cars 1960-1964
Porsche Cars 1964-1968
Porsche Cars 1968-1972
Porsche Cars in the Sixties
Porsche Cars 1972-1975
Porsche 356 1952-1965
Porsche 911 Collection No. 1
Porsche 911 Collection No. 2
Porsche 911 1965-1969
Porsche 911 1970-1972
Porsche 911 1973-1977
Porsche 911 Carrera 1973-1977
Porsche 911 SC 1978-1983
Porsche 911 Turbo 1975-1984
Porsche 914 1969-1975
Porsche 914 Collection No. 1
Porsche 924 1975-1981
Porsche 928 Collection No. 1
Porsche 944 1981-1985
Porsche Turbo Collection No. 1
Reliant Scimitar 1964-1982
Rolls Royce Silver Cloud 1955-1965
Rolls Royce Silver Shadow 1965-1980
Range Rover 1970-1981
Rover 3 & 3.5 Litre 1958-1973
Rover P4 1949-1959
Rover P4 1955-1964
Rover 2000 + 2200 1963-1977
Rover 3500 1968-1977
Saab Sonett Collection No. 1
Saab Turbo 1976-1983
Singer Sports Cars 1933-1934
Studebaker Hawks & Larks 1956-1963
Sunbeam Alpine & Tiger 1959-1967
Thunderbird 1955-1957
Thunderbird 1958-1963
Triumph 2000-2.5-2500 1963-1977
Triumph Spitfire 1962-1980
Triumph Spitfire Collection No. 1
Triumph Stag 1970-1980
Triumph Stag Collection No. 1
Triumph TR2 & TR3 1952-1960
Triumph TR4.TR5.TR250 1961-1968
Triumph TR6 1969-1976
Triumph TR6 Collection No. 1
Triumph TR7 & TR8 1975-1981
Triumph GT6 1966-1974
Triumph Vitesse & Herald 1959-1971
TVR 1960-1980
Volkswagen Cars 1936-1956
VW Beetle 1956-1977
VW Beetle Collection No. 1
VW Golf GTi 1976-1986
VW Karmann Ghia 1955-1982
VW Scirocco 1974-1981
Volvo 1800 1960-1973
Volvo 120 Series 1956-1970

BROOKLANDS MUSCLE CARS SERIES
American Motors Muscle Cars 1966-1970
Buick Muscle Cars 1965-1970
Camaro Muscle Cars 1966-1972
Capri Muscle Cars 1969-1983
Chevrolet Muscle Cars 1966-1972
Dodge Muscle Cars 1967-1970
Mercury Muscle Cars 1966-1971
Mini Muscle Cars 1961-1979
Mopar Muscle Cars 1964-1967
Mopar Muscle Cars 1968-1971
Mustang Muscle Cars 1967-1971
Shelby Mustang Muscle Cars 1965-1970
Oldsmobile Muscle Cars 1964-1970
Plymouth Muscle Cars 1966-1971
Pontiac Muscle Cars 1966-1972
Muscle Cars Compared 1966-1971
Muscle Cars Compared Book 2 1965-1971

BROOKLANDS ROAD & TRACK SERIES
Road & Track on Alfa Romeo 1949-1963
Road & Track on Alfa Romeo 1964-1970
Road & Track on Alfa Romeo 1971-1976
Road & Track on Alfa Romeo 1977-1984
Road & Track on Aston Martin 1962-1984
Road & Track on Audi 1952-1980
Road & Track on Audi 1980-1986
Road & Track on Austin Healey 1953-1970
Road & Track on BMW Cars 1966-1974
Road & Track on BMW Cars 1975-1978
Road & Track on BMW Cars 1979-1983
Road & Track on Cobra, Shelby & Ford GT40 1962-1983
Road & Track on Corvette 1953-1967
Road & Track on Corvette 1968-1982
Road & Track on Corvette 1982-1986
Road & Track on Datsun Z 1970-1983
Road & Track on Ferrari 1950-1968
Road & Track on Ferrari 1968-1974
Road & Track on Ferrari 1975-1981
Road & Track on Ferrari 1981-1984
Road & Track on Fiat Sports Cars 1968-1981
Road & Track on Jaguar 1950-1960
Road & Track on Jaguar 1961-1968
Road & Track on Jaguar 1968-1974
Road & Track on Jaguar 1974-1982
Road & Track on Lamborghini 1964-1985
Road & Track on Lotus 1972-1981
Road & Track on Maserati 1952-1974
Road & Track on Maserati 1975-1983
Road & Track on Mazda 1978-1986
Road & Track on Mercedes Sports & GT Cars 1970-1980
Road & Track on MG Sports Cars 1949-1961
Road & Track on MG Sports Cars 1962-1980
Road & Track on Pontiac 1960-1983
Road & Track on Porsche 1951-1967
Road & Track on Porsche 1968-1971
Road & Track on Porsche 1972-1975
Road & Track on Porsche 1975-1978
Road & Track on Porsche 1979-1982
Road & Track on Porsche 1982-1985
Road & Track on Rolls Royce & Bentley 1950-1965
Road & Track on Rolls Royce & Bentley 1966-1984
Road & Track on Saab 1955-1985
Road & Track on Toyota 1966-1986
Road & Track on Triumph Sports Cars 1953-1967
Road & Track on Triumph Sports Cars 1967-1974
Road & Track on Triumph Sports Cars 1974-1982
Road & Track on Volkswagen 1951-1968
Road & Track on Volkswagen 1968-1978
Road & Track on Volkswagen 1978-1985
Road & Track on Volvo 1957-1974
Road & Track on Volvo 1975-1985

BROOKLANDS CAR AND DRIVER SERIES
Car and Driver on BMW 1955-1977
Car and Driver on BMW 1977-1985
Car and Driver on Cobra, Shelby & Ford GT40 1963-1984
Car and Driver on Datsun Z 1600 & 2000 1966-1984
Car and Driver on Corvette 1956-1967
Car and Driver on Corvette 1968-1977
Car and Driver on Corvette 1978-1982
Car and Driver on Ferrari 1955-1962
Car and Driver on Ferrari 1963-1975
Car and Driver on Ferrari 1976-1983
Car and Driver on Mopar 1956-1967
Car and Driver on Mopar 1968-1975
Car and Driver on Pontiac 1961-1975
Car and Driver on Porsche 1955-1962
Car and Driver on Porsche 1963-1970
Car and Driver on Porsche 1970-1976
Car and Driver on Porsche 1977-1981
Car and Driver on Porsche 1982-1986
Car and Driver on Porsche 1956-1985

BROOKLANDS MOTOR & THOROUGHBRED & CLASSIC CAR SERIES
Motor & T & CC on Ferrari 1966-1976
Motor & T & CC on Ferrari 1976-1984
Motor & T & CC on Lotus 1979-1983
Motor & T & CC on Morris Minor 1948-1983

BROOKLANDS PRACTICAL CLASSICS SERIES
Practical Classics on MGB Restoration
Practical Classics on Midget/Sprite Restoration
Practical Classics on Mini Cooper Restoration
Practical Classics on Morris Minor Restoration

BROOKLANDS MILITARY VEHICLES SERIES
Allied Military Vehicles Collection No. 1
Allied Military Vehicles Collection No. 2
Dodge Military Vehicles Collection No. 1
Military Jeeps 1941-1945
Off Road Jeeps 1944-1971

CONTENTS

ACKNOWLEDGEMENTS

Twenty years ago, in October 1966 the new Jensen Interceptor made its debut at the London Motor Show where it received acclaim from the press and admiration from the public. It is a credit to the stylists who created it, that it looks as fresh and modern today as it did then. Proof of this, if it is needed, is the fact that the Interceptor 4 is still being produced by Ian Orford and Jensen Cars Ltd in West Bromwich.

It is not necessary here to write a detailed history and introduction as this has been done expertly and entertainingly by Mike Taylor and Peter Nunn in their Profile from Classic and Sportscar called 'Gentlemans Carriage' which can be found on page 164. I suggest you to turn there immediately.

Brooklands Books are a reference series for enthusiasts. We are privileged in that the worlds leading publishers generously allow us to reissue lost and hard to locate articles for the benefit of todays owners and others that share in the hobby. We are especially indebted in this instance to the management of Autocar, Autosport, Australian Motor Manual, Cars, Classic and Sportscar, Competition Car, Modern Motor, Motor, Motor Sport, Motor Trend, Road & Track, Road Test, Sports Car Graphic, Sports Car World, Thoroughbred & Classic Cars, The World Car Catalogue, and Worlds Fastest Sports Cars for their on-going support.

R.M. Clarke

Our cover illustration is a 1971 MKI Interceptor owned by Peter Williams and is the subject of the article 'Owner's View' on page 179. Classic and Sportscar kindly allowed us to reproduce the photograph.

There will be no mistaking the lines of the new Interceptor when it is encountered on the road.

NEW CARS

Jensens in a brand new shape

Entirely new Italian styled bodies for Interceptor and FF models

AFTER introducing all-plastic body construction with the 541 model exactly a dozen years ago, Jensen have now returned to all-steel bodies for their two 1967 models. These are a new edition of the 6¼-litre Interceptor and a similarly bodied version of the FF model which attracted so much attention at Earls Court last year as the first private car in the world with four-wheel-drive. The body styling is by Superleggera Touring of Milan, with prototypes for the production models (which will be made at West Bromwich) carried out by Vignale.

These two models—the Interceptor and FF—will form the complete Jensen programme for the coming season and will supersede both the open Interceptor introduced at last year's Motor Show and the FF model in the plastics-bodied form in which it was first shown. The C-V8 also disappears from the list.

In view of Jensen's very successful use of glass-fibre body work over a period of 12 years, the change back to steel may seem surprising, but has been decided upon to facilitate production. Both the Interceptor and FF bodies have the same basis and differ only in such matters as frontal treatment, equipment details and the finish of the roof panel. The latter represents a striking innovation in the case of the FF because the entire panel is of brushed stainless steel, giving a most distinctive appearance.

The Interceptor

The new Interceptor is virtually the C-V8 with a new body. The same big V-8 Chrysler engine is used, and this is normally linked with a Chrysler Torqueflite automatic transmission, although the car may be obtained with a straightforward all-synchromesh gearbox. The transmission is normal, with an open propeller shaft to a rigid rear axle located by the semi-elliptic springs. As one expects (because Jensen were pioneers in the use of disc brakes all round) the Dunlop system on all four wheels is retained. The chassis, as on the C-V8 but modified in detail, is an immensely strong affair built up of steel tubes and pressings.

As will be seen from the illustrations, the new body is very modern, typically Italian and is slightly longer, lower and wider than the one it replaces. It is designed to give very roomy and comfortable accommodation for four, with access to the rear seats via two very wide doors and reclining front seats which incorporate a quick release for access to the rear.

The very deep front windscreen has a pronounced slope and this is continued into a curved roof which sweeps rearwards to meet the enormous sloping and curved window which is virtually a "fastback" in itself. It swings open on spring-loaded hinges to give access to an outsize parcel shelf which is easily removable if additional space is needed. A total of 16 cu. ft. of luggage space is available.

Considerable attention has been paid to heating and ventilation. The fresh-air heating system incorporates a thermostat in the water supply to the radiator matrix so that the latter is maintained at a constant temperature according to the setting of the controls. Following modern practice, individually controlled fresh-air outlets at face level are provided but, unusually, there are three of them; in addition, fresh-air outlets are arranged to the front foot wells. This flow of cool air can be boosted by a fan which is quite separate from the two-speed fan of the heating system. So far as windows are concerned, there are hinged ventilating panels on the doors and the rear quarters open to give an extractor effect. The possibility of the large rear window becoming misted is dealt with by twin electric demister fans which blow air over the surface.

Jensens in a brand new shape

continued

The FF four-wheel-drive model has a brushed stainless steel roof and twin vents behind the front wheel arches as easy identification points.

Various safety measures are included such as a dished steering wheel (with wooden rim), safety belts as standard in the front and red warning lights in the trailing edges of the doors.

Very full equipment has for many years been a Jensen feature and details in this case include a transistorized radio with twin speakers, lights in the engine compartment and boot, two-speed screen wipers, screen washers, cigar lighter and electrically operated windows.

Luxurious cockpit of the automatic: note the rest for that idle left foot.

The FF model

The FF model is, in effect, a four-wheel drive version of the Interceptor. Externally, it can be distinguished by the stainless steel roof already mentioned, deeper fluting on the bonnet with a raised air intake and different styles for the air intakes on the sides of the front wings. In other respects, the design and furnishings follow the same lines.

The FF chassis was described in very considerable detail on its introduction last year and the following is a brief outline. The engine and automatic gearbox are normally located, but behind the gearbox is the heart of the Ferguson four-wheel-drive system in the shape of a unit comprising a transfer chain drive to the front propeller shaft and the unique Ferguson limited-action differential which acts between this and the normal rear propeller shaft; the unit also includes the Dunlop Maxaret device.

The unique feature of the central differential is that it permits the front wheels to run slightly faster than the rears, or vice versa, but only to a strictly controlled extent—the limitation being purely on relative speed and not on the relative positions of the differential components. The permitted action is adequate to cater for cornering effects or other conditions which could cause tyre scrub, but much too limited to allow all the torque to pass uselessly through one or other of the propeller shafts if a wheel at one end of the car strikes a slippery surface and loses adhesion. In that event, the torque transmitted by that wheel and its counterpart on the opposite side of the car will be nil because normal differentials are used on front and rear; but the drive will be continued through the pair of wheels at the other end of the car.

Only if one front and one rear wheel strike an exceptionally slippery surface simultaneously can spin occur—and even then it is less likely because the driving torque is being shared out so that the spin point is reached less easily.

This differential action also makes individual wheel-locking under braking impossible, although it cannot prevent all four wheels locking simultaneously on, for example, ice. This is when the Dunlop Maxaret comes in and, sensing a sudden deceleration in the drive system as a whole, cuts off the brake servo action.

One final point is that virtual elimination of wheelspin and wheel-locking—important as they are in a car so fast and powerful as the Jensen—is still not quite the end of the story. Tyres can transmit just so much driving, braking or cornering force in any given conditions and no more. It follows that if all the driving torque has to be transmitted through one pair of wheels, the available cornering force is that much less. With four-wheel drive, the torque is shared out and the risk of running into trouble correspondingly reduced. **M**

Driving the new Jensens

An opportunity to drive the new Interceptor and the FF left me with two overriding impressions. One is what an excellent thing four-wheel drive is in bad conditions and the other is that, like the Mark III C-V8 before it, the new Interceptor is a very fine car by any standards, even if it can't compare with the FF on slippery surfaces. The trials were laid on at Goodwood where both the racing circuit and a grass-grown area were used—both, as luck would have it, nicely wet for the occasion. First I took the new Interceptor for a lap of the racing circuit, followed immediately by a lap in the FF. Then, still in the FF, I put in a few laps of a short circuit on wet grass and then went on to a re-start on a grass-grown embankment. Finally, just to get things back in perspective, an opportunity was given for trying the Interceptor on the grass.

The Interceptor is a very fast car, with a probable

Above: under-bonnet scene with the Chrysler V-8 hiding beneath the large air-cleaner. Below is a drawing showing the general layout of the Ferguson four-wheel-drive and Maxaret system of the FF.

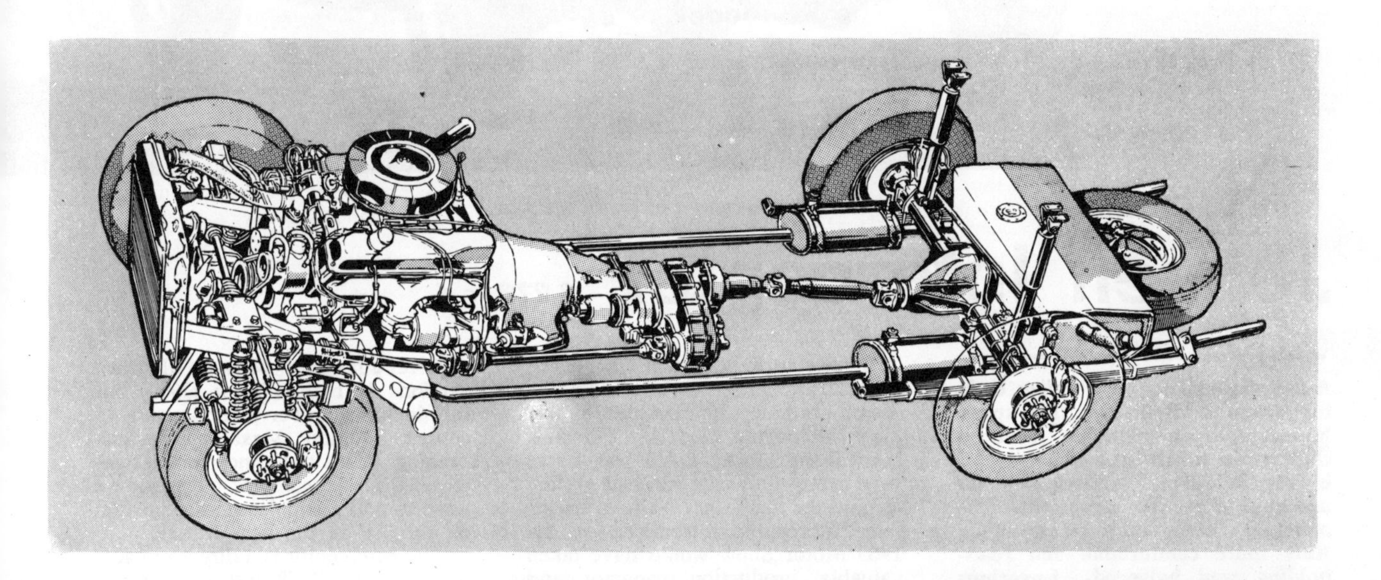

maximum in the 130-140 m.p.h. bracket and a power/weight ratio that discourages taking liberties in the wet: but once under way, everything feels so essentially well balanced that it is no liberty for an experienced driver to put in some quick motoring right away. The FF, on the other hand, called for a little more playing-in because it has power-assisted steering and one always needs to get used to a particular application; a few more laps on both cars would have been much more revealing.

What did very much impress me with the FF was being able to brake really hard at around 85 m.p.h. in the wet, knowing that wheel locking was nearly impossible. I say "nearly impossible" because the Maxaret can be beaten by very heavy pedal pressure, but no one could do so unknowingly because the pedal kicks back unmistakably when the wheels are near to locking and actual locking can be achieved only by "fighting" the pedal.

On wet grass, the difference between the cars was astonishing—not just in the vastly improved adhesion of the FF for get-away and acceleration, but in the way splitting the torque among four wheels instead of two enables one to lap the grass circuit appreciably faster without break-away.

Harold Hastings

Specification

The Interceptor

Engine

V-8 (Chrysler). 108 mm. x 86 mm.; 6,276 c.c.; o.h. valves (pushrods); Carter 4-barrel carburetter; 330 b.h.p. (S.A.E.) at 4,600 r.p.m.; 425 lb. ft. torque at 2,800 r.p.m.

Transmission (automatic)

Chrysler Torqueflite fully automatic system with torque convertor and 3-speed-and-reverse epicyclic gearbox; ratios, 3.07, 4.44 and 7.50; reverse, 6.74; final drive by open propeller shaft and hypoid-bevel rear axle with Powr Lok limited-slip differential to rear wheels. Road speed at 1,000 r.p.m., 25.6 m.p.h.

Transmission (manual)

$10\frac{1}{2}$-in. s.d.p. clutch and 4-speed, all-synchromesh gearbox; ratios, 3.07, 4.26, 5.86 and 8.16; reverse, 7.92. Otherwise as with automatic transmission.

Running gear

Dunlop disc brakes all round; independent coil-and-wishbone front suspension; semi-elliptic rear springs; rack-and-pinion steering; pressed-steel five "spoke" wheels and Dunlop Road Speed 6.70-15 tyres.

Dimensions

Length, 15 ft. 8 in.; width, 5 ft. 9 in.; kerb weight, $31\frac{1}{4}$ cwt.

FF saloon

Engine

As Interceptor.

Transmission

Chrysler Torqueflite fully automatic transmission as on Interceptor but with open propeller shafts driving front and rear wheels from Ferguson controlled central differential; final drive by hypoid bevel (with differential) at front and rear.

Running gear

Dunlop disc brakes all round with servo and Dunlop Maxaret anti-locking device; independent coil-and-wishbone front suspension; semi-elliptic rear springs with Panhard rod axle locations; power-assisted rack-and-pinion steering; wheels and tyres as Interceptor.

Dimensions

Length, 15 ft. 11 in.; width, 5 ft. 9 in.; kerb weight, 34 cwt.

PRICES

Interceptor: £3,742 11s. 2d. (inc. £699 3s. 3d. PT)

FF: £5,339 19s. 9d. (inc. £996 19s. 9d. PT)

Jensen Interceptor 6,276 c.c.

AT A GLANCE: New Italian body for Jensen C-V8 in steel. Top speed higher, but acceleration reduced slightly up to 100 m.p.h. Powerful brakes fade-free. Superb, smooth and quiet American engine with well-matched automatic transmission. Ride more comfortable and road-holding well balanced. Luxurious interior, but heating and ventilating could be better. Very satisfying high-performance touring car with practical seating for four plus luggage.

MANUFACTURER

Jensen Motors Ltd., West Bromwich, Staffordshire.

PRICES

Basic	£3,043 7s 11d
Purchase Tax	£699 3s 3d
Total (in G.B.) ..	£3,742 11s 2d

PERFORMANCE SUMMARY

Mean maximum speed	133 m.p.h.
Standing start ¼-mile	15·7 sec
0-60 m.p.h.	7·3 sec
30-70 m.p.h. (through gears	6·2 sec
Fuel consumption ..	14·2 m.p.g.
Miles per tankful ..	225

IT was entirely logical for Jensen to rationalize their production programme into just two almost identical looking models. The bulbous shape of the C-V8 was never very pretty and that kind of styling is now on the wane. The convertible Interceptor introduced at the 1965 Motor Show would have taken valuable production capacity and with the acute interest in four-wheel drive to the Ferguson formula, Jensen settled for just one body with the most sleek and graceful lines to come from Italy for some time. Superleggera construction by Touring to Vignale patents is used and although the first few cars have been built in Milan, the tools will soon be installed in the West Bromwich plant.

In order to keep costs low the ordinary (if that word can be applied to such a car) two-wheel-drive Jensen is identical with the FF (Ferguson Formula) except for an extra 4in. length ahead of the windscreen to accommodate the transfer gears for the front-wheel-drive take-off. Differentation is by name plates (JFF on the four-wheel-drive) and a double ventilation grille just behind the front wheels each side. The FF also has a stainless steel roof.

Price difference between the two versions is high, almost £600, but this includes power steering and, of course, Dunlop Maxaret anti-lock braking. This test concerns the two-wheel-drive Interceptor only, but we hope to add a supplementary portion on the FF in the near future.

The Interceptor is a direct replacement for the C-V8 and in its mechanical specification is much the same. There is a massive steel chassis fabricated from sheet steel welded into box sections, but instead of a separate composite body made up from glass-fibre and aluminium panels, an all-steel body is welded to a tubular framework which all forms a structural part of the main hull. The result is tremendous strength and stiffness at the expense of an 11 per cent increase in weight, the Interceptor being nearly 3½cwt heavier than the C-V8.

Such an increase, fortunately, is not much of a problem, as the 6·3-litre Chrysler vee-8 engine develops more than enough horse-power to give dynamic performance still. To say that the acceleration is electrifying is something of an understatement. The TorqueFlite automatic transmission is standard and really cannot be faulted at all; for those who

Autocar road test number 2113

Make: JENSEN
Type: Interceptor
6,276 c.c.

TEST CONDITIONS

Weather: Drizzle. Wind: 3-8 m.p.h.
Temperature: 7 deg. C (44 deg. F)
Barometer: 29·45in. Hg.
Surfaces: Wet concrete and asphalt

WEIGHT

Kerb weight: 33·0cwt (3,697lb-1,680kg) (with oil, water and half-full fuel tank)
Distribution: per cent F, 50; R, 50
Laden as tested: 35·3cwt (3,947lb-1,794kg)

Figures taken at 6,000 miles by our own staff at the Motor Industry Research Association proving ground at Nuneaton.

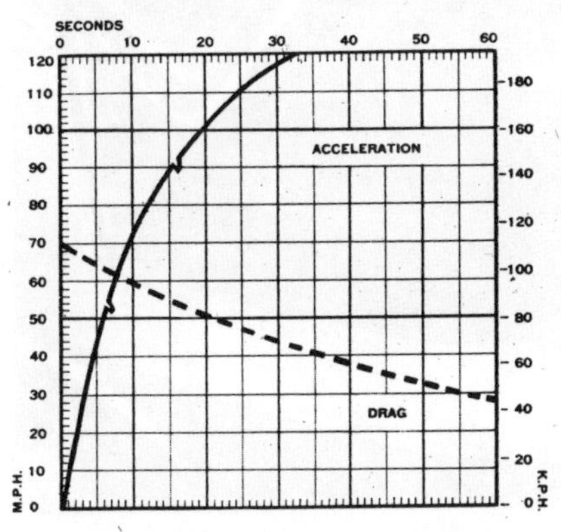

MAXIMUM SPEEDS

Gear	m.p.h.	k.p.h.	r.p.m.
Top (mean)	133	214	5,100
(best)	133	214	5,100
Inter	92	148	5,100
Low	54	87	5,100

Standing ¼-Mile 15·7sec 92 m.p.h.
Standing Kilometre 28·4sec 115 m.p.h.

TIME IN SECONDS	3·3	4·3	5·9	7·3	9·5	12·1	15·4	19·0	24·9	32·2
TRUE SPEED M.P.H.	30	40	50	60	70	80	90	100	110	120
INDICATED SPEED	30	40	50	60	70	80	90	99	109	117

Mileage recorder 2 per cent under-reading.

Test distance 1,203 miles.

Speed range, gear ratios and time in seconds

m.p.h.	Top (3·07-6·75)	Inter. (4·44-9·77)	Low (7·5-16·5)
10— 30	—	3·0	2·1
20— 40	4·4	3·3	2·4
30— 50	4·5	3·9	2·7
40— 60	5·1	3·5	—
50— 70	5·9	3·9	—
60— 80	6·1	5·1	—
70— 90	6·4	6·1	—
80—100	8·0	—	—
90—110	9·5	—	—
100—120	12·2	—	—

FUEL CONSUMPTION

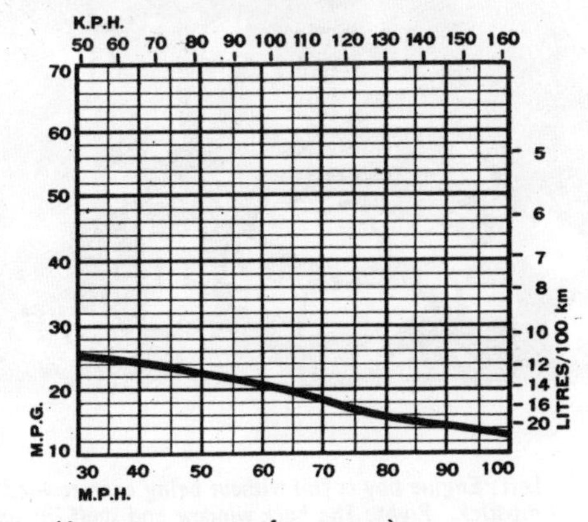

(At constant speeds—m.p.g.)

30 m.p.h.	25·8
40	24·5
50	22·3
60	20·6
70	18·7
80	15·8
90	14·9
100	12·8

Typical m.p.g. 14·2 (19·9 litres/100km)
Calculated (DIN) m.p.g. 17.0 (16·6 litres/100km)
Overall m.p.g. 13·6 (20·8 litres/100km)
Grade of fuel, Super Premium (99·4—101·7 RM)

OIL CONSUMPTION

Miles per pint (SAE 20W/40) .. 400

PEDAL PRESSURE (lb) FOR 0·5g

STOPS AT ¼ MILE INTERVALS FROM 70 M.P.H

BRAKES (from 30 m.p.h. in neutral)

Load	g	Distance
25 lb	20%	150 ft
50 „	40%	75 „
75 „	60%	50 „
100 „	85%	35 „
125 „	90%	33·4 „
Handbrake	35%	000 „

Max. Gradient, 1 in 4.

TURNING CIRCLES

Between kerbs L, 36ft 7in.; R, 38ft 5in.
Between walls L, 38ft 3in.; R, 40ft 1in.
Steering wheel turns, lock to lock .. 3·5

HOW THE CAR COMPARES:

MAXIMUM SPEED (mean) M.P.H.

Jensen Interceptor
Aston Martin DB6
Jaguar E-type 2 2
Pontiac GTO
Porsche 911S

0–60 M.P.H. (secs.)

Jensen Interceptor
Aston Martin DB6
Jaguar E-type 2 2
Pontiac GTO
Porsche 911S

STANDING START ¼-MILE (secs.)

Jensen Interceptor
Aston Martin DB6
Jaguar E-type 2 2
Pontiac GTO
Porsche 911S

M.P.G. OVERALL

Jensen Interceptor
Aston Martin DB6
Jaguar E-type 2 2
Pontiac GTO
Porsche 911S

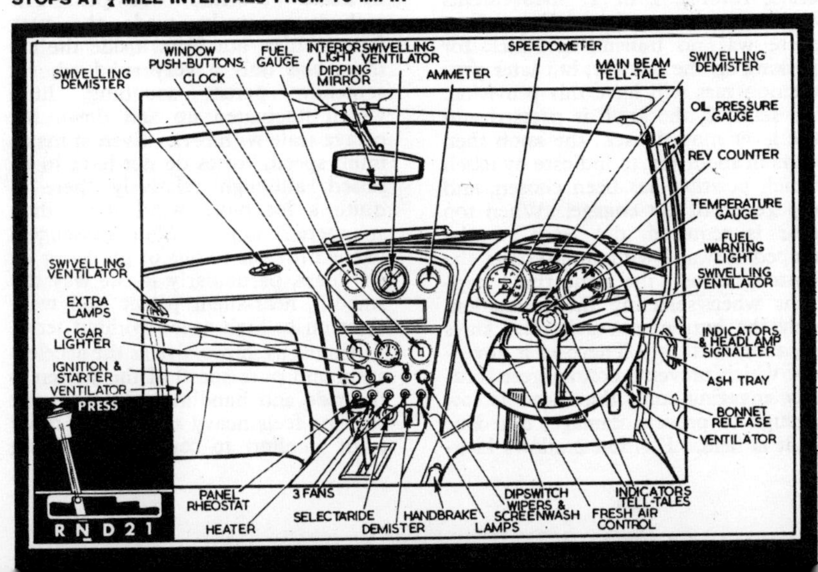

PRICES

Jensen Interceptor	£3,743
Aston Martin DB6	£5,084
Jaguar E-type 2+2	£2,284
Pontiac GTO	£3,474
Porsche 911S	£3,556

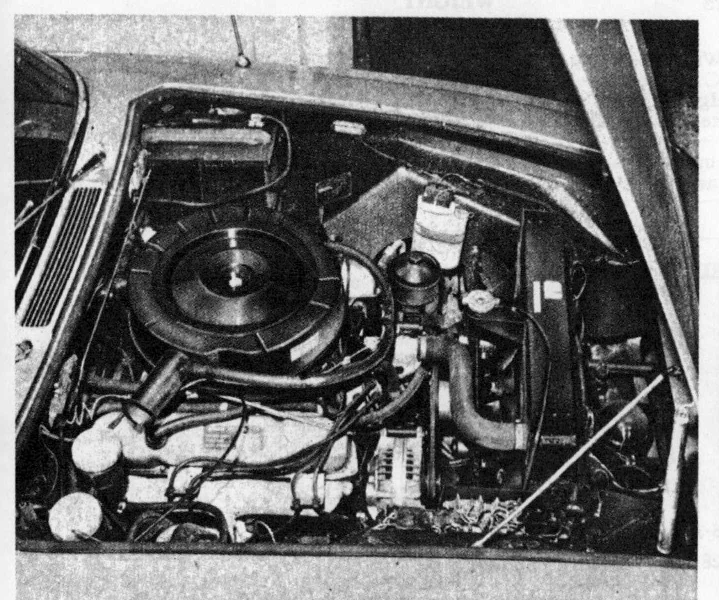

Left: Engine bay is full without being overcrowded. All fillers are easy to reach, but the bonnet stay is on the opposite side from the dipstick. Right: The back window and shelf lift up together and the boot is fully carpeted

Jensen Interceptor...

like more work there is the option of a 4-speed manual box at extra cost.

In terms of acceleration there has been a slight loss up to 100 m.p.h. compared with the C-V8, but above 100 the better shape of the Interceptor plays its part more and the top speed is higher with the new car. From rest to 120 m.p.h. now takes just over half a minute (32·2sec) instead of 29·8sec measured previously, but this speed still comes up in comfortably under one mile, and 100 can be reached in 19sec and not much over a quarter of a mile. From 70 m.p.h. to 120 m.p.h. takes just under 23sec, so very high cruising speeds can be regained quickly after traffic hold-ups.

We took the Jensen to the Continent for maximum speed measurements and covered vast distances in remarkably short time intervals, such is the speed and nature of the machine. Even on a week-end trip to the West Country shortly afterwards an average of 45 m.p.h. on a 3-hour journey took very little effort and certainly involved no risks. Many roads in Northern France have now been improved to about British trunk road standards and it was here that the Jensen regularly shot up to three-figure speeds as soon as a short straight unwound from a turn. On *autoroutes* 120 m.p.h. is a comfortable and very relaxed cruising speed, and even on a blustery day with teeming rain the stability was excellent.

There is a red sector on the rev counter from 5,100 to 6,000 r.p.m. and the beginning of this mark is the limit to which one should take the engine. During maximum speed runs we were impressed by the quickness with which the needle swung to this point and then stopped dead, on opposite runs on quite a windy day. Our fifth-wheel speedometer showed 133 m.p.h. each time, proving the rev counter exactly accurate; the car's speedometer .suddenly became quite wildly inaccurate and read only 126 m.p.h. at maximum speed. Throughout the range from 30 to 90 m.p.h. it had no error we could measure. Top speed of the C-V8, by the way, was 129 m.p.h.

With the big central selector lever in D, the gearbox changes up with full throttle at 3,500 r.p.m. out of low, and at 4,000 r.p.m. out of intermediate. It therefore pays to use the over-riding provision when maximum acceleration is required, and we found we gained a second right through by running up to maximum revs. On the road this sort of difference is hardly worth the trouble of working the lever, but one does develop a habit of using it to hold intermediate for fast cornering and smooth downward changes.

The lever has a large press-in knob whch releases the safety catch to select reverse, 2 or 1. Movements between N (neutral) and D are free; there was no transmission lock for parking on the test car, but later production cars will have this provision. To select 2, the knob is pressed and the lever moved back; the knob then stays in about ¼in. to indicate by touch which position has been chosen, and top gear will not engage. When top gear is required, the lever can be tapped forward without pressing the button. Much the same thing happens when selecting the 1 position, only the button moves in, and stays in, even further. There is a governor which prevents bottom gear actually engaging until the speed is low enough to prevent damage, but once in it is held. Position 2 allows kick-down changes into bottom and out again.

With some 425 lb. ft. torque on tap and a converter ratio of 2·2 to 1, a kickdown change is bound to produce a surge. It is much less tiring for passengers, therefore, to pull the lever back into 2 on the approach to an obstacle and then accelerate smoothly past in intermediate, selecting top when appropriate. On the over-run, downward changes are imperceptible except by a flick of the rev counter needle and slight pitch increase in the hum of the engine. Automatic upward changes are perfectly smooth and free from hesitation and surge.

The engine itself performed faultlessly throughout the 1,200 miles we drove in seven days. Starting hot or cold is always instantaneous and the automatic choke phases out progressively without over-speeding or making the mixture too rich. Big vee-8s are always very smooth and this one was entirely free from vibrations and practically silent in operation. There was certainly no mechanical noise from it ever, and only a very faint exhaust beat could be heard if a window was open. The carburettor intake made the very faintest hiss, but from inside the car there was only a very subdued, yet somehow potent sounding, hum which fluctuated up and down the octave scale with revs. Even at maximum speed, voices do not have to be raised, although relatively there is quite a lot more wind noise than at a mere 70 m.p.h. Many passengers likened the car to one of the latest jet air liners, particularly in the way the smooth, near-silent power pull went right on to high speed without jerks.

Almost as impressive as the acceleration and pure speed of the Jensen is the ride and handling. In town the steering feels heavy and it takes quite a lot of effort to counter the strong

Bumpers follow the wings right round and there are stainless steel rubbing strips along the body sills. Wheels are pressed steel with chrome plating relieved by matt black. Twin exhaust pipes are 2½in. dia.

Jensen Interceptor...

self-centring. As soon as the speed builds up, however, the steering lightens considerably and the quick, positive response enables the car to be placed very precisely. There is almost a violent kick-back to the driver's hands when the front wheels hit a sharp ridge or pot-hole, but on slippery undulating roads the feel from the steering is much appreciated.

With the C-V8 we thought the ride too firm, particularly at the back. On the Interceptor dual-rate rear springs are used and their initial stiffness must be less, for the ride is much more accommodating. The new car takes all manner of unevennesses in its stride, with just a kind of galloping motion of the wheels vaguely detectable, somewhere underneath. We experimented with the Armstrong Selectaride four-position adjustable dampers at speed on some notorious sections of French *chaussée* and found the softer settings increased the front end plunge noticeably and substituted some float for vertical jerk. Driven fast the car felt more stable switched to the firmest damping.

So many high-performance cars are now fitted with radial-ply tyres, it was interesting to go back, so to speak, to Dunlop RS5s on the Jensen. An immediate impression is how much more comfortable they are, and with the perfectly equal 50:50 loading of the Interceptor their adhesion was hard to fault. On some badly drained tarmac we only began to aquaplane at speeds over 120 m.p.h. and on wet concrete full power take-offs caused only a yard or two of wheelspin, overcome no doubt with the assistance of the Powr-Lok limited-slip differential. During braking tests from 30 m.p.h. we recorded 0·9g as the limit on a wet track and could not better this when the roads had dried.

The road-holding characteristics of the Interceptor are as well balanced as one would expect, and the car behaves neutrally on a steady throttle through a turn. The mount of tail-out attitude can be varied as desired by the accelerator foot, and the whole procedure is so progressive and controllable that we really enjoyed a lot of high-speed cornering during the test period, which was almost entirely wet. As a slippery bend is entered, the steering sends back a signal of how much adhesion there is from its lightness and the driver then knows how early he can turn the power on, or how late he must wait to prevent too much of a tail slide.

Big disc brakes on all four wheels give reassuring stopping power and our fade tests showed no deterioration with hard use. Pedal loads are not heavy and there is a nice "hard" pedal feel which is effective without being vicious. A servo fault we found on the C-V8 did not repeat itself, and it took only 125 lb to produce maximum stopping power from 30 m.p.h. The handbrake held with the car facing up the 1-in-3, but not facing downwards.

In some ways the Jensen is unique among GT cars, because it is a real four-seater with a vast luggage boot. The big back window lifts up almost like an estate car tailgate for loading and the parcels shelf, which lifts with it, can be detached easily if anything really bulky needs to be carried. Back seats are shaped for two, with a central folding armrest, although we carried a family of four plus driver for several miles without any complaints.

Perhaps because the whole of the

The interior is fully trimmed in soft black hide with reclining front seats and the rear backrest is shaped for two. The steering wheel has a wood rim and there are matching panels in the doors and on the centre console

Interceptor is so exciting, two features were disappointing. First, the four headlamps gave a really miserable light output with poor penetration even on main beams and were no match for the performance of the car. The beam pattern seemed straggly and Continental iodine vapour units would be very desirable if much night driving were anticipated. Next, the heating and ventilating system, although versatile with separate hot and cold supplies at the front and two blowers to demist the huge back window, did not function efficiently and we found temperature control insensitive and misting of windows still a problem with so much glass area. Heating wires would be a much better solution for the back window, because the rear blowers were very noisy in use.

For a new model the Interceptor feels fully mature and extremely well built. It is an eye-catcher everywhere and its looks are a clever combination of practicalities and an efficient shape. The performance is satisfying, with enough for any situation, and used with discretion in experienced hands the Interceptor represents one of the safest forms of road transport. At about 14 m.p.g., fuel bills are high, but, judged against the pleasure the car gives, these costs are worth every penny. ■

SPECIFICATION: JENSEN INTERCEPTOR (FRONT ENGINE REAR-WHEEL DRIVE)

ENGINE

Cylinders	8, in 90-deg vee
Cooling system	Water; pump, thermostat and twin electric fans
Bore	108mm (4·25in.)
Stroke	86mm (3·38in.)
Displacement	6,276 c.c. (383 cu. in.)
Valve gear	Overhead, hydraulic tappets
Compression ratio	10-to-1
Carburettors	Carter 4-barrel progressive
Fuel pump	Mechanical
Oil filter	Full-flow, renewable element
Max. power	325 b.h.p. (gross) at 4,600 r.p.m.
Max torque	425 lb. ft. (gross) at 2,800 r.p.m.

TRANSMISSION

Gearbox	Torque Flite Hi-performance, 3-speed automatic with torque convertor
Gear ratios	Top 1·0-2·2; Inter. 1·44-3·19; Low 2·44-5·39; Reverse 2·19-4·91
Final drive	Hypoid bevel with Powr-Lok limited slip differential, 3·07 to 1

CHASSIS and BODY

Construction	Steel body and tubular frame welded together

SUSPENSION

Front	Independent, twin coil springs, wishbones, lever-arm dampers, anti-roll bar
Rear	Live axle, dual-rate half-elliptic leaf springs, Panhard rod, telescopic Armstrong Selectaride dampers

STEERING

Type	Cam gears, rack and pinion
	Wheel dia. 17in.

BRAKES

Make and type	Dunlop discs front and rear, divided circuits
Servo	Vacuum type
Dimensions	F, 11·25in. dia.; R, 11·25in. dia.
Swept area	F, 249·1 sq. in.; R, 249·1 sq. in. Total 498·2 sq. in. (282 sq. in. per ton laden)

WHEELS

Type	Pressed steel disc, chrome plated and pierced, 4·5in. wide rim
Tyres—make	Dunlop
—type	RS.5 tubed cross-ply
—size	6·70—15in.

EQUIPMENT

Battery	12-volt 72-amp. hr.
Alternator	40 amp
Headlamps	4 Lucas sealed beam 37·5/50 watt
Reversing lamps	2
Electric fuses	5
Screen wipers	2-speed, self-parking
Screen washer	Standard electric
Interior heater	Standard, water-valve control
Safety belts	Standard in front
Interior trim	Leather seats, p.v.c. headlining
Floor covering	Wilton carpet
Windscreen	Laminated
Starting handle	No provision
Jack	Bevelift
Jacking points	4, 2 each side
Underbody protection	Bitumastic on all surfaces exposed to road
Other bodies	None

MAINTENANCE

Fuel tank	16 Imp. gallons (low level warning lamp) (73 litres)
Cooling system	32 pints (including heater) (18·2 litres)
Engine sump	8·5 pints (4·7 litres) SAE 20W/40 Change oil every 4,000 miles; Change filter element every 8,000 miles
Gearbox	17 pints SAE ATF Type A. No change
Final drive	3 pints Shell Limited Slip diff. S6721A. Change oil every 12,000 miles.
Grease	6 points every 1,000 miles. 4 points every 4,000 miles
Tyre pressures	F, 24; R, 28 p.s.i. (normal driving). F, 30; R, 36 p.s.i. (fast driving)

PERFORMANCE

Top gear m.p.h. per 1,000 r.p.m.	25.6
Mean piston speed at max. power	2,600 f.p.m.
B.h.p. per ton laden (gross)	184

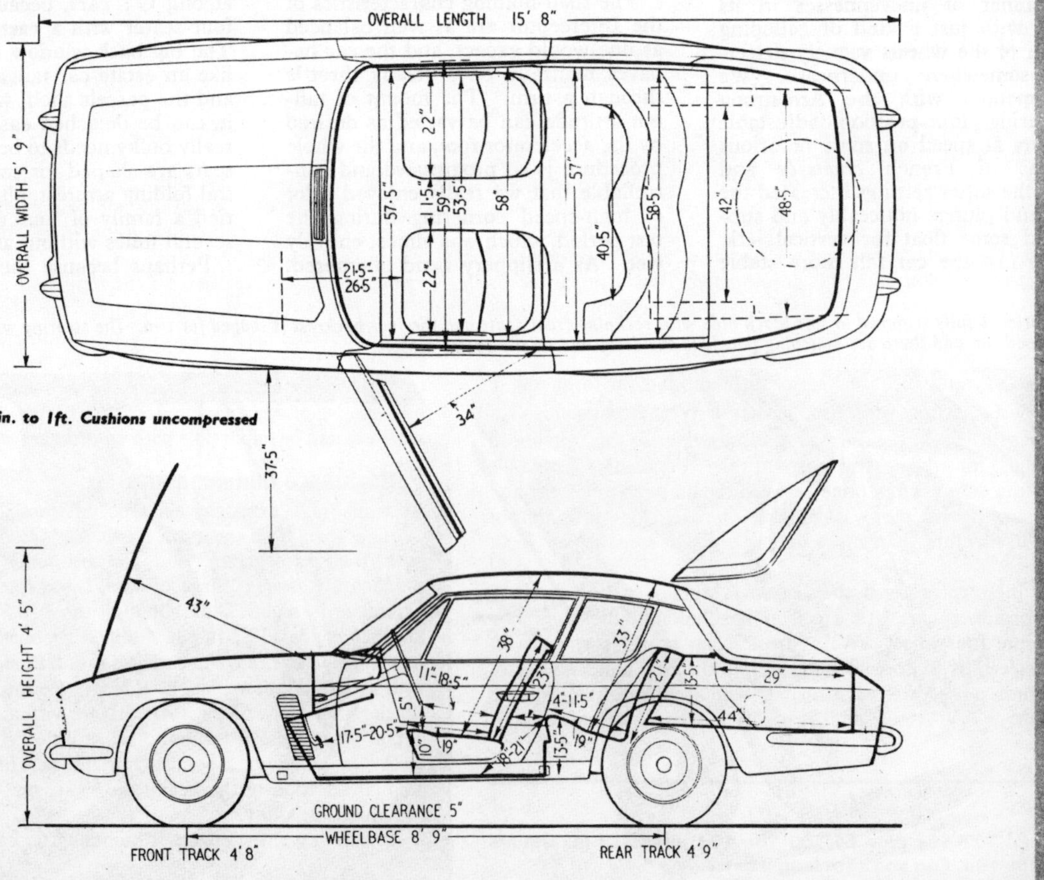

Scale: 0.3in. to 1ft. Cushions uncompressed

Performance with safety

Four-wheel drive does not significantly reduce performance . . . superb power steering . . . best handling car of its size and power we have tested . . .

FOR the second time in a matter of weeks *Motor* has tested one of the first production examples of a new car which embodies outstanding advances in automotive technology. But almost the only features common to the two cars are superb power steering and magnificent handling, for while the technical interest of the NSU Ro80 derives mainly from its Wankel engine, the Jensen FF is distinguished by its Ferguson Formula four-wheel-drive and anti-lock braking system. More significantly, while a substantial German car maker took up the Wankel invention and forcefully pushed through its development, the British motor industry seems to have turned its back on the equally important ideas of the FF system, leaving their evolution to the relatively slender resources (financially speaking) of Harry Ferguson Research Ltd., and their realization in a production form to the courage of a tiny lone-wolf firm, Jensen of West Bromwich. As a result the British buyer has to pay heavily for his advanced engineering, for the extra cost of the Ferguson system is £1,499—the difference in price between the more complex car and the ordinary Interceptor. What does he get for this sum of money—itself more than most people are prepared to pay for a complete car?

In its Interceptor form the Jensen is already an outstanding high-performance car with excellent roadholding; the combined effect of the four-wheel drive and first-class power steering with excellent "feel" is to make it quite simply the best handling car of its size and power we have tested, with tremendous cornering power, wet or dry. Above all it is wieldy and can be thrown about as if it were a car of half its size and weight. To make a large car weighing 36 cwt. behave in this way is a very considerable feat. And of course the system has other advantages: no FF owner is likely to get stuck in a muddy field; nor should he ever need such aids to adhesion as chains or studded tyres.

Our approval of the Dunlop-Maxaret anti-locking system is a little more cautious. It does its job of preventing the wheels from locking under wet and slippery conditions, but the rate of release and re-application seems to us to be a little slower than we remember it to have been on the Ferguson R5 prototype and the whole car bounces up and down as the Maxaret does its work. Our test staff found this bouncing action rather disconcerting at first, but having grown to accept it, we feel that the system could be a life-saver, especially in a really high-speed emergency, as it is possible to brake, steer and corner at the same time in a way which would be impossible with an ordinary car.

Performance and economy

With all those extra drive-shafts, differentials and gears to turn—quite apart from the extra 3 cwt they weigh—one might expect both the performance and the economy of the FF to be significantly worse than of the Interceptor, but in fact the difference is slight. Thus although the 130.5 m.p.h. top speed is lower than the 138.5 m.p.h. attained by our Interceptor, we have reason to believe that the earlier car had an unusually good engine with a bit more power at the top end. Certainly the standing start acceleration times of the two cars are virtually identical until 100 m.p.h. when the FF begins to fall a little behind. Hence with the ability to get from a standstill to 60 m.p.h. in 8.1s. (7.7s with manual selection of the gears) the FF is one of the very quickest cars available today.

At 100 m.p.h. the engine is humming unobtrusively at less than

PRICE: £4,707 15s plus £1,309 15s 10d purchase tax equals £6,017 10s 10d. Fog and spot lamps extra.

Jensen FF *continued*

4,000 r.p.m. making the Jensen one of the most restful cars we have ever driven. Above 4,000–4,200 r.p.m.—the speed at which the automatic transmission changes up—engine noise becomes a little more noticeable and the car is just beginning to work hard at 110 m.p.h. but still in a very calm relaxed way with a noise level that allows the radio to be heard in comfort. For acceleration there is little point in using much more than 4,000 r.p.m., since the peak of the power curve is attained at 4,600 r.p.m. and the engine runs abruptly out of urge at its 5,100 r.p.m. red-line limit, perhaps because the critical "pump up" speed of the hydraulic tappets is being approached.

Almost the only evidence of increased weight and rolling resistance is in the poor constant speed fuel consumption at the lower end of the range—30 and 40 m.p.h. But as the increase in consumption with increased speed is from then on very gradual, and as the maximum speed is slightly lower than the Interceptor's, the touring consumption works out more or less the same at 14.8 m.p.g. Similarly our 11.5 m.p.g. overall fuel consumption was actually a trifle better than for the Interceptor—not that petrol economy, if you can call it this, will be of too much concern to an FF buyer. A 10:1 compression ratio means, of course, that only the best fuels will do: although the car ran quite happily on French 98 octane super, certain 99 octane petrols bought in England produced quite marked pinking.

Transmission

Just as satisfying as the effortless performance was the character of the Chrysler Torqueflite automatic transmission which usually changed gear smoothly and neatly. So long as kickdown was selected below about 50 m.p.h., the attendant downward shift was performed with equal neatness, but above that speed the change

The front seats have an adequate range of fore-and-aft adjustment but are not very comfortable. The lever at the bottom of the photograph locks and releases the reclining backrest, but is difficult to reach with the door shut. The knurled knob above it controls the tension of the spring which forces the backrest forward when released.

The back seats are deep and comfortable with a central armrest and ashtrays on each side. Rear-seat legroom is limited unless the front seats are pushed well forward.

Performance

Performance test carried out by *Motor's* staff at the Motor Industry Research Association proving ground, Lindley.

Conditions:

Weather: Cold with light snow showers. Wind 10-20 m.p.h.
Temperature 32°-36°F. Barometer 29.4 in. Hg.
Surface: Damp concrete and tarmacadam.
Fuel: Super premium 101 octane (RM). 5-star rating.

Maximum speeds

	m.p.h.
Mean opposite runs	130.5
Best one-way kilometre	131.0
Intermediate } At 5,100 r.p.m. limit	90.0
Low } At 5,100 r.p.m. limit	53.8

Acceleration times

m.p.h.	(D1 and D2 Hold) sec.	automatic sec.
0-30	2.9	3.0
0-40	4.2	4.3
0-50	5.8	6.0
0-60	7.7	8.1
0-70	10.4	10.8
0-80	13.4	14.1
0-90	17.3	18.4
0-100	22.4	23.6
0-110	30.9	32.8
Standing quarter mile	16.1	16.3

m.p.h.	Kickdown sec.
20-40	2.3
30-50	3.0
40-60	3.8
50-70	4.8
60-80	6.0
70-90	7.6
80-100	9.5
90-110	14.4

Brakes

Pedal pressure, deceleration and equivalent stopping distance from 30 m.p.h.

lb.	g	ft.
25	0.39	77
35	0.80	37½
45	0.95	31½
Handbrake	0.32	94

Fade test

20 stops at ½g deceleration at 1 min. intervals from a speed midway between 30 m.p.h. and maximum speed (=80.3 m.p.h.)

	lb.
Pedal force at beginning	28
Pedal force at 10th stop	28
Pedal force at 20th stop	28

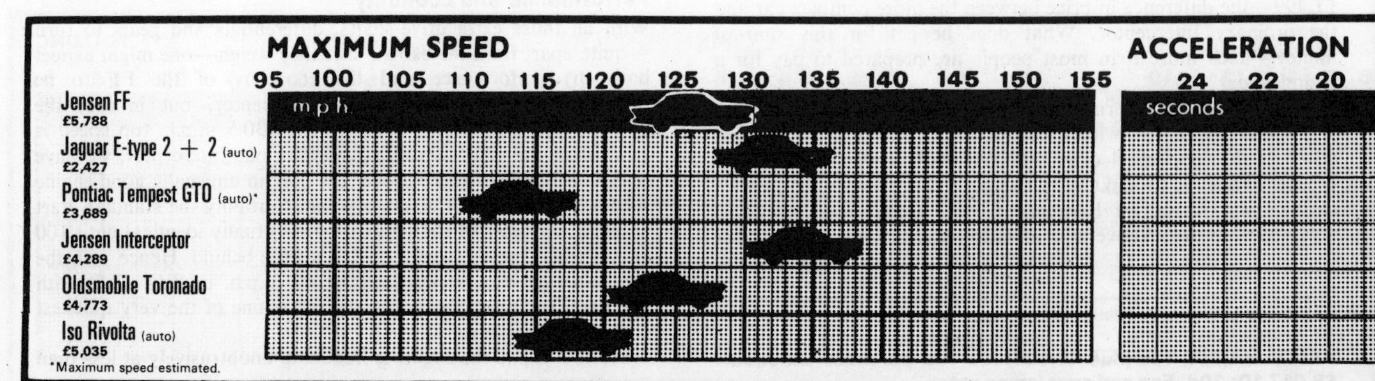

Braking when cornering hard like this only caused the tail to swing out on a track dampened by a thin layer of melting snow.

became rather violent and jerky. Manual downchanges on the over-run were inclined to be rather sudden, too.

Although 37 and 70 m.p.h. may seem rather low change-up speeds for a car with a maximum of 130 m.p.h., not much improvement in acceleration is to be gained by resorting to manual control which is mainly needed for holding a gear on roundabouts, twisty roads etc. On the Jensen this is a simple matter of selecting 1 or 2 as marked on the selector quadrant, although the lever was initially stiff until adjustment was carried out.

The Ferguson four-wheel drive system has already been described at length in *Motor* and needs no more than a brief re-cap here. Behind the conventional automatic gearbox is the Ferguson control differential which distributes the drive to a normal live rear axle via a short prop-shaft, and to the front wheels through a chain drive and another prop-shaft which runs forward beside the engine. The control differential apportions 63% of the torque to the rear wheels; 37% to the front, but more important prevents the front wheels from overrunning the rears by more than 16.5% and the rears from overrunning the fronts by more than 5.5%. The Dunlop-Maxaret brake sensor is driven off the differential and transmits electrical signals to a solenoid which in turn controls the action of the powerful vacuum servo.

Handling and brakes

If further evidence be needed to explode the theory that power steering systems are incapable of providing "feel" it is supplied by the Adwest rack-and-pinion system fitted to the FF (optional on the Interceptor). Few drivers—unless they had considered the

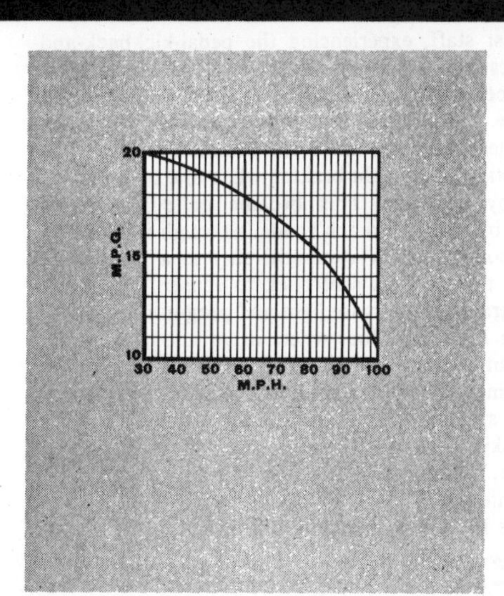

Fuel consumption

Touring (consumption midway between 30 m.p.h. and maximum less 5% allowance for acceleration) . . . . . 14.8 m.p.g.
Overall . . . . . 11.5 m.p.g.
(=24.6 litres/100 km.)
Total test mileage . . . . . 1,871 miles
Tank capacity (maker's figure) . . . . . 16 gal.

Speedometer

Indicated	20	30	40	50	60	70	80	90
True	18	27	37	46	56½	67½	76	86

Indicated	100	110
True	95	106

Distance recorder . . . . . 1% fast

Weight

Kerb weight (unladen with fuel for approximately 50 miles) . . . . . 36.0 cwt.
Front/rear distribution 53/47
Weight laden as tested . . . . . 39.75 cwt.

Steering

Turning circle between kerbs:	ft.
Left	37
Right	38
Turns of steering wheel from lock to lock	3.5
Steering wheel deflection for 50 ft. diameter circle	1.2 turns

Parkability

Gap needed to clear 6 ft. wide obstruction parked in front:

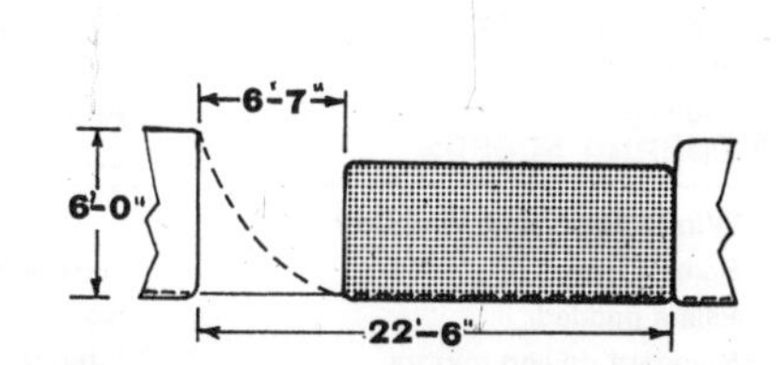

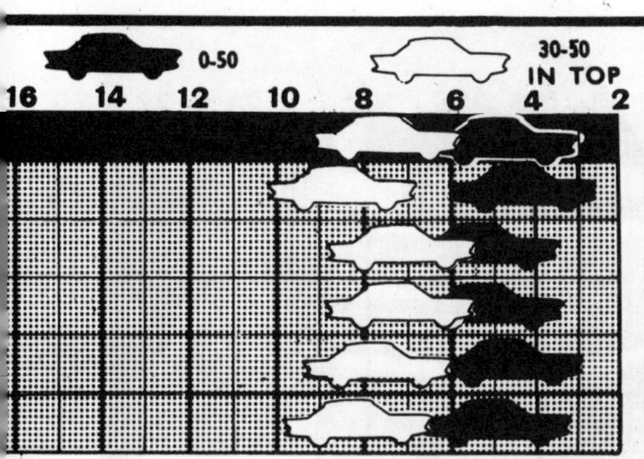

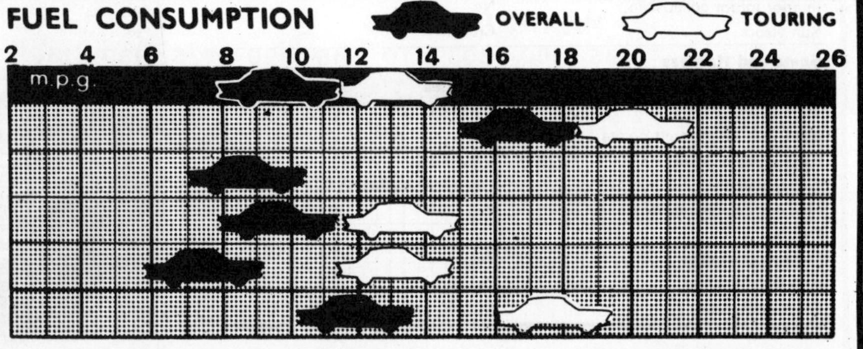

problem of coping with fat tyres and a front axle weight of nearly a ton—would detect power assistance were it not for the occasional slight twitchings and hissings that sometimes betray its presence in the car park. Splendidly light for parking—yet without that almost total lack of resistance at the wheel rim characteristic of many power steering systems—there is always enough feel to let the driver know what is happening to the front wheels. When driving along iced-up ruts in a snow-covered Welsh mountain road, for example, the forces exerted by the ruts on the front wheels were always faithfully reflected at the steering wheel allowing the appropriate rapid corrections to be made; with a normal "feel-less" system almost the only indication of "rut-steering" would have been an actual change in the direction of the car. On bumpy roads there was also a certain amount of kickback.

Despite a ratio which requires a little over $3\frac{1}{2}$ turns from lock to lock the steering seldom feels low-geared. More than anything it was this twirlability—coupled with the excellent feel—that inspired confidence in our drivers to chuck all 36 cwt. of the Jensen around as if it were an Imp. And the addition of front-wheel drive has made no difference to the (rather poor) turning circle.

What the Jensen does on a corner is complex but consistent and always in the driver's favour. Consider first the behaviour in the dry when cornering under power. The first thing most drivers noticed was the ability to accelerate on full throttle through a right angle from T-junctions and the like with no more than a faint grumble from the tyres. Such decorum is in marked contrast to the nasty manners of most other very powerful cars whose antics during such a maneouvre range from a tantrum of tyre-smoking wheel-lift to instant rotation about a polar axis.

What happens at higher speeds up to 60-70 m.p.h. depends very much on how much surplus power is used, for the 37:63 front/rear torque distribution ensures that the FF to some extent handles like a conventional rear-wheel drive car, so that pressing the accelerator tends to point the car into a corner, requiring a little lock to be unwound. It is, however, genuine oversteer rather than tail-slide, even at low speeds with a lot of right boot: the kind of opposite lock circumnavigation of a steering pad with the car lined up almost radially that is described in our test of the Interceptor is quite alien to the fastidious nature of the FF. At higher speeds the behaviour is more like that of a front-wheel drive car and there is mild understeer, until eventually the whole car slides bodily sideways for a brief moment before scrubbing off speed and regaining its grip. Actually understeer is not the proper term to use here, since it refers to a situation in which the front of the car tends to run wide with respect to the rear; all four of the Jensen's wheels tend to run wide simultaneously, a phenomenon which one member of our test staff suggested might be called "crab-steer".

Lifting off while cornering hard creates a mild degree of front-end tuck-in which the hardest likely combination of simultaneous braking and cornering does little to aggravate into anything worse than an easily controllable change of line. It is only when the driver gets to the stage of adding 0.5g braking to 0.5g cornering —in the wet—that the laws of nature can no longer be defied and the tail of the car swings out—but still in a readily controllable way.

Perversely, our period of tenure coincided with what must surely be a British meteorological all-time record: ten or so days with little or no rain, but fortunately enough for an accurate assessment. In the wet the Jensen does the same things that it does in the dry but naturally the breakaway points occur at slightly lower speeds. There is a limit—albeit a very high one—to the improvement that four-wheel drive can bring to the roadholding of a car, and the handbook does well to point out that the car should still be driven "with due regard to the prevailing conditions".

Everyone now knows that an anti-skid device works by alternately releasing and re-applying the brakes, but at first we were all rather disconcerted to find that the Dunlop-Maxaret system as fitted to the FF did so in a way which bounced the whole car on its springs and more slowly than we remember to have been the case for the Ferguson R5 prototype. On smooth roads, however, we gained enough confidence in the system to attempt in the dry a brutal panic stop from 120 m.p.h.—which in any normal car would have inevitably ended in a hospital ward if not the mortuary—to find that the car was brought to a controlled if rather bouncy stop without any skidding or loss of directional control. The cycling rate of the system for those conditions worked out at a little more than two per second, but it speeds up on slippery surfaces.

Some of our test staff, experiencing the pedal-kickback-and-bounce on surfaces both slippery and bumpy, felt that under certain circumstances during straight-line braking this could put the car off balance. In addition, the system tended to show up shortcomings of the suspension since the Maxaret would sometimes be set into action under light braking when one of the wheels was thrown up by a bump. This became quite a common occurrence on dry but rough French roads, although it may have been triggered in some way by excessive play in a front wheel bearing (for which the car was sent back to Jensen) which was affecting the pedal travel—otherwise light and progressive.

Nevertheless the combined four-wheel drive and anti-locking systems displayed an impressive ability to cope with a wide variety of conditions making it impossible to lose steering control. In particular, the FF system dealt magnificently with wet and dry patches when braking heavily in a corner. In a high-speed avoidance situation, therefore, the Dunlop-Maxaret arrangement could well prove a life-saver.

The brakes of the FF were completely free of fade.

Safety check list

Steering Assembly	
Steering box position	Well forward
Steering column collapsible	No, but has universal joints
Steering wheel boss padded	No
Steering wheel dished	No
Instrument Panel	
Projecting switches	Yes
Sharp cowls	Yes
Padding	Above and below facia and on parcel shelf edge
Windscreen and Visibility	
Screen type	Laminated
Pillars padded	No
Standard driving mirrors	Interior
Interior mirror framed	Yes
Interior mirror collapsible	No
Sun visors	Crushable
Seats and Harness	
Attachment to floor	On slides
Do they tip forward?	Backrests only
Head rest attachment points	Yes
Back of front seats	Unpadded
Safety harness	Lap and diagonal
Harness anchors at back	Yes
Doors	
Projecting handles	Yes
Anti-burst latches	Yes
Childproof locks	No, but only two doors

The tailgate lifts well up to facilitate loading of the boot—the glass is hidden in this picture by the parcel shelf which swings up with it. The toolkit shown is incomplete.

Specification

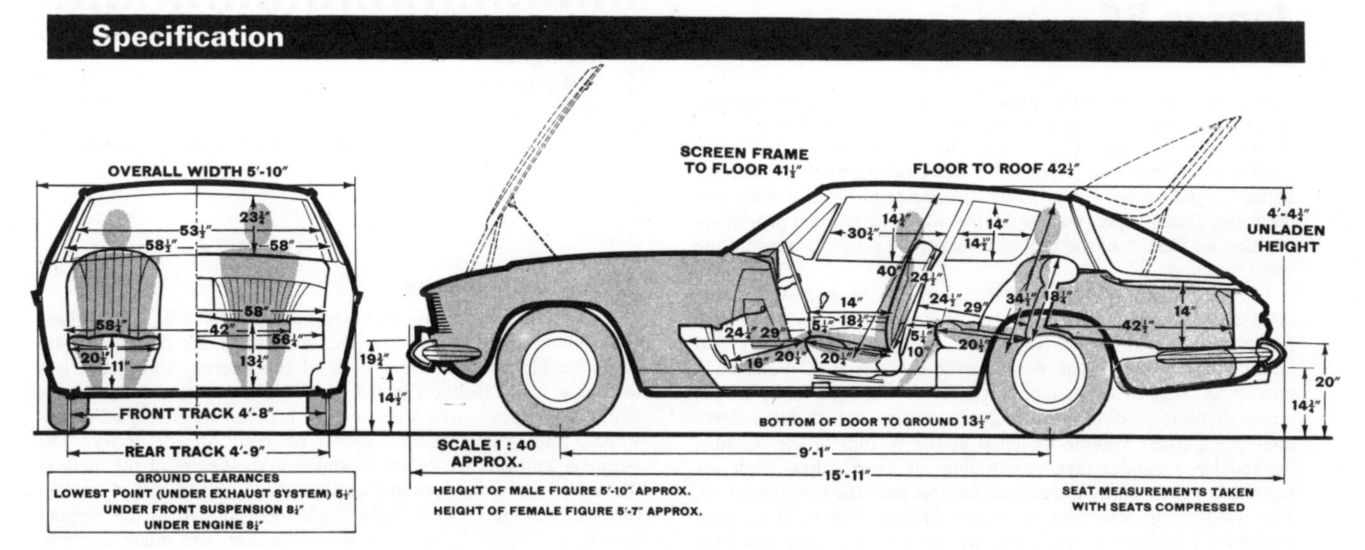

Engine

Cylinders	8
Bore and stroke	108 mm. x 86 mm.
Cubic capacity	6,276 c.c.
Valves	pushrod o.h.v. with hydraulic tappets
Compression ratio	10.0:1
Carburetter	Carter 4-barrel
Fuel pump	Carter mechanical
Oil filter	Mopar full flow
Max. power (gross)	325 b.h.p. at 4,600 r.p.m.
Max. torque (gross)	425 lb.ft. at 2,800 r.p.m.

Transmission

Chrysler Torqueflite 3-speed automatic

Top gear	1.0:1
Intermediate	1.45:1
Low	2.45:1
Reverse	2.20:1
	Final drive 3.07:1

M.p.h. at 1,000 r.p.m. in:—

Top gear	25.8
Intermediate	17.7
Low	10.6

Chassis

Construction	Unitary steel body and tubular frame

Brakes

Type	Girling discs with Dunlop Maxaret anti-skid device.
Dimensions	11.38 in. dia. front; 10.75 in. dia. rear.
Friction areas:	
Front	28 sq. in. of lining operating on 231 sq. in. swept area of discs
Rear	21.1 sq. in. of lining operating on 197 sq. in swept area of discs

Suspension and steering

Front	Independent by twin coil springs and wishbones
Rear	Live axle on semi-elliptic leaf springs with Panhard rod location.
Shock absorbers:	
Front	Armstrong telescopic
Rear	Armstrong telescopic Selectaride
Steering gear	Adwest power assisted rack and pinion
Tyres	6.70-15 Dunlop RS5
Rim size	5J

Coachwork and equipment

Starting handle	No
Jack	Screw pillar
Jacking points	Two each side in sills
Battery	12 volt negative earth, 67 amp hrs. capacity
Number of electrical fuses	2
Indicators	Self-cancelling flashers
Screen wipers	Lucas two-speed with anti-lift blades
Screen washers	Lucas electric
Sun visors	Two
Locks	
With ignition key	Glove locker
With other key	Doors, boot, fuel filler cap
Interior heater	Fresh air
Extras	Fog and spot lights, whitewall tyres, etc.
Upholstery	Leather
Floor covering	Carpet
Alternative body styles	None

Maintenance

Sump	8 pints SAE 20W-40
Gearbox	17 pints SAE Type A Suffix A
Final drive:	
Front	3 pints SAE EP90
Rear	3 pints Shell S6721A
Steering gear	Retinax A
Cooling system	32 pints (one drain tap)
Chassis lubrication	Every 4,000 miles to 3 points
Minimum service interval	4,000 miles
Ignition timing	12.5° b.t.d.c.
Contact breaker gap	0.014-0.019 in.
Sparking plug gap	0.035 in.
Sparking plug type	Champion J-13Y or J-11Y
Tappet clearances	Hydraulically operated—no adjustment needed
Valve timing:	
Inlet opens	18° b.t.d.c.
Inlet closes	58° a.b.d.c.
Exhaust opens	66° b.b.d.c.
Exhaust closes	14° a.t.d.c.
Front wheel toe-out	Parallel to ⅛ in.
Camber angle	1°
Castor angle	1°
Kingpin inclination	7°

Tyre pressures:

	Normal-110 m.p.h.	Occasionally over 110	Sustained over 110
Front	24	30	36
Rear	28	36	40

1, left-hand window control. 2, spotlight switch. 3, fuel gauge. 4, ignition/starter lock. 5, face-level air vent. 6, clock. 7, spotlight switch. 8, wiper/washer switch. 9, right-hand window control. 10, ammeter. 11, speedometer. 12, main beam warning light. 13, mileometer. 14, trip mileometer. 15, demisting vent. 16, oil pressure and water temperature gauge. 17, rev-counter. 18, fuel warning light. 19, indicator/flasher stalk. 20, face-level air vent. 21, cigar lighter. 22, panel light rheostat. 23, rear window heater. 24, heater temperature control. 25, heater fan control. 26, Selectaride adjustment. 27, heater distribution control. 28, ventilation fan. 29, lights switch. 30, heater air volume control. 31, dipswitch. 32, bonnet release.

Comfort and controls

On British roads the ride was firm and well damped, with small amplitude movements and a trace of pitch. When subjected to the far bumpier French "routes de communication importante" the Jensen lived up to both its GT and luxury images by allowing us to drive at around 100 m.p.h. without excessive movement of the car or any trace of bump-steering. It was only when driving at such speeds on roads of this kind that we noticed an increase in the amount of movement and some float on undulations when the Selectaride was turned to its softest setting; under all other conditions we could detect little difference.

The large, high-backed seats with reclining backrests—slotted to receive optional headrests—provided reasonable lateral support but the shape of the cushion tended to make the occupant slide forward, promoting back-ache and fatigue on long journeys. A steering wheel adjustable for reach allowed anyone to adopt a straight-armed driving position if he wished, although a little more fore-and-aft adjustment would have been appreciated by the taller members of our staff, and the lever controlling the reclining mechanism is almost trapped between the seat and the door so that it is very difficult to use on the move. At the rear the legroom is barely adequate for small children, making it difficult to take advantage of the depth of the shaped rear seats, unless the front seats are pushed well forward.

Major controls such as the steering wheel and gear-selector are well located in relation to each other, but the driver's footwell is rather narrow—the brake pedal is of normal, "non-automatic" width—and some of our test staff complained that the left foot resting place (near the footrest-sized dipswitch) was uncomfortable. The more important minor controls, such as the horn button in the centre of the wheel, the indicator/flasher stalk and the rotary/push wiper/washer control which occupies a prominent position on the left of the central console, are similarly easy to find when required.

For all other controls, however, it is to be hoped that the intellectual attainments of the typical FF owner are on a par with his income, for there are almost as many switches, levers and knobs sticking out of the panel beside the driver as quills on a porcupine. Part of the trouble arises from the complexity of the comprehensive heating and ventilating system, which has a lever controlling water volume mounted at the bottom of the console, flanked by a similar lever controlling air distribution, while air volume is governed by a quadrant control near the steering wheel. The windscreen demisting vents can further separately be controlled by knurled nuts and there are three eyeball type face-level vents on the facia. Then there is a two-speed fan for the heater and another to boost the flow from the fresh-air vents, and a third switch for the electrically heated backlight. Perhaps we did not get enough practice to master so many controls for we found that on the move continual adjustment was needed to maintain the interior at an even temperature.

Our test car suffered slightly from an imperfectly sealed front quarterlight which raised the otherwise low level of wind noise. Engine noise was very slight, but the cross-ply tyres made a muffled roar on coarse surfaces (which a Peugeot-owning passenger noticed immediately) and subdued thumps when the wheels contacted larger irregularities.

The long, wide bonnet made placing of the car in confined spaces a very simple business; visibility is excellent and the goldfish-bowl rear window splendid for rearward vision. Equally good was the tremendous blaze of light on main beam produced by the four Lucas quartz-iodine headlamps.

Cooling is by twin electric fans. The right-hand front drive-shaft is just visible.

1, radiator filler cap. 2, cooling fan. 3, oil filter. 4, brake servo control solenoid. 5, power steering reservoir. 6, brake servo. 7, oil filler cap. 8, dipstick. 9, 10, twin master cylinders.

Insurance

AOA group rating	7
Lloyd's	On application

Fittings and furniture

A clear and reasonably accurate speedometer with a matching rev-counter are mounted straight in front of the driver and are easily visible through the spokes of the steering wheel, but less fortunate in its location is the combined oil pressure and water temperature gauge which nestles low between them, angled downwards, and which cannot easily be read on the move. The ammeter and fuel gauge are mounted in the centre of the facia at the top of the switch console and are more readily seen. For map reading there is a rather feeble light incorporated in the dipping mirror, but this is backed up by two further, and much brighter, individually controlled lights on either side of the roof. Neatly styled into these is a pair of grabhandles for the rear passengers, while at the front there are armrests on the doors. Also on the doors are small pull-out ashtrays, matching a similar pair in the rear quarters—naturally there is a cigar lighter on the central console. Both front windows are electrically operated, and the standard equipment includes reversing lights and a very good radio installation with two speakers.

The arrangements for the stowage of odds and ends are a little less satisfactory. The under-facia parcel shelves are small and shallow, as is the lockable glove box (which can foul your elbow when changing gear) on the transmission tunnel. The map pockets on the doors and the backs of the front seats are some compensation for this lack of space, and the large rear parcel shelf is fine until you remember that everything rolls off as it rises with the tailgate. Accommodation for heavy luggage is much better: the Jensen's carpeted boot accepted 8.1 cu.ft. of our test boxes—and you can get in more by temporarily removing the boot cover—and on one journey swallowed up our test kit, a lot of photographic gear as well as some rough weather clothing with sundry pairs of wellington boots.

Servicing and accessibility

The jack is easy to use without getting one's hands dirty, but it is both slow and heavy in operation. Although it should be possible to get at the nut in the floor of the boot to lower the spare wheel tray without taking out any luggage, the wheel itself is heavy and difficult to remove from the tray without kneeling on the ground.

Despite the added complexity of front-wheel drive the long bonnet provides ample room for the engine and all the servicing points are easy to get at. Servicing is required every 4,000 miles and is surprisingly modest in its demands for so complex a vehicle, the main jobs being a change of engine oil, a top-up for front and rear axles plus greasing of three nipples. **M**

Maintenance summary

Every 4,000 miles: Change engine oil; clean and check alternator, air cleaner element and sparking plugs; check and lubricate distributor; check and top up front and rear final drives; grease brake balance lever and rear hubs.

Every 8,000 miles: Clean and check air cleaner element and sparking plugs; inspect and lubricate distributor; inspect prop-shaft UJs for leakage; check and top up automatic transmission, power steering system and centre differential.

Every 12,000 miles: Drain and refill front and rear final drives; check and repack front hubs; grease front prop-shaft sliding spline.

Every 32,000 miles: Clean and repack hubs and prop-shaft joints; change automatic transmission fluid and adjust.

Every 36,000 miles: Drain and refill centre differential unit.

MAKE: Jensen. MODEL: FF. MAKERS: Jensen Motors Ltd., West Bromwich.

JENSEN FF

(6,276 c.c.)

AT-A-GLANCE: Unique four-wheel-drive GT. Big, lazy American engine gives sparkling performance. Smooth automatic transmission, slow to change down. Almost unlimited traction and incredible roadholding from Ferguson 4-wd system. Anti-lock braking not yet perfect. Well equipped and comfortable four-seater.

MANUFACTURER
Jensen Motors Ltd., West Bromwich, Staffordshire.

PRICES

Basic	£4,707 15s 0d
Purchase Tax	£1,309 15s 10d
Total (in G.B.)	£6,017 10s 10d

EXTRAS (inc. PT)

Cibie quartz-iodine fog lamps (fitted)	£19 14s 8d

PERFORMANCE SUMMARY

Mean maximum speed	130 mph
Standing start ¼-mile	15.9 sec
0-60 mph	8.4 sec
30-70 mph (through gears)	7.7 sec
Typical fuel consumption	14 mpg
Miles per tankful	224

ADVERTISED as "the world's most advanced car" and with a price tag slightly more than £6,000, the Jensen FF seems formidable at first acquaintance. Its 16ft length and angular Italian styling make it impressive (to say the least) as it sits by the kerb, and the deep throb of its 6.3-litre vee-8 engine suggests there is power to spare. In themselves, these qualities are not so unusual; but under the skin there is something much more, something unique that makes this the safest high performance car available today: four-wheel drive and anti-lock braking.

When we first drove the Oldsmobile Toronado we were apprehensive about how a large American car would behave with front-wheel drive. We were surprised at how much earlier the 500 lb.ft. of torque could be applied in a bend and how controllable, and therefore safe, the Toronado was. Steering the Jensen FF into a corner is uncanny, because the car seems to pull itself round with a combination of all the best front-drive and rear-drive characteristics. It is as much in advance of the Toronado as the Toronado is ahead of the rear-drive Americans.

All this is the natural result of transmitting drive to all the wheels, but if it were as simple as just that there would be far more four-wheel drive cars in production. Ferguson Research have taken many, many years to develop the split-torque system to the present state where it is sufficiently viable for Jensen to put it into production and for a converted Ford Mustang to be under active assessment for police work by the Swedish Government. After almost 3,000 miles of testing in England and on the Continent, we feel the Ferguson Formula four-wheel drive gives the Jensen a tremendous advantage.

To recap on the fundamentals, the FF has a tubular chassis welded to its steel-panelled body, with a live rear axle and double-wishbone front suspension. The engine and automatic gearbox come from Chrysler and the integrated all-disc anti-lock braking system has been developed by Ferguson Research and is made jointly by Dunlop and Girling. At the back of the gearbox is a differential which splits the torque in a ratio of 37 : 63 per cent between the front and rear wheels. There is a standard Salisbury rear axle and at the front a chassis-mounted differential with double-jointed drive shafts; the front propeller shaft passes along the left-hand side of the engine and gearbox.

Just over a year ago we tested the two-wheel drive Jensen Interceptor, which is exactly the same as the FF except that it has no four-wheel drive and is therefore a little shorter in the wheelbase. This was a truly dynamic car with a top speed of 133 mph and a 0 to 100 mph acceleration time of only 19 sec. With extra gears to churn, the FF loses a little of this performance, but not much. Maximum speed was again identical in both directions, at exactly 130 mph, and 0 to 100 mph took 22.5 sec.

PERFORMANCE

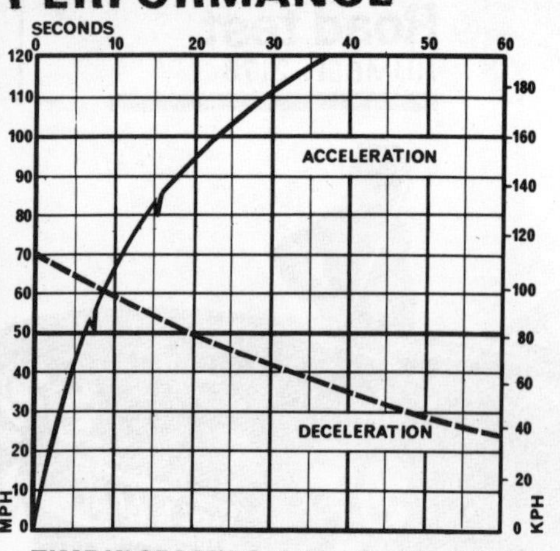

MAXIMUM SPEEDS

Gear	mph	kph	rpm
Top (mean)	130	209	5,080
(best)	130	209	5,080
Intermediate	88	142	5,000
Low	52	84	5,000

Standing ¼-mile 15.9 sec 86 mph
Standing Kilometre 29.3 sec 111 mph

TIME IN SECONDS	3.1	4.4	6.2	8.4	10.8	13.8	17.5	22.5	28.2	37.2	
TRUE SPEED MPH	30	40	50	60	70	80	90	100	110	120	130
INDICATED SPEED	31	42	52	63	73	83	94	104	115	126	136

Mileage recorder 1.7 per cent over-reading.
Test distance 2,922 miles.

SPEED RANGE, GEAR RATIOS AND TIME IN SECONDS

mph	Top (3.07-6.76)	Inter (4.45-9.79)	Low (7.52-16.55)
10-30	—	—	2.2
20-40	—	—	2.6
30-50	4.8	3.8	3.2
40-60	5.6	3.8	—
50-70	6.3	4.6	—
60-80	6.9	5.0	—
70-90	7.3	5.5	—
80-100	8.3	6.5	—
90-110	10.7	—	—
100-120	15.1	—	—

CONSUMPTION

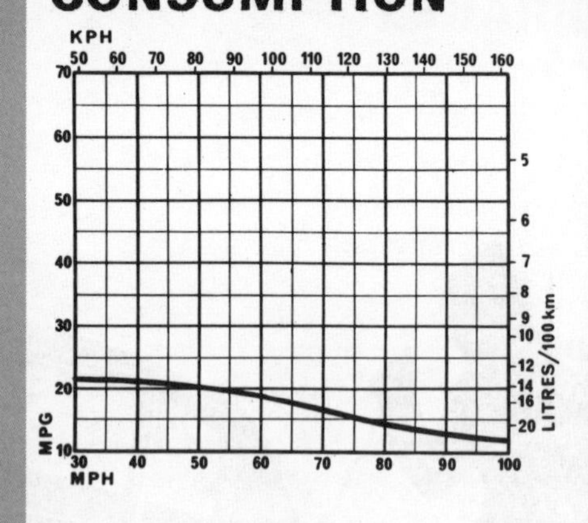

FUEL

(At constant speeds—mpg)

mph	mpg
30	21.9
40	21.9
50	20.6
60	19.3
70	16.6
80	14,8
90	13.1
100	11.5

Typical mpg . . . 14 (20.2 litres/100km)
Calculated (DIN) mpg 15.1 (18.7 litres/100km)
Overall mpg . . 13.6 (20.8 litres/100km)
Grade of fuel, Super Premium, 5-star (min 100 RM)

OIL

Miles per pint (SAE 20W/40) . . . 600

HOW THE CAR COMPARES

Maximum Speed (mean) mph

110 120 130 140 150

Jensen FF
Aston Martin DB6
Jaguar E-type 2 + 2
Jensen Interceptor
Porsche 911S

0-60 (sec)

20 10

Jensen FF
Aston Martin DB6
Jaguar E-type 2 + 2
Jensen Interceptor
Porsche 911S

Standing Start ¼-mile (sec)

30 20

Jensen FF
Aston Martin DB6
Jaguar E-type 2 + 2
Jensen Interceptor
Porsche 911S

MPG Overall

10 20

Jensen FF
Aston Martin DB6
Jaguar E-type 2 + 2
Jensen Interceptor
Porsche 911S

PRICES

Jensen FF	£6,018
Aston-Martin DB6	£4,229
Jaguar E-type 2+2	£2,458
Jensen Interceptor	£4,460
Porsche 911S	£4,122

TEST CONDITIONS Weather: Cloudy, fine. Wind: 0-5 mph. Temperature: 0 deg. C. (32 deg F). Barometer: 29.3in. Hg. Humidity: 78 per cent. Surfaces: Dry concrete and asphalt.

WEIGHT Kerb weight 35.7cwt (3,981lb-1,806kg) (with oil, water and half-full fuel tank). Distribution, per cent F, 52.5; R, 47.5. Laden as tested: 39.3cwt (4,403lb-1,998kg).

TURNING CIRCLES
Between kerbs L, 39ft 10in.; R, 39ft 4.5in.
Between walls L, 41ft 8.5in.; R, 41ft 1in.
Steering wheel turns, lock to lock 3.6

Figures taken at 8,000 miles by our own staff at the Motor Industry Research Association proving ground at Nuneaton and on the continent.

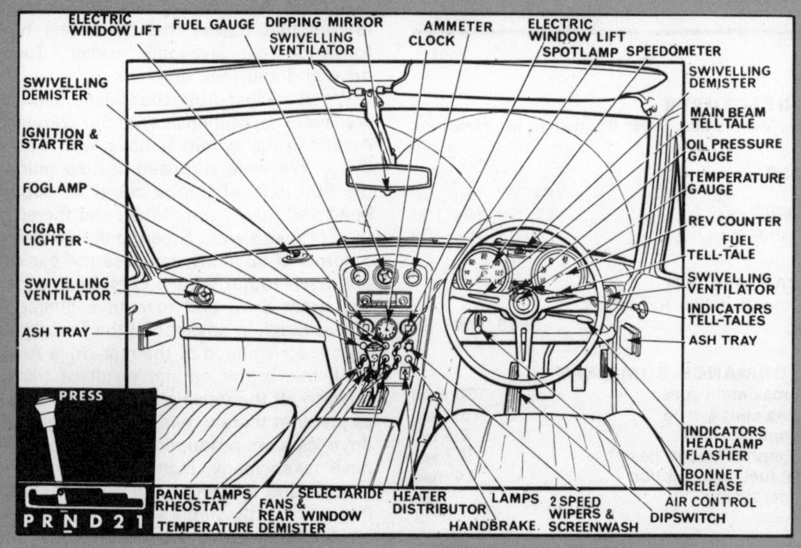

Jensen FF (6,276 c.c.)

BRAKES

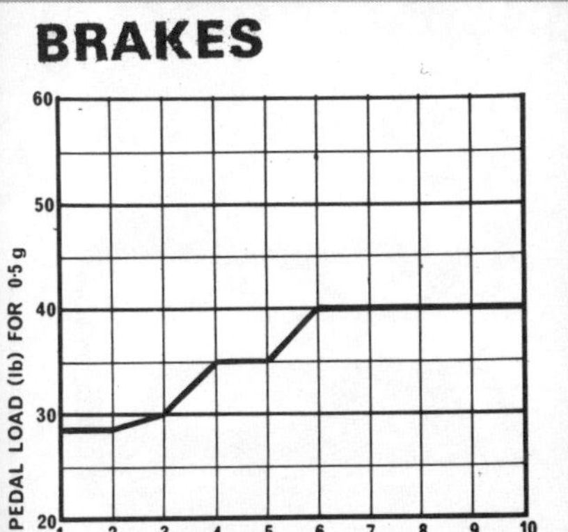

(from 30 mph in neutral)

Load	g	Distance
20lb	0.28	107ft
40lb	0.65	46ft
50lb	0.83	36ft
60lb	0.90	33.4ft
Handbrake	0.40	75ft

Max. gradient 1 in 4

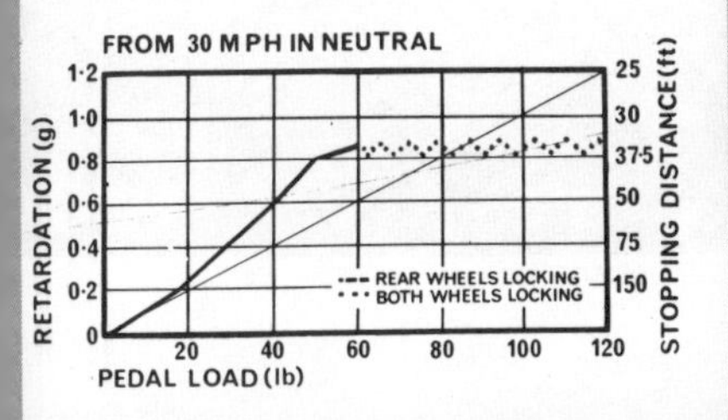

SPECIFICATION

FRONT ENGINE, FOUR-WHEEL DRIVE

ENGINE

Cylinders	8, in 90-deg vee
Main bearings	5
Cooling system	Water; pump, thermostat and two electric fans
Bore	108mm (4.25in.)
Stroke	86mm (3.38in.)
Displacement	6.276c.c (383 cu.in.)
Valve gear	Overhead, hydraulic tappets
Compression ratio	10-to-1 : Min. octane rating : 100 RM
Carburettor	Carter 4-barrel progressive
Fuel pump	Carter mechanical
Oil filter	Mopar full flow, renewable element
Max. power	325 bhp (gross) at 4,600 rpm
Max. torque	425 lb.ft. (gross) at 2,800 rpm

TRANSMISSION

Gearbox	Chrysler Torque-Flite Hi-performance 3-speed automatic with torque converter
Gear ratios	Top 1.0-2.20 Inter 1.45-3.19 Low 2.45-5.39 Reverse 2.20-4.84
Final drive	Hypoid bevel with Powr-Lok limited slip differential at rear only, 3.07-to-1

CHASSIS and BODY

Construction	Steel body and tubular frame welded together

SUSPENSION

Front	Independent, twin coil springs, and telescopic dampers, wishbones, anti-roll bar
Rear	Live axle, dual-rate half-elliptic leaf springs, Panhard rod, Armstrong Selectaride adjustable telescopic dampers

STEERING

Type	Adwest power-assisted rack and pinion
Wheel dia.	17in.

BRAKES

Make and type	Girling discs front and rear, divided hydraulic circuits, Dunlop Maxaret anti-lock system incorporated
Servo	Vacuum
Dimensions	F. 11.38in. dia.; R. 10.75in. dia.
Swept area	F. 237.2 sq.in.; R. 197.4 sq.in. Total 434.6 sq.in. (221 sq.in./ton laden)

WHEELS

Type	Pressed steel disc, chromium plated and pierced, 5in. wide rim
Tyres—make	Dunlop
—type	RS5 cross-ply tubed
—size	6.70-15in.

EQUIPMENT

Battery	12 volt 67 Ah
Alternator	40-amp a.c.
Headlamps	Lucas 4-lamp iodine vapour 110/220-watt (total)
Reversing lamp	2 standard
Electric fuses	5
Screen wipers	2-speed, self-parking
Screen washer	Standard, electric
Interior heater	Standard, water-valve type
Heated backlight	Standard
Safety belts	Standard
Interior trim	Leather seats, pvc headlining
Floor covering	Wilton carpet
Starting handle	No provision
Jack	Bevelift
Jacking points	2 each side under sills
Windscreen	Laminated
Underbody protection	Bitumastic compound on all surfaces exposed to road

MAINTENANCE

Fuel tank	16 Imp gallons (no reserve) (73 litres)
Cooling system	32 pints
Engine sump	8.5 pints (4.7 litres) SAE 20W/40. Change oil every 4,000 miles. Change filter element every 8,000 miles.
Gearbox	17 pints ATF type A. No change needed
Centre and front differentials (each)	3 pints SAE 90EP. Change oil every 12,000 miles
Final drive	3 pints Shell Limited Slip Diff. oil S6721A. Change oil every 12,000 miles.
Grease	3 points every 4,000 miles
Tyre pressures	F. 24; R. 23 p.s.i. (normal driving) F. 30; R. 36 p.s.i. (short bursts to 110 mph) F. 36; R. 40 p.s.i. (sustained 110 mph and above)
Maximum load	750lb (341kg)

PERFORMANCE DATA

Top gear mph per 1,000 rpm	25.6
Mean piston speed at max. power	2,600ft/min
Bhp per ton laden (gross)	165.3

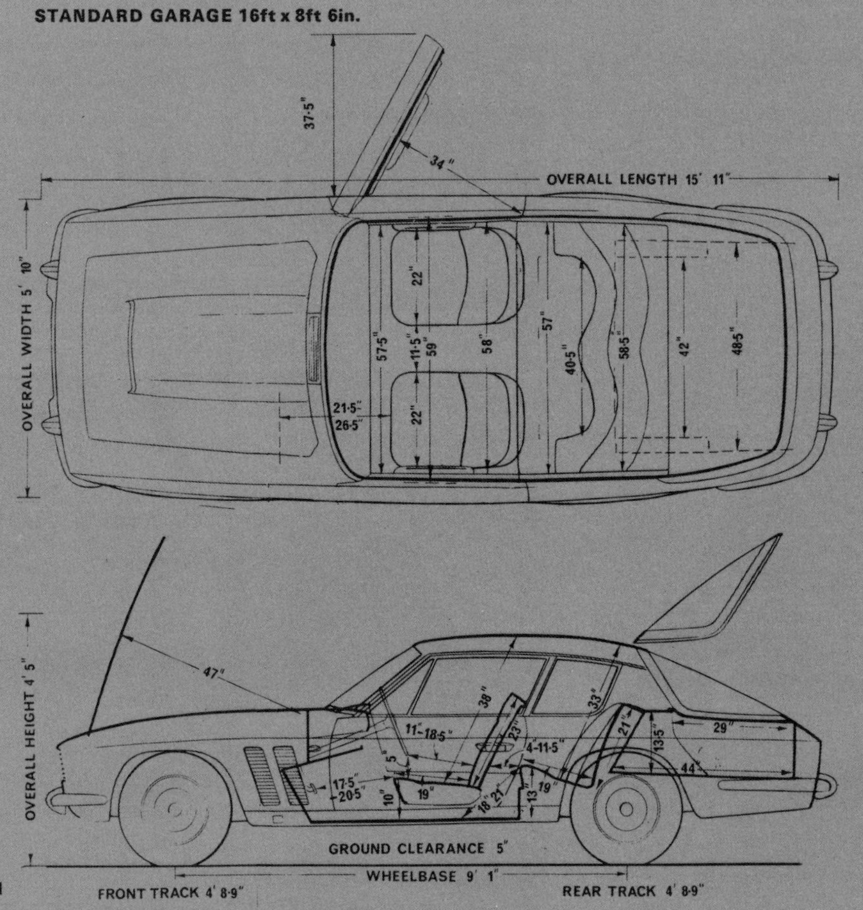

SCALE
0.3in. to 1ft
Cushions uncompressed

1 **2**

1. *Front seat backrests have reclining adjustment and tip forward for access to rear compartment*
2. *The four headlamps all have iodine vapour bulbs and give magnificent night driving illumination*
3. *Boot lid incorporates the wrapround rear window and reveals a really spacious carpeted compartment*
4. *Four-wheel drive aids handling on dry roads as well as wet*
5. *Well contoured rear seats give excellent location and are comfortable for adults in spite of some restriction on leg room*

3

4

5

Luxurious aircraft-type interior, with minor switches and controls on centre console

JENSEN FF ...

While the FF may lose a bit in a straight line on a dry road, it more than makes up for this on twists and turns or if there is any rain about. After a dry day in the Midlands we drove back to London where there had just been a heavy shower and the streets were in that ultra-greasy state which causes unexpected skids and a lot of crumpled wings. As one set of traffic lights turned green, we gingerly opened the first pair of carburettor butterflies, expecting wheelspin and possibly some snaking, but the FF simply surged forward as if the road were dry. At the next lights we gave it full throttle and the same thing happened; it was impossible to spin the wheels.

A few days later, we were trying the car on fresh snow in Switzerland, still equipped with ordinary cross-ply Dunlop RS5 high-speed tyres at normal pressures. During a standing start with full power, the rear wheels and the right front one would just spin for a moment, but there was enough traction to climb a 1-in-4 nursery ski slope to the total amazement of the *piste* patrol. Only the rear differential has a Powr-Lok mechanism and there is enough lateral torque reaction at the front when accelerating hard to give the left wheel grip.

Steering universal joint and rubber gaiter round front drive shaft can be seen just ahead of the alternator. The compartment is not too crowded, but access to sparking plugs is difficult

All Wheel Control

Cornering the Jensen fast is terribly easy because it seems to steer itself round every turn, exactly on line. Initially the front tyres scrub a bit, particularly on a light throttle, but often this is because the driver has put the lock on too suddenly thinking there would be some under-steer. The power-assisted steering takes a little getting used to; it is light and very sensitive with just the right degree of feed-back from the road surface.

Driving to one's accustomed standards, there is always a tremendous margin of spare cornering power in hand. As the dramatic picture we published three weeks ago showed so well, it looks as if the tyres would pull off the rims of the wheels before the car lost its grip on a dry road. In the wet there may be slightly greater slip angles front and rear, but the balance remains the same and still the FF just goes round each corner on line.

Harking back to the test of the Interceptor, we commented on how well the driver could sense when it would be safe to apply full power without generating a tail slide. With the FF he can floor the accelerator as he enters a blind curve and know the front will always pull in as tightly as required and the back will simply follow round without hanging out. When one becomes used to these characteristics, it is possible to storm along twisty roads at seemingly impossible speeds, barely lifting for the kinks and bends. Passengers though, need breaking in gently to the new phenomenon, or they are liable to become alarmed.

Eventually, and only on snow, we reached the limits of adhesion for the FF. With more torque to transmit, and without enough grip to give full weight transference rearwards, it is the tail of the car which slides first. Smoothly and progressively the rear ends swings out, in just the same way as a conventional rear-wheel-drive car would at a much slower speed. The difference, and it is a big one, comes in the correction: because the front wheels are pulling as well as steering, opposite lock is much more

Traction on fresh snow is incredibly good, on wet roads, wheel spin is impossible despite cross-ply tyres and 425 lb/ft. of torque

JENSEN FF . . .

effective and the FF straightens up with a quicker response than we have ever experienced.

While we are fully converted to the advantages of four-wheel drive, we must retain our reservations about the Maxaret anti-lock braking system. The way this works is to sense as soon as the wheels are about to lock (and with four-wheel drive they can lock only together) and reverse the action of the vacuum servo to reduce the pressure in the hydraulic lines. Because the servo works directly as assistance to the pedal, the driver feels this action as a firm kicking-back under his foot. Our pressometer leapt from 60 to 180 lb. during this cycling.

With the non-Maxaret Interceptor we obtained a maximum retardation on a dry road of 0.9g and we were able to repeat this figure on the FF merely by standing on the pedal and letting the mechanism do its work. With practice on the Interceptor, a skilled driver could hold this g figure for the whole of his stop, whereas on the FF there is nothing he can do but leave himself in the hands of the unit, which pulsates down from this peak and back again. The cycling rate is quite slow, about two or three times a second, which has the advantage of giving better steering control—while the wheels are unlocked—during emergency braking.

On wet roads the pedal kicks back at much lower pressures, because the wheels try to lock earlier. We never achieved the claimed cycling rate of five or six per second though, and we felt the system responses were too slow.

Two or three times the brake pedal kicked back at us without apparent reason when we were braking only gently from high speed. Psychologically it is disturbing to have automatic control take over in a panic situation such as a crash stop, even though the system may be bringing the car to rest in a shorter distance. On this last point we are not yet convinced, and we look forward to carrying out some further more elaborate braking tests at an early opportunity.

Luxury Interior

The rest of the FF is well up to what one has a right to expect for the price. Inside there is sweet smelling Connolly hide; a twin-speaker radio with electric aerial is standard. Windows drop and lift by electric motors and there is an impressive, but not very tidy, array of instruments and switches. On the back window is a new type of heating element which is applied to the inner surface and effectively prevents misting up. It cannot cope with frost or snow on the outside though, since toughened glass is too good a thermal insulator.

Although the heating and ventilating system is comprehensive, with separate hot and cold air ducting, it lacks temperature sensitivity and the short levers poking through the central console panel are stiff to adjust. There is a two-speed booster fan for the hot-air system and a separate single-speed fan for the cold-air inlets, which take the form of adjustable nozzles in the centre and at each end of the facia.

Surprisingly, there is no ignition warning lamp and the indicator tell-tales are too dim and almost hidden under the edge of the padding between the speedometer and rev counter. The horns are far too polite and melodious for a high performance GT, and they do not carry at speed.

Seating is very comfortable, although it is a bit of a struggle to climb in behind the wheel, especially when another car or a wall prevents the wide door from opening fully. Backrest angle can be adjusted and the steering column telescopes to suit different arm lengths and different driving attitudes. Back seats are well shaped, but the limited dimensions here prevent one getting really comfortable.

All too often high speed cars are reduced to a crawl at night because of poor lighting equipment. In our Interceptor test we criticized the four headlamp system and suggested iodine vapour units. These are now standard on both Jensen models, and Lucas are to be congratulated on supplying by far the best set of lamps we have driven behind. Even on dipped beams it is possible to sustain very high speeds in the dark with confidence, and on main beams it is just as though the road ahead is flood-lit.

We have purposely concentrated in this test on the peculiar aspects of the four-wheel drive. The engine and transmission performed faultlessly, although we would have liked less delay in the manual over-ride mechanism. Noise levels were very low, and the FF makes no more fuss at 120 mph than it does around town. On the Continent it is truly a grand touring car with a huge appetite for gobbling up the miles, hundreds at a time. In England it is a relaxing car, which gets you there much earlier than you expect. Somehow the big, lazy engine and supreme cornering security with automatic gears and power steering take all the work out of driving and bring back much of the pleasure, despite restrictions and congestion. □

JENSEN INTERCEPTOR

ENGINE CAPACITY 383 cu in, 6,276.22 cu cm
FUEL CONSUMPTION 15 m/imp gal, 14.2 m/US gal, 16.6 l × 100 km
SEATS 4 **MAX SPEED** 135 mph, 217.3 km/h
PRICE IN GB basic £ 3,488, total £ 4,289

NGINE front, 4 stroke (Chrysler); cylinders: 8, Vee-slanted at 90°; bore and stroke: .25 × 3.38 in, 107.9 × 85.8 mm; engine capacity: 383 cu in, 6,276.22 cu cm; compression ratio: 10; max power (SAE): 330 hp at 4,600 rpm; max torque (SAE): 425 b ft, 58.6 kg m at 2,800 rpm; max engine rpm: 5,200; specific power: 52.6 hp/l; cylinder block: cast iron; cylinder head: cast iron; crankshaft bearings: 5; valves: per cylinder, overhead, in line, push-rods and rockers, hydraulic tappets; camshafts: 1, at centre of Vee; lubrication: rotary pump, full flow filter; lubricating ystem capacity: 9 imp pt, 10.78 US pt, 5.1 l; carburation: 1 Carter downdraught -barrel carburettor; fuel feed: mechanical pump; cooling system: water, 2 electric hermostatic fans; cooling system capacity: 32 imp pt, 38.47 US pt, 18.2 l.

RANSMISSION driving wheels: rear; gearbox: Torqueflite automatic, hydraulic torque convertor and planetary gears with 3 ratios + reverse, max ratio of convertor at stall 2, possible manual selection; gearbox ratios: I 2.443, II 1.446, III 1, ev 2.195; selector lever: central; final drive: hypoid bevel, limited slip; axle ratio: .070.

HASSIS tubular; front suspension: independent, wishbones, coil springs, antioll bar, lever dampers; rear suspension: de Dion rigid axle, semi-elliptic leafprings, telescopic dampers electrically adjustable while running.

STEERING rack-and-pinion; turns of steering wheel lock to lock: 3.83.

RAKES disc (diameter 11.50 in, 292 mm), independent front and rear circuits, ervo; area rubbed by linings: total 498 sq in, 3,212.10 sq cm.

LECTRICAL EQUIPMENT voltage: 12 V; battery: 72 Ah; generator type: alernator, 40 Ah; ignition distributor: Chrysler; headlamps: 4.

IMENSIONS AND WEIGHT wheel base: 105 in, 2,667 mm; front track: 55.80 n, 1,417 mm; rear track: 56.90 in, 1,445 mm; overall length: 188 in, 4,775 mm; overall vidth: 69 in, 1,753 mm; overall height: 53 in, 1,346 mm; ground clearance: 5.50 in, 40 mm; dry weight: 3,501 lb, 1,588 kg; turning circle (between walls): 38 ft, 11.6 m; yres: 6.70 × 15; fuel tank capacity: 16 imp gal, 19.3 US gal, 73 l.

ODY coupé; doors: 2, seats: 4; front seats: separate, reclining backrests.

ERFORMANCE max speeds: 56 mph, 90.2 km/h in 1st gear; 95 mph, 153 km/h n 2nd gear; 135 mph, 217.3 km/h in 3rd gear; power-weight ratio: 10.6 lb/hp, 4.8 kg/hp; carrying capacity: 706 lb, 320 kg; acceleration : standing ¼ mile 14.6 sec; speed in direct drive at 1,000 rpm: 26.5 mph, 42.7 km/h.

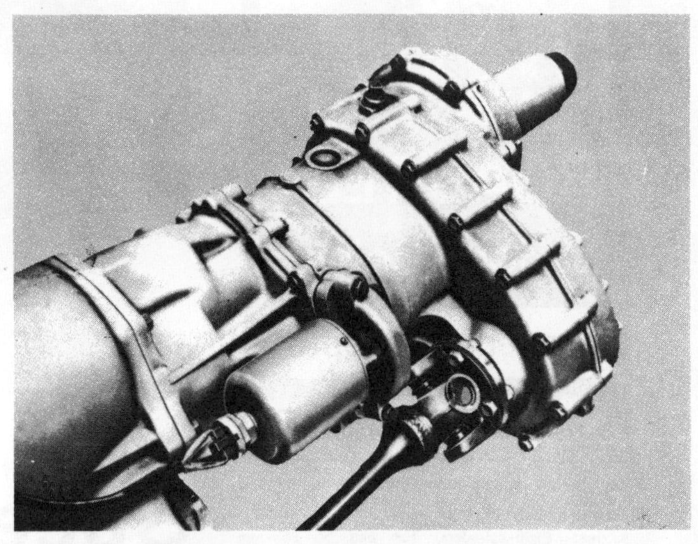

Dunlop-Ferguson anti-skid braking control system

PRACTICAL INSTRUCTIONS fuel: 100 oct petrol; engine sump oil: 8.50 imp pt, 10.15 US pt, 4.8 l, SAE 20W-40, change every 4,000 miles, 6,400 km; gearbox oil: 20 imp pt, 24.10 US pt, 11.4 l, automatic transmission fluid type A, change every 36,000 miles, 58,000 km; final drive oil: 6 imp pt, 7.19 US pt, 3.4 l, SAE 90, change every 12,000 miles, 19,300 km; greasing: every 4,000 miles, 6,400 km, 4 points; valve timing: inlet opens 18° before tdc and closes 58° after bdc, exhaust opens 66° before bdc and closes 14° after tdc; normal tyre pressure: front 24 psi, 1.7 atm, rear 28 psi, 2 atm.

VARIATIONS AND OPTIONAL ACCESSORIES power-assisted steering; 4-speed mechanical gearbox (I 2.658 II 1.909, III 1.388, IV 1, rev 2.580) **V** FF, Ferguson 4-wheel drive without limited slip final drive, automatic gearbox, front suspension with telescopic dampers but without anti-roll bar and rear suspension with transverse linkage bar, power-assisted steering, 2.57 turns of steering wheel lock to lock, brakes with Dunlop-Maxaret anti-skid device, wheel base 109 in, 2,769 mm, front and rear tracks 56.90 in, 1,445 mm, overall length 191 in, 4,851 mm, ground clearance 5 in, 127 mm, dry weight 3,808 lb, 1,727 kg, turning circle (between walls) 39 ft, 11.9 m, power-weight ratio 11.5 lb/hp, 5.2 kg/hp.

SPECIFICATION AND PERFORMANCE DATA

Car tested: Jensen Interceptor 2-door, 4-seater coupé, price £4459 12s 0d including PT. Power assisted steering £100 extra.

Engine: Eight-cylinders, 108 mm × 86 mm (6276 cc). Pushrod-operated overhead valves. Compression ratio 10:1. 325 bhp (gross) at 4600 rpm. Carter 4-barrel progressive carburetter.

Transmission: Torque Flite 3-speed automatic gearbox with fluid torque converter, ratios 1.0, 1.44, and 2.44:1. Maximum converter multiplication 2.2:1. Hypoid level rear axle with limited slip differential, ratio 3.07:1.

Chassis: Steel tubular chassis frame welded to steel body. Independent front suspension with wishbones, twin helical springs, lever-arm dampers, and anti-roll torsion bar. Rack and pinion power-assisted steering. Rigid rear axle on dual-rate semi-elliptic springs with Armstrong Selectaride telescopic dampers and Panhard rod. Disc brakes 11.25 ins diameter all round. Pressed steel plated disc bolt-on wheels fitted with Dunlop RS5 tyres 6.70-15 ins.

Equipment: 12-volt lighting and starting with alternator. Speedometer, rev counter, oil pressure, water temperature and fuel gauges. Ammeter, clock, heating, demisting and ventilation system. Rear window demister, flashing direction indicators, cigar lighter and reversing lamps. Radio (extra).

Dimensions: Wheelbase 8 ft 9 ins; track (front), 4 ft 8 ins; (rear), 4 ft 9 ins. Overall length, 15 ft 8 ins; width, 5 ft 9 ins. Weight 1 ton 13 cwt.

Performance: Maximum speed 133 mph. Standing quarter-mile 15.5 s. Acceleration: 0-30 mph, 3.2 s; 0-50 mph, 5.8 s; 0-60 mph, 7.4 s; 0-80 mph, 12 s; 0-100 mph, 18.8 s.

Fuel consumption: 13 to 17 mpg.

Speed, acceleration, luxury

THE Jensen Interceptor is a logical development from the well-known CV8. It has a similar Chrysler 6276 cc V8 engine and Torque Flite transmission, though a manual 4-speed gearbox is now available at a saving of £250 or so. This hefty engine gives massive torque and a gross output of 325 bhp, so the appreciable extra weight of the new car is not a serious consideration. There is still a steel chassis but instead of a glass-fibre body the structure is now of pressed steel. The body and chassis are welded together, becoming a single unit of immense strength, and the suspension remains conventional, with wishbones and helical springs in front and a rigid axle on semi-elliptic springs behind.

The steering is by rack and pinion with power assistance, and large disc brakes all round are designed to cope with the considerable weight. Tyres for heavy, fast cars are a problem and for safety at sustained high speeds it has been decided to standardize Dunlop RS5 tubed cross-ply tyres. The body is of Italian design and is very handsome indeed, attracting considerable attention everywhere in spite of quiet colours and an absence of decoration. The interior is delightfully furnished, with genuine Connolly leather and plenty of proper round instruments. Only the oil pressure gauge is recessed and difficult to read.

I believe that the impressive array of switches has been criticized elsewhere, but personally I always found the one I wanted

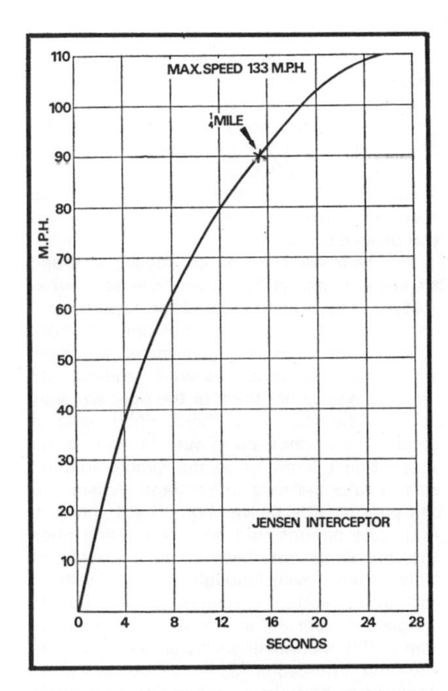

without conscious thought, so the layout must be logical. The ventilation system has plenty of capacity, with three large adjustable outlets, and the heating and demisting are easy to control, plus a much appreciated electrically heated rear window. The body is perhaps too close coupled to be called a genuine four-seater for long journeys. It has an ingenious arrangement for concealing the luggage, which is loaded by opening the enormous rear window.

The car is easy to enter through the large doors and it does not have the low roof and cramped space of the typical sports car. It is in fact a luxury car first and foremost, and the shattering performance which is in reserve is almost incidental. When the big engine starts, there is a deep but subdued burble from the exhaust which exactly suits the character of the machine.

On the road, the Interceptor feels less sporting than the CV8. This may to some extent be due to the extra weight, but it is mostly thanks to completely different settings in the automatic gearbox. The original CV8 had a very fierce box with an ultra-rapid kickdown that was great fun but could be exciting in the wet. There is now a delay on the kickdown, and the box is much smoother in action. As the delightful little gearlever is very well placed, I usually changed down manually instead of using the kickdown. For an engine of this character, the Torque Flite transmission could hardly be improved, and it can be treated as a manual box whenever the driver so wishes. As second gear is good for well over 80 mph, it is useful both for overtaking and cornering.

The car is almost unbelievably effortless, drifting along in silence at 100 mph on a mere whiff of throttle and slipping rapidly up to 120 mph with no increase of sound. Above 120 mph, the vivid acceleration begins to tail off a bit, but by staying just short of the red section of the rev counter it is safe to drive at 133 mph.

The tyres must be inflated to high-speed pressures, which in any case I always used on the Continent, and I kept the Selectaride dampers permanently on the hardest setting. I think the car would go on to 135 mph or a little more, but I did not wish to tangle the tappets, which are hydraulic, and it would take an extremely long road to reach such a speed, so there is normally not the slightest chance of over-revving.

Very vivid acceleration is a notable feature and though I used manual selection in recording the road test figures, very creditable results are obtainable by allowing the automatic changes to occur quite early, with a worthwhile improvement in fuel consumption, for the big Chrysler produces massive torque. In normal fast touring, using a 100 mph cruising speed with short bursts up to 120 mph, one achieves about 15 mpg, which is more than reasonable in view of the weight of the car.

I used the Jensen to cover the Le Mans test weekend, having the opportunity therefore to drive it on some most variable road surfaces, some of which were atrocious. The car rides extremely well, treating bad roads with contempt, while very little noise is transmitted into the interior. The ride feels fairly hard in England, and it takes a long, fast drive on the Continent to bring out the excellence of the suspension.

The power-assisted steering is not excessively light, but parking is very easy. At first, I tended to over-correct skids when I put too much power through the rear tyres on wet roads, but this was a matter of practice. Normally, the car under-steers consistently and is remarkably stable, ignoring changes of camber and side winds. It is not as fast through a corner as some modern light cars on radial ply tyres, but one would not expect it to be. The rear wheels stick down remarkably well on bumpy roads though the suspension is entirely orthodox. The Jensen is too big and heavy to be flung around like a single-seater but it is entirely controllable when handled reasonably.

Quite hard driving caused the brakes no embarrassment and no wheel locking was ever experienced. The hand brake is rather tucked away on the left of the driver's seat, but it is reasonably effective, and of course it is reinforced by the parking lock on the gearlever. Four headlamps of great potency make fast night driving a pleasure.

The standard of construction is very high throughout, and there is all the difference in the world between this and a quantity production car. The way in which the doors close, the fit of the boot lid, and the standard of the leather upholstery, all testify to the excellence of the engineering and body building. Except for the fuel pump, which is rather tucked away, the mechanical parts are accessible for inspection and routine maintenance. The big air cleaner can be removed by unscrewing one wing nut, when the carburetter can be got at with the greatest ease.

Most of my driving of the Interceptor took place in France, where it could be extended to the full. However, I also covered a fair mileage in England, where it still proved to be a most likeable car. It has easy manners in heavy traffic and its silent running makes it an untiring companion for a long journey. The executive, engrossed with his problems, can let the automatic transmission take over the chores of driving, while the enthusiast can add interest to the trip by handling the gearlever himself.

The new Jensen cars are more than worthy of the reputation which the CV8 has established. To the solid virtues of that car they add a beauty of line which greatly increases the owner's price of possession. Production has reached a level which is highly satisfactory for such expensive cars and the name now has a prestige value which makes a Jensen a very good investment.

Why I left home

It took 12 years and a Jensen Interceptor to find out

Words and pictures by Rab Cook

SEA . . . and FISH. There must be a pun in there somewhere. Note quaint local character disguised as journalist.

Records established

(Subject to official condemnation)

First	G-registration Jensen Interceptor to go over Lecht Road.
Shortest	time between consecutive 12-gallon fill-ups at Banff Road Service Station, Fraserburgh (2 hrs. 58 min.).
Longest	distance travelled while "Hey Jude" being played on radio (7.2 miles).
First	visit of Jensen to Insch, Maggieknockater, Oyne, Pitcaple, Ugie Motors (Strichen), Kirktown of Clatt, Pittulie, Inverallochy and Linkwood Distillery.
Biggest	lythe caught by a Jensen driver at Rosehearty during 1968.
Most	flies killed in any fortnight during August/September by a passenger car (1,785,367 plus 1 swatted inside and 2 killed on rear window during rapid reversing).

IT WAS a mild Saturday evening towards the end of August. I was completely alone in a public car park in Auchterarder, just south of Perth, about to attack a brand new Jensen Interceptor with one of the three screw-drivers from its splendid tool-kit—the driver's side screen-washer jet was half a degree out.

A small tweak—try—oops, too much—another tweak—try—GOOD HEAVENS! I looked around and found myself totally surrounded by three coach-loads of Glaswegians (properly Glasgovians, but who wants to be proper?). Here, finally, I had support for my theory that the natives of Glasgow are actually descendants of visitors from outer space—I suspect the Andromeda galaxy, but that's merely a wild guess. They have this ability to materialize in large numbers from nowhere and are quite unlike any other form of life on earth. Their speech is also totally different.

Their spokesman approached me: "Therra rerr carr, surr," he said, pressing his nose against the Jensen's Sundym window. I should explain here that there is another give-away about their outer-space origins. While they inhale oxygen like us, *they do not exhale carbon dioxide* like earth creatures: it is a form of alcohol vapour instead.

Following up his initial approach, the spokesman said: "Whuttl she dae whan ye tak th' brakes aff?" and this was backed up by another observing: "Aye, she'll dae gallons tae th' mile, that yin." Then they all disappeared as quickly as they'd come, leaving only the lingering smell of their breath on the soft summer air. I don't *think* I imagined it.

I didn't really want to be in Auchterarder anyhow; we'd set out about 9 a.m. from London, heading for Fraserburgh at a steady 70 (it says here in the script) and with over 420 miles on the trip reading of this astonishing vehicle we felt so fresh that it seemed silly to stop anywhere but better to keep going for the remaining 160. So I pulled up at a phone box in Auchterarder, got through to The Saltoun Arms Hotel, outlined the problem and was most sorry to hear that they were fully booked that night (our booking ran from the morrow, of course). So the Jensen was rested—not for long, actually, because to fill in the evening we went for a run!

Quite definitely, this is the most comfortable car I have ever driven. The multi-hour grind up the length of Britain in intermittent thunderstorms is the real test. And here I was with no pain in the back, no tightness in the muscles across the back of the shoulders, no stiffness in the legs—completely relaxed. The beautifully controlled suspension, tremendous rigidity of the car, the latest seats, the power steering, the featherlight brakes . . . but above all, I think it is the feeling of complete confidence that makes the biggest contribution to comfort. And, incidentally, I have never known another car so totally unaffected by blustery side winds.

A quick burst of acceleration the following day and we were in Fraserburgh once more and being subjected to a few witty remarks such as: "Foo muckle does this ane cost? Five thoosan'? Aye, wi' a ful' tank, like?"

It's on my conscience that I did the 6.3-litre Interceptor a terrible injustice in the North-East because a miscalculation produced a ridiculously low fuel consumption figure, which I mentioned to a few wide-eyed citizens. The true gobblation was 14.9 m.p.g., and over 800 miles to the pint of oil. In the fortnight we did 2,520 miles—which leads to interesting thoughts such as if one kept on at this rate it would total 66,000 miles per year and cost £1,300-odd for petrol. I've never done so many miles on holiday before yet never felt so hungry for more more more. One feels that here is the sort of car for which one would sell one's mother (able to knit, cook—of course—type, tell funny stories, and good for several decades yet. Offers should be sent in a plain envelope). Certainly, it's the only car over £3,000 which I have really felt to be worth the money and if I had £5,000 to spend on a car . . . if I had £5,000 . . . would you believe £500?

This year we went on an angling kick and an ancient monument kick—both somewhat inadvertently. I hadn't fished for 12 years but last winter I found my old rods and set about refurbishing them as a form of harmless amusement. Some spares were required and the only way to get them of the right size was to take the rods to a tackle shop—and in London you can't park outside any tackle shops that I know of so the simple solution was to take the rods to Scotland. Where you can park outside tackle shops that I know of. And, sure enough, we got the missing rings and things in Peterhead; then a couple of reels; then, even though it was salmon and trout tackle, it seemed a pity not to dangle a rubber eel in the sea on the end of some 20lb. monofilament nylon. And that was how the Interceptor came to be parked in Rosehearty harbour in a howling gale while Cook swept away 25 years by catching his first lythe for heavens knows how long. If you've never heard of such fish, they're lythes to the Scots, pollacks to the English.

It was here that I had a nerve-racking experience. While I was out at the point of the pier lashing the Moray Firth into a lather some fishermen laid nets out to dry between me and the shore with only a space $J + 2 \div n$ left between them and the water, where J = Jensen, 2 is 2 feet and n is the factor which unaccountably makes 2 seem like 0.2 because there is a drop on one side and you are reversing anyhow. But I made it and, stopping for breath, was infuriated to see the inevitable small-boy-on-a-bicycle go straight over the nets—until one pedal got caught in the mesh and he became a flailing blurr of cycle wheels and grey stockings.

At this stage I must issue a warning to all employees and directors of Jensen Motors Limited and to any potential customers who go for a demo run in SEA300G. If you feel a sudden, sharp, shooting pain **DO NOT MOVE.** It may be a fish hook.

Shortly after this incident I fell victim to some mysterious hay-fever type allergy which made further fishing seem unwise and, anyhow, there couldn't really have been many fish left in the sea around there. So we went motoring all over the place. I have written before that I go to North East Scotland not just because I can understand the language, but mainly because it is the last place left in the world where you can go motoring on well-surfaced empty roads just for the hell of it. Things are better than ever now, thanks to the breath tests, and in a few years' time there will thus be no drivers left at all apart from ministers, whisky salesmen and district nurses. It's an ill breath, you see, that nobody blows any good.

Having an allergy naturally brought thoughts of country churchyards . . . you see . . . and: well, no. The truth of the matter is that we caught sight of a large pile of stones by the roadside and just after I had laid forth about them being gathered off the fields by the farmers, we came on a blue sign that said it was a burial cairn so I shut up for a bit and we read all these blue notices instead. Actually, they are very annoying notices because apart from giving the name of the thing they tell you nothing more than that you musn't damage it!

Having gone to all that expense they could surely to goodness add: "Built circa 2,000 BC" or whatever. This was particularly infuriating in the case of an underground "earth house" about which I could discover nothing whatsoever.

So, we Jensened to Huntly Castle, Deer Abbey, Balvenie Castle, the three huge cairns near Culloden and other things with no special plan in mind—just stopped when a blue notice was spotted. Back in London I find from the "Shell Guide to Scotland" that we missed some good things and often drove past them within a megalith's throw. By the way, unless someone commissions me, I doubt if there will ever be a better guide to Scotland than this Shell one; oddly enough, the equivalent Irish volume is dreadful.

Isn't it splendid to be free to do what you like for a fortnight and whisk from A to Z in the grandest possible style? I'm convinced that the Interceptor isn't just a good car but a *great* one. I spent quite some time just sitting in it trying to think of things I would have changed were it mine. At first I thought I'd swap over the fuel gauge and ammeter to bring the former nearer me—then I realised that the fuel warning light is straight ahead of the driver, so the dial arrangement is quite correct. At a steady 70 the speedo and rev-counter needles are exactly lined up with each other on a flat road—probably coincidence but it does make for at-a-glance reading: 2,500 revs, by the way, which is sort of ticking over.

Perhaps: yes, I would definitely bring the accelerator pedal up more in line with the brake; and I would fit a slightly longer winker/flasher stalk and put the horn switch on a twin one at the other side instead of in the wheel-centre button; and I would have the optional leather-covered steering wheel—I don't like these converted tennis racket things which people seem to think are sporty. Back to old-fashioned plastic for me and no more grooves on my palms. By the way, if you're still wondering about that "2,500 revs at 70 on a flat road" remark above, remember the torque converter which causes the rev-counter to go faster than the speedo up hills and when accelerating.

Reading the instruction book before setting out I was startled to find a stern warning about drilling any holes at all in the chassis tubes. *There's* fragile for you now boy-o, I thought (I'd just had lunch with two half-Welshmen) but I read on: ". . . because they are used as vacuum reservoirs for the brakes". And such splendid brakes: tell you what, let's borrow from the experts and run over the car using *Motor's* standard road-test sub-divisions and headings.

Performance and economy: From 0 to 100 in 19 seconds with a top speed of 140. What really counts on the road is that in many situations you have a choice between kick-down and just a squirt with the accelerator pump and, whichever way you do it, you will effectively hurtle towards the horizon in the most satisfying way imaginable. And with this sort of performance I certainly don't grumble at nearly 15 m.p.g.

Transmission: I've said before that the Chrysler Torqueflite automatic box is just about the ultimate because it obeys you instantly and its changes can hardly be sensed—much better than any manual. Nothing more to say there.

Handling and brakes: Early on in the holiday I had one or two moments when I thought: "It took a little bit of doing to get through that corner" followed by a pop-eyed glance at the speedometer which clearly showed that I'd come through the bend at a speed I wouldn't normally contemplate; and once or twice a look in the mirror revealed other cars I'd just overtaken travelling at much lower speeds with their suspensions all undignified at one side, and chopping about madly. The Interceptor has this trick of scaling everything else down—at 70 you get the same dream-like feeling of hovering as in a Viscount floating in just before the wheels go *Owk Owk* on the runway. Hills don't make any difference to anything. If you've never experienced this scaling down business you'll find it very hard to imagine—maybe impossible.

At first I thought that the brakes weren't progressive enough—that too little extra pressure brought in too much extra stoppery. Two things altered this situation: one was that the linings changed their character a little as they were used more and got nearer

"The lonely SEA and the sky . . . and all I ask is a tall glass . . ." or is it ". . . a few sips"?

Spot for wonder and indignation (above). The Culsh Earth House might be a prehistoric barrow, or a less ancient robbers' hide-out, or all sorts of things, but the Ministry of Works merely warns you not to damage it. Perhaps some reader knows?

Right: The little children play with pebbles—the big ones with Jensen Interceptors and boats. . . . The harbour at Pennan, on the Banffshire/ Aberdeenshire border.

Why I left home

to the "harder" state which I prefer—one of the things I have in common with Graham Hill is a preference for heavy brakes. (The others? Well, we both live north of the Thames; and that's about it.) Then, as the mileage increased, I realised that the faint tyre howl which had made me ease the pressure had nothing to do with wheel locking, but just the Dunlop RS5s singing to themselves under braking. Once this had sunk in I slammed them on happily and found them every bit as king-size as the performance.

Comfort and controls: We seem to have done that one, except for the allegedly complicated heating/fresh-air system of the Jensen. It is nothing of the sort—once you realise that the heating and fresh-air systems are totally separate, with their own blower motors, and that the marvellous idea of getting a controlled blast of cool air across your feet is also quite on its own and not interconnected with anything but the forward speed. *And* the heater has a thermostat that keeps it constant irrespective of the air flow. The passenger can control her own environment to a large extent, which leads to happy families, and minute changes in the temperature and air flow can be made very simply. One constantly finds new combinations of the controls with a pleasure akin to that of discovering a new face in the bathroom linoleum's marbled pattern (there was a Viking chief carrying a sword on ours this morning).

Fittings and furniture: The trim is superb and I couldn't fault it. Next please.

Servicing and accessibility: Once you have removed the air cleaner (one wing-nut) you find a Carter four-barrel carburetter that you couldn't possibly even begin to understand. It has things on it that carburetters don't have. The plugs might be a little bit tricky to change but the rest seems easy enough to get at, if you want to, but milling over at 2,500 most of the time seems a sort of ideal life for an engine and it should last a few hundred years. Tappets are hydraulic, so no adjustment needed there.

* * *

Generally, I don't think I've ever been so proud to be seen with a car, or so delighted with its practical features, and this is where the grand design really scores: no folding yourself up double before getting in, and plenty of luggage space; yet lines which look as though you had splashed the money purely for turkey-cock reasons. Of course, pride cometh . . . . Driving out of Fraserburgh on the Banff road one morning I waved to someone I knew and slammed my foot down—only, the engine was too cold, it went blatt-blatt in the twin pipes and we had what jet pilots refer to as a flame-out. And with an automatic you can't restart on the over-run, and you have to move the lever to N before turning the key, and I got a bit confused, and my friend laughed and laughed and laughed. The pig.

But pride returned. In Banff, shopkeeper Sinclair Young said: "You can leave that parked outside my door just as long as you like". Very sensible people in the Royal and Ancient Burgh of Banff . . . where I was born and schooled . . . and they've got ancient monuments, and fishing, and splendid roads. But no Jensens.

That, really, must have been why I left.

JENSEN FF TO SWISS SNOW

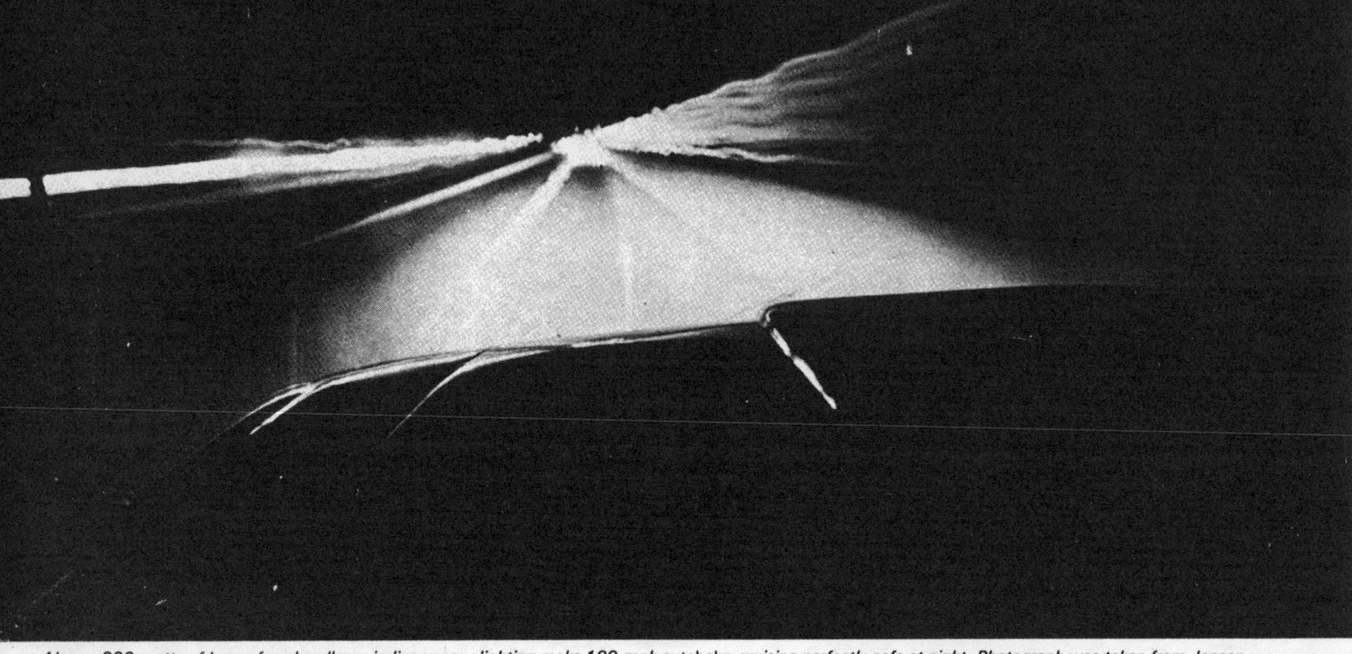

Above: 330-watts of Lucas four-headlamp iodine vapour lighting make 100-mph autobahn *cruising perfectly safe at night. Photograph was taken from Jensen passenger seat on a 15-sec exposure; streaks are opposing traffic. Below: Snowploughs had left their mark on the dazzling snow walls of the road down from the Col du Pillon*

TO SEE how the four-wheel-drive Jensen FF behaved on snow and ice, it was taken to Switzerland last winter. A full description of its tremendous performance was given in the Road Test in AUTOCAR 28 March. This short account describes the trip and how such a car—a true Grand Tourer, unlike some of the tarted-up saloons which debase the letters GT—makes short work of long journeys.

KEEN drivers seem to envy the job of a motoring journalist and without any thoughts about the less glamorous side of press dates, hours behind a typewriter instead of a steering wheel and the relentless pressure on time, they ponder only on the fine foreign trips in fast cars. Such a trip, perhaps, as the rare plum which fell our way earlier this year: to take the Jensen FF to Switzerland and try to find some snow on which to assess its four-wheel drive. Not until we were safely on the night boat for the Hook and out of reach of recalling telephones could we believe the Editor really meant it.

Craned on like a crate of oranges was "our" deep blue Jensen FF, worth nearly a pound for each of its 6,276 c.c. and with its 16-gallon tank full of pre-Budget fuel. Pending hovercraft, this Harwich-Hook night crossing is one of the less tiresome ways of crossing the moat, and as our brief also included "Wot'll she do?", a starting point on Dutch motorways seemed to suit well. Unless almost free of other cars two-lane Continental motorways are inevitably less safe for maximum speed runs than Britain's 36-footers, so when we emerged from a fairly calm night in one of ss *Arnhem's* first class "cupboards" our first task was to find an empty stretch of motorway on which to unleash the full 325 bhp.

Early morning proved a bad time for Holland, busy with rush-hour traffic and swarms of sleepy cyclists, and although we found it easy to cruise at 90-100 mph on the *autoweg,* allowance had to be made for such contingencies as traffic lights, a cheap substitute for a flyover at the Utrecht junction. So after an hour and a half of effortless progress we found ourselves bearing down on a Douane/Zoll sign at 110, and that was Holland, that was.

Arnhem, near the border, generates a lot of traffic, but once into Germany the *autobahn* from Emmerich to Wesel carries only sparse traffic crossing from the one country to the other. We had no difficulty at all in holding the Jensen at full throttle for long enough to be sure there

A PLEASANT AFTERNOON'S RUN

By STUART BLADON AND MICHAEL SCARLETT

A lazy 110 mph cruise needs only 4,300 rpm from the $6\frac{1}{4}$-litre Chrysler engine

Above: Glorious sun glints on a glorious car in a typical Swiss village near Gstaad. Horse in the background is harnessed to a hefty sledge. Below: It was the way back that demonstrated how close Swiss snows are to Southend. Despite autobahn road works and the non-motorway stretch from Liège to Brussels, the Jensen covered 522 miles in $6\frac{1}{2}$ hours running time (Basle to Ostend)

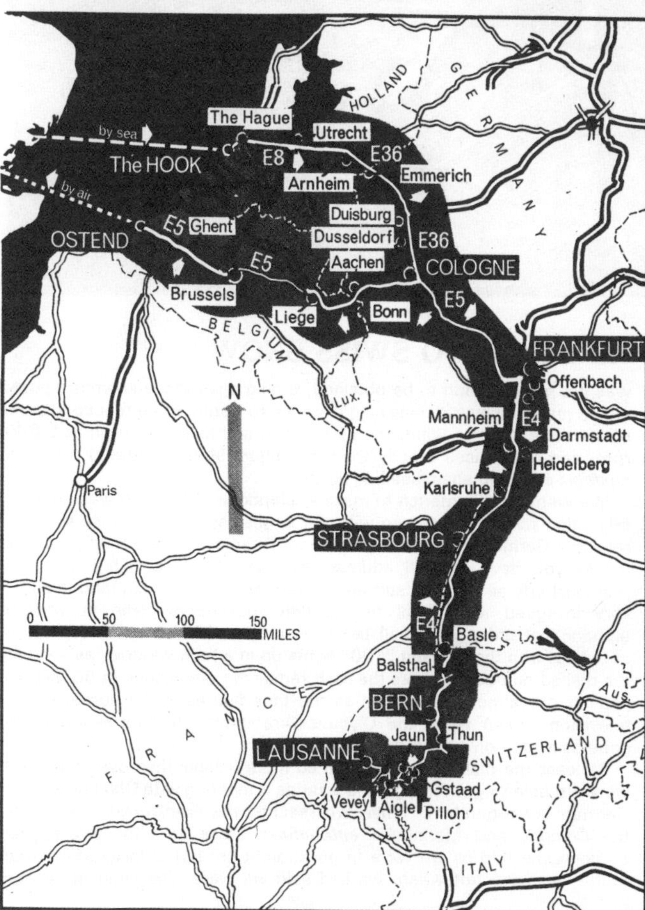

Above: Everybody was interested in the Jensen. We thought of charging a Swiss franc per Swiss look but decided this might look like a swiz. Below: A booted Bladon makes a 12-minute dash round the Beautiful Vignale body before photography in the snow

JENSEN FF TO SWISS SNOW

was not another mph to be obtained, timing against the kilometre posts which mark the ever-diminishing distance to Berlin. In perfect conditions of sunshine with no wind, the FF reached and held 130 mph at 5,080 rpm, and reproduced exactly the same figure after we turned off at an *ausfahrt* and tried again heading north.

We went into Emmerich to make a telephone call, which was quite an education for anyone fed up with the English system, because in many respects German telephones are worse. Directories are virtually useless unless you have the full address, as they break up a big area like Frankfurt into all the little sub-areas. German visitors to England must be very intrigued to find all the London subscribers given in straight alphabetical order. At a call box, you drop a 1DM piece (now worth about 2s) into the slot and "100" lights up in a little window; as soon as the dialled number answers the cash remaining diminishes to 90, 80, 70 and so on, almost as quickly as the time figures in the corner of the television screen when the Olympics are shown. A mark seems to be gone in a trice on a long-distance call.

At least the dialling system seemed more reliable than over here, and we were able to get through and arrange a meeting with Olaf Fersen, our German correspondent. When we reached the *Frankfurtekreuz,* where the Cologne and Mannheim *autobahnen* cross at a massive flyover complex, he told us we were to go straight on; but unfortunately—our fault—we were not where we had said we were. The snag of Jensen rates of progress is that in the brief five minutes it takes to feel you have gone wrong, consult the map, and realize the error, you are nearly nine miles down the wrong road; and by the time a flyover has been found to turn round on, at least a couple of gallons of fuel have been wasted.

We spent the night at the university city of Heidelberg, obtaining directions to our hotel from a somewhat drunk and disorderly party of students in a Volkswagen, which the most sober one was clumsily refuelling from a can and smoking at the same time.

After a leisurely start next day we cruised on down the magnificently straight and traffic-free Basle *autobahn.* So as not to be too hard on the car's fuel consumption we kept the speed down most of the time to a leisurely 100 mph, but did allow ourselves an invigorating burst for a few miles at 120 to shake off a police helicopter which had insisted on sitting almost on the roof of the car. In Switzerland the *autobahn* stops at Basle, but there is a choice of splendid all-purpose roads to Olten, where the new Swiss *autoroute* (N1) with advisory 75 mph speed limit leads down to Bern.

Neither of us had been to Switzerland in winter before, and we wondered what it would be like. Would all the small passes be *geschlossen* as would the big ones like the Susten? To find out, we diverted over the Jaunpass but although snow was piled high beside the road, the surface was only wet. Under a deep blue sky and warm sunshine it was an absolutely beautiful run, and only the gathering dusk eventually sent us gliding along the Geneva road to stop for the night at Lausanne. Next morning we upset the local tourist bureau somewhat by asking which was the nearest pass that was closed so that we could try driving over it, and were directed to the nearby Col des Diablerets and Col du Pillon.

Again a magnificent blue sky and hot, unbroken sunshine greeted us as soon as the dawn mist had cleared, and we slipped quietly through Montreux and again back up to 4,500ft to the saddle of Les Diablerets. The fantastic spectacle of the ever-mounting banks of snow beside the road, the surrounding snow-clad mountains, and all the time the dazzling sunshine glaring back from the whiteness really made one understand why people go winter sporting—yet why not by car? They must miss so much. At the top of the pass a triangular circuit of deeply snow-covered roads between high banks of packed snow gave us all the opportunity we needed to experiment with four-wheel-drive handling characteristics. The Col du Pillon was indeed signposted as closed, but the ploughs had been through and it did not really need four-wheel-drive to prove the notice lied.

At the foot of the pass we stopped at Gstaad, thronged with skiers, but still felt we had not really put the car to the test. But at about 5 pm the ski lift stopped, and shortly afterwards the sun dipped behind the peaks and the temperature started falling rapidly. As fast as the mercury dropped, the skiers disappeared, and the sudden realization that the nursery slopes were almost deserted gave us the idea to try the car on the steep ski slope. Although prepared for four-wheel-drive traction, we were absolutely staggered at the way the Jensen on ordinary Dunlop R55 tyres at motorway pressures would climb and even stop and restart on a gradient of 1-in-4 on snow polished and compressed by skiers.

We were so impressed we decided to stay the night there, and carry out more tests at the top of the pass next morning, then venture on to the ski slopes again so that we could take photographs. After bitter overnight frost this was a real test for four-wheel drive, and gave us the heading picture for the Road Test (28 March).

Lunchtime found us still lingering at Gstaad, although we were due on an aircraft at Ostend first thing next morning; so we set off to find out if Switzerland to the Channel port was "on" in an afternoon, or whether it would need the night as well. We cleared the Swiss border at 4 pm, and our comfortable $6\frac{1}{2}$ hours running time for the 522 miles to Ostend (80 mph average) showed that if one really tried it should be possible in 6 hours by Jensen. Speeds of the order we were using are everyday in Germany and Belgium; how they and other Continental drivers must laugh at our 70 mph motorway speed limit. But not even the anti-climax of 40 mph traffic all in the right-hand lane on the Southend road on return to Britain could spoil the memories of our superb Jensen journey. □

Welcome home to Sunday on the Southend road. Not once on any autobahn was the Jensen ever obstructed unnecessarily—Continental drivers moved over quickly and safely after one flash of the headlamps

TWO JENSENS

Some Notes on the Four-Wheel-Drive, Dunlop-Maxaret-Braked FF and The Interceptor. Luxury Cars with 6.3-litre Chrysler V8 Engines

ENGINEERING SOPHISTICATION.—The four-wheel-drive Jensen FF, with anti-lock brakes, may mean nothing to the birds but is a splendid technical achievement, Jensen being the only manufacturer to adopt the Ferguson Formula for safer motoring to a production car, giving Britain a significant lead.

MY PREVIOUS association with Jensen Motors of West Bromwich was four years ago, when I visited the factory and road-tested the then current 6.3-litre CV8 saloon. Recently I was able to bring my knowledge of Jensen affairs up to date, by driving the advanced FF (Ferguson Formula) model for a long weekend and a modern Interceptor—a very smart maroon one—for a longer period.

Richard and Allan Jensen entered the Motor Industry in the early 1930s as specialist bodybuilders, achieving fame with their Avon Standards, etc. Like Sir William Lyons, of Jaguar, they later built complete cars, such as the Ford V8-powered tourers and saloons (they were very cagey in those days as to the origin of the engine!), and subsequent models using 22 h.p. Ford V8 and 4.2-litre straight-eight Nash power units. Steyr and Lincoln engines were also used, and after the war there was an imposing 3.9-litre Meadows-engined car, until the Interceptor arrived in 1950, powered with an Austin A135 4-litre engine.

Jensen were pioneers of disc brakes on all four wheels in 1957, were early users of safety belts fitted as standard, and the 5.9-litre Chrysler-powered CV8 of 1963 led on to the current models and the innovation of four-wheel-drive and Dunlop Maxaret anti-skid braking on the Jensen FF by 1967, the comparatively-small West Bromwich company thus making one of the world's most advanced cars.

Because it sells safety of the kind which makes a driver to avoid accidents, instead of safety that protects the car's occupants *during* an accident, the four-wheel-drive Jensen is a great advance in automobile engineering technique. I was naturally anxious to try it, and have waited a very long time for the privilege. Taking an FF away from the factory, the first impression (after a thoughtful and observant pedestrian had stopped me to say the fuel tank was leaking—the cheap and nasty A.C. bayonet-type cap had not been replaced after replenishing) was that there is absolutely no way of telling that there is anything at all unconventional about the Jensen FF's Laystall-made transmission, although it is extraordinarily unusual, with four-wheel-drive on the Ferguson system, using hypoid drives front and rear, that additional differential, and a drive shaft passing along the n/s of the engine, and transfer to this shaft by means of a chain drive.

Yet, in action, there is no transmission noise and the very good power steering gives no hint that the front wheels are being driven. On dry roads, likewise, the Dunlop anti-lock Maxaret braking feels entirely normal. Fortunately, going up to Silverstone for the V.S.C.C. Driving Tests the roads were wet, and I was able properly to appreciate the superiority of the FF over conventional motor cars. It is possible to turn on the power of the 325 b.h.p. Chrysler V8 engine with impunity, because the car goes exactly where it is pointed. Corners can be negotiated under power—you just turn the front wheels and the FF goes where it is pointed. With the power of an average American automobile at your command, this is not only impressive and reassuring—it makes for excellent cross-country average speeds. My experienced passenger remarked: "It must feel very safe", realising that I would not be driving a rear-wheel-drive car as quickly without courting a shunt.

The Maxaret braking, with Mintex M74 pads, is likewise of immense value on slippery roads. The knowledge that the wheels will not lock until the car is stationary gives great confidence—you approach a road junction, or tuck-in between two moving vehicles, and just stamp on the brake pedal, no matter how wet or greasy the road surface. If the wheels attempt to lock up they release automatically, before so doing, at the expense of kick-back from the pedal. On normally slippery going, or if a wheel becomes air-borne on a wet patch, this pedal reaction is no worse than that we used to experience on certain vintage cars whose chassis frames flexed over rough roads—a 6½-litre Bentley, for example. It is on abnormally gripless surfaces, such as wet grass, that the action could be alarming, both from the aspect of violent kick and clunking from the system, unless the driver has been forewarned. But the car stops in a straight line, without any need for cadence braking on the driver's part. On a dry road the Maxaret stopping distances may not be quite so short as with a normal system. But the FF's foolproof braking is entirely satisfactory and this insurance against wheel locking reduces driving tension—and *should* reduce insurance charges!

Couple this safe braking with four-wheel-drive and you have one of the safest slippery-road cars yet put on the market. The FF costs £1,809 more than the Interceptor; whether this is worthwhile will depend on how a driver rates his skid-avoidance skill and how much fast driving under skid-prone conditions is likely to be undertaken. From my limited experience of the FF I can say that it transformed my method of driving, and the pleasure I derived from driving, this powerful and large motor car.

The Jensens are well made, fully-equipped cars. They do not challenge the Rolls-Royce market in respect of either quietness or absolute refinement of detail, being essentially high-performance cars for four passengers rather than the epitome of luxurious travel for up to five occupants. The FF, incidentally, suffered from a few shortcomings which should not be found in a £7,000 car. For example, the driver's (electric) window-lift worked jerkily and stuck down on one occasion, the front passenger's seat was of a most uncomfortable shape, the engine tended to stall at parking speeds with the power steering on full lock (the Silver Shadow isn't exempt from this), the l.h. heater control was at times absurdly stiff to move, and at speed the boom from the twin exhaust pipes became somewhat irritating—more so on the

The two Jensens together, showing the twin vents and air-intake on the bonnet top which distinguish FF from Interceptor.

The "cockpit" of a modern Jensen, with clock, switches, electric window-lift controls and heater levers, etc., on the central console.

Interceptor than on the FF. In addition, the o/s screen wiper blades did not properly clean the glass, even after the washers had been used, and I cannot imagine the owner of an FF, perhaps while listening to the Warsaw Concerto on the Voxson stereo-player (which I was able to do while driving the Interceptor), liking to have to get out and wipe the screen with the backs of his gloves. Both cars suffered from reflections in their windscreens.

Having disposed of these criticisms, most of which, curiously, were not present on the less expensive Interceptor, I am free to pay tribute to the excellence of the FF's speed, acceleration, comfort, good driving position and, above all, its impeccable controllability. Its cornering tendency is neutral, with a trace of oversteer if power is taken off in mid-corner—and it takes even an experienced driver quite a time before he is willing to exploit to the full the remarkable adhesion of this remarkable car.

The FF and Interceptor, four-wheel-drive and Maxarets apart, are virtually the same, except that the frame tubes are slightly heavier, and further outboard, on the former, as the transmission tunnel is wider. The FF is recognisable by two vents on the bonnet sides instead of one on each side and an air-intake on the bonnet lid. Its body is slightly less aerodynamic, so the top speed of the Interceptor, 133 m.p.h., is higher by perhaps three m.p.h. The FF is also somewhat heavier, the transmission weighing about 180 lb. and the Maxaret unit approximately 20 lb. But it would be the faster car in point of average speed, especially in the rain, and to drive it in these conditions is to add a new experience to the motoring repertoire. I was unable to do a full fuel-consumption check in the time available, but a brief test showed 10.9 m.p.g. of 100-octane petrol.

The Interceptor did rather better, giving 14.5 m.p.g. on a long journey. As the low-level warning light shines with only 30 to 36 miles to go before the tank is dry, refuelling is needed about every 200 miles and the FF even more frequently, in spite of a 16-gallon tank. This will represent less than 2½ hours' motoring on Continental roads, so these Jensens are not true GT cars! There was a little difficulty about refuelling the Interceptor in Herefordshire, and thereby hangs a short tale. A Shell garage was closed, a Regent garage had only regular gas in stock. So I arrived at a B.P. filling station with about a pint in hand and was obliged to take on 99-octane fuel, on which the engine pinked like a prudish young bride. This suggested one of three things—the ignition was abnormally far advanced, B.P. super grade fuel is inferior to other brands, or B.P. Superblend pumps can cause the customer to receive the wrong octane fuel.

The Interceptor, like the FF, has a steel-panelled four-seater body welded-up and upholstered by Jensen, using some panels imported from

VIGNALE-STYLED.—An impressive rear view of the Jensen Interceptor, with its sloping back window which lifts up to give access to the luggage boot.

Italy, the styling being by Vignale. Whereas the CV8 had a fibre-glass body, this material is confined to interior body parts on modern Jensens.

Dealing now with the Interceptor, the concept is a fairly "close-coupled" saloon, two fully-adjustable bucket front seats, separated by a wide veneer-finished tunnel and console, with a shaped and generously upholstered back seat, having a folding centre arm-rest. The wide screen sill, central facia and speedometer and tachometer nacelles are upholstered in black anti-dazzle Amblia-cum-leather, veneered wood being confined to the console. A multitude of flick-switches conveniently located on the console confuse a driver unaccustomed to a Jensen, but are generally satisfactory, except for the insensitive action of such controls when applied to rheostat panel lighting. The switch nearest to the driver in the bottom row puts on the lamps (foot-dipper), and half the big sloping back window is demisted by a Triplex heater. There is a comprehensive cold/hot air system of ventilation and heating, each with its own fan, supplemented by fresh air from three swivelling facia vents and foot-level inlets.

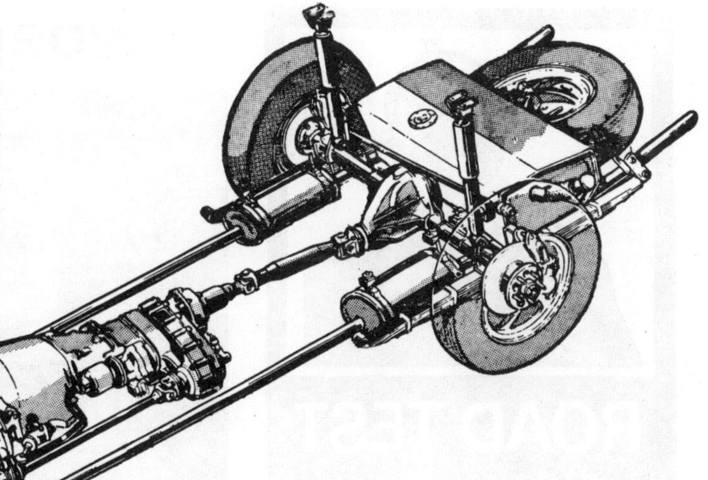

CHAIN AND SHAFT DRIVE AND THREE DIFFERENTIALS.—A drawing showing how four-wheel-drive is contrived on the Jensen FF.

The instruments comprise Jaeger speedometer and tachometer before the driver, the former calibrated every 20 m.p.h., and the latter "going into the red" from 5,000 to 6,000 r.p.m.—this Chrysler engine does not "rev" as fast as more modern American V8 engines, but peaks at 4,600 r.p.m. and is comfortably under 3,000 r.p.m. cruising at our pathetic top speed-limit. (The top axle ratio on both cars is 3.07 to 1.) Between these two big dials is a combined oil/temperature gauge, not altogether easy to read. It is intended, I think, that the needles shall lie in line when all is well—in fact, in recording normally just under 50 lb./sq. in. and just above "N", they don't quite do this. Of the warning lights, those for oil pressure low and hand brake on are right in front of the driver. A reasonably accurate Jaeger electric fuel gauge and a Lucas ammeter occupy the facia, angled towards the driver, and at the top of the console there is a loud Smith/Jaeger clock, flanked by the electric window-lift controls.

The horizontal area of the console contains the rather ornamental, short lever controlling the commendably smoothly-functioning Chrysler Torqueflite-8 three-speed automatic transmission, which has 1st and 2nd gear "hold" positions and a kick-down which postpones the change into top until around 80 m.p.h. has been reached.

Both Jensens have plenty of creature comforts—Connolly leather upholstery, push-down internal door locks (the doors are sill-less and unincumbered by woodwork) openable side windows (fixed front ¼-lights), deep vizors with vanity mirror, Jensen/Britax safety-belts, cigar lighter, first-aid kit, pull-out ash trays upholstered to match the leather trim, electrically retracting radio aerial, lift-up inside door handles conveniently below the arm-rests, provision for fitting head-rests to the front seats, anti-dazzle mirror, etc. The carpeted boot is spacious, the spare wheel being below it and the rear window constituting its lockable lid. But luggage has to be humped up into the boot. If bulky luggage is to be carried the rear-window shelf can be removed, after undoing seven nuts, giving more "roof" space in the boot, but the attachment of this shelf, and the cover plates giving access to the rear-lamp wiring, leave something to be desired in a £7,000 car, or even in a £4,700 one! One of the covers was difficult to replace, for instance. For stowing small objects there is a very long, lockable lidded well behind the console, two rather shallow under-facia shelves (pipe-racks, perhaps?) and covered wells forming outboard arm-rests, at each end of the back seat, as well as pockets on the back-seat squabs. A data panel is provided under the lid of the stowage well, and a good handbook accompanies the car. The petrol filler flap requires a key to open it and the ignition and boot-lid keys are the same shape, which is confusing. The bonnet lid is self-supporting, with a prop for safety, and the boot opens nicely and stays open—both compartments are illuminated. The car can be wired for stereo, or front/rear radio speakers. The bumpers are rubber-tipped, and the radiator grille is of solid alloy sections. The Lucas duel headlamps, the outboard ones iodine quartz lamps, gave a ridiculously cut-off beam on both Jensens, when dipped. A l.h. stalk controls turn-indicators and headlamp flashing and an old-fashioned button sounds a genteel horn note. The small steering wheel has column adjustment, is sensibly low-set, and has a non-slip leather-bound rim.

The tyres fitted are tubeless, nylon Dunlop Road Speed RS5s, 6.70 × 15 (H15 on the FF), Jensen not having come to grips with radial-ply tyres. The Rubery Owen pressed steel wheels were originally made specially for Jensen.

In both cars the 108 × 86 mm (6,267 c.c.) D-series engine, with 10 to 1 c.r., gives very effortless, impressive and useful acceleration and easy fast cornering, at the cost of some exhaust boom. The Interceptor ran 550 miles without needing oil (sump capacity 8½ pints). The automatic choke of the Carter carburetter gives prompt cold starting.

It is in handling that the Interceptor falls from grace to go with the pace, especially when sampled immediately following the super-safe FF. On both cars the rack-and-pinion steering is entirely free from lost movement and is geared 3½ turns lock-to-lock, with a small turning circle. The FF's power steering is excellent. On the Interceptor the harsher, rather heavier action of the power-assisted steering is immediately apparent, nor do the handling characteristics encourage

CONTINUED ON PAGE 163

A BONNETFUL OF FINE MACHINERY.—Chrysler power for the Jensen FF.

Four-wheel-drive *plus* anti-lock braking *equals*

WORLD'S SAFEST CAR

ROAD TEST by John Bolster

Jensen FF

The elegant Italian-style lines have made the Interceptor/FF series the best ever from Jensen. Wheels are the BRM/Rubery Owen Rostyle components. 39-5-3

THERE is nothing new about four-wheel drive. The first 4wd car was the six-cylinder Spyker, built in Holland just after the turn of the century, and it was followed a few years later by the Badger, a very powerful American car. The firm that built the Badger also produced the famous 4wd lorry that performed so magnificently in the mud of the first world war, and subseqently Bugatti and Miller constructed four-wheel-drive racing cars. Those of us who owned Jeeps after the second war can vouch for the many advantages of the principle.

Early four-wheel-drive cars suffered from the lack of any method of sharing out the power between the front and rear wheels. Owing to rearward weight transfer on acceleration, the back wheels can take nearly twice as much power as the front, so if an ordinary differential is used between the forward and rear pairs of wheels, the front ones will spin first and rob the rear ones of traction, such a car being actually less effective than a normal rear drive vehicle under some conditions. The alternative is to delete the master differential, as on a Jeep, but the transmission then "winds up," which is most undesirable. Other cross-country vehicles use a free wheel, but this removes the advantages of four-wheel-drive during braking.

In the case of the Jensen, a much more sophisticated solution has been worked out, based on the Ferguson Formula. This system, the result of many years of research, incorporates a "lopsided" differential, which divides the torque between the front and rear wheels, so that 37 per cent goes to the front and 63 per cent to the rear. In addition there are two multi-plate clutches which permit the front wheels to over-run the rears by 16.5 per cent, and the rear wheels to overrun the fronts by 5.5 per cent. If either pair of wheels begins to slip more than this, the appropriate clutch locks up automatically, temporarily converting the differential to a solid drive.

It must be realised that the correct functioning of this master differential, and the freedom of the differential between the front wheels, are essential to the car's roadholding on fast bends. Cross-country vehicles are often very dangerous when cornered fast on hard roads, because any winding up of the transmission can produce alarming changes in the steering behaviour. The complexity of the Ferguson Formula is thus fully justified in the case of a very fast car like the Jensen.

In addition to its greater traction, four-wheel-drive also improves braking because the back wheels cannot lock without the front locking too. This means that a single aircraft type anti-locking device can be applied to the transmission and control all the brakes. The Dunlop Maxaret works on the servo, through which it cuts down the braking effort as soon as signs of locking are indicated. A panic-stricken driver can continue to press the pedal, but he will be prevented from precipitating a skid, be the road wet or dry. Since I last drove the Jensen the Maxaret has been modified to work closer to the limit as the result of experience.

To take full advantage of four-wheel-drive, plenty of power is required. This is provided by a Chrysler V8 of 6.3 litres, giving 325 bhp, which is in unit with its own three-speed automatic transmission. The Ferguson Formula components are behind the box, and from the rear of this assembly an ordinary propeller shaft goes to a rigid rear axle with a limited-slip differential. The drive to the front wheels passes on the left of the engine, which is slightly offset to the right in consequence. An enclosed chain—actually three Morse "Hyvo" chains side by side—conveys 37 per cent of the torque from the master differential to the front propeller shaft, which drives a chassis-mounted hypoid unit with a plain differential for the front drive.

The independent front suspension is by hefty wishbones and twin helical springs with an anti-roll bar, the rack and pinion steering naturally having power assistance. At the rear the rigid axle is on semi-elliptic springs, and at first one is rather surprised that such a conventional chassis is used to carry all that advanced engineering. For reasons that are not at all clear, the four-wheel-drive system completely transforms the roadholding of this very straightforward suspension design, the results being much better than one would believe possible.

An idea of the traction provided can be gathered from the excellent performance figures, for these were timed in pouring rain! Obviously no car driven by two of its wheels could approach these results, and there was literally no sign of wheelspin, the standing starts being made on full throttle. I exceeded 130 mph on a road running with water, and there was no sign of aquaplaning. This is logical, because films taken of aquaplaning show that the front wheels slow down and even stop, so driven wheels are much less likely to suffer from this terrifying effect, though we must give due credit to the Dunlop tyres.

Theoretically four-wheel-drive cannot increase the cornering power of a car, but by reducing the disturbing effect of putting power through one pair of wheels it does in effect do just that. For this reason a Jensen FF would out-corner an Interceptor, although it is a little longer and appreciably heavier. Even the Ferguson magic stops short of miracles, and it cannot make a heavy luxury-car corner like a light racing machine, but it removes so much skill from the proceeding that a moderate driver could safely corner at speeds not normally within his grasp. Cornered on full power, the car retains the same balance as it does on a light throttle, with no tendency to lose one end or the other. It corners geometrically, to use Dehane Segrave's phrase, and the driver need learn no tricks.

The only unusual thing that one notices is that the steering must be pulled straight pretty smartly after taking a sharp corner on full throttle. There is not much castor action and the car can come out of a corner so fast that it must be straightened up as quickly as possible, though this is only disconcerting at first and rapidly becomes instinctive.

Most good drivers learn by experience to brake almost to the limit on any surface without going too far. For them the Maxaret will probably not give a spectacular improvement in braking performance, but when used by a less experienced driver it will literally prove to be a life-saver. Even an excellent driver may find it necessary to have his car driven by other people from time to time, and the protection provided by the Maxaret can then give him peace of mind. The powerful brakes are undaunted by the considerable weight of the car and do not tend to fade, though the hand brake has not much stopping power.

The suspension gives a fairly firm ride and, while small bumps are felt, the bigger ones are quite well absorbed. The front seats are very comfortable, though they do not hug the occupants like rally seats, and the rear seats are fairly close-coupled, lacking space for really tall passengers. There is a marked absence of road noise, except for some thump over bad potholes, and the complete elimination of wind noise is almost incredible. The engine is as smooth and quiet as one expects a big Chrysler to be, but only remarkable engineering could achieve the outstanding silence of the transmission. The use of a chain drive instead of the more usual train of gears is abundantly justified by these results, and neither of the two hypoid drives is audible.

The automatic transmission changes up very smoothly, but there is a curious delay in the kickdown, which prevents the driver from taking the fullest advantage of the fantastic traction. When making manual up-changes for acceleration testing, I sometimes found it difficult to change from first to second, the lever tending to slip straight through into top. Apart from that, all the controls work easily and smoothly and are well placed. The power-assisted steering is not ultra-light, and some feeling of the road has been retained.

The finish of the coachwork is superb, and the beautiful Connolly leather adds greatly to the luxurious character of the interior. Quartz-iodine headlamps are now fitted and they are immensely effective, the all-round view being assisted by the electrically heated rear window. There are three eyeball ventilators for cool air, and the heater, which is very powerful, is unusually easy to control. The windows are raised and lowered electrically, as one would expect nowadays with a car of this calibre. The rear window lifts up like an estate car tailgate, raising a shelf that covers the contents of the large, carpeted luggage boot.

Four-wheel-drive adds to the cost and weight of a car, and any simplification of the design would certainly affect the roadholding. For light, low-powered cars, it would not offer much advantage, but with six healthy litres of engine the benefits are tremendous. Though there are good reasons for using the system on racing cars, it is the unpredictable nature of fast journeys on the road that bring out its greatest virtues. It is possible that, in years to come, a powerful GT car will have four-wheel-drive as a matter of course, and the Jensen FF is certainly the leader in this important field.

The interior is extremely well laid out, with clear speedometer and rev counter dials and the bulk of the controls grouped in the centre console. 39-5-4

The powerful and extremely torquey 6.3-litre Chrysler V8 gives tremendous acceleration and is not at all overcrowded in the Jensen's engine bay. 39-5-5

SPECIFICATION AND PERFORMANCE DATA

Car tested: Jensen FF 4-seater coupé, price £7007 including tax.

Engine: Eight cylinders, 108 mm × 86 mm (6276 cc). Pushrod-operated overhead valves. Compression ratio 10:1. 325 bhp (gross) at 4600 rpm. Carter four-barrel downdraught carburetter.

Transmission: Three-speed automatic gearbox with torque converter, ratios 1.0, 1.45 and 2.45:1. Ferguson Formula four-wheel-drive with controlled master differential splitting torque 37 per cent to front and 63 per cent to rear. Rear drive by open propeller shaft and hypoid axle with limited slip differential. Front drive by divided propeller shaft driven by triple Morse chains, to chassis-mounted hypoid with free differential. Ratios of both hypoids 3.07:1.

Chassis: Tubular frame welded to steel body. Independent front suspension by wishbones and twin helical springs with anti-roll bar. Power-assisted rack and pinion steering. Rigid rear axle on semi-elliptic springs with Panhard rod. Telescopic dampers all round with Selectaride control at rear. Girling servo-assisted disc brakes all round with Maxaret anti-lock system. Bolt-on disc wheels fitted Dunlop RS5 6.70-15 ins tyres.

Equipment: 12-volt lighting and starting with alternator. Speedometer. Rev-counter. Ammeter. Oil pressure, water temperature and fuel gauges. Clock. Reversing lights. Heating, demisting and ventilation system with electrically heated rear window. Electric window lifts. Windscreen wipers and washers. Flashing direction indicators. Extra: Voxson radio and tape player.

Dimensions: Wheelbase, 9 ft 1 in. Track, 4 ft 8.9 ins. Overall length, 15 ft 11 ins. Width, 5 ft 10 ins. Weight: 1 ton 15 cwt 3 qrs.

Performance (wet road): Maximum speed, 132 mph. Standing quarter-mile, 15.7 s. Acceleration: 0-30 mph 2.8 s, 0-50 mph 5.8 s, 0-60 mph 7.9 s, 0-80 mph 12.4 s, 0-100 mph 20.2 s, 0-120 mph 33.6 s.

Fuel consumption: 12 to 15 mpg.

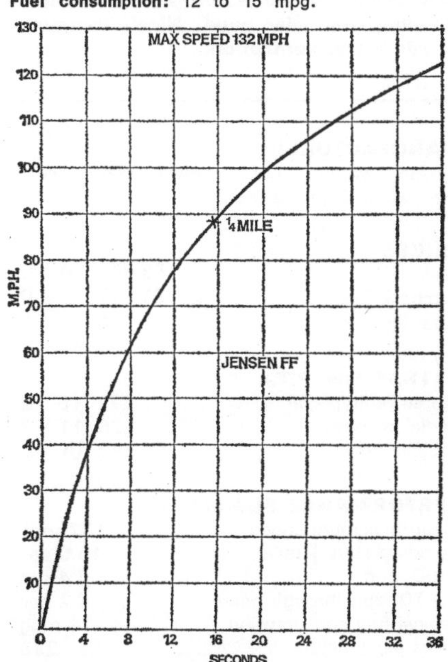

Autotest

JENSEN INTERCEPTOR (6,276 c.c.)

AT-A-GLANCE: Latest version of British GT with Italian styling and American engine. Lots of performance; light fade-free brakes; very smooth transmission. Power steering. Handling normally good. Nicely trimmed. Needs better ventilation.

MANUFACTURER

Jensen Motors Ltd., Kelvin Way, West Bromwich, Staffordshire.

PRICES

Basic	£3,980	0	0
Purchase Tax	£1,218	8	0
Total (in G.B.)	£5,198	8	0

EXTRAS (inc. P.T.)

Stereo radio/player	£71	16	2
Radial ply tyres	£20	11	3
Price as tested	£5,290	15	5

PERFORMANCE SUMMARY

Mean maximum speed	137 mph
Standing start ¼-mile	15.0 sec
0–60 mph	6.4 sec
30–70 mph through gears	6.2 sec
Typical fuel consumption	14 mpg
Miles per tankful	225

THE recovery of Jensen Motors from a very shaky position in 1966 has been something of an industrial marvel. New management and a good product have been responsible, and Jensen now rates as number one in the specialist car field. Over 1,200 Interceptors and FFs have been made in only 2½ years and production is now averaging 17 cars per week. In the light of this we decided it was time to reappraise this exciting American-engined GT.

It was 5 January 1967 when we first tested the Interceptor with its Chrysler 6.3-litre vee-8, TorqueFlight automatic transmission, conventional suspension and beautiful Vignale body. Since then there have been detail changes to the engine (better torque and clean air combustion package), a redesign of the front suspension, refinements to the gearbox and improvements in the tyre equipment (with a revised axle ratio to suit different rolling radii). Power steering has been added to the standard specification, ventilation and demisting are improved and the headlamps now have quartz-halogen bulbs.

Even before one opens a door there are obvious signs of better quality compared with the early cars. Working from panels shaped in Italy, Jensen reform the rough flanges, weld up and fill to make a body which as well as being elegant is free from blemish and ripple long before it enters the paint spray booth. Inside there is an extremely high class of finish, with a luxurious smell of real Connolly hide and satisfying fits to the complex trim around the instruments and facia.

Like all Americans, the engine starts easily and idles smoothly at only 500 rpm, with a sporty burble to its exhaust. At the peak of 4,600 rpm it now develops 330 bhp compared with 325 previously and although the torque is still quoted as 425 at 2,800 rpm, the shape of the curve is a lot flatter.

With a power output like this in a car weighing 33 cwt unladen, the results of pressing the accelerator are pretty electrifying. From rest 60 mph is reached in only 6.4sec and 100 mph comes up in 18.2sec. Compared with our earlier test car, the latest one is slightly quicker, but only to the extent of less than 2sec all the way to 120 mph. This was one of the rare cars which could reach 130 mph from rest comfortably within the mile length of the MIRA horizontal straights. Even on a dreadfully wet day, when we had eventually to abandon our test measurements, the Interceptor (which has only two-wheel drive remember) shot to 100 mph in only 19.4sec with remarkably little wheelspin.

Radial-ply tyres are now optional, Dunlop Sport being fitted. These are slightly smaller than the cross-ply RS5s which used to be obligatory, so the axle ratio is changed from 3.07 to 2.88 to 1 to compensate. In fact, top gear mph per 1,000 rpm goes up a little from 25.6 to 26.4.

During acceleration runs we found that the hydraulic valve gear did not "pump up" at 5,100 rpm as on the earlier car, and 5,500 rpm was possible and usable. There is a red sector on the rev counter from 5,100 to deter the use of high revs and most of the time there is an abundance of torque much lower down the rev band. But it made quite a difference on top and this time we recorded 137 mph in two directions with the rev counter reading 5,400 rpm.

The latest TorqueFlight transmission has a cushion clutch to reduce the snatch when changing up or down and it is a real example of how smooth an automatic box can be. There is hardly a pause in the steady accelerative pull during upshifts, and the kickdown quality is particularly good. The selector has a big round knob, well placed and easy to hold, with a push-button in the top to unlock it. Holding the lower gears with the over-ride we ran to 95 and 55 mph at 5,100 rpm.

Girling now make the brakes instead of Dunlop and sizes are altered slightly. With discs front and rear there is no fade what-so-ever and

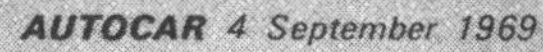

the response is much lighter than before. It now takes only 60 lb effort to get a maximum (0.98) g stop, about half the previous figure. There is always a very reassuring bite to the pedal.

Our previous criticisms of the steering have been heeded, and a power-assisted system is now fitted. It is a special installation by Adwest, with a servo rack and pinion and a steering oil cooler up front. The big (17in. dia.) wood-rimmed steering wheel has been replaced with a 15½in. leather one with the same number of turns (3½) between rather cumbersome and uneven turning circles of 41ft left, 37ft right, between kerbs.

All the work has now gone out of parking but there is a dead patch around the straight ahead position which leads to slight instability at speed. Turning the wheel a few degrees in this region made the car deflect all right, but it stayed on the chosen rate of turn without pulling straight on its own. This kind of behaviour is often caused by too much friction in the steering swivels rather than insufficient castor. To improve the whole front end and give adjustments not previously provided for, the front suspension is now by means of Alford and Alder ball-jointed wishbones with telescopic dampers, instead of by lower wishbones and upper lever-arm dampers with bushed king-pins.

One of the additional benefits claimed is better front end damping. Our car had covered almost 12,000 miles by the time we had completed our test and the dampers at the front were too weak. In relation to those at the rear they were out of balance, causing the car to float and pitch at the front about the rear end as a pivot. This behaviour spoilt what would otherwise be a very good ride. Armstrong Select-a-ride rear dampers are fitted and experiments with their four settings altered only the fierceness of the disturbances without reducing the discomfort.

The relative rear end stiffness, especially in roll, caused us serious concern about the ulti-

Left: The small steering wheel has a leather rim and instruments are well placed and easy to read. The centre console and tunnel are covered with highly polished wood veneer. Right: Seats are trimmed in real hide and adjustable for rake in the front

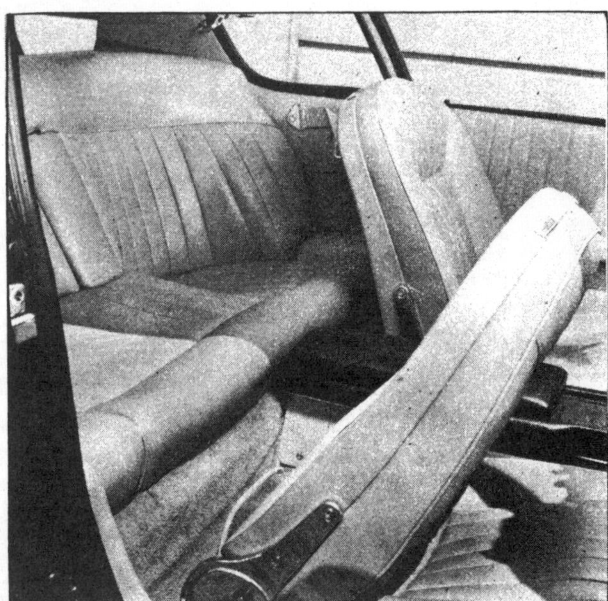

ACCELERATION

SPEED MPH TRUE	INDICATED	TIME IN SECS
30	29	2.5
40	39	3.7
50	49	5.0
60	60	6.4
70	71	8.7
80	82	11.2
90	93	14.3
100	105	18.2
110	116	23.7
120	130	30.6
130	145	40.6

SPEED RANGE, GEAR RATIOS AND TIME IN SECONDS

mph	Top (2.88)	Inter. (4.17)	Low (7.06)
10–30	—	2.5	2.6
20–40	3.4	2.7	2.1
30–50	3.5	2.8	2.6
40–60	4.1	3.3	—
50–70	5.0	4.3	—
60–80	6.0	5.0	—
70–90	6.8	5.6	—
80–100	7.8	—	—
90–110	9.9	—	—

Standing ¼-mile
15.0 sec 92 mph
Standing kilometre
27.7 sec 116 mph
Test distance
1,005 miles
Mileage recorder
7 per cent
over-reading

PERFORMANCE

MAXIMUM SPEEDS

Gear	mph	kph	rpm
Top (mean)	137	186	5,100
(best)	137	186	5,100
Inter.	95	153	5,100
Low	55	88	5,100

BRAKES

(from 70 mph in neutral)
Pedal load for 0.5g stops in lb

1	45	6	35
2	40	7	35
3	37	8	35
4	35	9	37
5	33	10	40

RESPONSE (from 30 mph in neutral)

Load	g	Distance
10 lb	0.12	251 ft
30 lb	0.42	72 ft
50 lb	0.92	33 ft
60 lb	0.98	30.7 ft
Handbrake	0.30	

Max. Gradient 1-in-5 (see text)

MOTORWAY CRUISING

Indicated speed at 70 mph	71 mph
Engine (rpm at 70 mph)	2,650 rpm
(mean piston speed)	1,495 ft/min.
Fuel (mpg at 70 mph)	18.3 mpg
Passing (50–70 mph)	3.7 sec

COMPARISONS

MAXIMUM SPEED MPH

Monteverdi 375L	152	(£10,250)
Aston Martin DBS	140	(£6,112)
Jaguar E-type 2+2	139	(£2,642)
Jensen Interceptor	**137**	**(£5,198)**
Porsche 911E	130	(£4,243)

0–60 MPH, SEC

Montverdi 375L	6.3
Jensen Interceptor	**6.4**
Jaguar E-type 2+2	7.4
Aston Martin DBS	8.6
Porsche 911E	9.8

STANDING ¼-MILE, SEC

Montverdi 375L	14.6
Jensen Interceptor	**15.0**
Jaguar E-type 2+2	15.4
Aston Martin DBS	16.3
Porsche 911E	17.0

OVERALL MPG

Porsche 911E	19.0
Jaguar E-type 2+2	18.8
Jensen Interceptor	**12.9**
Aston Martin DBS	12.7
Monteverdi 375L	11.6

GEARING (with 185-15in. tyres)

Top	26.4 mph per 1,000 rpm
Inter.	18.7 mph per 1,000 rpm
Low	10.8 mph per 1,000 rpm

TEST CONDITIONS: Sunny. Wind: 0 mph. Temperature: 25 deg. C. (77 deg. F). Barometer: 29.95 in. hg. Humidity: 40 per cent. Surfaces: dry concrete and asphalt.

WEIGHT:
Kerb weight 33.0 cwt (3,695 lb–1,675 kg) (with oil, water and half full fuel tank.) Distribution, per cent F, 50.7; R. 49.3. Laden as tested: 37 cwt (4,105 lb–1,865 kg).

TURNING CIRCLES:
Between kerbs L, 39ft 6in.; R, 34ft 11in. Between walls L, 41ft 1in.; R, 36ft 9in. steering wheel turns, lock to lock 3.5.

Figures taken at 11,800 miles by our own staff at the Motor Industry Research Association proving ground at Nuneaton and on the Continent.

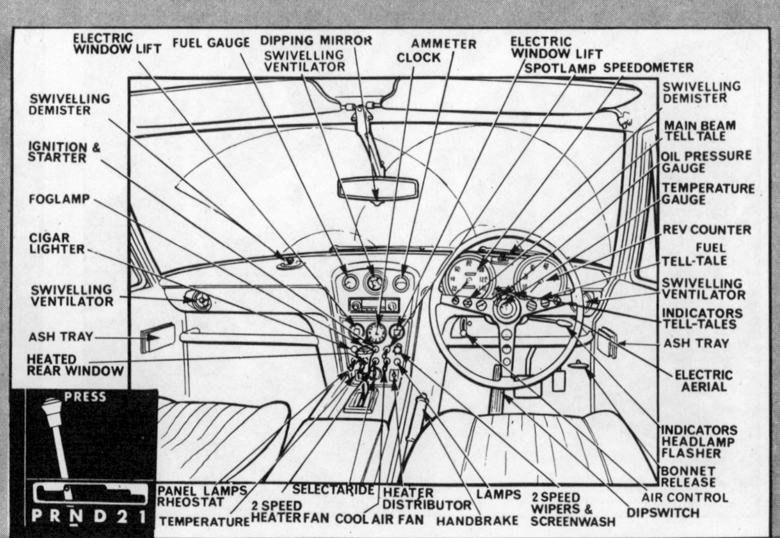

JENSEN INTERCEPTOR (6,276 c.c.)

CONSUMPTION

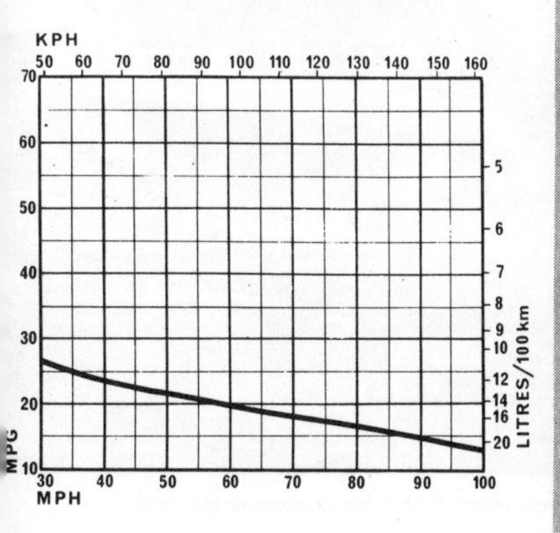

FUEL

(At constant speeds—mpg)

30 mph	26.7
40 mph	24.0
50 mph	21.6
60 mph	19.7
70 mph	18.3
80 mph	16.7
90 mph	14.9
100 mph	13.0

Typical mpg 14 (20.2 litres/100km)
Calculated (DIN) mpg 16.6 (17.0 litres/100km)
Overall mpg 12.9 (21.9 litres/100km)
Grade of fuel
Super Premium, 5-star (min. 99 RM)

OIL

Consumption (SAE 20W/40) . . . Negligible

SPECIFICATION

FRONT ENGINE, REAR-WHEEL DRIVE

ENGINE

Cylinders	8, in 90-deg. vee
Main bearings	5
Cooling system	Water; pump, thermostat and twin electric fans
Bore	108mm (4.25in.)
Stroke	86mm (3.38in.)
Displacement	6,276c.c. (383 cu.in.)
Valve gear	Overhead, hydraulic tappets
Compression ratio	10-to-1 Min. octane rating: 100
Carburettor	Carter AFB 4-barrel progressive
Fuel pump	Carter mechanical
Oil filter	Mopar full flow, renewable element
Max. power	330 bhp (SAE) at 4,600 rpm
Max. torque	425lb.ft (SAE) at 2,800 rpm

TRANSMISSION

Gearbox	Chrysler Torque Flite Hi-performance 3-speed automatic with torque converter
Gear ratios	Top 1.0 Inter 1.45 Low 2.45 Reverse 2.20
Final drive	Hypoid bevel with Powr-Lok limited slip differential, 2.88 to 1 with radials

CHASSIS and BODY

Construction	Steel body and tubular frame welded together

SUSPENSION

Front	Independent, double wishbones, coil springs, telescopic dampers, anti-roll bar
Rear	Live axle, dual-rate semi-elliptic leaf springs, Panhard rod, telescopic Armstrong Selectaride dampers

STEERING

Type	Adwest rack and pinion, power assisted
Wheel dia.	15.5in.

BRAKES

Make and type	Girling discs front and rear, divided circuits
Servo	Girling Type 100 vacuum
Dimensions	F. 11.38in. dia.; R. 10.75in. dia.;
Swept area	F. 234sq.in., R. 199sq.in. Total 433sq.in. (234sq.in./ton laden)

WHEELS

Type	Pressed steel disc, chrome plated and pierced, 5.0in. wide rim.
Tyres—make	Dunlop VR
—type	Radial ply tubed
—size	185-15in.

EQUIPMENT

Battery	12 Volt 74 Ah
Alternator	60 amp.
Headlamps	Lucas 4-lamp tungsten-halogen 110/220 watt (total)
Reversing lamps	2, standard
Electric fuses	5
Screen wipers	2-speed, self-parking
Screen washer	Electric, standard
Interior heater	Water-valve type, standard
Heated backlight	Standard
Safety belts	Standard for front seats, anchorages built-in at rear
Interior trim	Leather seats, pvc headlining
Floor covering	Carpet
Jack-type	Bevelift
Jacking points	2 each side under sills
Windscreen	Laminated
Underbody protection	Bitumastic compound on all surfaces exposed to the road

MAINTENANCE

Fuel tank	16 Imp. gallons (no reserve) (73 litres)
Cooling system	32 pints (including heater)
Engine sump	8.5 pints (4.7 litres) SAE 20W/40 Change oil every 4,000 miles. Change filter element every 8,000 miles.
Gearbox	17 pints SAE ATF type A. No change needed
Final drive	3 pints Shell Limited Slip diff. S6721A. Change oil every 12,000 miles
Grease	3 points every 4,000 miles
Tyre pressures	F. 28; R. 32 psi (normal driving) F. 36; R. 40 psi (fast driving)
Max. payload	800lb (363kg)

PERFORMANCE DATA

Top gear mph per 1,000 rpm	26.4
Mean piston speed at max. power	2,595ft/min.
Bhp per ton laden	177 (gross)

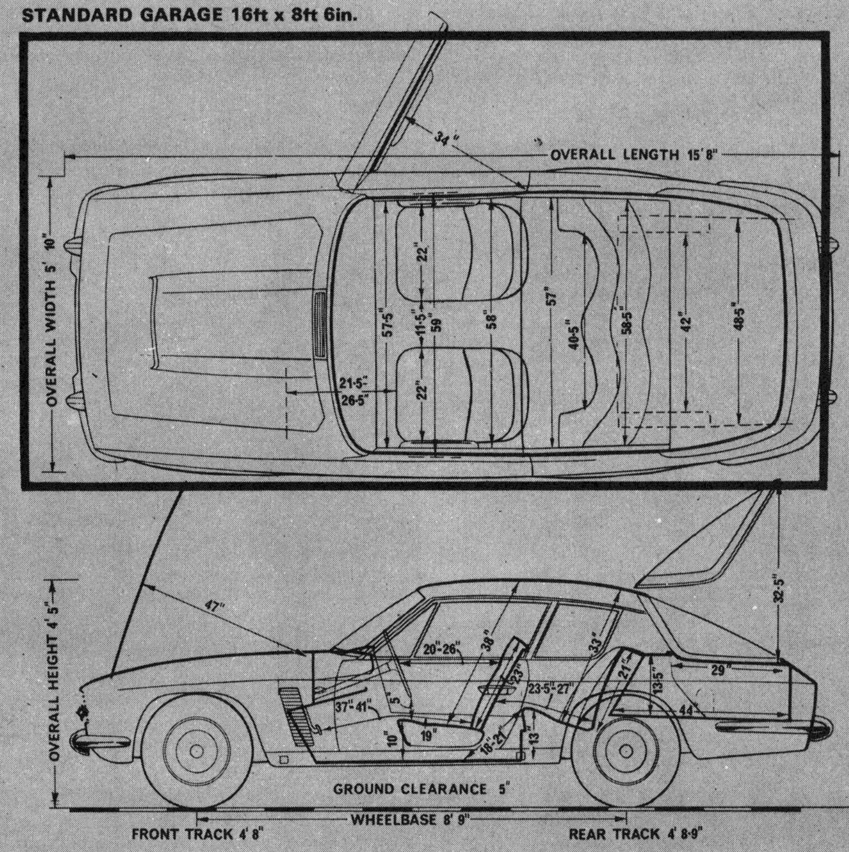

SCALE 0.3in. to 1ft.
Cushions uncompressed

Left: Up to a very high cornering rate there is safe predictable understeer. Right: Breakaway at the limit is sudden and very hard to catch

mate handling. Up to a very high cornering speed there was predictable understeer, but beyond what we found to be a very critical and sudden limit the back end would break away regardless of the amount of power being applied to the rear wheels. To put this criticism in perspective we should qualify it by saying that one expects a car of this calibre and price to have unusual roadholding powers at least the match for its considerable power. We should also add that only an idiot is ever likely to encounter this limit on public roads under normal driving. It is the behaviour in an emergency which worries us, because once adhesion has been lost, recovery takes too long and when correction does take effect it is with a sudden whip which is very hard to catch.

If the going is slippery or one wants to make good time, the best way in this Jensen is to adopt the slow-in, fast-out technique in corners and to treat it as a point-and-squirt machine. With all that torque on tap and such excellent brakes willing to take any punishment, there are no problems in getting along very fast indeed. When required, the selector can be flicked back a notch to give engine braking, and the eager beat of the dual exhausts is somehow indicative of unleashed power.

Even when pressing on at a lesser rate, the seats seem to be too slippery and rather lacking in lateral support. They are comfortable and well shaped for sitting on, but not for holding one in place. The smaller steering wheel is much more manageable, and its leather rim is nicer to touch.

Instrument and switch layout is unchanged but the rear fan demisters have been replaced by a Triplex Hotline heated element in the glass. It is confined to the area seen in the mirror, which is small, but it works well. There is a measure of through-flow air, but not nearly enough to counter the considerable heat of the big vee-8 in our recent spell of hot weather. Face-level fresh-air ducts definitely do not pass enough volume and the air picks up heat on the way through. Separate fans boost the independent systems, but these are noisy. Temperature control for the heater is by a crude water valve with poor sensitivity.

Flick switches on the wood veneered central console are identified by symbols and there is a double scale temperature gauge and oil pressure gauge right under the driver's eyes between the matching rev counter and speedometer.

There is a limited amount of room in the back for two more people, but this is a 2 + 2 rather than a four-seater. Getting into the rear compartment is a game only for children and those with supple muscles and small feet.

One of the most enjoyable extras fitted on the test car was a Voxson radio and stereo tape player with four speakers. Tape cassettes are slotted-in where tuning push-buttons normally fill the face, so radio stations must be found by hand. The extra dimension of stereo in a car like this adds tremendously to the pleasures of driving it.

Noise levels on the whole are low and it is barely necessary to raise one's voice or the volume of the radio when cruising at 70 mph or 100 mph for that matter. Overall the exhaust seemed louder than we remembered on other Jensens and road noise seemed less.

The quartz-halogen bulbs in the four headlamp system add a lot of brilliance, especially on main beams when there is a white blaze of light scorching its way through the night.

Overall the Interceptor is a very refined car, with tremendous performance and a high standard of finish. It is more for the successful tycoon than sporty playboy, and treated with the respect such a powerful machine deserves it is an invigorating way to get about. All it lacks at the moment is better ultimate handling and a more sophisticated heating and ventilation system □

Left: The Chrysler engine fits snugly under the bonnet and it is well back in the car. Right: The whole rear window and shelf lift up for access to the fully carpeted boot

Jensen refinements

Mk. II Interceptor and FF

Above: New "American safety" dashboard—and a collapsible steering column too.

Left: Higher bumper, squared over-riders, parking lights lowered, black lamp surrounds—Mk. II identification points.

Below: A new fuse box—but the big interest point is the air conditioning unit ahead of the air cleaner.

It is an open secret that, following the loss of sub-contract work for Austin Healey and Volvo two or three years ago, Jensen found themselves in the unenviable position of having a large factory and only the very small output of Jensen cars to sustain it. Not surprisingly, the balance sheet went into the red. Now, thanks both to the high quality and performance of the product and the foresight and energy of Mr. Carl Duerr, the American who took over control in January last year, the company is again profitable. Production (which was only two/three cars a week when he joined the company) is now approaching 20 a week, which is quite substantial for cars in the £5,000–£8,000 bracket.

For 1970, Mk. II versions of both the Interceptor and the four-wheel-drive FF models are being introduced. In neither case are any fundamental changes being made, but both cars have a large number of detail improvements and an even wider range of luxury equipment, which is already among the most comprehensive offered by any manufacturer anywhere.

Externally, the Mk. II can be distinguished by modified frontal treatment in which the bumpers have been raised, "square" overriders substituted for the pointed type, the headlamp surrounds finished in black instead of body colour, and new-style side lamps and flashers fitted below instead of above the bumper. At the rear, the new overriders have also been adopted and are the only obvious feature although other points of identification are "II" badges and low-profile tyres.

Further improvements include an increase in fuel capacity from 16 to 20 gallons, the fitting of new cast-aluminium rocker covers to the 6¼-litre, V-8 Chrysler engine, a modified electrical system incorporating 12 fuses, the inclusion of hazard flashers, the replacement of the ammeter by a battery condition indicator, a higher axle ratio (2.88:1 in place of 3.07:1), the fitting of Dunlop ER 70 VR 15 (approximately equivalent to 205-15) low-profile radial tyres on 6in. wide rims, and the adoption of a lattice-type collapsible steering column surmounted by a new wheel with a large padded centre.

The interior has been completely restyled so far as trim and facia-board treatment are concerned. The front seats are also new and fitted on runners with increased travel; they have a stepless reclining mechanism and headrests to U.S. specifications. At the rear, the squab and cushions have also been restyled and three-point rear seat belt anchorages are now incorporated as standard.

The new instrument board is unusual and, in addition to the speedometer and large-dial rev counter in front of the driver, has a row of smaller instruments above the console, carefully angled towards the driver and hooded to cut out reflections.

A small detail which was dropped on last year's cars but is now fitted again, is a remote control of the fuel flap which can again be operated from the driving seat by means of a solenoid; the system incorporates a warning light. Another remote control—cable-operated in this case—is used for the boot lock, which can be released by operating a lever on the door jamb. Minor refinements include a changeover switch to control the volume of the horns, and a razor-charging point.

Air conditioning is now offered as an option on the Mk. II models. The system used has been evolved by Jensen engineers in co-operation with Smiths Industries. A feature is that it can be switched to operate on re-circulated air when required so as to achieve a quick result if a car has been parked in the sun, subsequently being changed over to a fresh-air condition. Other details include a three-speed blower, four demisting nozzles for efficient defrosting and four face-level vents of which two serve the front-seat occupants and two the rear.

As already mentioned, both Jensen models have a quite exceptional range of accessories and equipment. Among other things, these include electrically operated windows and radio aerial, transistor radio, parking lights, fire extinguisher, first-aid kit and steering-column lock.

Prices of the new models are: Interceptor II, £5,838 2s. 6d. (including £1,368 2s. 6d. purchase tax), FF II, £7,705 1s. 5d. (including £1,805 1s. 5d. purchase tax). The extra charge for full air-conditioning is £220 6s. 3d. (including £51 11s. 3d. purchase tax).

H.C.H.

In brief

Engine: V-8, 108 mm. x 86 mm., 6,276 c.c.; o.h. valves (push rods); Carter 4-barrel carburetter; 10:1 compression ratio; 325 b.h.p. gross at 4,600 r.p.m.; 425 lb. ft. torque at 2,800 r.p.m.

Transmission: Torqueflite 3-speed fully-automatic transmission with torque converter; ratios, 2.88, 4.16 and 7.05; reverse, 6.32; top gear m.p.h. per 1,000 r.p.m., 26.3 m.p.h.

Running Gear: Hydraulic disc brakes with tandem master cylinder and servo; independent coil and wishbone front suspension; semi-elliptic rear springs; power assisted rack-and-pinion steering; Dunlop ER 70 VR 15 radial tyres.

Dimensions: Length, 15 ft. 8 in.; width 5 ft. 9 in.; turning circle, 38 ft.; kerb weight 31½ cwt.

FF II

As above except: four-wheel drive by Ferguson system; brakes include Dunlop Maxaret anti-skid device; length, 15 ft. 11 in.; turning circle, 39 ft.; kerb weight, 34 cwt.

2500 MILES IN A JENSEN FF

MODERN MOTOR **road** TEST

four wheels that work

Four-wheel-drive GT car adds new dimension to motoring, says European ed. Dvoretsky

AFTER 2500 miles through three countries in all types of conditions, I find that the Jensen FF effortlessly lives up to its ambitious advertising slogan of "the world's most advanced car".

Its main theme of safety through technical advancement can hardly be faulted, although there are a couple of minor irritations present which should not appear in a car with a basic price of £5400 Stg.

The FF (for Ferguson Formula) is the world's first production four-wheel-drive car. But it is more than that. With a top speed of 130-plus mph, acceleration to 60 mph in 7.5 sec., and 100 mph in 21 sec., the ability to cruise in extreme silence and safety at 115/120 mph on a motorway, it is a GT car of the first water.

Now, with one a day rolling down the assembly line at Jensen's Bromwich plant, it is daily bringing to a few lucky individuals scattered around the world a new dimension in motoring.

It is a dimension I hope won't take too long getting to the rest of the world's populace. The additional safety brought about by four-wheel-drive coupled with the Dunlop Maxaret anti-lock braking system, is possibly the biggest safety step forward in the history of the motor car.

A heartening aspect of the development of the Ferguson Formula is that some of the big manufacturers are at last getting round to developmental work, with a view to making it available in relatively cheap cars.

That day is still some time off, but it is coming, and in the meantime those privileged few who get to drive the Jensen FF can let their colleagues know what they can look forward to.

How it works

To recap on the basics of the Ferguson Formula: behind the conventional automatic gearbox is a Ferguson control differential which distributes drive to a normal live rear axle and also to the front wheels via a short prop-shaft which runs forward alongside the engine.

The differential apportions 63 per cent of the torque to the rear wheels, 37 per cent to the front. But, more important, it prevents the front wheels from over-running the rear wheels by any more than 16.5 per cent and the rears from over-running the fronts by more than 5.5 per cent. (Details, diagram: page 61).

The Maxaret brake sensor is driven off the differential and, by electric signals to a solenoid, controls the action of a powerful vacuum servo.

The Interceptor (i.e., non-FF) version of the Jensen, styled by Vignale and powered by a 6.3 litre Chrysler V8 and Torqueflite automatic transmission, is no mean car.

But, like all high-powered conventional cars, particularly those with a live rear axle (even a well-located one), it can be driven into a situation where it becomes what I call, for want of a better word, "brutish". It is then a case of the tail wagging the dog.

The FF is just not like this. Although it is bigger (three inches longer) than the Interceptor, and grosses about two tons, it remains completely docile under almost any condition.

No matter how hard the foot is clamped to the accelerator, the FF just goes round the corner without drama. The tyres hardly murmur, the body hardly leans; just about the only indication of the violence of the cornering is the extreme g-force exerted. That alone makes passengers very nervous until they grow confident in the car's tremendous cornering ability.

The extent to which the throttle is opened in corners depends entirely on the nerve of the driver.

My honest opinion is that few drivers will ever dare match the car's cornering potential — either because they have upwards of £5500 invested (likely Australian price: around $16,000) or simply because caution will overcome bravery.

Driving the FF through corners is an effortless business, thanks to a quick (3.5 turns of lock) Adwest power-assisted rack and pinion steering system.

The Adwest gives so much "feel"

TOP: FF can be thrown at corners with great abandon, hangs on incredibly well. Ultimate cornering power is well above skill of most drivers. LEFT: Front end treatment is neat, conservative, uses quartz halogen lighting. BELOW: Sumptuous boardroom interior leaves nothing to chance. Ventilation could be better, says Harold Dvoretsky.

LOOSE surface cornering — the four-wheel-drive gives tremendous grip.

four wheels that work

to the driver that it is difficult to believe that the steering is assisted. Just about the only giveaway was the odd grunt or hiss heard when the front wheels went to full lock in parking manoeuvres.

Steering characteristics are almost dead neutral. Full throttle in corners produces nothing but a desire for the car to go exactly where it is pointed. Up to 60 or 70 mph the FF handles just like a normal rear-wheel-drive. Put a bit more power on and under some conditions (an uneven surface perhaps?) there's a slight trace of oversteer.

Certainly, you have to take a little lock off coming out of fast corners. But at really high speeds, there's more of a tendency to understeer. It's the nearest thing to "going round on rails" I've ever encountered.

When the car is pedalled really hard, as I did for the action pictures, there is no "breakaway" in the accepted sense.

Another writer has described the attitude of the FF at the limit as "crab-steer", and that sums it up pretty well. At the limit, all four of the Jensen's wheels seem to run wide simultaneously.

The "crab-steer" continues fractionally until the tyres take another bite at the road. This might sound odd, but you hardly notice it happening, even if the right foot is lifted. Lifting off produces fractional tuck-in, but it is so slight that I feel guilty mentioning it.

I do so only because should you have to apply brakes hard in a corner it does nothing to aggravate the condition. Of course, if you are cornering hard and you brake hard at the same time, gravity takes over and the tail starts to go (in the wet this is, naturally, a bit quicker and more pronounced than in the dry).

I should mention here that there is a "limit", high though it may be. As the instruction book points out, the ultimate limitation of car control is the grip between the tyres and the road surface.

The Ferguson system of all-wheels-control helps the driver to use this grip to the best advantage under all conditions, but "it cannot increase the available grip. Therefore, the car should always be driven with due regard to the prevailing conditions".

This means that if you push hard enough on a slippery surface (but it has to be **very** slippery), you can get the tail to break away and lose adhesion. Fortunately, it takes but a little correction to bring the 36 cwt. car on course again.

The Dunlop Maxaret anti-locking device is another thing. As yet I don't think it is entirely perfected, although it works exceedingly well.

It is a little unnerving in your first emergency stop to feel "kick-back" on the brake pedal.

The anti-skid effect works by alternately releasing and re-applying the brakes. If a wheel tends to stop, the brake is released and re-applied as it starts to roll again.

The "pulse rate" is said to be six a second, but I doubt if I ever achieved this. But it certainly works, as I was to find out towards the latter end of my 2500-mile run.

Hurrying back to Calais to catch my Townsend ferry across the Channel on one of those drizzly northern France mornings, I met a lot of traffic coming the opposite way as the few French citizens not on holiday wended their way to work. My speed was just over the 'ton'.

One Mustang driver with a death wish and no conceivable idea of approach speeds suddenly left the line of traffic coming the other way and looked me head on at very close distance. He would have been travelling around 80 to 90 mph—perhaps more.

Our combined closing speed was nearing 200 mph.

As I stomped on the anchors, my immediate reaction was to wonder what way the skid would start. There are very few cars (if any) of that weight, travelling at that speed on a wet surface, which could guarantee to brake in a straight line.

I reckon I have as much feel of a car and its braking potential as most drivers, yet the feel of the Maxaret giant anchor has been tossed out was as the car lost speed—as though a giant anchor has been tossed out—was something I would have found hard to emulate.

Angela, in "the seat nearest the accident", forgot to be nervous and commented as the Mustang driver slewed badly back into the queue what a wonderful feeling of safety there had been during the whole episode.

On another occasion I worked my way up on a smooth road, eventually trying a real crunching panic stop from 115 mph.

It's a manoeuvre I'd attempt with few cars, no matter how wide the testing facility. The fact that the discs and pads by that time (20 brutal stops and starts) must have been red-hot didn't go to make matters any better.

SWITCHERY is a little hard to read, but Jensen is superbly comfy.

But, whereas in lesser cars I could have expected a failure on one wheel or another, the Jensen bumped its way to a stop in a dead straight line.

It has been suggested by some of my learned colleagues that the brakes coming off and going on again might under certain conditions (say, corrugated surfaces) put the car off balance. It could be there is a situation when this might happen. I certainly couldn't find it.

The four-wheel discs, 11.38 in. front and 10.75 in. diameter rear with a total of 434 sq. in. swept area, are fade free, though they squealed a bit after really heavy use.

The suspension, with its independent-by-twin-coil-springs-and-wishbones at the front, and live axle on semi-elliptic leaf springs with panhard rod location at the rear, provides a very good ride over all types of surfaces.

Armstrong telescopic "Selectaride" rear shock absorbers are a very useful standard accessory.

A simple four-position switch on the central panel gives varying rates of stiffness from boulevard softness to the firmness required for more spirited and loaded-car driving.

The body by Vignale with wide window areas, particularly the big wrap-around at the rear, may not be to everyone's taste. I liked it. So, apparently, do a lot of others.

In traffic the big window areas are a boon, and, despite a 39-ft. turning circle, the car is easy to place and to park.

Comfort Department

The seats (designed to the personal taste of Jensen's bossman and old (English) car fancier, American Carl Duerr) are the best I've had the pleasure of sitting in for many a long day.

The combination of the finest of Connelly leathers and good adjustment to squab and seat (plus a telescopic steering column) made for a superb driving position. I did more than 800 miles one day in very hot conditions.

Despite the heavy August French traffic and the extreme concentration of high-speed running, I was fresher than I can ever remember after such a run.

In Spain, where the car was left out in temperatures of 100/105 degrees, the seats took but a moment to cool down.

The Jensen will carry four (we even carried three in the rear seat for one 40-mile excursion) at a pinch. Three could go a long way — even four, providing the driver wasn't too long-legged and didn't mind driving a little closer to the wheel. Two children would have comfort indeed.

The big Chrysler V-8 of 6276 cc. churns out 325 bhp, and though a lot of this is lost on the way through the automatic and all the coggery of the four-wheel-drive, there's still a useful amount getting down through the wheels on to the road.

Taking the FF from the lights in a hurry is surprising — particularly in the wet. Try to get that amount of horsepower down on to the road through just the rear wheels of any car and you'll get all sorts of drama.

FF TECHNICAL DESCRIPTION

THE basis of the Ferguson all-wheel control formula is a master differential and two one-way clutches. In this particular design the master differential is a planetary gear that permits a speed variation between front and rear output and also divides the torque unequally in the ratio of 37 per cent to the front, 63 to the rear.

Drive is taken to the master differential by mounting the planet carrier onto the output shaft of the gearbox, in this case the Chrysler "TorqueFlite" automatic. Three planet gears are in mesh with an annulus and a sun gear. Chain sprockets on the sun gear shaft drive the front output shaft through a set of three Morse "Hyvo" chains.

Also mounted on the sun gear shaft is a gear that drives the main shaft of the control unit. This unit consists of two one-way clutches that are controlled by two gears driven from the input shaft (gearbox output). Each clutch has a multiplicity of plates, the inner ones being splined to the main shaft and the outer plates held in an outer casing.

An abutment ring with a chamfered end race bears against the chamfered ends of six radial plungers. An inner sleeve prevents the plungers from being pressed inwards as the result of end thrust on the abutment ring(s). Light spring pressure between the rings ensures that the clutch plates are held in contact with one another.

Between the outer casing of each clutch and its control gear are three balls positioned in ramps formed in both faces.

It will be appreciated that the friction in the clutch pack, due to the spring pressure, will cause the outer casing to lag behind the speed of its control gear. Under normal conditions this will ensure that the clutch is inoperative.

However, should the speed of the control gear equal that of the outer casing, the balls will travel up the ramps and so exert an axial thrust that engages the clutch.

The control gear and the mainshaft will now revolve together and so lock the sun gear and planet carrier. This effectively couples both pairs of road wheels together, although they are running at different speeds.

In this particular design the front wheels are permitted to over-run the rears by 16.5 per cent and the rear wheels over-run the fronts by 5.5 per cent.

To obtain these speed differences one clutch and its control gear revolves faster than the main shaft while the other clutch and gear turns slower.

Front wheelspin under traction is prevented by the faster running clutch which also prohibits rear wheels locking during braking. The slower running clutch controls the rear wheels under traction and the front ones during braking.

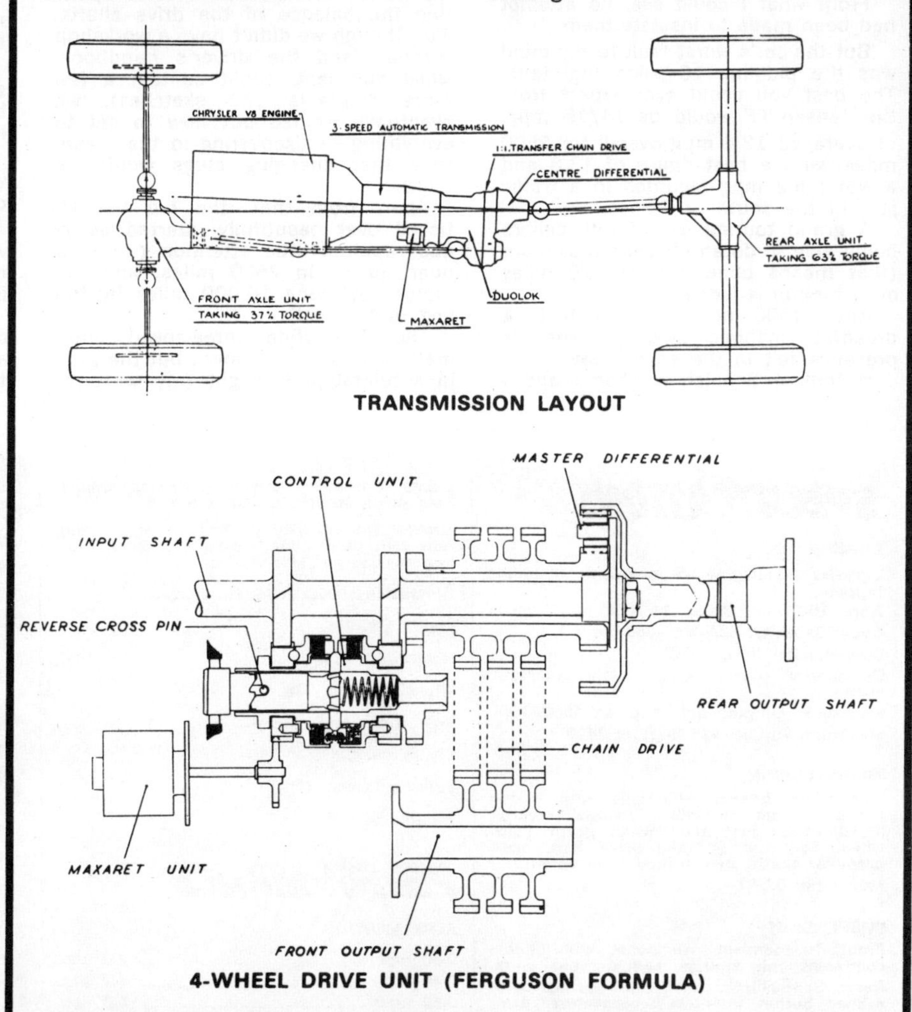

TRANSMISSION LAYOUT

4-WHEEL DRIVE UNIT (FERGUSON FORMULA)

four wheels that work

There's nothing like that in the Jensen FF — no wheelspin, no slide. The power gets right down to the road, wet and dry, without any rubber burning.

The Jensen isn't perfect — but what car has ever been? The instrument layout and interior generally has been revised subsequently for the benefit of U.S. safety regulations.

On the Mark One I drove, some of the minor instruments like fuel gauge were a little hard to read and the switchery was a great conglomeration which I never did get completely used to.

Another mod for 1970 is a bigger radiator — the big Chrysler needs it. You could cruise down the motorway in the Mark One at 115 mph — for 40 or 50 miles on a hot day.

Then the water temperature gauge started hunting the red line.

I trust the new and bigger radiator will allow for air conditioning, because the Jensen needs it. There are three dashboard outlets (in addition to the demisting slots), two outlets to the feet and two for direct fresh air at the side of the cockpit.

But in anything above 90 degrees you've got to have the electrically-operated windows down to keep cool, and this is a pity.

Half the heat problem, I think, stems from the fact that the big twin exhaust pipes run directly under driver and passenger seat.

From what I could see, no attempt had been made to insulate them.

But the car's worst fault to my mind was the piddling 16-gallon fuel tank. The best you could ever expect from the Jensen FF would be 14/15 mpg.

I averaged 12.4 mpg overall for 2500 miles, with a best figure of 13.8 and a worst 8.2 mpg recorded in a traffic jam in the south of France.

A grand touring car of this calibre being able to do an absolute maximum (that means bone dry) of 220 miles on a tankful is ludicrous.

After 1400 miles of the test, a dreadful rhythmic tinkling made its presence felt in the engine bay.

It took a Spanish mechanic and I 90 minutes to discover the sound wasn't from overhead, but from underneath, where a swash plate between the starter motor and the flywheel housing had worked loose, the worm of the starter fouling it and making the peculiar sound.

BIG 6.3-litre V8 Chrysler gives the Jensen 325 bhp. It overheated, despite twin-fan radiator, on hot days.

This meant dismantling the front drive, the shafts of which are supported by a bracket mounted on the same bolts as the starter motor.

One thousand miles from home, I dreaded the idea of interfering with the front drive train for fear of upsetting the balance of the drive shafts. But, though we didn't have a workshop manual (and the driver's handbook, while sufficient, could contain a few more diagrams and sketches), we eventually worked out how to get to everything — discovering in the meantime that changing plugs would be murder.

Apart from that, the big "donk" ticked over beautifully, started easily and required little attention (under a quart of oil in 2500 miles, and the motor had done 10,000 miles by the end of the test).

The Torqueflite three-speed automatic can be over-ridden, but the gain in acceleration is slight (my performance figures are the mean of six runs, half of which were using the D1 and D2 "hold" position).

The quartz-iodine headlamps by Lucas are fabulous. This is one of the few cars I've ever driven that I could use almost full potential at night. Terrific. Not so the floor-mounted pedal dipswitch.

Mounted down to the left of the brake pedal, it interferes with the stretch of the long-legged driver's left foot.

Whatever U.S. regulations might say, my advice to Jensen is to get the dip back on a stalk off the steering column.

The steering wheel of 16-inch diameter is Sorbo padded and leather bound. Even on the stickiest day gloveless hands can grip it with confidence.

I didn't go for the big sunvisors, which could be skull-cutters in times of crash and were annoying to use.

These faults aside, I can recommend wholeheartedly this car to anyone who has that sort of money to spend and is looking for something different.

What you're paying for is a new dimension in motoring — a dimension, as I've said before, I trust won't take too long getting to every family car. •

SPECIFICATIONS

ENGINE:

Chrysler 90 degree V8 ohv. with hydraulic tappets.
Bore: 108 mm. Stroke: 86 mm.
Cubic Capacity: 6276 cc. (383 cu. in.).
Compression Ratio: 10:1.
Carburettor: Carter 4 bbl with automatic choke.
Maximum Output: 325 bhp at 4800 rpm.
Maximum Torque: 425 lb. ft. at 2800.

TRANSMISSION

TorqueFlite 3-speed automatic with torque converter and over-riding manual control. Kickdown on first and second gears. Four-wheel Ferguson Formula drive unit, open propeller shafts, hypoid final drive units.
Axle ratio: 3.07:1.

SUSPENSION

Front: Independent. Wishbones with double combined coil springs and damper units.
Rear: Semi-elliptic dual rate springs with rubber button inter-leave separators. Armstrong telescopic driver controlled adjustable shock absorbers. Panhard Rod.

Brakes: Dunlop disc (11.30in. front, 10.75in. rear with duplicated hydraulic system. Dunlop Maxaret anti-skid device.

Dimensions: Overall length 15ft. 11in.

Width: 5ft. 9in.

Height: 4ft. 5in.

Wheelbase: 9ft. 1in.

Track front and rear: 4ft. 9in.

Clearance: 5in.

Turning Circle: 39ft.

Weight: 34 cwt.

PERFORMANCE

ACCELERATION

0-30 mph	2.9 sec.
0-40 mph	4.2 sec.
0-50 mph	5.3 sec.
0-60 mph	7.0 sec.
0-70 mph	9.0 sec.
0-80 mph	12 sec.
0-90 mph	16 sec.
0-100 mph	20.9 sec.
0-110 mph	27.9 sec.

Top recorded speed: 131 mph.

Speeds in gears: D1 53; D2 90 mph.

20-40 mph (kickdown)	2.3 sec.
30-50 mph	3.0
40-60 mph	3.0
50-70 mph	4.0
60-80 mph	3.5
80-100	5.0

Speedo: 5 percent error at 100 mph.

Fuel Consumption Overall: 2500 miles — 12.4 mpg (Best 13.8 mpg). Full 100 octane.

THE WORLD'S SAFEST CAR

Now available in Australia a new form of luxury motoring . . . provided you have the necessary cash to qualify.

From J. F. J. Kuipers

YET another British thoroughbred is available in Australia. With 40 years of experience, Jensen is currently manufacturing the Interceptor II, a high speed four-seater coupe, and the FFII, the world's safest car — this is not a slogan from a Jensen brochure, but the description nearly every motor journalist uses when describing this car.

Some manufacturers know better than others, the way to make their marque synonymous with prestige and performance. One is Jensen, a small British firm.

The company was founded as Patrick-Jensen Motors Ltd in 1931 by the brothers Richard and Allan Jensen, with financial assistance from the Patrick family, well-known motor car distributors. A year later, the Jensen brothers resigned and started building special bodies on Wolseley Hornets, Morris Eights, Ford Eights and Singers. They also bodied R. T. Horton's record-breaking MG Midget. In 1934, a one-off Ford V-8, based on an American chassis, was built for movie star Clark Gable.

The first car to bear the name Jensen came in 1936. Powered by an American Ford V-8 3.5-litre engine, it was the world's first car to fit

The Jensen Interceptor II, described as . . . quick as a flash, beautiful as a Greek goddess and as comfortable as a Louis XIV bed. It's luxury plus.

The smooth-flowing body was originally designed by Vignale and built in Milan. However, Jensen is now building bodies in England.

The rear window of the Jensen hinges up allowing access to the quite spacious boot. The full glass canopy at the rear was originally designed by Vignale and built initially by Touring, Milan.

self-contained overdrive as standard. It had a remarkable performance for the time: the top speed was 90 mph at 3000 rpm, with a fuel consumption of only 20 mpg. 0-60 was achieved in 13 seconds.

This new panther of the road held faithfully to the design ideas shown in the first car built by the Jensens: a modified Austin Chummy, showing a long, low-raking body, wide-view windscreen, and something plus in special springing. It was of this Jensen-Ford that motor-ace Sir Malcolm Campbell wrote, "I have nothing but praise. This car is something out of the ordinary, particularly noticeable to someone like myself who is continually driving all kinds of different makes."

In 1938, a 4.5-litre straight-eight, featuring the same range of bodywork, was added to the 3.5-litre. Power was delivered by an American Nash pushrod ohv engine with dual downdraught carbs which gave off 120 hp at 3500 rpm. The torque at low speeds was excellent. By modern standards the car was not light: the chassis alone weighed 23½ cwt, the complete tourer 30½ cwt and the sedan 34 cwt. However, the performance was quite brisk and the great charm of the car was its high cruising speed at low revs: at 85 mph, with high speeds engaged on the dual ratio back axle, the engine was only running at 2800 rpm.

A few years after World War II the famous Interceptor was introduced, equipped with a 4-litre Austin engine. This model lasted until 1958, though only 88 were built.

In 1962 came the C-V8, powered by a V8 Chrysler. This was succeeded in October, 1966 by the current Interceptor and FF. Until recently Jensens never specialised on the manufacture of cars alone: in 1938 a lightweight commercial vehicle was introduced fitted with daylight alloy frame. This stayed in production till 1960. For some years, the bodies of the Austin Healey six cylinder sports cars were manufactured by

the Jensens, and during the early 60s they assembled the Volvo P 1800. The sales of cars never were very high.

American Carl F. Duerr joined the staff and fully reorganised the company. The FF and Interceptor were mainly his work, as was the change from fibreglass bodywork to full-steel body. The output of cars rose from five to 20 units weekly within less than four years. By the end of 1968, all the assets owned by the Norcrosse group, could be bought back. Jensens are now again on their own. Recently the Mark

Except for the fitting of the front wheel drive system and extra air vent on the front mudguard, FFII is almost identical with Interceptor.

This detailed drawing of the Jensen Interceptor shows the dimensions and the smooth flowing Vignale lines. Originally of fibreglass the body is now assembled in steel by Jensen.

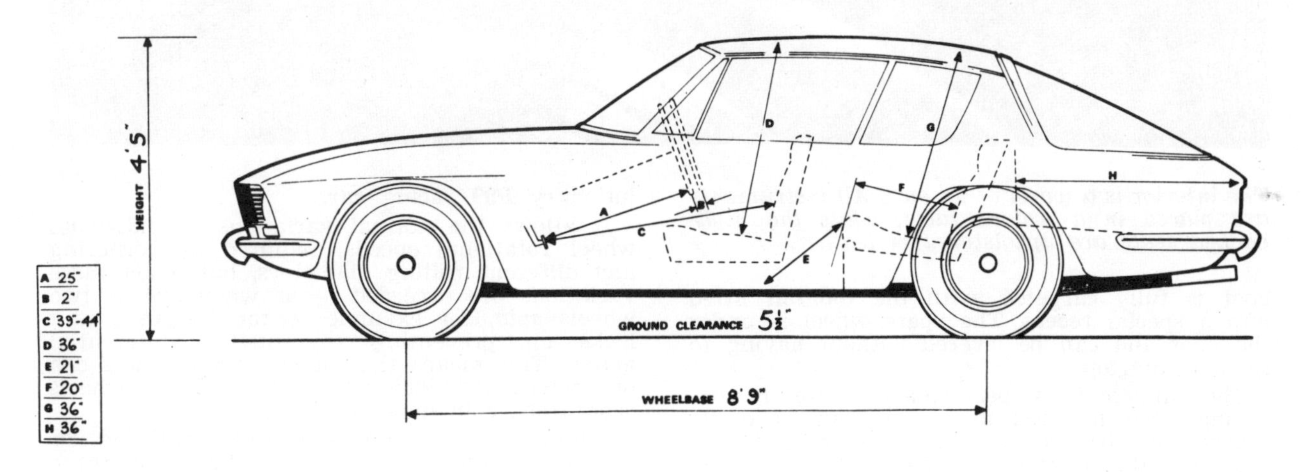

II version of both the Interceptor and FF were announced.

The Interceptor II is as quick as a flash, beautiful as a Greek goddess, and comfortable as a Louis XIV bed. This might sound overdoing it, but perhaps you would believe it if we throw in a Chrysler as power unit, a Vignale-designed full-steel body, real leather upholstery and deep Wilton carpets.

The Chrysler V8 unit is one of the best power packs for high-speed luxury limousines. Its cylinder dimensions are very much oversquare with a bore and stroke of 108 x 86 mm, resulting in a capacity of over 6¼-litres. The compression ratio is 10 to 1 and the combustion chambers are fed from a Carter 4 bl downdraught carburettor through overhead valves operated by hydraulic tappets. The total output delivered is 325 bhp at 4600 rpm, while maximum torque of 425 lb/ft is given at 2800 rpm.

In its standard outfit, the engine has two thermostatically-controlled electric cooling fans which come into use on engine-demand. The Torqueflite three speed automatic transmission with torque converter changes gears with imperceptible smoothness and also allows the driver full overriding control.

The suspension at front is independent with coil springs and wishbones; the rear axle, however, is of the live type, located by semi-elliptic springs and a Panhard rod.

Armstrong hydraulic shock absorbers — at rear of the adjustable Selectaride type — are mounted all round. The hydraulic Girling disc brakes have a divided circuit and servo-assistance. Steering is by a power-assisted Ardwest rack-and-pinion unit with collapsible steering column. The immensely rigid chassis frame is of tubular construction.

The roadholding and handling characteristics of the car are so good that it could be equipped with the 425 hp version of the Chrysler engine.

The smooth-lined body with its all-around character line and the full glass canopy was designed by Vignale and initially built by Touring of Milan. Jensens now assemble the body.

A world on its own is the car's interior with the high-backed, very comfortable separate front seats and the wrap-around rear seat, both upholstered in the finest Conally leather and fitted with headrests. The floor is covered with deep Wilton carpets.

Mounted in front of the driver are the speedometer and rev-counter. All other instruments and switches are placed on a walnut-finished central console. The Interceptor is equipped with a four-speaker radio, electrically-operated aerial, door windows and fuel filler cap, two-speed wipers with anti-lift blades and electric washers, double quartz iodine headlamps, a first-aid kit, fire extinguisher and safety belts.

The heating and ventilating system is complicated: It has 24 different operations. A Smiths air conditioning system can be installed as well.

The boot under the counterbalanced fastback canopy has 16 cu ft of space. The parcel shelf may be removed for additional cubic feet. The

The interior is a world of its own. All instruments are placed in a walnut facia, while the high-backed seats are upholstered in leather.

boot is fully carpeted, with the tool-roll fitted into a special recess. The spare wheel is under the boot and can be levered without having to remove luggage.

The Interceptor's performances are breathtaking. One hundred miles an hour is easily reached in 20 seconds. Maximum speed is 140 mph and the overall fuel consumption is about 12 mpg.

On the whole, the Interceptor is a tremendous car, with its superb engine and transmission, enthralling performance, comfortable interior and well-balanced handling, though it has its small vices, like all things produced by men. But who would like an infallible car?

The Miraculous Jensen FF II

The magical FF is the world's first luxury car fitted with four-wheel-drive.

During the early 60s the Jensens and their chief engineer, Kevin Beattie, were caught by an all-wheel-drive system for cars under development at the Harry Ferguson Research Laboratories of Coventry. This resulted in an agreement for the joint development of a Jensen car, the Ferguson Formula system of all-wheel-drive. A prototype vehicle was shown in 1965, based on the then-current C-V8.

A year later, an entirely new range of cars was introduced, featuring the Interceptor and its 4-wd companion, the FF. Both have the same body, though the latter can be distinguished by its longer bonnet, the double louvres behind the wheel-arches and an additional air inlet in the bonnet hood.

Except for the fitting of additional front-wheel-drive to the FF, both cars are technically almost identical. The most important part of the 4-wd system is the automatically-controlled centre differential, incorporated in the transfer box, behind the gearbox.

This device has been tried and tested over millions of miles, and caused a sensation in motor racing circles some years ago on the revolutionary P99 racing car.

It allows the normal variations in individual wheel rotational speeds, required by cornering and different rolling diameters, but when these variations are exceeded — as when one or two wheels spin, for example — the Ferguson unit locks up, preventing any further differential action. This means that in no circumstances can one wheel individually, or any pair of wheels separately, spin under drive.

Additionally, a Dunlop Maxaret anti-skid device is mounted, operating on the brake servo system, in order to prevent the locking of any wheels when braking.

The results are twofold: the FF has the exceptional acceleration and cornering power of all-wheel-drive, but without the tyre scrub and mechanical wind-up inherent in other systems. Furthermore, two of the main causes of skidding — wheelspin when accelerating or cornering, and wheel-lock when braking — are reduced to an absolute minimum, if not fully abolished. This achievement yielded the FF the designation of 'safest car in the world'.

Driving an FF is an extraordinary experience. Wet or slippery roads don't cause troubles any more when accelerating or braking. The road-holding of the car can only be described as sensational: under-or-over steering tendencies are nearly fully absorbed by the car itself, while jiggling with the steering wheel when accelerating from a corner is no longer necessary: the car keeps its line without any trouble.

Even under the most arduous conditions, not the slightest sign of fading can be noticed. The value of the Maxaret anti-skid device — it came from the aviation industry, where it was mounted on heavy planes — and the automatically locked differential is clearly shown when the brakes are applied at very high speeds with the steering wheel released (it is possible): the car won't deviate one inch from its course.

The four-wheel-drive Jensen FF matches power to safety as no car has ever done. All its qualities are so remarkable that it seems reasonable to think one's safety can be guarded automatically. #

JENSEN INTERCEPTOR II

Chrysler engine and transmission clothed in an elegant European GT car shape

THERE IS NOTHING like horsepower. The 6.3-liter V-8 engine in the Chrysler Newport sedan whisks that substantial 4100-lb 6-seater along at over 115 mph fully loaded. Put the same power package in a smaller coupe weighing 700 lb less, carrying two in utter luxury or four in discomfort, and you get a stimulating 140-mph maximum and acceleration in complement, like a standing ¼-mile in 15 sec and 0 to 100 in 18.2. That's the Jensen Interceptor II, and although the number of Chrysler engine/transmission units shipped to West Bromwich is a mere trickle from Detroit's overall output, a lot of them will be returning across the Atlantic this year, elegantly clothed in Jensen suits to be sold by selected Chrysler dealers.

It is a remarkable human faculty that we so often forget the unpleasant things and remember the good. Our three days with one of the first federalized Interceptor IIs were distinctly marred by dismal British winter rain and a defective alternator, yet the glorious gobbling forward rush when one gave the Chrysler V-8 its head, and the superb ease, comfort and precision of driving the car remain our chief memories of it. Interceptor I, born in 1966, showed that Jensen was on to a good design formula, but Interceptor II is still better. The front suspension, by ball-jointed A-arms, coil springs and tube type shock absorbers, has been further refined; low-profile wide base Dunlop SP Sport radial ply tires are now fitted, the ventilation and demisting equipment has been revised, a sophisticated air conditioning system is a new option, fuel tank capacity is raised from 16 to 20 gallons, and the latest detoxed Chrysler 6.3 engine with smoother torque curve is used in conjunction with Chrysler Torqueflite 3-speed automatic transmission.

To extoll the virtues of automatics to Americans is to preach to the converted. The Jensen's Torque-Flite is remarkably smooth all the way up, with almost imperceptible changes and a swift kickdown, plus over-ride control to hold 1st or 2nd gear when desired. The acceleration figures were taken on a sticky wet track with slight wheel-spin and all would show improvement in the dry. Jensen themselves claim 0 to 60 mph in 6.4 sec, but our best of 7.0 sec to an indicated 60 is still substantially quicker than the 2-plus-2 E-type Jaguar or Aston Martin DBS over the same distance.

Handling and steering proved excellent under the unpleasant circumstances of our test. The rack and pinion power steering makes maneuvering in tight spots an easy matter, without loss of feel at higher speeds, although on bumpy roads there was a certain indecision about the steering at speeds when pointing straight ahead, perhaps suggesting weak caster action. Wet roads and limited visibility, aggravated in our case by lack of electrics for adequate demisting, inhibited enterprise in fast cornering, but the Jensen with its classic cart-sprung back end proved a nice safe understeerer and very much an aim-and-squirt machine, with the SP Sport Dunlops keeping it commendably stable under sudden power out of turns. The Girling disc brakes were equally impressive, requiring only light pedal pressure for very effective stopping without fade or wheel lock. Engine and wind noise at speed are both well subdued, while the engine ticks over with a pleasant sporty burble.

The interior layout, restyled for 1970 around federalizing redesign, has been well worked out, with a 160 mph speedometer and 6000 rpm tachometer (5 to 6 thou in the red) readily to eye, the wiper/washer knob on the far right readily to hand, other instruments—voltmeter, fuel gauge, oil pressure and water temperature—angled at the driver, and other control buttons marshalled in a neat row below.

GEOFFREY GODDARD PHOTOS

JENSEN INTERCEPTOR II

They include the head and side light switch, which some of us would prefer as a stalk control on the steering column. Located centrally is that Jensen specialty, the Voxson combined radio and 8-track stereo unit which offers music to choice through the standard four speakers. There is a large central console embodying a lockable compartment, and between it and the driver's seat is the handbrake, accessible through a rather narrow slot.

Trim throughout is in impeccable real leather, door handles inside and out are sensibly simple, and the trunk is opened, not by key but by an internal lever set flush in the offside door jamb. The seats are fully adjustable, have detachable headrests, and are well contoured for long-distance comfort. We cannot vouch for the quality of Jensen's new ventilation and demisting gear, since the defaulting alternator meant living entirely off the 12-volt battery.

Jensen's plastic days seem well over and the steel body, styled by Vignale (recently taken over by Rowan-Ghia) is superbly finished, as are the external accessories. As for styling and trim, we didn't care for that vast one-piece rear window with stainless steel surround accentuating it, but appreciated the way it opened and resultant accessibility of the trunk. The makers call the Interceptor a "full 4-seater" but we'd say a 2-plus-2, for as long-legged, long-suffering cartoonist Brockbank found, there's little legroom at the rear. The way we see it, the Interceptor II is an elegant, top quality, high performance Grand Tourer ideal for the drive-yourself executive, offering all the latest pleasure of tremendous power reserve, and the confidence of a lightly stressed power unit.

Last of all, the price. The Interceptor II is not cheap in its mother country at £5,838 (about $14,000) inclusive of *that* tax, but the basic figure is £4,470 or around $10,700. Right now the U.S. price is not known. *—Cyril Posthumus*

JENSEN INTERCEPTOR II

PRICE

List price (not including British purchase tax).... $10,440
U.S. price.........not established

IMPORTER

To be sold through selected Chrysler dealers in the U.S.

ENGINE

Engine..............Chrysler V-8
Bore x stroke, mm.......108 x 86
Equivalent inches....4.25 x 3.38
Displacement, cc/cu in...6276/383
Compression ratio..........10:1
Bhp @ rpm..........330 @ 4600
Equivalent mph............122
Torque @ rpm, lb-ft...425 @ 2800
Equivalent mph.............74
Carburetion........4V Carter AFB
Type fuel required.......premium
Emission control.....engine mods

DRIVE TRAIN

Transmission: Chrysler Torqueflite automatic (3-speed with torque converter)
Gear ratios: 3rd (1.00)......2.88:1
2nd (1.45)..............4.17:1
1st (2.45)..............7.03:1
Final drive ratio..........2.88:1

CHASSIS & BODY

Body/frame.......tubular frame, steel body
Brakes: Girling disc, 11.38-in. dia. front, 10.75-in. dia. rear; power assisted
Swept area, sq in...........433
Wheels..........steel disc, 15 x 5
Tires:...Dunlop radial ER 70 VS 15
Steering type: rack & pinion with power assist
Turns, lock-to-lock..........3.4
Turning circle, ft..........39.5
Front suspension: unequal-length A-arms, coil springs, tube shocks, anti-roll bar
Rear suspension: live axle, leaf springs, panhard rod, tube shocks

INSTRUMENTATION

Instruments: 140-mph speedo, 6000-rpm tach, fuel level, voltmeter, clock, oil pressure, water temperature
Warning lights: high beam, directionals, fuel level, hazard, handbrake on, brake fluid level, oil pressure

GENERAL

Curb weight, lb........(mfr) 3695
Test weight, lb..............4100
Weight distribution (with driver), front/rear, %....51/49
Wheelbase, in.............103.0
Track, front/rear.......55.8/56.5
Overall length.............188.0
Width...................69.9
Height...................53.0
Ground clearance.............5.0
Trunk space, cu ft......not taken
Fuel tank capacity, U.S. gal.....20

ACCOMMODATION

Seating capacity, persons..2 plus 2
Seat width, front/rear...2 x 22/55
Head room, front/rear......39/33
Seat back adjustment, degrees..30
Driver comfort rating (scale of 100):
Driver 69 in. tall..........100
Driver 72 in. tall............95
Driver 75 in. tall............90

SPEEDOMETER ERROR

30 mph indicated is actually...28.0
40 mph....................39.1
60 mph....................59.8
80 mph....................80.1
100 mph...................101.0

SPEEDS IN GEARS

3rd gear (4600).............122
2nd (4600)....................84
1st (4600)....................50

ACCELERATION

Time to distance, sec:
0-100 ft....................3.3
0-250 ft....................5.9
0-500 ft....................9.2
0-1000 ft...................11.2
0-1320 ft (¼ mi).......... 15.7
Speed at end of ¼ mi, mph....91
Time to speed, sec:
0-30 mph....................3.5
0-40 mph....................4.2
0-50 mph....................5.3
0-60 mph....................7.1
0-70 mph....................9.2
0-80 mph...................12.0
0-100 mph..................19.5

FUEL CONSUMPTION

Normal driving, mpg.........12.4
Cruising range, mi...........248

BRAKES

Panic stop from 80 mph:
Deceleration rate, %g........90
Control.................excellent
Overall brake rating.....very good

Faster than ever

Refined interior, slightly modified suspension plus radial ply tyres on wider rims; more speed

Probably no other car in the world can claim to offer more primary safety on the road than the Jensen FF with its special kind of 4wd and Maxaret anti-lock braking. Yet to meet the ever-tightening American Federal Regulations—mostly concerned with secondary safety—and thus to assure sales in the US, Jensen were obliged to bring out a revised version of the FF at last year's London show, three years after the car was first introduced. Most of the changes—which have also been built into the FF's stablemate the Interceptor—are to the interior styling and safety, like the facia padding and collapsible steering column.

So the FF II retains its unique transmission which apportions 63 per cent of the engine torque to the rear wheels and 37 per cent to the front ones which allows the front wheels to overrun the rear wheels by no more than 16.5 per cent and the rear wheels to overrun the front ones by a maximum of 5.5 per cent. Only the final drive ratio has been changed, from 3.07:1 to 2.88:1, partly to compensate for the smaller rolling radius of the low-profile radial ply tyres now fitted as standard (on 1in. wider rims) and partly to give even more restful cruising at high speeds. Also retained, naturally, is the Maxaret system which prevents the wheels from locking and the car from skidding under heavy braking.

The remaining mechanical changes are small ones. The front suspension has been slightly modified to give increased roll stiffness, while at the back the rear spring eyes have been raised to promote roll understeer. Both these changes were effected to make the car understeer a little more under a wider variety of conditions. The Selectaride dampers (no longer in production) have been replaced by fixed-setting dampers, also made by Armstrong.

The facia has been completely revamped, the front seats redesigned, and the equipment augmented by such items as a hazard warning light switch, a city/country tone control for the horns, and an electric release to the fuel filler cap of the sort fitted to earlier cars of the series but subsequently dropped. An important new option (costing £220 6s.) is air conditioning.

Since we last tested an FF we have been lucky enough to drive such cars as a Ford GT40 and various Ferraris as well as some more recently introduced vehicles like the Aston Martin DBS and the Jaguar XJ6. It is against standards raised by the general march of progress and such particular experiences of the excellent that the FF II must now be judged.

PRICE: £5900 plus £1805 1s. 5d. purchase tax equals £7705 1s. 5d. Air conditioning £220 6s. 3d., Sundym glass £50 6s. 11d., Voxson radio/stereo tape player £71 16s. 2d., air horns £16 12s. 11d. —all including tax. Total as tested £8064 3s. 4d.

By such standards we must confess ourselves a little disappointed in the FF II when judged purely as a machine for cornering in the dry. We feel that the sum of the small changes to the suspension has if anything had a small adverse effect on the cornering, cancelling out the advantage of more and stiffer rubber on the ground. One factor which may account for the FF's slightly lurchy behaviour on corners is the adoption of dampers with a fixed setting corresponding to position three on the Selectarides previoulsy fitted.

We tried Pirelli and Dunlop radials during our test, and found both squealed loudly; a little less if pressures were raised to the high speed level. The Pirellis—never very quiet—then transmitted a lot of thump and roar and set up drumming in the body structure. The Dunlops were a little quieter both in squeal and in road noise.

The lavish cockpit now conforms with American safety standards —the controls are recessed, the facia thickly padded, the steering wheel collapsible. Externally the car is little changed

Thus we don't think the FF II corners any quicker in the dry than some comparable two-wheel drive cars like a Ferrari or the Aston Martin DBS or even the Jaguar XJ6 at one third of the cost. The XJ6 of course, undermines the whole concept of the high-priced low-volume luxury performance car, but it is not the price of the FF II that we object to—since it is no more expensive than some of its rivals—but we wonder whether its mechanical complexity is technically justified.

But after some braking tests at Dunlop's skid pan carried out with the help of Jensen and Harry Ferguson Research Ltd we were no longer in much doubt that the Maxaret system must be a real life saver in slippery conditions. Using brutal, panic braking which raised pedal pressures to at least 160lb. we were able to stop the car in 151ft. from 50mph on a very low-mu surface. The car weaved a little as the Maxaret cyclically released and reapplied the brakes, but kept a straight course without the need for any correction. Then we tried the same exercise with the conventionally braked Interceptor, and our test driver found himself able to beat the Maxaret system to get a stopping distance of around 137ft. The essential point, however, was that he had to apply full lock to keep the car in a straight line, and that even under the artificially safe conditions of a private test track he could not bring himself to indulge in a really heavy stamp on the brakes fearing an expensive encounter with the iron spray pipe running alongside the track. Equally, had he tried the same gentle and well judged braking technique in the FF the stopping distance would have been about the same or better. In real-life emergencies such judgement is often very difficult to exercise.

Strictly speaking the Maxaret and 4wd systems interact so their effects cannot be separated; nevertheless, considering four-wheel drive only, we feel that its advantages only become really significant on snow and ice or when the car is driven off normal surfaced roads.

Although the Chrysler engine produces nominally the same power as before, in its latest versions the speed at which the hydraulic tappets pump up has been postponed and it has become capable of revving to 5600 rpm. Unusually for a big American V8 it continues to produce useful power up to its new limit, giving considerably improved acceleration if the gears are selected manually to take advantage of it, though the tachometer is still red-lined at 5100 rpm where formerly the power cut off sharply. As a result the 0-100 time is now down to 19.1sec!

This slight increase in power together with the raised final drive ratio and the much reduced rolling resistance of radial ply tyres at high speeds means that the overall maximum has been considerably increased. We had no opportunity to measure this properly on a Continental motorway, but we did reach 129.0 mph through MIR's timing lights after accelerating from 120+ mph off the banking (which has a hands-off speed of no more than 85-90 mph) and the car was still accelerating strongly. We are therefore inclined to accept Jensen's claim for a true maximum of 140 mph, compared to the top speed of 130.5 mph that we achieved with our original FF.

If you have to ask how much fuel the FF consumes you cannot, like the prospective ocean yacht owner, afford it; but thrifty millionaires may like to know that at 11.4 mpg overall (11.5 mpg before) the thirst has not been affected by the improved performance.

Chrysler's torqueflite three-speed automatic transmission is the smoothest and most refined of all the American automatics. Last time we criticized it a little for the jerkiness of manual downward changes, but on the FF II these changes were smooth and the transmission a delight to use.

We liked the new seats (especially their built-in headrests on which you really can rest your head) but still found them to be slightly of the slide-down sort; a cloth insert with a higher friction might solve the problem nicely. Rear seat legroom, however, remains negligible.

Wind noise is very low; it builds up after 100 mph but it is still possible to listen to the radio without aural discomfort at 120 mph. We were not very convinced by the ventilation system as warm air came through the ducts when the optional air conditioning was not running. Even when it was operating, the coolness was not impressive, perhaps because most of the unit's energies were being expended in dissipating the tremendous waste heat from the engine. It is also worth recording that our test car had very stiff door locks, a loose sealing strip (the design has since been modified) and an alternator that vibrated on its bracket when its belt drive became loaded by the air conditioning compressor. ■

PERFORMANCE AND SPECIFICATION

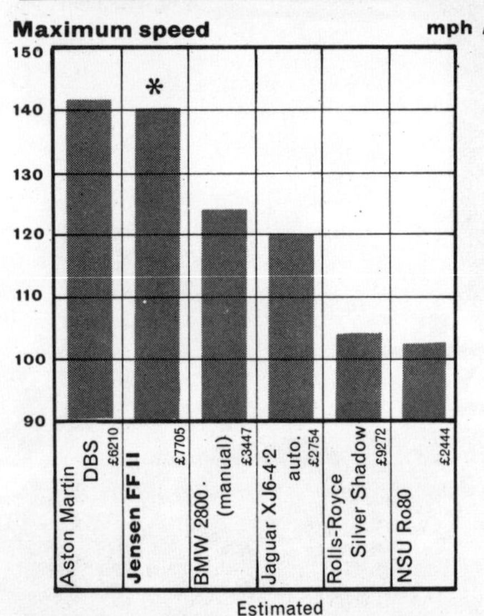

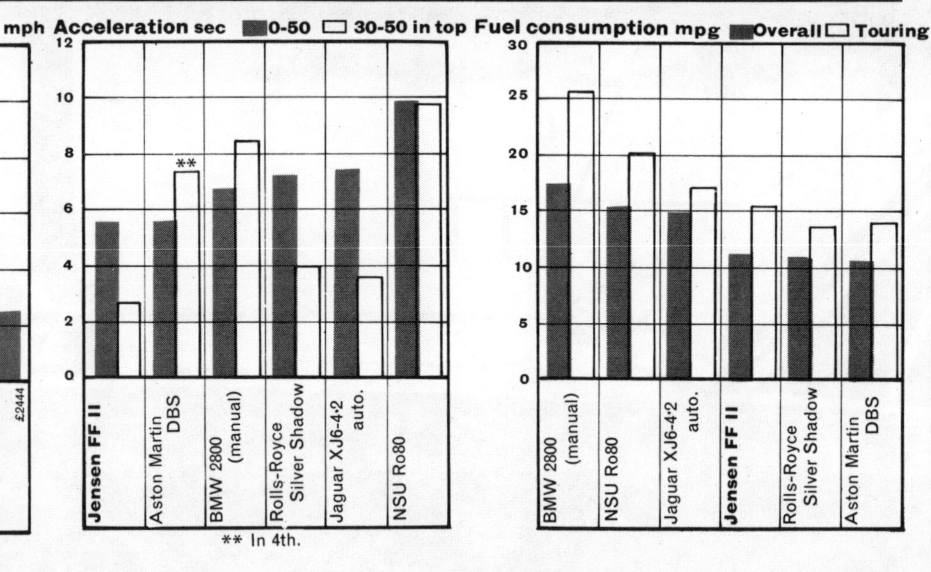

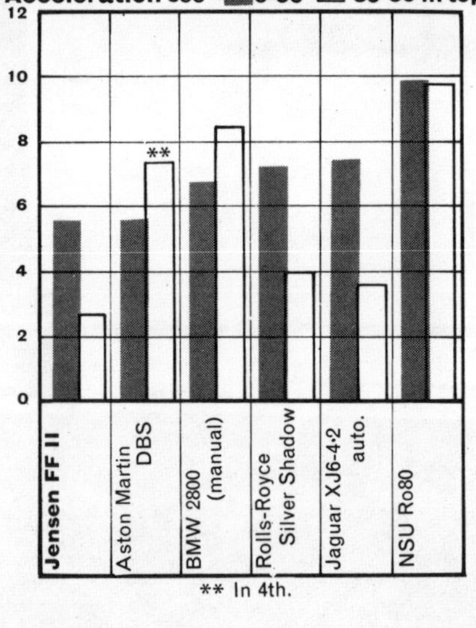

Performance tests carried out by *Motor's* staff at the Motor Industry Research Association proving ground, Lindley.

Test Data: World copyright reserved; no unauthorized reproduction in whole or in part.

Conditions

Weather: Warm and dry
Temperature: 56-60°F
Barometer 29.4in. Hg.
Surface: Dry tarmacadam
Fuel: Super 101 octane (RM), 5 Star rating

Maximum Speeds

		mph	kph
See text		140	225
2nd gear Intermediate	at 5600 rpm	104	167
1st gear Low	at 5600 rpm	61	98

Acceleration Times

mph	Auto sec.	Manual select sec.
0-30	3.2	2.9
0-40	4.6	4.1
0-50	6.1	5.6
0-60	7.9	7.4
0-70	10.6	9.5
0-80	13.4	12.3
0-90	17.0	15.3
0-100	21.9	19.1
0-110	27.7	24.8
Standing quarter mile	16.3	15.8
Standing kilometre	29.4	28.6

mph	Kickdown auto sec.
10-30	—
20-40	2.6
30-50	2.9
40-60	3.3
50-70	4.5
60-80	5.5
70-90	6.4
80-100	8.5
90-110	10.7

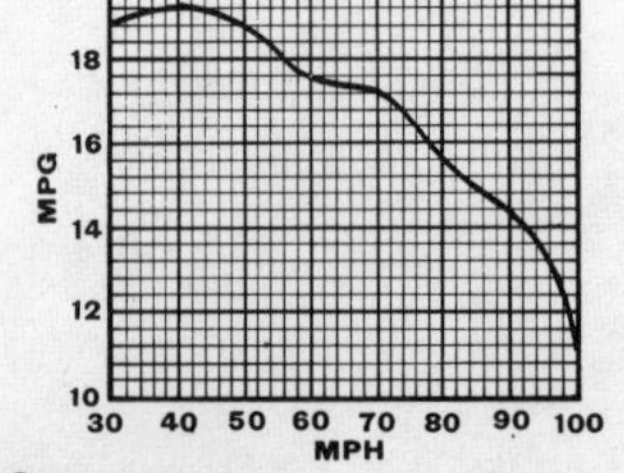

Fuel Consumption

Touring (consumption midway between 30 mph and maximum less 5% allowance for acceleration)	15.3 mpg
Overall	11.4 mpg
	(=24.8 litres/100km)
Total test distance	1139 miles

Speedometer

Indicated	10	20	30	40	50	60	70
True	10	20	30	40	50	60	69
Indicated	80	90	100				
True	79	89	97				

Distance recorder accurate

Engine

Cylinders	8 in vee
Cooling system	Water
Bore and stroke	108mm (4.25in.) 86mm (3.39in.)
Cubic capacity	6276 c.c. (383 cu. in.)
Valves	Pushrod ohv
Compression ratio	10:1
Carburetter	4-barrel Carter
Fuel pump	Mechanical
Oil filter	Full flow
Max. power (gross)	325 bhp at 4600 rpm
Max. torque (gross)	425 lb.ft. at 2800 rpm

Transmission

Chrysler automatic

Internal gear box ratios	
Top gear	1.00:1
Intermediate	1.45:1
Low	2.45:1
Reverse	2.20:1
Overdrive type	
Final drive	2.88:1
Mph at 1000 rpm in:—	
Top gear	26.8
Intermediate	18.5
Low	10.9

Jensen

The coachwork for current Jensens was designed by Vignale in 1967 and is not likely to change before importation begins. Bodies are steel.

The less expensive Interceptor with conventional two-wheel drive will be imported to the U.S. beginning January, 1971, with the FF following a year later.

The English Jensen firm has had a curious if prosperous history, starting by designing lovely tourer bodies for pre-WWII Fords, graduating from these to their own chassis with Nash dual-ignition engines and finally, after a brief flirtation with an Austin truck engine, settling on the familiar and durable Chrysler 383 V-8 coupled to an automatic transmission. Then recently, when the Jensen brothers, who owned the small firm in its entirety, retired, the assets were taken over by a Norwegian-American named Kjell Qvale who distributes MG, Austin and Lotus cars in the eleven Western states. Mr. Qvale plans to bring in about 20 of the two-wheel-drive Jensen Interceptor models starting in January, 1971, and perhaps in another year, after it passes its safety tests, the unique four-wheel-drive Jensen FF.

Mr. Qvale plans national if limited distribution of the Jensens and not necessarily just through Chrysler dealers as has been reported, the connection probably being derived from the use of Chrysler powerplants and transmissions. The Interceptor, with a four-passenger Vignale-designed body, will list at $13,500 with no extras being either offered or necessary. Air-conditioning, electric windows and even a stereo-tape player are standard equipment. The Jensen version of the Chrysler 383 V-8 (made in Canada) is rated at 330 horsepower, giving the car grand tourer capabilities.

In fact, in FF form with the Ferguson system of all-wheel drive combined with Dunlop's "Maxaret" skid-proof braking, which also acts on all wheels, the Jensen is considered the world's safest if not finest grand tourer. Though not priced as yet, this will probably cost about $3,500 more than the Interceptor as it does now in England. Modern Jensens are seldom seen on these shores, particularly the FF, as Jensen was understandably reluctant to let a complex, essentially experimental car stray too far away from factory service facilities.

While not a large car, with a wheelbase of 109 inches and an overall length of 191 inches, Jensens are fairly heavy with the FF weighing in at approximately 4,050 pounds. Thus, they are not capable of the 150 mph plus speeds served up by Ferraris, Lamborghinis and other exotics and they are also not generally considered a sports car. However, these facts are academic in this speed-limited country because even *prima-facie* Nevada is inclined to take umbrage if you exceed 100 mph by much. Also to be remembered is that the engine and transmission may be attended to in any of thousands of Dodge and Chrysler-Plymouth dealerships whether they sell Jensens or not. Ferrari owners are limited to only 18 official clinics as of this writing.

The Jensen firm has survived because it is highly practical in all of its undertakings. The relatively low price for the Interceptor is obtained by opting for perfectly adequate but cheap Canadian-made drive-train components and eschewing such erotica has a wood inlay dash finish and a variety of custom-made body styles. Jensen is a custom builder in its own right, having made the prototype Volvo 1800 and Austin-Healeys. On that latter note, Mr. Qvale has recently obtained the services of the famous Donald Healey and his son, Jeffrey, whose contracts for their sports car had not been renewed by British Leyland Motors. Six prototype two-seater Healeys are under construction right now in the Jensen shops and production versions are expected to be available in the U.S. for under $4,000 within 14 months.

Data in Brief

(based on Jensen FF, European)

ENGINE: V-8 cylinder ohv (Chrysler), 383 cu. ins., 330 hp at 5000 rpm, 425 lb.-ft. of torque at 2800 rpm, four-throat Carter carburetion.

DRIVELINE: 4-speed manual or Torqueflite automatic, all-wheel-drive via chain transfer with Ferguson system positive limit slip on center differential.

SUSPENSION: Coil front, leaf rear.

BRAKES: Girling discs front and rear, power assisted, Dunlop Maxaret skid control.

STEERING: Rack and pinion, power assisted.

DIMENSIONS: Wheelbase 109.0 ins., overall length 191.0 ins., width 69.0 ins., height 52.4 ins., weight 4050 lbs.

AUTOTEST

JENSEN FF II (6,276 c.c.)

AT-A-GLANCE: Luxury GT capable of carrying four adults. Chrysler vee-eight an impressive and refined performer. Exceptionally effortless high-speed cruising. Ferguson all-wheel-control gives remarkable traction and excellent handling. Anti-lock braking still controversial, but ensures control during panic stopping. Very good power steering. Air-conditioning leaves scope for improvement.

MANUFACTURER

Jensen Motors Ltd., Kelvin Way, West Bromwich, Staffordshire

PRICES

Basic	£5,900	0s	0d
Purchase Tax	£1,805	1s	5d
Front seat belts	standard equipment		
Total (in G.B.)	£7,705	1s	5d

EXTRAS (inc. P.T.)

*Air conditioning	£220	6s	3d
*Air horns	£16	12s	11d
Fog or spot light (Cibié)	£8	15s	7d
White wall tyres	£19	3s	6d
*Sun-dym glass	£50	6s	11d
Static safety belts in rear	£10	19s	4d
Special upholstery	£48	6s	2d
Special paint	£65	5s	6d
Duo-tone paint	£26	2s	2d
*Voxson radio and stereo tape player	£71	16s	2d

*Fitted to test car

PRICE AS TESTED £8,064 3s 8d

PERFORMANCE SUMMARY

Mean maximum speed	137 mph
Standing start $\frac{1}{4}$-mile	15.8 sec
0-60 mph	8.1 sec
30-70 mph through gears	7.1 sec
Typical fuel consumption	12 mpg
Miles per tankful	240

WITH its sophisticated four-wheel-drive transmission and anti-lock braking, the Jensen FF II is undoubtedly one of the most technically advanced cars in current production. Although the FF has remained unchanged fundamentally since its debut in October 1966, numerous detail improvements have been made since then. The appearance of the FF II in October 1969 marked a significant step in the model's development. New features included extensive interior restyling, improved seating, low-profile radial-ply tyres on wider rims, higher overall gearing, greater fuel capacity, a larger radiator, improved heating, full air-conditioning as an optional extra, plus a host of lesser items. The rear suspension was also modified slightly and the Selectaride dampers dropped in favour of conventional fixed-setting ones.

As described in the 24 September issue of *Autocar,* there are still more improvements for 1971. Among them are improved refrigeration, with a larger evaporator and a pair of additional facia outlets. The seats have been further improved and the instruments made easier to read. There are also a number of new safety features, primarily to satisfy American GFA requirements. Our test car, now some seven months and 9,000 miles old, was built before the introduction of these latest changes, and is to be the subject of a long-term report in next week's issue.

Performance

The big vee-8, aided by its automatic-choke Carter carburettor, starts instantly from cold, but sometimes stalls almost immediately afterwards. It subsequently restarts without trouble to settle down to a reliable and consistent idle. Hot-starting, on the other hand, is sometimes embarrassingly difficult. A 10 minute stop in hot weather can mean anything up to 20 sec "cranking" before the engine fires. There is, however, no trace of fuel vaporization, something we have often experienced with large American-engined cars during performance testing at MIRA. The provision of a pair of electric cooling fans helps a great deal in this connection. Controlled by a thermostatic switch, they are unusual in not being wired through the ignition. This arrangement undoubtedly helps to keep down under-bonnet temperatures during the heat-soak period immediately following switching off, but the considerable noise from the fans (they frequently operate under these circumstances) often excites comment from bystanders. From inside the car, however, the noise is modest unless a window is lowered.

Air-conditioning (an optional extra, as previously mentioned), wider rims and tyres, and slightly more fuel all contribute to an increase of just over 2 cwt in kerb weight compared with the FF tested by *Autocar* in 1968 (Mk I model—report published 28 March 1968). In the form tested, the FF II scales 37.8 cwt, 51.6 per cent of it on the front wheels, 48.4 per cent on the rears. Despite the additional mechanism associated with the drive to the FF's front wheels, this compares favourably with the 50.7—49.3 distribution of the Interceptor tested last year (*Autocar,* 4 September 1969) largely because of the FF's 4 in. longer wheelbase and slightly more rearward engine-gearbox disposition.

Minor engine changes have raised the peak of the power curve some 5 bhp and 400rpm, but the FF II as tested has a slightly less favourable power-weight ratio than the earlier car. This, together with marginally higher gearing, may well account for a slightly less brisk step-off. However, the 0-50 mph time (6.2 sec) is the same for both, and the FF II has a slight advantage at higher speeds. Its top speed, too, is better (137 mph mean, 141 mph best, compared with the earlier car's 130 mph). To a considerable extent, this is due to the Dunlop SP radials having appreciably less rolling resistance than the RS5 cross-plies formerly used.

As our comparison tables show, there are cars capable of out-performing the FF II, but they are few and far between. We must also point out that it may well be possible to better our through-the-gears times by holding low and intermediate gears to 5,500 rpm or so. Although revs of this order are within the engine's capacity (the FF can exceed 5,400 rpm in top), we chose to observe the tachometer red-line (5,100 rpm) during the acceleration runs. Leaving the transmission to its own devices, with the selector lever in D, results in earlier changes (at 4,500 rpm indicated). The acceleration suffers slightly as a result, an additional 1.3 sec being taken to reach 100 mph. There is usually such a splendid reserve of power that holding in this way is quite unnecessary.

A spectacular performance on paper is one thing—using it under give-and-take conditions on public roads is an entirely different matter. This is where the FF II really excels: Even on a damp and greasy surface, the odds are that it will achieve *exactly* the same times as in the dry, and with absolutely no fuss or drama. Its superb traction really has to be experienced to be believed. Even on loose gravel, stalling the convertor on full throttle before releasing the brakes, there is rarely a trace of wheelspin. Damp and greasy London streets even fail to catch it out. We can think of no other production car, let alone one with 330 bhp under its bonnet, that can remotely compare with the FF II in this respect.

Even by luxury car standards, it is an astonishingly effortless car. When cruising at around 120 mph (122 mph on the clock), the power train is remarkably unobtrusive. Wind noise, too, is modest. Allied to excellent straight-line stability and first-class brakes, these qualities make for a quite exceptional journey car. Yet it is just as much at home on winding country roads or crowded city traffic.

Inevitably, one has to pay for performance of this order from a car weighing more than 2 tons (41.1 cwt, laden as tested). Overall petrol consumption during the 1,400 mile test period (entirely divorced from the long-term appraisal) was 11.9 mpg. Moderate driving on a journey to North Wales returned 12.2 mpg, but we could not approach the calculated (DIN) figure of 14.8 mpg. Consumption, in fact, seems little affected by the way the car is driven and around 12 mpg would seem a typical figure. With a 20 gallon tank, this gives an absolute range of 240 miles, not a lot for a car of this calibre. On the credit side, the fuel gauge and low-level warning light (3 gallons remaining) are both exceptionally accurate, enabling most of the tank's contents to be used with safety. Reference to the comparison tables shows that the fuel consumption, in fact, is similar to that of other cars in this class. Oil consumption during the test was negligible.

Automatic Gearbox

Chrysler's Torqueflite transmission is a particularly smooth unit. Our only criticism concerns its reluctance to kick-down on part-throttle. One can, of course, change down manually, but some of our testers thought the selector lever a little too high and too far back. Full-throttle kick-down into intermediate is possible at speeds below 66 mph and into low at 28 mph. Unlike some automatic gearboxes, holding intermediate does not interfere with kick-down operation into low (and subsequent changing back into intermediate).

All-wheel-control

A great deal of the FF II's magic stems from the Ferguson system of all-wheel-control, now handled by GKN. Briefly, what it does is divide engine torque between front and rear wheels in a 37:63 ratio (in this particular instance). Furthermore, it allows the front wheels to overrun the rears by a maximum of 16 per cent, and the rears to overrun the fronts by a maximum of 5 per cent. This arrangement allows the degree of freedom between front and rear wheels necessary to prevent transmission wind-up, rapid tyre wear and handling peculiarities, but ensures that optimum traction is available at all times.

The system is only partly effective in reverse; torque is still divided between front and rear in the same proportions, but the one-way clutches which control the permissible speed differentials are inoperative. This means that one should avoid situations where the car has to be reversed up a particularly slippery gradient. Apart from the Ferguson control unit, a Salisbury Powr-Lok limited-slip differential is used at the rear. Steering and handling considerations render the use of such a unit undesirable at the front.

Also forming part of the Ferguson Formula is the Dunlop Maxaret anti-lock braking system. This, in principle, consists of a small flywheel geared to the output side of the car's transmission. As the car (and therefore the transmission) decelerates, the flywheel is forced to follow suit. In doing so, it tries to overrun its driving spindle. If the deceleration should exceed a pre-determined rate (as would happen if incipient locking of any one wheel took place), this overrun action causes a cam mechanism to actuate a micro-switch. This, in turn, controls a solenoid-operated valve which modulates the vacuum applied to the brake servo unit.

Handling and steering

Mention had already been made of the FF II's remarkable traction, but we make no apologies for stressing the point. A great deal more power can be used in any given circumstances than would be possible with conventional drive. Even when deliberately provoked, the FF II rarely puts a foot wrong. Indeed, we found the limiting factor on a right-handed airfield circuit to be lack of engine power, caused by fuel starvation—a good indication of the cornering forces involved. We hasten to add that such cornering rates are well in excess of what is likely to be indulged in on normal roads. For all practical purposes, the Jensen can be relied on to go exactly where it's pointed.

Despite the unorthodox layout, there are no handling peculiarities. When cornered sufficiently hard, the FF adopts a slightly tail-out attitude, feel being much the same as that of a well-balanced rear-drive car. Lifting-off in such circumstances does not upset the balance in any way. Pushed to the limit, front and rear break away together, usually without any detectable change in attitude. On those occasions when slight correction is required, response to steering movements is extraordinarily rapid. Just about the only criticism we can level at the handling concerns a very occasional tendency for the live rear axle to bump-skid on rough corners, but this almost amounts to being hyper-critical.

The excellent Adwest power-assisted rack-and-pinion steering adds greatly to the enjoyment of driving the FF II. Although not particularly light at town speeds (for a power system), it is beautifully quick and precise on the open road. There is just a trace of kick-back on rough surfaces, again at low speeds, but this is a small price to pay for the excellent feel the system affords. Steering wheel diameter, at 16 in., seems just right and telescopic adjustment for reach is provided. Drive to the front wheels, plus a lengthy wheelbase, result in a mean turning circle diameter of just over 40 ft between kerbs. This we consider to be approaching the limit of acceptability.

Ride

Considerable bump-thumping at low speeds tends to create an impression of harshness. This disappears as the speed rises and the suspension, in fact, is ideally tailored for high-speed cruising. The Armstrong Selectaride rear dampers of the Mk I have been replaced by conventional fixed-setting ones (also of Armstrong manufacture). Damper-settings, inevitably, are a matter of compromise, and we feel that those chosen for the FF II are well suited to its character. It is undoubtedly at its best during high-speed cruising on open roads. Seldom have we experienced such rock-steady stability.

Brakes

The Maxaret anti-lock braking system still excites considerable controversy. In the main, this concerns its response time—in other words, the frequency with which the pedal pulsates when too much effort is applied. In the case of our test car, the cycling frequency certainly did not exceed 2 cps. This, of course, means that braking torque is appreciably below optimum for much of a panic stop. While we acknowledge that a skilful and alert driver can equal or better the Maxaret system, the latter does ensure that a measure of steering control is maintained no matter how clumsily the brake is applied.

Our test car achieved an excellent 1.05 g from 30 mph, this with a modest 60lb pedal effort. All four wheels appeared to be on the point of locking and the pedal, in fact, kicked just as the car came to rest. To satisfy ourselves that this was not a freak result, the performance was repeated without trouble.

There was relatively little increase in pedal effort during our 70 mph fade test (from 35 to 45lb), but there was slight judder, accompanied by an increase in pedal travel, during the last two stops. Judder was also experienced when braking from 110 mph at the end of the through-the-gears acceleration runs. On the road, however, braking behaviour was impeccable.

The firmest possible pull on the hand-brake produced a deceleration of 0.3g, but its performance on the test hills was poor. With the transmission selector in 'D', it would just hold the car when facing up a 1 in 4 gradient. In neutral, the best it could achieve was 1 in 5. In sharp contrast, a 1 in 3 restart was achieved with contemptuous ease, again, of course, without a trace of wheelspin.

Fittings and furniture

With its Connolly-hide upholstery and Wilton carpeting, the Jensen is the epitome of luxury. Seat backrests, of course, are adjustable for rake and there is separate provision (with levers both sides of each seat) for tilting them forward. Head restraints (detachable) are standard, with Velcro-fastened pads for maximum comfort. The seats, both front and rear, are shaped to provide ample sideways support, a particularly important point in a car capable of generating high lateral forces. Although not particularly soft, the seats proved very comfortable on long journeys. Making room for adults in the rear, however, involves some sacrifice on the part of the front seat occupants, particularly the driver.

Smiths air-conditioning, integrated with the heating system, was fitted to the test car. It proved a real boon during the warm weather that prevailed during the test but it suffered limitations which subsequent changes may well have overcome. There were, in fact, occasions when warm air was fed through the refrigeration outlets at traffic speeds, this with the control knob at its minimum-temperature setting. Normally, however, it coped quite adequately. An irritating detail is the need (according to the instruction book) to switch off the three-speed blower, thus declutching the compressor), before operating the starter. A better scheme would be to arrange for the compressor to be declutched automatically when the key is turned to the start position.

The Jensen FF II is well constructed and beautifully finished. However, nothing is perfect, and we noted some minor shortcomings while the car was in our hands. For instance, the left-hand private-lock button is difficult to reach from the driver's side. A central locking system would be nice to have in such a luxury machine. Another fault, and an irritating one, is the difficulty experienced in raising the bonnet. A pair of hairpin-type springs are intended to raise it enough to enable one's fingers to be inserted below the edge, but these are hopelessly inadequate. The compression struts, designed to provide a measure of counterbalancing, are also too weak. Another grouse is that the oil pressure and fuel-flap warning lamps are partly obscured by the steering wheel spokes. One last point; we feel that an ammeter is a more informative instrument than a voltmeter (or "battery condition meter"). An ignition warning lamp should also be provided—by the time one has noticed a low-reading voltmeter, the battery may well be flat. □

Top left: The big Chrysler vee-8 is mounted well back in the frame. Note the refrigeration compressor ahead of the air cleaner. The Maxaret vacuum-control unit is to the rear of the battery

Bottom left: Luxury interior, upholstered in Connolly hide. A large console separates driver and passenger. Beneath glove locker is non-standard Air Call radio-telephone

Below: Squatter tyres and restyled bumpers have improved the looks. Wheel rims now have enamelled finish. Stout electric-aerial does not wilt at speed

JENSEN FF II (6,276 c.c.)

ACCELERATION

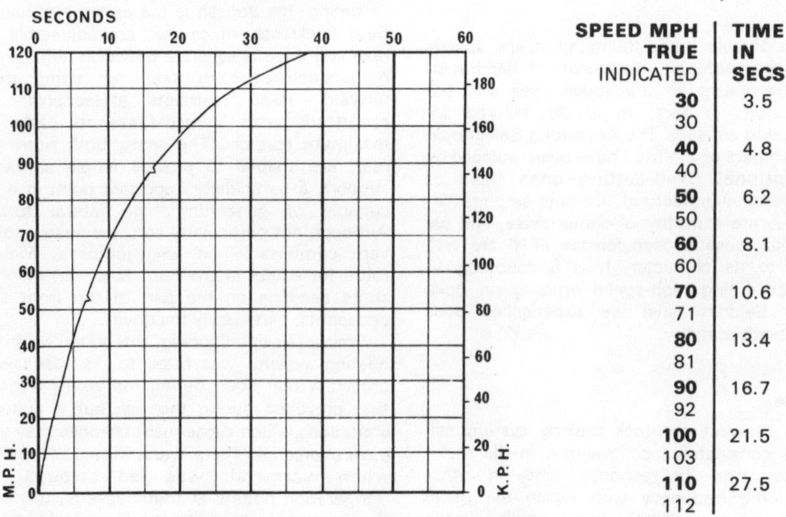

SPEED MPH TRUE	INDICATED	TIME IN SECS
30	30	3.5
40	40	4.8
50	50	6.2
60	60	8.1
70	71	10.6
80	81	13.4
90	92	16.7
100	103	21.5
110	112	27.5

SPEED RANGE, GEAR RATIOS AND TIME IN SECONDS

mph	Top (2.88-6.34)	Inter (4.18-9.20)	Low (7.06-15.53)
0-20	—	—	2.4
10-30	—	—	2.6
20-40	—	3.5	2.4
30-50	—	3.8	2.8
40-60	5.4	4.2	—
50-70	6.0	4.8	—
60-80	7.0	5.3	—
70-90	7.9	—	—
80-100	9.0	—	—
90-110	10.7	—	—

Standing ¼-mile
15.8 sec 88 mph

Standing kilometre
28.9 sec 112 mph

Test distance
1,400 miles

Mileage recorder
2.6 per cent
over-reading

PERFORMANCE

MAXIMUM SPEEDS

Gear	mph	kph	Theoretical rpm
Top (mean)	137	221	5,200
(best)	141	227	5,350
Inter	93	150	5,100
Low	55	89	5,100

BRAKES

(from 70 mph in neutral)
Pedal load for 0.5g stops in lb

1	35	6	40
2	35	7	40
3	35	8	40
4	35	9	40
5	40	10	45

RESPONSE (from 30 mph in neutral)

Load	g	Distance
20lb	0.28	107ft
40lb	0.65	46ft
60lb	1.05	29ft
Handbrake	0.30	

Max. Gradient 1 in 5 (see text)

MOTORWAY CRUISING

Indicated speed at 70 mph	71 mph
Engine (rpm at 70 mph)	2,650 rpm
(mean piston speed)	1,500 ft/min.
Fuel (mpg at 70 mph)	16.3 mpg
Passing (50-70 mph)	4.4 sec

TEST CONDITIONS:
Weather: Fine and sunny. Wind: 7-15 mph. Temperature: 20 deg. C. (68 deg. F). Barometer 29.7 in. hg. Humidity: 44 per cent. Surfaces: Dry concrete and asphalt.

WEIGHT:
Kerb weight 37.8 cwt (4,230lb—1,920kg) (with oil, water and half full fuel tank). Distribution, per cent F, 51.6; R. 48.4. Laden as tested: 41.1 cwt (4,608lb—2,092kg).

TURNING CIRCLES:
Between kerbs, L, 40ft 10in.; R, 39ft 6in. Between walls L, 42ft 9in.; R, 41ft 5in., steering wheel turns, lock to lock 3.6.

Figures taken at 7,500 miles by our own staff at the Motor Industry Research Association proving ground at Nuneaton and on the Continent.

COMPARISONS

MAXIMUM SPEED MPH

Monteverdi 375 L	(£10,450)	152
*Ferrari 365 GTC	(£7,901)	151
*Aston Martin DBS	(£6,210)	140
Jensen FF	**(£7,705)**	**137**
Mercedes-Benz 300 SEL 6.3	(£6,210)	134

0-60 MPH, SEC

*Ferrari 365 GTC	6.3
Monteverdi 375 L	6.3
Mercedes-Benz 300 SEL 6.3	7.1
Jensen FF	**8.1**
*Aston Martin DBS	8.6

STANDING ¼-MILE, SEC

*Ferrari 365 GTC	14.5
Monteverdi 375 L	14.6
Mercedes-Benz 300 SEL 6.3	15.5
Jensen FF	**15.8**
*Aston Martin DBS	16.3

OVERALL MPG

Mercedes-Benz 300 SEL 6.3	15.1
*Aston Martin DBS	12.7
Jensen FF	**11.9**
*Ferrari 365 GTC	11.9
Monteverdi 375 L	11.6

* Manual transmission

Theoretical GEARING
(with ER70VR 15in. tyres)

Top	26.4 mph per 1,000 rpm
Inter	18.2 mph per 1,000 rpm
Low	10.8 mph per 1,000 rpm

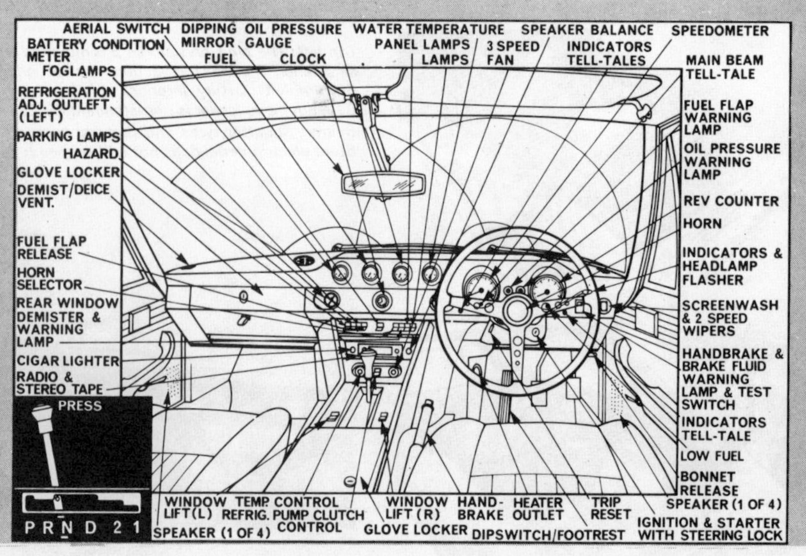

JENSEN FF II (6,276 c.c.) *AUTOCAR 22 October 1970*

CONSUMPTION

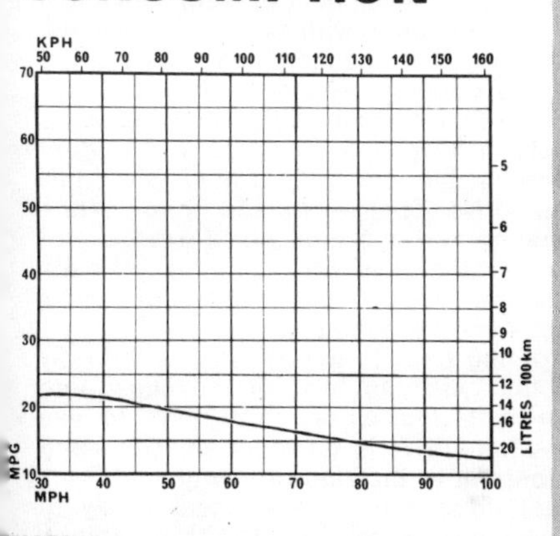

FUEL

(At constant speeds—mpg)

30 mph	21.8
40 mph	21.4
50 mph	19.6
60 mph	17.8
70 mph	16.3
80 mph	14.8
90 mph	13.7
100 mph	12.6

Typical mpg 12 (23.5 litres/100km)
Calculated (DIN) mpg 14.8 (19.1 litres/100km)
Overall mpg 11.9 (23.8 litres/100km)
Grade of fuel
Super Premium, 5-star (min. 100 RM)

OIL

Miles per pint (SAE 20W/40)
Negligible consumption

SPECIFICATION FRONT ENGINE, FOUR-WHEEL DRIVE

ENGINE

Cylinders	8, in 90-deg vee
Main bearings	5
Cooling system	Water; pump, thermostat and two electric fans
Bore	108mm (4.25 in.)
Stroke	86mm (3.38 in.)
Displacement	6,276 c.c. (383 cu.in.)
Valve gear	Overhead, pushrods and hydraulic tappets
Compression ratio	10-to-1 Min. octane rating: 100 RM
Carburettor	Carter 4-barrel progressive
Fuel pump	Carter mechanical
Oil filter	Mopar full-flow, renewable element
Max. power	330 bhp (SAE) at 5,000 rpm
Max. torque	425 lb.ft (SAE) at 2,800 rpm

TRANSMISSION

Gearbox	Chrysler Torqueflite 3-speed automatic with torque convertor
Gear ratios	Top 1.0-2.20 Inter 1.45-3.19 Low 2.45-5.39 Reverse 2.20-4.84
Final drive	Hypoid bevel, 2.88-to-1. Powr-Lok limited-slip differential at rear only

CHASSIS and BODY

Construction	Steel body welded to tubular steel frame

SUSPENSION

Front	Independent, double wishbones, with twin coil springs and telescopic dampers each side. Anti-roll bar
Rear	Live axle, semi-elliptic leaf springs. Panhard rod

STEERING

Type	Adwest power-assisted rack-and-pinion
Wheel dia.	16in.

BRAKES

Make and type	Girling discs front and rear. Divided hydraulic circuits. Dunlop Maxaret anti-lock system
Servo	Girling vacuum
Dimensions	F 11.38 in. dia. R 10.75 in. dia.
Swept area	F 237.2 sq.in., R 197.4 sq.in. Total 434.6 sq.in. (212 sq.in./ton laden)

WHEELS

Type	Pressed-steel "Rostyle", 5-stud fixing, 6in. wide rim.
Tyres—make	Dunlop
—type	SP radial-ply tubeless
—size	ER70VR 15 in.

EQUIPMENT

Battery	12 Volt 69 Ah
Alternator	60 amp
Headlamps	Lucas 4-lamp quartz-halogen 110/220 watt (total)
Reversing lamps	2 standard
Electric fuses	12
Screen wipers	2-speed, self-parking
Screen washer	Standard, electric
Interior heater	Standard, water-valve type
Refrigeration	Optional extra
Heated backlight	Standard
Safety belts	Standard front, extra rear
Interior trim	Leather seats, pvc headlining
Floor covering	Carpet
Jack	Bevelift
Jacking points	2 each side, in sills
Windscreen	Laminated
Underbody protection	Bitumastic compound on all surfaces exposed to road

MAINTENANCE

Fuel tank	20 Imp. gallons (no reserve) (91 litres)
Cooling system	28 pints (including heater)
Engine sump	8.5 pints (4.7 litres) SAE 20W/40. Change oil every 4,000 miles. Change filter element every 8,000 miles
Gearbox	15.5 pints ATF type A. Change oil every 36,000 miles if operating under severe conditions. Otherwise, no change needed
Final drive	3 pints SAE 90EP in front unit, limited-slip lubricant in rear. Change oil every 12,000 miles
Grease	4 points every 4,000 miles
Tyre pressures	F 28; R 32 psi (normal driving) F 36; R 40 psi (fast driving or full load)
Max. payload	750 lb (341 kg)

PERFORMANCE DATA

Top gear mph per 1,000 rpm	26.4
Mean piston speed at max. power	2,820 ft/min
Bhp per ton laden	160.6 (gross)

STANDARD GARAGE 16ft x 8ft 6in.

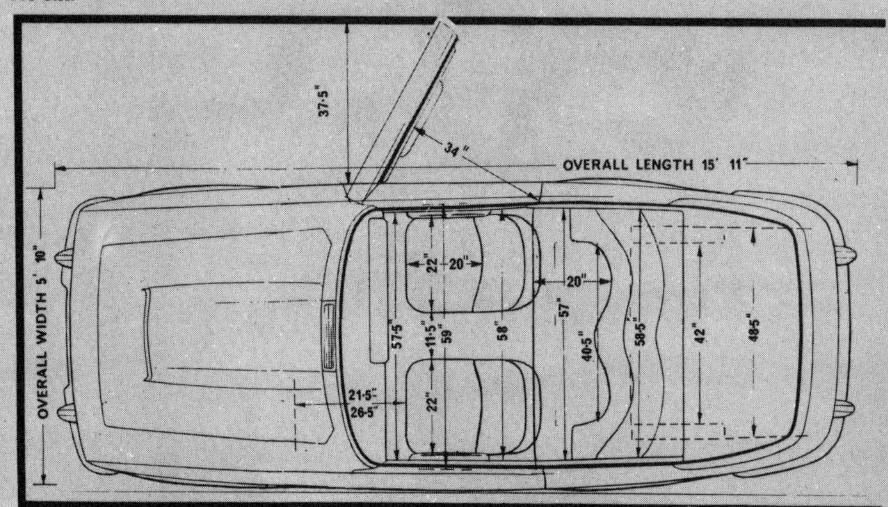

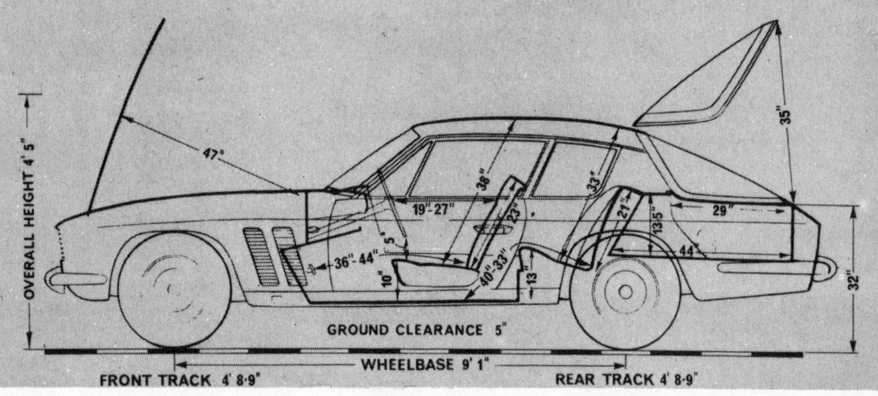

SCALE 0.3in. to 1ft
Cushions uncompressed

ETM

Executive Transport Module

Long-term Report on a Jensen FF II *by Maurice Smith*

WHERE men and their machines are concerned, the more advanced they become the more specialized and costly also. Though space and lunar exploration top the list for specialized hardware, in the down to earth areas of travel also there are the special and exotic vehicles which fit into the pattern. "The most technically advanced car in the world", claim Jensen for their FF. Car seems such a small and mundane term for this complex machine; it is more of an executive transport module. We have been operating such an ETM for the past six months and quite an experience it has proved to be. Like an airline passenger who concerns himself mainly with safety, comfort, punctuality and could seldom say what the engines were or even how many or how positioned, we have found ourselves attracted by the gilt while taking the Jensen's gingerbread for granted.

Clearly the FF has a big, unobtrusive source of power and an automatic transmission which gets on with its job without the occupants really knowing. The driver aims the car and it obeys with exceptional precision. No question of effort or deep concentration, even when the car is going faster than most. Touch the brake pedal and the speed is instantly checked, whether the roads are wet or dry. No one is suggesting that there is any magic, but simply that for all ordinary—and extraordinary within reason—driving this car handles impeccably and with an exceptional margin of safety. In the end you still depend upon four very small areas of rubber pressed on to the road surface. The ultimate grip they can give is your lot and, as a Swiss tester discovered last winter, if you lose all sense of judgement of the conditions, you can lose your four foot-holds and then even your Jensen will go. If you want still more grip, apply to Jim Hall for a suction skirt. Our normal road test assessment with performance figures was published last week so we will take that as read.

We have heard most of the arguments about four-wheel drive and at one time or another have taken both sides of most of them to keep the talk going. The cautious ask why they should pay hundreds of pounds extra when their present cars seem to go well enough with two driving wheels. The "Coventry Knockers" say "If I wanted a cross-country vehicle I'd buy a Land-Rover." The formula racing fraternity, some of whom have had their financial fingers burned a bit, are quite voluble on four-wheel drive. Their views add up to "When someone makes a four wheel drive Grand Prix car that can go round the circuits faster than a two-wheel drive one we'll have to take another look at it."

Coming back to the FF, this is the only car that you can buy off the showroom floor with four-wheel drive built in like two-wheel drive is on other vehicles—and in contrast to the kind of low-geared four-wheel drive you engage occasionally in special circumstances. The New Range Rover will have another kind of permanent, three-differential, four-wheel drive. FF, of course, stands for Ferguson Formula, a feature of which is to split the engine torque 37 per cent to the front wheels and 63 per cent to the rear to give optimum drive (in this case). The nose of the FF is 3in. longer than that of the Interceptor's to help make room for the front wheel part of the drive ahead of the engine. It is very different in other respects too, but looks very similar because the bodies are the same from the windscreen rearwards. The wheelbase is 4in. longer, the front track 1 in. wider and the engine-transmission assembly is further back, with some disadvantage to interior space, but giving almost a mid-engine weight distribution. The FF weighs $2\frac{3}{4}$ cwt (308 lb) more.

An incidental advantage of this 4-w.d. is to make practical the fitting of Maxaret anti-skid brakes (Coventry Knockers: "I can stop quicker without them in the dry") which is another safety feature peculiar to the Jensen. Perhaps we should add here that most other manufacturers could do all this on a one-off basis and a number of Ford cars such as Mustangs, Zodiacs and Capris have been converted to Ferguson Formula four-wheel drive at not less than £1,000 a throw with, in our opinion, marked improvements to their traction, braking and stability. Their engines being mounted a bit higher than that in the Jensen, the front drive shafts can pass under or through the sumps.

We had no cause to use this particular Jensen on ice and snow and only seldom on very slippery roads, so we had little experience of the Maxaret in operation. What it does, of course, is to cause the brake pedal to kick back momentarily, easing pressure at the instant the wheels reach locking point. In this way you get the maximum retardation that the particular road surface will permit, but no skidding. On dry roads you can exceed 1g. With the Ferguson Formula drive, no single wheel can lock or turn in the forward direction without the others. So infrequently does one approach the hardness of braking required to lock the wheels of a FF that a driver might go for months without "Maxaretting." On the other hand, it is always there guarding against possible dramatic loss of adhesion and steering control in the event of a panic stop, particularly on a wet road.

Prospects for wider adoption of the Ferguson system were much increased when the GKN transmission division took it up. They are now actively promoting it as the All Wheel Control system and a part of GKN's contribution to safety on the roads.

All this detail sinks into the background

Continued

The front seats, head rests here removed, are contoured to locate as well as support. There are both a central locker and a drop-drawer (carrying the radio telephone) and both are locking. Red warning lamps show when the doors are open

Rear passengers have comfortable bucket seats but require the front seats to be about two notches forward of their back-stops to give sufficient legroom. There are separate air conditioning ducts to the back. Note the locking boot release catch in the door pillar

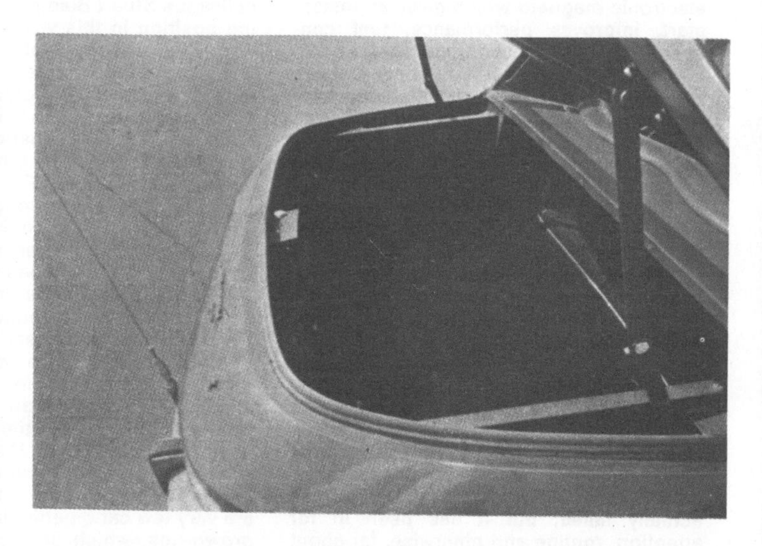

A big, regular, carpeted boot with a rather high edge to load over. The rear shelf rises with the huge electrically heated window but is removable to make way for tall packages

Left: Both the front grille with FF motif and the twin extractor grilles on the flank distinguish this car from the shorter Interceptor. Over-riders have rubber inserts and halogen head lamps fitted

EXECUTIVE TRANSPORT MODULE . . .

after a few weeks experience with your ETM. There is the comforting knowledge in the back of your mind that come ice, snow, mud or high-speed sunshine you are better equipped than the rest. You do not spin to a standstill in snow or dig in when trying to leave muddy-field car parks.

Air conditioning with refrigeration comes with the complete package and very welcome it can be all the year round. No-one should believe that this is for hot climates only. Fresh air is delightful when it can be found, but unhappily these days there are increasingly often good reasons for keeping car windows closed and controlling your own ambience. On our private list of features to be improved on the FF III, if one materializes under the new Donald Healey-Kjell Qvale regime, is the conditioning system. For example, the compressor should declutch automatically when the starter is being engaged. It should be possible to get fresh ram air through without using the blower fan; the temperament should be taken out of the refrigeration system, which suffers periods of *ennui* during hot weather journeys and must be given an occasional rest. Air-flow through the cooler is insufficient for traffic jams.

An associated item for the list would read: 'Douse those electric cooling fans and reduce the under bonnet temperature,' which would be both contradictory and very difficult. As it is, the whirr of fans heard from outside is at times intolerable in such a refined car. Associated with the oven in which the engine and equipment must function is the reluctance of the engine to start when hot. The starter sometimes churns noisily for up to 20 seconds before the engine bites and the more embarrassing the circumstances the longer it seems to take. It may also die again if you have to reverse out.

The solution we were told is a Judson electronic magneto which gives an instant start, improves performance, fuel consumption, etc, etc, into the bargain. An attractive looking device for only £25, we fitted one. Not a scrap of difference have we been able to measure or detect. In fact, after some later top-end-of-performance hesitation we were tuned and wired back to the original coil by a slightly reproachful Jensen engineer. There has been no further trouble but the hot starting continues to be bad.

We have now reported the only two faults that continue to irritate. During the running-in period we suffered noisy and leaking powered steering, units of which were replaced. The brake servo needed attention for lag and an audible clonk. Recently a metallic rattle in the area of the torque convertor alarmed us and the car was driven back to the works for fairly major attention. We have never been let down by the FF and nothing important has actually failed, but it has been in for attention, routine and otherwise, for about three weeks in the first six months and 9,000 miles. Incidentally, there is an informative owners' instruction manual.

The nearest we came to being stranded was when a fan belt broke. A weakness of battery condition indicators in place of ammeters is that one seldom notices the change in needle position until the battery is pretty flat. The long belts are difficult to keep properly tensioned. We recall that colleague Stuart Bladon lost a very promising position in this year's Mobil Economy Run when his Interceptor had this trouble and he could not restart. Our earlier road test Interceptor suffered the "torque-convertor tinkle" which in fact arises from a crankshaft thrust washer fault of the Chrysler engine—now cured by a modification, we are told. For a time we had difficulty with starter engagement which all the checking of connections did not cure. Next time in for service the motor was changed and all has been well since.

When you list faults and incidents like this, things begin to sound bad. In fact, we have had very little real trouble and are aware that expensive and complicated cars are, if anything, more likely to need minor attentions than simple mass-produced ones. Take the FF to the European Continent, get on the open roads and *autoroutes* and you would forgive it anything. We have done just this and there are very few cars, particularly carrying four grown-ups, which are so fast, effortless, safe and comfortable. The fairly firm GT suspension which in Britain, at low speeds, is sometimes quite thumpy, seems transformed abroad. In spite of the usually poorer surfaces (and the fact that the tyre pressures should be up by no less than 8 psi all round for sustained speeds of over 110 mph) the Jensen whisks over the roads between 80 and 120 mph, the high averages being owed more to the eager acceleration than flat-out speed capabilities. It is seldom indeed that we touch 120 on any roads other than *autoroutes*, where 120 feels and sound no more than 80, and you can talk normally or listen to the radio. To answer the inevitable question, we did have a go and just topped 140 mph. It is significant that in 9,000 miles of Jensen FF driving this spring and summer there has not been a single dicey moment of our own or other people's making.

It took some weeks to learn to take a sweeping bend fast and dead on line. The steering is so precise and positive that you find yourself slightly overcorrecting. You are also likely to be travelling 10-15 mph faster than normal. The steering is one of the joys of the FF and practically all our drivers rate the power assistance, response and ratio near perfect for the type of car. It is very difficult indeed to induce a slide even on wet roads, so you can accelerate hard out of a bend, pouring the power on much earlier than with a rear wheel drive car. It is reassuring to know that with so much torque and even in the event of unintentional kick-down you will not flip your tail coming out of a bend or corner. Couple this with the knowledge that emergency braking cannot lock your

Above: Heating and refrigeration are responsible for most of the complication of pipes, belts and fans, but there are also power steering, brake servo and ignition connections. The fuses in the foreground are beautifully set out and labelled. Everything that needs to be checked or topped up is accessible but the engine oil dip stick is difficult to read. An adjustable inspection lamp is fitted above the radiator. Left: An elegant tail with large area lamps neatly fitted. The rear window serves as the boot lid and is almost big enough to be regarded as a tail gate. Right: It is hard to make the FF roll on corners. The lean-over angle here shows that it is rounding the bend very fast indeed

wheels nor deprive you of steering control and you have the makings of very safe and rapid all-weather transport.

For its uses in speed-restricted Britain we shall probably remember our ETM quite differently as the town and commuting car *par excellence*. It does not feel large when you are accustomed to its width and seems to park easily in tight corners. After a trying day in the office you sink into the elaborately shaped seat, the adjustable head cushion easing the ache in your neck. The cold engine starts first push and you select Drive. You direct cool air on your face, turn on the four-speaker stereo so you get soothing music very softly all round you and glide off. If you wish, you can steer with thumb and finger of one hand and there is no cause to remain taut, prove anything or do other than smile benignly at the taxi driver who carves you up. There was that boxer dog grinning across from the car beside me. I had to make a boxer face back at it. The driver wasn't at all amused. He was all tensed up in his old rattletrap; a unit of mobile aggression.

On the list of luxuries in a mature ETM such as the Jensen are of course electric window operation, electrically-heated rear window and a fuel filler cap release switch on the panel. The boot lid—almost a fifth glass door on the Jensen—releases from a locking lever in the door jamb. This is another safe and convenient system. For tall packages you can take out the rear shelf. Tinted glass is restful, particularly for the screen, which is so large. The forward view, with all the right ingredients, is exceptionally good. You sit high enough, the adjustable steering wheel is below the line of the car's nose to your eyes. The bottom frame is low, the pillars are thin and curve outwards so there are no blind spots. You sit near enough (but not too near) to the screen to be unaware of it. There are virtually no reflections.

The main instruments are in front of the driver, with markings that are clear but could be easier to read. The secondary instruments are in the middle of the panel, angled towards the driver, and easy to check at a glance. You soon learn to hit the right rocker switch by feel alone and though far from being ideal these switches are quite positive. A "town" horn is a bit of a luxury, since it is so seldom wanted; we keep on "country" and like the high Italian type screech on the few occasions a horn is needed. In our opinion an electric aerial is well worth the money. Now we want a central door locking system, because it is difficult to reach across the Jensen behind the seat to the passenger side lock button. In the rain, to have to use a key on more than one external lock is a nuisance. The 1971 FF's will have some detail improvements.

We have already reported on the Air Call radio telephone (*Autocar* 10 September). For us it was a luxury fitting since we could not make full use of the services offered, but there were several occasions when it was very convenient indeed. The truth is that you grow to like having it available and on a solo drive, particularly at night, it is comforting to see the red tell-tale and know you are in contact.

Petrol consumption is pretty heavy; an average of 10.1 mpg in and around London, 11.5 on short journeys out of town and 12.2 on the Continent, cruising in the 70-110 mph bracket. Oil consumption is negligible, but the battery needs topping up regularly, as does the power-steering reservoir.

Wear and tear has been slight. The leather looks and smells new. The exterior paint picks up tiny surface scratches rather easily and there are a couple of chips on the edges of the big doors, but otherwise it is very good. The tyres front and rear are about half worn and hold their pressures well.

No car we have owner-tested over a period of months has given more satisfaction, more exhilarating driving and a greater feeling of security and well-being. Its capacity is convenient, there being sufficient room for four grown-ups on a journey and ample luggage space. Clearly, it is eye-catching and, according to some of our drivers, bird-catching, too. Head porters in London have a way of finding parking space *in front of* the hotel for a Jensen. □

PERFORMANCE CHECK

Maximum speeds

Gear	mph Staff	kph Staff	rpm Staff
Top (mean)	137	221	5,200 indicated
(best)	141	227	5,350 indicated
Intermediate	88	142	5,100 indicated
Low	52	84	5,100 indicated

Standing ¼-mile, Staff: 15.8 sec 88 mph

Standing kilometre, Staff: 28.9 sec 112 mph

Acceleration, Staff:

Time in seconds	3.5	4.8	6.8	8.1	10.6	13.4	16.7	21.5	27.5		
True speed mph	30	40	50	60	70	80	90	100	110	120	130
Indicated speed MPH Staff:	30	40	50	60	71	81	92	103	112	122	133

Speed range, Gear Ratios and Time in seconds.

Mph	Top (2.88—6.34)	Inter. (4.18—9.20)	Low (7.06—15.52)
0-20	—	—	2.4
10-30	—	—	2.6
20-40	—	3.5	2.4
30-50	—	3.8	2.8
40-60	5.4	4.2	—
50-70	6.0	4.8	—
60-80	7.0	5.3	—
70-90	7.9	—	—
80-100	9.0	—	—
90-110	10.7	—	—
100-120			

Fuel Consumption
Overall mpg, **Staff:** 12 mpg (23.5 litres/100km)

NOTE: No comparison figures available.

COST and LIFE of EXPENDABLE ITEMS

Item	Life in Miles	Cost per 10,000 Miles
		£ s. d.
One gallon of 4-5 star fuel, average cost today 6s. 7d.	12	274 5 0
One pint of top-up oil, average cost today 3s. 8d.	3,000	12 0
Front disc brake pads (set of 4)	8,000	included in second service below
Rear brake linings (set of 4)	8,000	included in second service below
tyres (front pair)	16,000	39 17 0
tyres (rear pair)	16,000	39 17 0
Service (main interval and actual costs incurred)	4,000	29 12 0
Total		344 6 0
Approx. standing charges per year:		
Depreciation (on £8,062)		1,300 0 0
Insurance		100 0 0
Tax		25 0 0
Total		1,769 6 0

Approx cost per mile—3s. 6d.

JENSEN INTERCEPTOR III

Jensen's new Interceptor sells for 13,500 strong American dollars . . . however, it's the car that impressed us, not the price

by Paul Van Valkenburgh

BLIMEY, MATE, wot a whippy set of wheels! (That's British-American for the most altogether pleasant hybrid we may have ever come across.)

You know, I used to have a dream about the most ideal vehicle for my purposes; to wit, a slightly styled-up BMW 2800 coupe with a smooth-and-healthy American V-8 and automatic. And now I have driven the ideal and there is nowhere left to go.

But it isn't built by BMW, it's built by Jensen Motorcars Ltd. in, believe-it-or-not, good old Mother G.B., where lazy-labor unions and careless craftsmanship encourage economic suicide. American capitalists are capitalizing on the situation by picking up controlling interests, such as Rootes Group becoming Chrysler U.K. But in that instance, it looks like a better buy might have been Jensen, since they've been using Chrysler engines and transmissions for years anyhow, and it would give Chrysler a sporty prestige car that they could *never* put together over here. So Chrysler gets a Cricket and Kjell Qvale of British Motor Car Distributors Ltd. (of San Francisco) picks up the heavy end of Jensen and becomes probably the only Norwegian owner of an automobile manufactory in the world.

I didn't know all that. And I wouldn't have cared to find out if our test car hadn't turned out to be such a delightful machine. However, I ought to point out right away that it sells (well) for 13,500 strong American dollars. Also, before you get the idea that we-all are impressed by the implied authority of tall prices, recall that we have told you when a $20,000 car was a poor dollar buy as often as a $2000 car.

For any price, this Jensen just doesn't hardly do anything wrong, under *any* conditions. I picked the car up at the Laguna Seca Can-Am and immediately got caught leaving the race in a two-hour per eleven-mile traffic jam. But it didn't *matter,* because it was so comfortable, quiet, cool, smooth, and relaxed inside. Then I followed John Cannon in his Firebird down corkscrewey highway one, and we arrived at San Simeon together, maintaining a healthy pace with ease while overcoming John's goading to race. Perhaps it is happenstance and possibly it comes from years of hard work, but the Jensen comes across with finely tuned and well developed suspension/tire/chassis that gives a superb combination of a just-right ride and secure handling. And you may quote me on that. In our standard skid-pad test it showed up well in spite of some oddities and deficiencies, producing maximum *g*'s equivalent to a more "pure" sports car. For example, it understeered heavily to the left and was neutral to oversteer in a steady-state right turn. Assuming that weight and springs are well-balanced about the centerline, that indicates the front camber is probably asymmetrical, with maybe both front wheels leaning to the right. Also, the oil level was sensitive to long, high-*g* corners, and oil ran up to the rockers and down past the valves — producing smoke — but only after 20 seconds in a corner, which is even abnormal in racing. And for really fine-edge handling on the limit, the throttle response and relatively slow power-steering are a little lacking in sensitivity. On the other hand, it *ain't* a racer, and the controls are faultless for normal-to-hard everyday cruising. It has a slightly firm, telegraphic ride and excellently smooth transition from corner to corner in switchbacks and esses. In the straightaways: effortless cruising, not hour after hour, but probably day after day . . . humalong happily, even through the pouring rain, la-la.

Weight could have a lot to do with softness and smoothness (near two ton all wet), although you don't really feel the pounds. There must be a good couple of hundred pounds of just sound-deadening material, since it's really difficult to get all the panel resonance out of an all-steel unit-construction body. Actually, it's part tube frame, as two large-diameter-tube longerons project forward beneath it to mainly support the engine and anchor the front A-arms and steering.

For all the weight, including what you know the Chrysler engine up front weighs, it is perfectly balanced front/rear, indicating something in back is also pretty heavy. Could be the trunk lid, since it includes the rear window and a healthy section of bodywork. Functionally, however, it's worth it to have both a large, unobstructed rear window, and a large, unobstructed opening over the baggage area. Another obvious advantage is that the window opens into the passenger area, allowing easy loading of your skis, shovels, stepladder, and what have you. Also, if you have taller bags, or get locked in the trunk, an access panel below the window can be removed. The only drawback to the whole scheme is that in the lighter colors, the lid seam shows up rather grotesquely, breaking up an otherwise very attractive shape. For all it weighs, it *is* well counterbalanced, but they might as well have made it power assisted since everything else is: windows, brakes, steering, antenna, gas cap . . . and all other known conveniences are standard also: automatic trans, air-conditioning, limited-slip, electric demister, airhorns and AM-FM 4-speaker stereo. No options are available. Sorry.

There's no way you could improve on the comfort anyhow, because either tactually or visually we just couldn't fault it. The seat shape/adjustment/material, the armrests, pedals, adjustable wheel positions, the visibility, the silence at any speed . . . exquisitely comfortable. And this car has a headrest that really *is*. A pillow-soft cushion is attached to the head-high seatback by Velcro tape, so that you can shift it to any position (even to the small of your back, occasionally) and it's so functional that it seems *natural* to lean back and use it. They have also installed the biggest sun visors you've ever seen, which are useful but not obtrusive. The dash and switches are very tastefully laid out, organized and well labeled, and at night the panels light up in multi-colors that give you the feel of a satellite cockpit. Damn! I can't wait to get back *in* it!

The rear seats are lovely to look at also, but with the fronts at a comfortable position there just isn't any rear legroom, which makes the car an obvious 2+2. Other miscellaneous small things for the owner/driver make up for that, though, such as door locks so silent you can't tell whether you did or not, and not one, not two, not four, but *three* electric cooling fans that are independent of the ignition and thermostatically controlled. After a long, hard run you can shut it down and walk off while the fans run on, which helps avoid heat-sink after-boil. And the exhaust note, for coming from a Chrysler V-8, is very excitingly un-American.

Numerically speaking, the performance is mediocre as a sports car, which speaks highly for it as a luxury coupe. Considering it's a 4000-pound vehicle with a 3-speed automatic transmission, the acceleration is well up there with American ponycars, and though the 2.88 rear-axle ratio is absurd for dragging, it produces an easy 140-mph plus, at a comfortable five grand on the tach. (We don't need it, but they sell in Europe also.) Braking in our car was only tolerably good in distance, but so smooth and stable it wouldn't shake the stiction out of our electronic accelerometer, and we kept getting flat spots in the recording. The aerodynamics wasn't too good, but for a relatively large and heavy "sports car," drag and lift weren't all that much out of proportion.

Though it's a *non sequitur* in a car of this ilk, fuel mileage is maybe a little indeterminate because of a small failure. Yes, father, it happens to the best of them. The odometer drive gear was slipping on the shaft, and occasionally we caught it stopping altogether, even though the *speed*ometer continued. Another tolerable failure was loose wires in the heating/a.c. fan and right window switches. A less forgiving sin in a bucks-up car was a couple of comengo rattles, but they were mostly occasional.

The biggest nuisance, though, was the continued question: "A Jensen, eh. Who makes it?" It's a shame they don't know, because it takes a long time for even the greatest cars to establish a reputation for automatic prestige. Now, in the case of Jensen, only the Very In know . . . *you* for example. Maybe unsophisticated V-8s with automatic aren't your teacup, but you take the guy who can afford a Jensen, and he probably doesn't appreciate finicky, small-liter, high-rpm engines with five-speed manual trick boxes. Well, sir, even me . . . now that I'm in the autumn of my years (creak) . . . I can appreciate a little hi-per luxury. And if you get all wet over technological safety, or even technological snobbery, you can get (in Europe) the same car with full four-wheel drive and four-wheel anti-skid, which John Blunsden goes into deeply in the next story.

Yes, reader, take heed. Considering all the five-figure luxury performance cars we have tested, the Jensen is the first one to seem functionally and esthetically worth its tag. Still, at a formidably grandiose $13,500 . . . "To dream the impossible dream . . . ."

JENSEN INTERCEPTOR II

PRICE

Base $13,500
As tested $13,500
With options .... Standard items include: air-conditioning; automatic transmission; power brakes, windows and steering; AM-FM 4-speaker radio, positraction

ENGINE

Type .... V-8, water-cooled, cast-iron block, cast-iron heads
Displacement .... 383 cu. in. (6276 cc)
Horsepower .... 330 hp @ 5000 rpm
Torque .... 425 lbs-ft. @ 3200 rpm
Bore & stroke .... 4.25 in. x 3.38 in. (108 mm x 85.8 mm)
Compression ratio .... 9.5 to 1
Valve actuation .... Pushrod/rocker arm, hydraulic tappets
Induction system .... Holley 4V
Exhaust system .... Cast-iron headers, 4 into 1
Electrical system .... 12-volt alternator, point distributor
Fuel .... Premium
Recommended redline 5200

DRIVE TRAIN

Torque converter

Transmission	Gear Ratio	Overall Ratio
1st	2.45	7.05
2nd	1.44	4.16
3rd	1.00	2.88

Differential .... Powr-Lok, 2.88 ratio

CHASSIS

Frame .... Unit steel, front engine, rear drive
Front suspension .... Double A-frame, coil springs, tube shocks, anti-roll bar
Rear suspension ..... Live axle, leaf springs, tube shocks, Panhard rod
Steering ...... Power assist, rack and pinion, 3.4 turns, overall ratio 17.1 to 1, turning circle 38 feet
Brakes .... Front and rear discs, power assist, dual systems, 11.7-in. dia. front, 10.7-in. dia. rear, swept area 433 sq. in.
Wheels .... 15-in. dia.; 6-in. wide
Tires .... Pirelli GR 70 VR 15, pressures F/R 32/36 (rec.), 36/40 (test)

BODY

Type ..... Integral steel, 2-door, 4-passenger
Seats .... Front buckets, rear buckets
Windows .... 2 power, 2 vents
Luggage space .... Rear trunk, 16 cu. ft.
Instruments .... 160 mph speedo, 6000 rpm tach
Gauges: .... temp, oil, fuel, alt
Lights: .... fuel, brake-warning

WEIGHTS AND MEASURES

Weight ...... 3895 lbs (curb), 4120 lbs (test)
Weight distribution F/R 50.0%/50.0%
Wheelbase .... 105.3 in.
Track F/R .... 56.3 in./57.5 in.
Height .... 53.0 in.
Width .... 70.0 in.
Length .... 187.0 in.
Ground clearance .... 5.5 in.
Oil capacity .... 5.0 qt.
Fuel capacity .... 24.0 gal.
Coolant capacity .... 15.0 qt.

MISCELLANEOUS

Weight/power ratio (curb/advertised) .... 11.8 lbs per hp
Advertised hp/cu. in. 0.86
Speed per 1000 rpm (top gear) .... 27.2 mph
Warranty .... 12 months/12,000 miles

AERODYNAMIC FORCES AT 100 MPH

CORNERING CONDITONS

PERFORMANCE

Acceleration .... 0-30 (3.0 sec.), 0-60 (7.5 sec.), 0-100 (19.8 sec.)
0-quarter mile (15.2 sec., 92.0 mph)
Top speed .... 142 mph (est.) at 5200 rpm (rpm limited)
Braking .... Distance from 60 mph: 150 ft. (0.80 g av)
Number of stops to fade: Not attainable
Stability: Excellent
Maximum pitch angle: 2.4°
Handling .... Maximum lateral: 0.77 g right, 0.74 g left
Skidpad understeer: 0° right, 7.1° left
Maximum roll angle: 6.0°
Reaction to throttle, full: Oversteer; off: Understeer

Speedometer	30.0	40.0	50.0	60.0	70.0	80.0	90.0	100.0
Actual mph	31.5	41.5	50.5	60.0	69.5	78.5	88.0	97.5

Mileage .... Average: 10.8 mpg
Miles on car: 1500-2300

Aerodynamic forces at 100 mph:
Drag .... 385 lbs (includes tire drag)
Lift F/R .... 575 lbs/115 lbs

TEST EXPLANATIONS

Fade test is successive maximum g stops from 60 mph each minute until wheels cannot be locked. Understeer is front minus rear tire slip angle at maximum lateral on 200-ft. dia. Digitek skidpad.

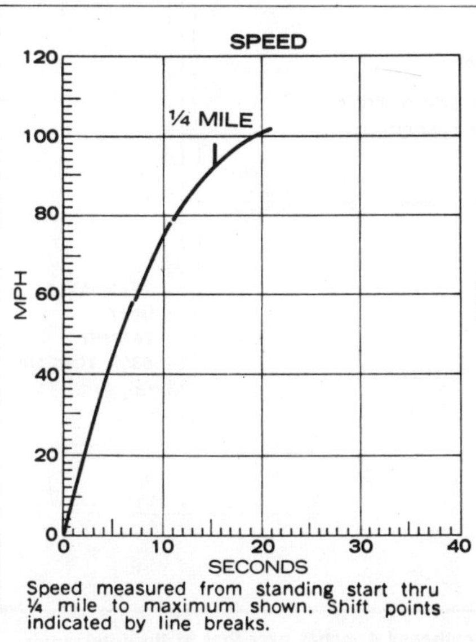

Speed measured from standing start thru ¼ mile to maximum shown. Shift points indicated by line breaks.

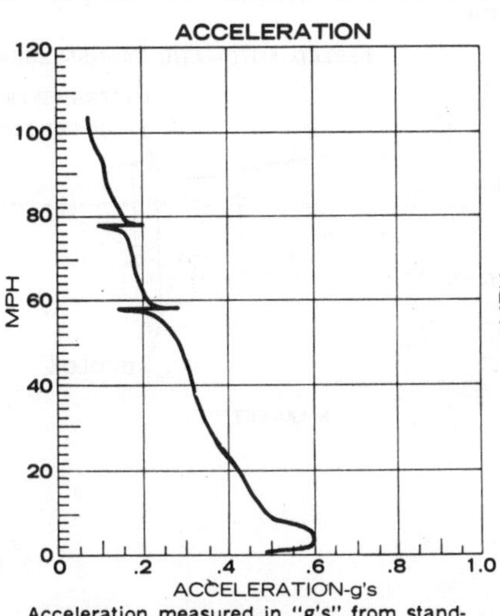

Acceleration measured in "g's" from standing start to speed shown. Shift points indicated by "spikes" on graph.

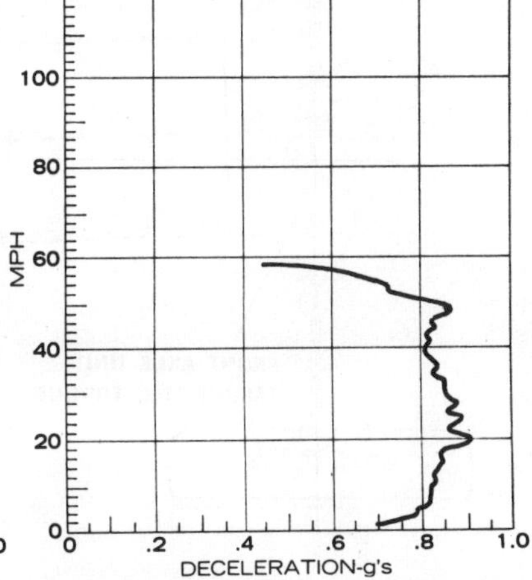

Brakes applied at 60 mph with maximum force, but using pedal "feathering" technique to prevent wheel lockup.

The Jensen FF is a motorcar of outstanding capabilities, but its four-wheel drive is more than a performance option / by John Blunsden

THE LATE HARRY FERGUSON is perhaps best known in the United States as the British tractor millionaire who took Henry Ford I to court . . . and won. But in his home country he is remembered for the pioneering work he performed as an automotive engineer, and particularly for his efforts to develop and popularize an efficient and practical system of four-wheel drive.

Its adoption by Jensen Motors — and that of the Maxaret anti-lock braking system developed by Dunlop, which is the second major constituent of the Ferguson Formula — coincided with Jensen's replacement of the fast-but-ugly Chrysler-engined C-V-8 coupe, by a mechanically similar but far more attractive Vignale-styled model, which was to mark the revival of one of the older Jensen model names, the Interceptor.

Since this car was aimed at the luxury GT market, it was obviously the right vehicle to be given the FF treatment, if only because it was already highly enough priced to make the considerable and inevitable extra cost of the Ferguson Formula a tolerable burden in terms of the percentage increase in price it would involve. It was decided, therefore, to supplement the Interceptor with an FF Jensen, which would become the company's great status symbol as the safest high-performance car in the world, as well as one of the most attractive.

As applied to the Jensen, the Ferguson transmission involves transmitting the drive from the 383-cubic-inch Chrysler V-8 directly to a center differential, which splits the torque in the ratio of 63/37 percent between the two output shafts. The shaft that runs toward the rear of the car takes the greater proportion of the torque. The shafts, which run down the left side of the car, connect to conventional front and rear differentials, of which only the rear is equipped with the Powr-Lok limited-slip feature, which is also standard on the Interceptor.

Some impressive demonstrations on snow, ice, soft mud and wet grass during the car's debut over four years ago proved convincingly the Jensen FF's superiority over the Interceptor under extreme conditions in terms of greater traction, greater controllability, and — through the medium of the Maxaret braking system, which prevents wheel lock by momentarily releasing the brakes at the point of loss of adhesion — greater stopping power. It was soon fulfilling its promise, and the FF was indeed one of the most prestigious cars in Europe.

With total production running at the rate of 15 units per week, the FF's exclusivity was assured, regardless of what percentage of total Jensen sales it would represent. In fact, on the average, only two of those 15 cars are FFs, which was roughly in line with the forecast. With a UK price of over £8000 ($19,200) compared with about £6000 ($14,400) for the Interceptor, it would have been unreasonable to expect more. In any case, this suited Jensen well, for the FF chassis had to be lengthened by 4 inches (to a 109 in. wheelbase and 192 in. overall length) to accommodate the special transmission. This meant a lot of additional fabrication. The extra 4 inches is "inserted" immediately forward of the cockpit bulkhead, where the FF can be identified at a glance by its dual extractor louvers in place of the single extractors on the Interceptor. From the cockpit back, the cars are identical in appearance.

It was Ferguson's great hope that Jensen's lead in adopting the transmission would be followed by other manufacturers with a larger production potential, which of course would enable the unit cost of the installation to be cut drastically. In this they may yet be successful, because Ford of Britain has been running Zodiacs and Capris for some time for research purposes and is currently supplying a batch of 50 cars to police forces for evaluation. This, in the words of a certain well-known song, could be the start of something big.

Meanwhile, the FF has reached a critical point in its production career. Because of the longitudinal driveshafts it is not practicable to equip Jensen FFs with left-hand drive, which of course

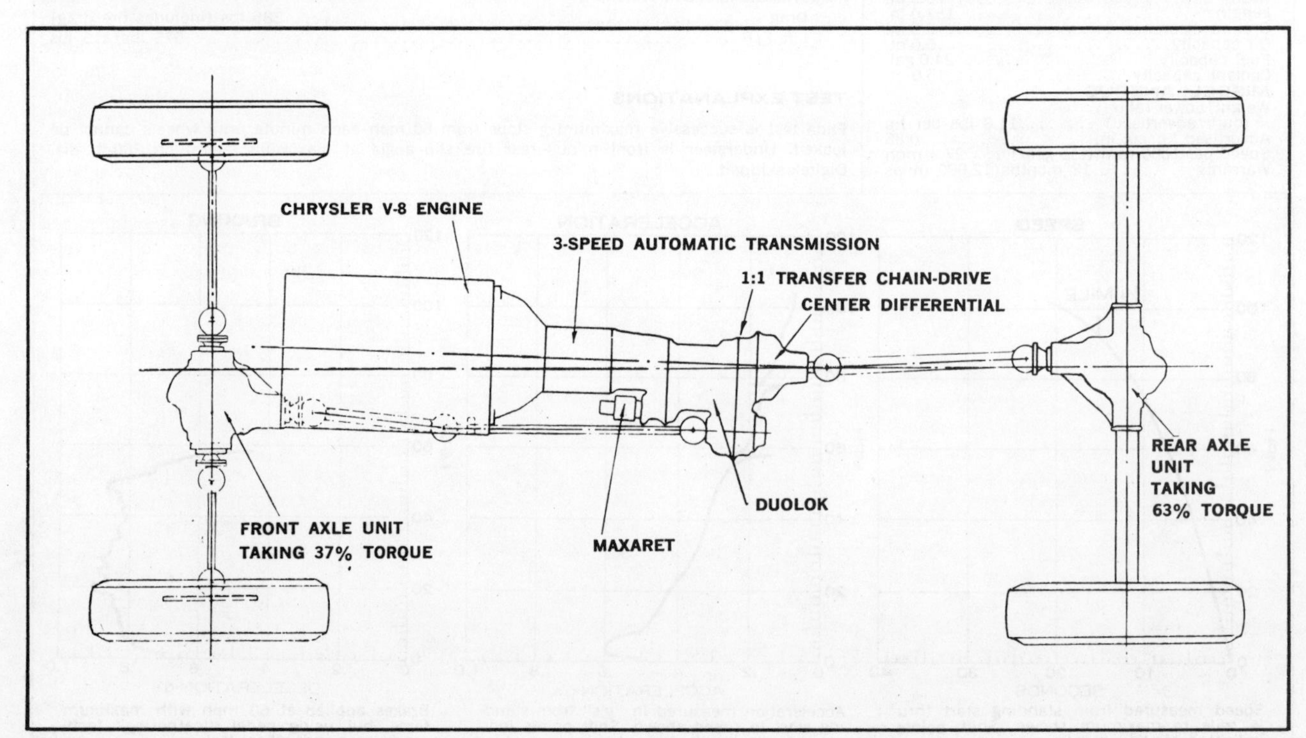

To accommodate the Ferguson 4-wheel-drive system, the chassis of the Jensen FF had to be lengthened 4 inches over that of the Interceptor.

would be essential for the United States market. This encumberance has not been too serious until recently, because the Jensen is a relative newcomer to the U.S. market. But the acquisition of majority shares in Jensen by Kjell Qvale and his backers (as a base for building a new, relatively low-cost Healey sports car, to be unveiled next summer) has meant a complete reorganization of the Jensen sales pattern. Exports have recently doubled to 43 percent of total production, and the United States, once a non-market, has suddenly become the key export territory. A Mark II version of the Interceptor has been developed (the modifications of which have been incorporated in the FF) in order to meet the U.S. federal safety regulations. Since the FF is not a marketable proposition in North America, its significance to Jensen's new marketing arrangements has inevitably been lessened. Nevertheless, in territories where right-hand drive is acceptable, it remains a magnificent prestige item, and will probably enjoy this privilege until such time as Ford or some other manufacturer offers a similar facility on a lower-priced car.

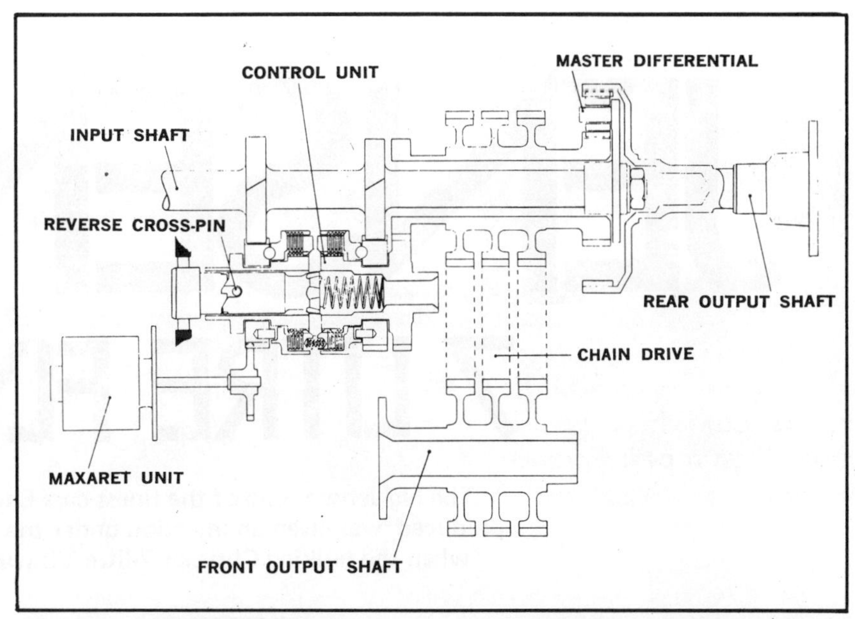

The basis of the Ferguson 4-wheel-drive unit is a master differential and two one-way clutches. The master differential is a planetary gear that permits a speed variation between front and rear output, and also divides the torque unequally, with 37 percent going to the front wheels and 63 percent to the rears. The Maxaret unit eliminates the possibility of all wheels locking.

Some time ago I carried out a series of "back-to-back" tests with an Interceptor and an FF in an effort to measure — as far as it was possible — the advantages of the layout. The tests took place under dry conditions, on a variety of road surfaces from smooth to badly broken, and revealed only marginal differences in performance.

A straight-line braking test from 60 mph on a moderately slippery surface produced a stopping distance of 168 feet for the Interceptor and 142 feet for the FF. The Interceptor slid a maximum of 2 feet to the right during the course of stopping, whereas the FF deviated less than a foot, first one way then the other, as the Maxaret unit kicked back through the brake pedal (with this unit you need only moderate foot pressure — firm enough to resist any loss of contact through kickback following a sudden loss of adhesion, but no more).

A second test, involving a lane change maneuver marked by soft pylons, involved completing a lane change to the right in 45 feet, covering 75 feet in the right-hand lane, then making a change to the left lane in another 45 feet. Each lane was 15 feet wide, and the car entered the test at 50 mph. With the Interceptor, a rear-end breakaway to the right occurred on completing the first lane-change, and the breakaway had to be maintained by only gradually applying corrective lock if the car were to be correctly lined up to make the second lane-change. If the breakaway was killed completely, there was insufficient time to re-enter the left lane without hitting one of the market cones. On the FF, however, there was ample time for all the conventional steering maneuvers because only very modest rear-end breakaway occurred at the end of each lane change. Nevertheless, the FF was no quicker than the Interceptor from start to conclusion of this test, even though it required a considerably reduced level of driving skill for a clean run, and a lot less work with the steering wheel.

The third test, simulating a skidpad of 100-foot radius, on which five clockwise and five anti-clockwise laps had to be completed at maximum speed, was abandoned because the Interceptor developed fuel starvation due to surge after two laps. Times were therefore taken for individual laps and showed a remarkable similarity for the two cars, usually varying by only about a fifth of a second over a mean lap time of about 15 seconds. However, whereas the Interceptor could only achieve its best time by being held in an oversteering slide through constant adjustment of corrective lock and occasional positive lock, the FF maintained an understeering attitude and a much higher cornering force; when a rear-end slide did eventually occur, it could not be maintained with the aid of corrective lock and power — even a reduction of positive lock was sufficient to "kill" it.

Most of these tests simulated extreme driving maneuvers or cornering speeds which would not normally be used on public roads. However, something of the sort could occur in an emergency situation, and in this case the FF showed up well. Not so much by its greater ability to contain the situation, but by the lower level of skill it required of its driver in order to do so. It is one thing for the average driver to carry out a test when "primed" for it, but another to do so because of an unexpected emergency.

Nevertheless, it is in the very wet, or on snow or ice, where the FF is seen at its best. Here, its value lies in its forgivingness. Imprudent arrival at a corner (too fast, or off-line), which could perhaps result in an Interceptor (or any other two-wheel-drive car) visiting a ditch, may mean no more than a spot of heartburn for the FF driver. For example, you can brake hard in the wet in the middle of a corner without plowing straight on (although the FF does have a moderate amount of understeer under most conditions). If you suddenly tighten a lock you might just get the back end to let go, but just a momentary flick on the wheel will restore adhesion.

The additional 400 pounds in the weight of the FF over the Interceptor has not made much difference in acceleration times or top-end performance. The following set of figures were obtained with a car equipped with 3.07 to 1 final drive, in place of the latest 2.88 to 1 unit, but the difference is partly offset by the slightly larger rolling radius of the earlier tires. Also the usable rev limit has been raised from 5100 to 5600 rpm on the Chrysler engine since these figures were taken, so that they remain well within reach of a 1971-specification FF.

Maximum speeds: low 54 mph; intermediate 92 mph; high 140 mph (Torqueflite transmission). Acceleration: 0-30 mph, 3.0 sec; 0-40, 4.2 sec; 0-50, 5.6 sec; 0-60, 7.2 sec; 0-70, 9.4 sec; 0-80, 12.0 sec; 0-90, 14.8 sec; and 0-100, 18.18 sec. Overall gas consumption, about 12 mpg.

Almost everyone who has driven one enthuses about the FF for obvious reasons, for it is — at least for the present — unique. Its price will never allow it to become a luxury best seller, but the threat to its future existence, its permanency within the Jensen range, lies not in its price, but in the all-around if less exclusive qualities of its stablemate, the Interceptor.

JENSEN SP
7-LITRE FLYER!

The big Jensen, one of the finest cars England has ever produced, was given an injection under the bonnet recently when the hulking Chrysler 7-litre V8 was dropped in.

Interiors don't come much more comfortable than the Jensen's. Instrument layout and seats are truly excellent.

Along with the new 7.2-litre engine for the SP, came fully-cast alloy wheels to improve looks and roadholding.

Getting into the Jensen's driving seat, you soon find that it has a good range of adjustment, gives good lateral support and, like all the other interior fittings, is beautifully made.

The pedals are a good reach away, and to get the driving posiion you want you set the seat for pedal reach and then adjust the length of the steering column, Jaguar-fashion, to get your arms comfortable.

Want to unlock the other door for a passenger to enter but it seems too far away? No problem — there's an electric unlocking button for it on the driver's door. Electric windows too, of course; heated rear window, built-in stereo tape deck, air conditioning, electric aerial, low or high-note horn selector switch. The list goes on and on, and is so complete that there's even a pair of gloves to don if you have to change a wheel.

The engine is an easy but not immediate starter. It has to be churned over on the starter a few times before the fuel finds its way into the pots, but then it booms into life with that marvellous Jensen VROOM. After that, it's a case of forgetting the engine — it's so quiet and fuss-free. The traction of the back wheels is superb, allowing the driver to use great bags of the car's power, even on surfaces as nasty as wet, oily cobblestones. Very rarely will you get wheel spin — the big Jensen just whistles forward to put away 0 to 60 mph in 7.4 seconds, 100 mph in 18.5 and 120 mph in a neat 30 seconds. Still whisper quiet, the car goes on accelerating hard all the way to 140, then slows down a bit to edge up to its maximum 147 mph. It's not so much the speed but rather the smooth, safe way it goes about it all that makes it exceptional.

JENSEN SP

If the Jensen SP can be summed up in one word, then that word unquestionably is "relentless". This big, beautiful car seems to flatten hills, ignore bends, smooth out bumps and just keep pounding on and on.

Driving it is rather like being in a jet aircraft with a remote hum somewhere beyond your reach, and when a bad stretch of road passes beneath the wheels the effect is exactly like a plane hitting bumpy air or flying through a rain cloud.

It is a car in which, as a passenger, you can be completely fooled into thinking that the speed is 40 mph less than the speedometer shows on a straight road because of the detached remote feeling and stable ride. Cruising at 120 mph, the driver is quite liable to find that his passenger has lost interest and has started to read a newspaper.

All these things have applied to previous Jensens, but they are even more true of the of the SP, the latest in the range. It is even quieter than before, something many people would have thought impossible, with the huge 7.2 litre Chrysler V8 blending so beautifully with the Torqueflite automatic transmission that it is almost impossible to pick the change points without looking at the tachometer.

The 410 lb/ft of torque, spread over a very wide band and peaking at 3600 rpm, is enough to leave you shaking your head in wonder as you tread on the throttle at speeds well over 100 and find great oomph still there as the second chokes of the three Holley carbies open up.

Below: The SP proves just how well the build-a-car-from-components idea can work. In this instance, it's an American engine in an Italian body all toted by a British chassis.

PHOTOS BY GORDON CHITTENDEN

JENSEN INTERCEPTOR

Ford invented the Thunderbird—
but Jensen has a better idea

[illegible] special- [illegible] roducts [illegible] dd per- [illegible] to cer- [illegible] to mar- [illegible] we are [illegible] contract [illegible] 0s and [illegible] ok over [illegible] Jensen [illegible] the end of 1967. It was the demise of the Healey that put Jensen into dire straits, but the little company has recovered financially and now enjoys a fresh injection of capital from San Franciscan Kjell Qvale. Jensen is now working toward the production of a successor to the Austin-Healey, the new Jensen-Healey, in 1972, under the direction of Donald Healey himself.

But for now we're interested in the Jensen model that Qvale's British Motor Car Distributors are selling on the west coast of the U.S., the Interceptor II. Introduced in late 1966 as a rebodied but mechanically similar successor to the Jensen CV-8 Mk III, the Interceptor has a Vignale-designed 2+2 body of steel laid over a tubular chassis structure, conventional coil-spring-A-arm front suspension and a live axle with leaf springs and Panhard rod at the rear, and a Chrysler V-8 engine with Torqueflite automatic transmission set well back in the chassis to give even front-rear weight distribution. It was upgraded to Interceptor II specification in late 1969 with balljoint steering (this is a clue to the vintage of the chassis design), wider wheels, power steering, air conditioning and several other changes to comply with U.S. safety regulations. In its home market a version called the FF is available, with Ferguson 4-wheel drive and the Dunlop Maxaret antiskid braking system, but BMCD has chosen not to market that much more expensive (by $3400) model.

As is the case with most small carmakers, Jensen buys its engines and transmissions. The Interceptor uses a current production Chrysler-Dodge-Plymouth 383-cu-in. (6.3-liter) engine, a pushrod ohv unit of typical American design developing modest power for its size and generous torque at low engine speeds. The big Chrysler engine and transmission provide exactly what everyone expects from an American V-8 powertrain: smooth, quiet and effortless performance throughout the legal speed range. Plus, thanks to Jen-

JENSEN INTERCEPTOR

sen, a lovely exhaust note that we rarely get in domestic cars. The gearing is very tall, which is good because the engine is redlined at 5100 rpm, and if it weren't for some driveline vibration and axle whine at highway speeds, the silence would be eerie. In our performance runs the Jensen got off the line with a tire chirp and a driveline shudder and we held the gears manually to 5100 rpm because the transmission would upshift automatically at 4500 and let the power curve fall on its face. From our mild-weather testing, in which the noisy electric cooling fans came on often and the temperature gauge climbed ominously during the performance testing, we might project marginal cooling for hot weather and use of the air conditioning, which is standard equipment for the U.S. market.

The Interceptor is a big car and not very efficient in its use of space. Setting the heavy engine well back in the chassis for good weight distribution has taken its toll in interior space. The front seats are sumptuous (though not well shaped) and spacious; the rear seats are also sumptuous but not spacious as there is simply no legroom left behind the driver's seat when a male of average height has adjusted it for a proper driving position. On the passenger side there is barely enough longitudinal space for two passengers, so we might call the car a 2+1 if we're getting persnickety.

Vision out of the car is good, even to the rear with a monstrous piece of glass (which is electrically heated if need be, and which raises to reveal the trunk) for a rear window. With the good vision and fairly agile handling the large size of the car doesn't make it a clumsy car in traffic.

As we said, the seats are sumptuous; and nearly all the upholstery is real, soft, good-smelling Connolly leather. The instrument panel is fascinating, with the usual British Smiths-Jaeger gauges and rocker switches in vast array; in the latter respect the Jensen is not up to the best current practice in controls that are easy to find and operate when driving (especially at night). There are other lapses in the interior

PRICE

List price, west coast $13,500
Price as tested $13,500
Price as tested includes (standard equipment) automatic transmission, power brakes, power steering, air conditioning

IMPORTER

BMCD-Jensen Motors Inc. 1200 Van Ness Ave., San Francisco, Calif. 94109

ENGINE

Type ..... ohv V-8
Bore x stroke, mm ..... 108.0 x 86.0
Equivalent in ..... 4.25 x 3.38
Displacement, cc/cu in 6276/383
Compression ratio 10.0:1
Bhp @ rpm ..... 330 @ 5000
Equivalent mph 133
Torque @ rpm, lb-ft ..... 425 @ 2800
Equivalent mph 76
Carburetion: one Holley R4668A (4V)
Type fuel required ..... premium
Emission control ..... engine mods

DRIVE TRAIN

Transmission ..... automatic; torque converter with 3-speed planetary gearbox
Gear ratios: 3rd (1.00) 2.88:1
2nd (1.45) 4.17:1
1st (2.45) 7.05:1
1st (2.45 x 2.0) 14.10:1
Final drive ratio 2.88:1

CHASSIS & BODY

Layout ..... front engine/rear drive
Body/frame ..... tube frame with integral steel body
Brake type: 11.4-in. disc front, 10.75-in. disc rear; vacuum assisted
Swept area, sq in 433
Wheels ..... styled steel, 15 x 6
Tires ..... Pirelli Cinturato CM GR70VR-15
Steering type ..... rack & pinion, power assist
Overall ratio 17.1:1
Turns, lock-to-lock 3.4
Turning circle, ft 38.0
Front suspension: unequal length A-arms, coil springs, tube shocks, anti-roll bar
Rear suspension: live axle on leaf springs, tube shocks, Panhard rod

ACCOMMODATION

Seating capacity, persons ..... 2+2
Seat width, front/rear ..... 2 x 19/2 x 18
Head room, front/rear 37.5/35.0
Seat back adjustment, degrees 45

INSTRUMENTATION

Instruments: 160-mph speedo, 99,999 odometer, 999.9 trip odometer, 6000-rpm tach, oil pressure, coolant temperature, fuel level, ammeter, clock.
Warning lights: oil pressure, generator, low fuel, handbrake, brake system, rear window heat, high beam, directionals

MAINTENANCE

Service intervals, mi:
Oil change 6000
Filter change 6000
Chassis lube 4000
Minor tuneup 6000
Major tuneup 12,000
Warranty, mo/mi 12/12,000

GENERAL

Curb weight, lb 3905
Test weight 4230
Weight distribution (with driver), front/rear, % 50/50
Wheelbase, in 105.3
Track, front/rear 56.3/57.5
Overall length 187.0
Width 70.0
Height 53.0
Ground clearance 5.5
Overhang, front/rear 31.7/50.0
Usable trunk space, cu ft 16.0
Fuel tank capacity, U.S. gal 24.0

CALCULATED DATA

Lb/bhp (test weight) 12.8
Mph/1000 rpm (3rd gear) 27.2
Engine revs/mi (60 mph) 2200
Piston travel, ft/mi 1240
R&T steering index 1.29
Brake swept area sq in/ton 205

planning: heat, apparently from the engine, pours through and air conditioning is necessary even on mild, overcast days; the workmanship around the instrument panel is decidedly shoddy; the inertia-reel Kangol belts don't tension dependably and tend to fall off the occupants' shoulders. The tape player in our car didn't work properly either.

Some more positive notes about the Jensen body are that the exterior finish is to a very high standard, that the trunk is large and well finished, that the electric window lifts are quiet and rapid (unusual for a transatlantic car), that the head restraints have stick-on, adjustable pieces that are actually head*rests,* and that there is generous storage space in the interior.

The Interceptor II has rack-and-pinion power steering, still a fairly unusual quantity, and generally it is satisfactory in feel and quickness, although one can hear it working when driving at low speeds. The handling is crisp and flat, even though the springing is soft enough that the car rides well over a variety of surfaces. But there are some odd problems. Under power, the car torque-steers to the right

ROAD TEST RESULTS

ACCELERATION

Time to distance, sec:
- 0–100 ft. 3.6
- 0–250 ft. 6.0
- 0–500 ft. 9.0
- 0–750 ft. 11.3
- 0–1000 ft. 13.4
- 0–1320 ft (¼ mi). 16.0

Speed at end of ¼ mi, mph. . . .89

Time to speed, sec:
- 0–30 mph. 3.3
- 0–50 mph. 5.8
- 0–60 mph. 7.4
- 0–70 mph. 9.7
- 0–80 mph. 12.8
- 0–100 mph. 16.5

Passing exposure time, sec:
- To pass car going 50 mph. . . .5.0

FUEL CONSUMPTION

Normal driving, mph. 12.0
Cruising range, mi. 288

SPEEDS IN GEARS

3rd gear (5100 rpm). 136
2nd (5100). 95
1st (5100). 56

BRAKES

Panic stop from 80 mph:
- Max. deceleration rate, % g. . .81
- Stopping distance, ft. 300
- Control. . . . . .fair

Pedal effort for 50%-g stop, lb. .24

Fade test: percent increase in pedal effort to maintain 50%-g deceleration rate in 6 stops from 60 mph. 25
Parking: Hold 30% grade?. . . . .no
Overall brake rating. . . . . .good

HANDLING

Speed on 100-ft radius, mph. .33.9
Lateral acceleration, % g. . . .0.750

SPEEDOMETER ERROR

30 mph indicated is actually. . .31.0
- 40 mph. 40.0
- 50 mph. 49.0
- 60 mph. 59.0
- 70 mph. 68.0
- 80 mph. 77.0
- 100 mph. 95.0

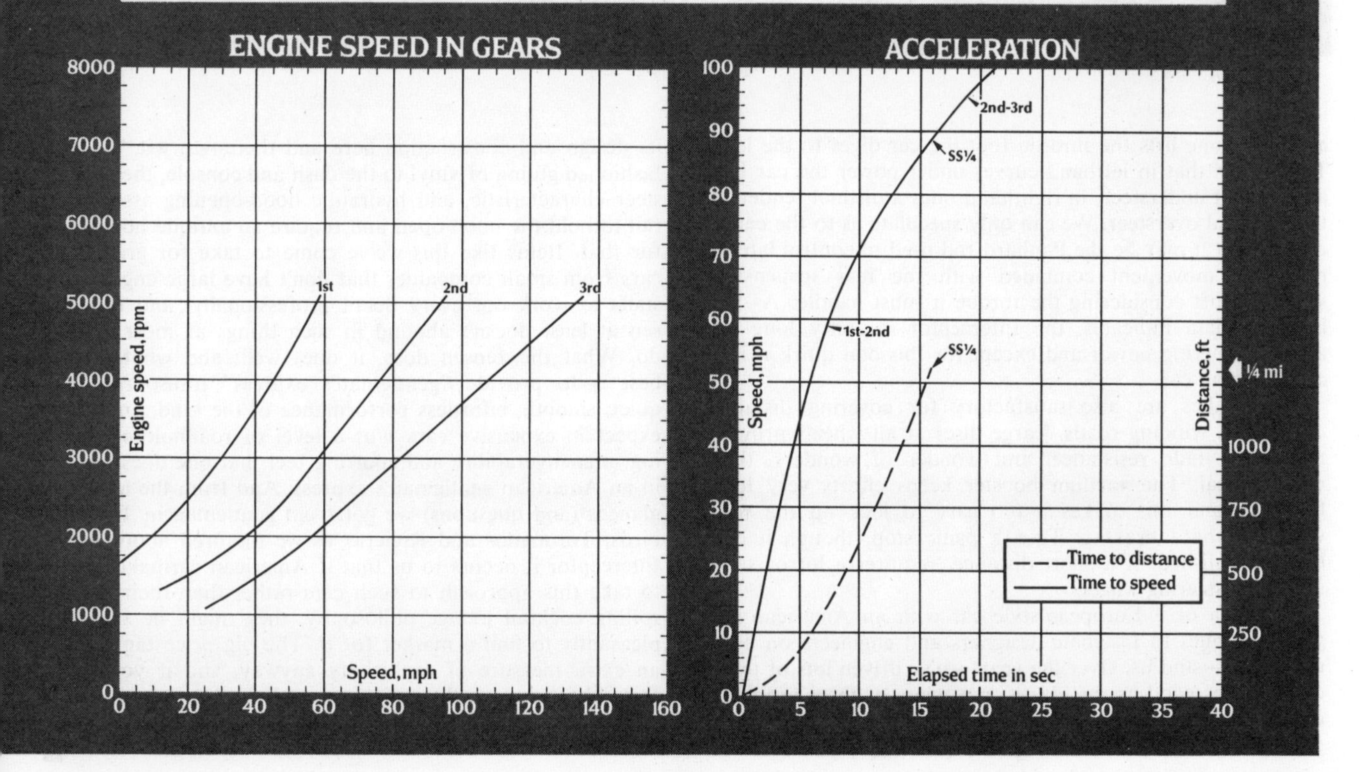

and when one lifts the throttle foot the car dives to the left. This means that in lefthand curves under power the car has a persistent understeer, in righthand ones a distinct tendency toward final oversteer. We can only speculate as to the cause of this, but it may be the Panhard rod used to control lateral rear axle movement combined with the rear suspension which is soft considering the torque it must handle. As the handling data indicates, the Interceptor is pretty long on actual cornering power and except for this odd quirk it is a capable road car.

The brakes are also satisfactory for covering distance quickly on winding roads. Large discs at all wheels provide reasonable fade resistance, and wonder of wonders, they don't squeal. The vacuum booster keeps efforts very low, however, and this makes it too easy to lock up the rear wheels in hard braking. Thus a panic stop, though it can be accomplished in a short distance, requires a lot of sawing at the steering wheel.

The idea of a European-style car with an American engine continues to fascinate designers and engineers on both continents—and us. Over the years we've driven lots of these cars, and as good as the idea is, not many of them are good cars. We're happy to report that the Interceptor II is a very good car, in fact, despite several touches of amateurism in its design and construction here and there—to wit, the old-fashioned gluing of vinyl to the dash and console, the torque-steer characteristic, and hydraulic hood-opening assists that fail to hold the hood open and require an antique hood prop for that. Items like this we've come to take for granted in cars from small companies that don't have large engineering staffs to work out every detail professionally, and the Jensen at least doesn't abound in such things as most hybrids do. What the Jensen does, it does well; and what it does best is to provide "gentleman's express" transportation—quiet, smooth, effortless performance of the kind Americans expect in expensive cars *plus* a level of roadholding, braking, maneuverability and sporting feel that one does not get in an American gentleman's express. And from the admiring glances (and questions) we got from gentlemen in Thunderbirds, Toronados and Rivieras as we motored about in the Interceptor it occurs to us that if American carmakers were to take this approach to such cars rather than their present rolling cocktail lounge philosophy, they might be surprised pleasantly to find a market for it. The big price tag gives it an extra measure of exclusivity anyway, and if you're the sort who admires the quietness and automation of a big American car but wants to go fast, we heartily recommend the Jensen.

All-steel body was designed by Vignale in 1967, is hand-built by Jensen in England with painting alone requiring 24 separate operations.

JENSEN INTERCEPTOR II

Relatively inexpensive at $13,500, the Chrysler-powered Interceptor is every inch a GT.

Probably only a few Americans have heard of Jensen Motors Ltd. until recently. However brothers Richard and Allan Jensen who founded the firm have kept U.S. ties since their beginning in the 'thirties, a beginning that saw essentially the same type of activity as their successor is carrying on now. This, in essence, is providing a small though standardized run of coachwork to fit around an American engine. At first, American chassis and most running gear were used; now, Jensen create much of this themselves.

The first product, aside from bodies for British chassis, was a striking open tourer based on '36-'37 vintage Ford V-8's. The late Edsel Ford, a noted perfectionist in styling, acquired almost the first one and Gary Cooper was another owner. Later, Jensen used the Lincoln-Zephyr 12 and still later, Nash twin-ignition 8's. After WWII, loyalty switched to Canadian Chrysler power of 383-cubic-inch displacement, aside from brief flirtations with Meadows and Austin.

Until 1967 the Jensen brothers styled their own bodies, but the Interceptor you see on these pages is a Vignale design built by Jensen. It thus is a four-year-old concept and to some extent, this explains why the car attracts little notice in traffic. If people compare it to anything, they are apt to be reminded of Plymouth's first Barracuda.

The Jensens retired a year or so ago and sold their small firm (16-20 cars a week plus odds and ends of custom coachwork) outright to a Norwegian American named Kjell Qvale who made his mint selling MGs and the like on the West Coast at the height of their popularity. He still does that along with assorted other products of what is now BLMC, plus Rolls-Royces and de Tomaso Panteras. If you're interested in a Jensen, British Motor Car Distributors, Ltd., headquarters are at 1200 Van Ness Ave., in San Francisco and the owner's name is pronounced *Shell Ke-vall-ee.* He's the type that's likely to answer the phone himself, if he's not in England at the moment supervising a new venture with Donald Healey involving a $4,000 two-seater to wear the Healey name.

Qvale has priced his Interceptor II at $13,500 which is either high or low, depending upon how you look at it. It is the lowest price currently being asked for a true grand tourer in the U.S. On the other hand, some people may feel that this is a lot of money for a somewhat dated design based on barely modified Chrysler components. In any case, the car neither causes you to instantly covet nor to turn away, as does the uncompro-

Styling is vaguely reminiscent of the first Plymouth Barracudas both front and rear. Car measures 186 inches overall on a 105-inch wheelbase.

Unlike the Italians in its class which cost much more, the Jensen is anything but fragile. Bumpers and overall size are well matched to U.S. traffic conditions.

mising Pantera displayed in the same showroom. The Jensen is best lived with a week before making a decision although with a target of just 400 of them the first year here, or four per dealer, you aren't likely to be offered this privilege.

Fortunately, we were. We flew to San Francisco to pick up the car (45 minutes) and drove it back to Los Angeles at posted limits via the scenic route through Carmel and Big Sur (9 hours). Returning it a week later, we chose the more usual route which is U.S. 101 Freeway, taking a little over seven hours for the 403 miles. Actually, it's somewhat more when you start in the suburbs south of L.A. and penetrate deep into S.F. where Qvale's shop is located. The point here is that we did this on one fill of the 24-gallon tank for an average of nearly 19 miles to the gallon, keeping to the maximum posted limit wherever possible! Try matching that in a Lincoln or even a 383 Chrysler.

The secrets, of course, are the 10 to one compression ratio in Jensen's version of the 383 engine plus an overall car weight of only 3,500 pounds. What aerodynamic efficiency it might possess could hardly have been a factor at legal speeds although absolute freedom from wind noise indicated a considerable measure of said efficiency.

The Big Sur area permitted plenty of chance to extend the car in turns that were always sharp and unbanked and mostly switchbacks. There also wasn't much between us and the ocean, many feet of jagged rocks below. Jensen use a proprietary servo assisted rack and pinion steering system with a 17.8 overall ratio and 3.4 turns lock-to-lock. While fast by U.S. standards, it doesn't quite match the cornering capabilities of the car. You are kept busy and sometimes, you don't have time to be quite busy enough. On freeways, though, it functions almost like an automatic pilot.

Also, the Interceptor is a biggish brute by grand tourer standards with its 186-inch overall length and 69-inch width. We must admit allowing an E-type Jag tagging us to pass rather than risk the hand-hammered Jensen sheetmetal on the decorative boulders that serve for a fence on the Coast route. The Jag is simply more lithe and easier to handle.

The Chrysler engine, which incidentally is disguised under lovely Jensen valve covers, is willing enough with 330 horsepower going through a 2.88 rear axle via a blueprinted Torqueflite automatic, the latter being your only choice in the U.S. We think a standing quarter in 13.82 seconds with a terminal speed of 103.4 mph proves this, as does zero to 60 mph in 5.9 seconds. These times were achieved with two aboard, using manual override and shifting at the rpm equivalent of 48 and 82 mph.

But ''dragging'' somehow is de-

Huge rear window is electrically heated and under it there's a cavernous truck complete with a full tool kit. Dual exhausts dispose of 330 horsepower.

Instrumentation is complete and attractive but the layout spreads too far away from the driver. Everything but the seats is automated.

Cornering is flat and level but the car is a little too bulky and loosely steered to qualify as a sports car. An E-Jag will outrun it in the mountains.

grading to a car like this. Its purpose is to give you upwards of 19 mpg in utter, quiet comfort and 100 mph plus cruising whenever that is possible. You aren't completely isolated while doing this, as in a Cadillac or Lincoln. You get some feedback every once in a while from the fat Dunlop radials. Engine mountings are not as flexible as the Chrysler originals, giving you an awareness of it working that's amazingly akin to the pre-WWII flat-head Ford V-8s. It's sort of a high-pitched vibration that you sense rather than feel.

The cockpit, and it rates that overworked description, is impressive but one must conclude that it was layed out for symmetry and builder's convenience in equal measure rather than with the driver solely in mind. The engine gauges are too far away and no provision is made for lighting the row of push-push switches. Despite vast blank areas where ashtrays could be built-in, these are illogically tacked onto the doors. We liked, though, the idea of putting the electric window switches on the console and ducting ventilating air out of the sides of same.

Achieving the right mixture of ventilation, heat or cool was not, however, easy whether you studied the explanation in the owner's handbook of the five-color coding system for the control or not. We couldn't master it completely even in a week and we also never quite figured out how to divorce the radio from its built-in tape deck, soundwise. Sometimes both would play at once, sometimes neither would work, and while the stereo phase of the radio would play admirably when you were able to capture the proper sequence of turning it on, the eight-track tape deck was incapable of separating "Porgy and Bess" from "West Side Story," resulting in an odd mixture of Southern drawl and Brooklynese, all of it earthy. This was the only tape in the car so we don't know whether it or the player was at fault.

Though there's a rear seat beautifully handcrafted in top-grain cowhide, the Interceptor must be basically looked upon as a two-passenger car, or perhaps three because the front passenger does have the room to move his seat forward far enough to allow a measure of legroom for the person in back of him on that side. A normal size driver can't move forward far enough to give someone in back of him any legroom at all. This is unfortunate and typical of Vignale, who puts seats inside his designs after they are styled, rather than styling around the accommodations desired by the client.

Our other minor complaint involved the unusual combination of a driver's left foot rest that's also used to operate the floorboard headlight dimmer. The pedal was too flabby to give any support and its travel precluded instant actuation of the dimmer. Maybe you could get used to it in time, but we'd rather see a solid block of rubber for the foot rest and the dimmer located in conjunction with the turn indicator on the steering column.

In the sense that every conceivable extra is standard Jensen equipment, the car can be considered a bargain at $13,500. Even the $17,500 Maserati Indy charges extra for an automatic transmission, power steering, radio and air-conditioning as does the $20,700 Ferrari GT2+2. What's not on a Jensen as it comes from the factory, you can't get except on the aftermarket.

Short of visiting the works in West Bromwich, it's hard to believe the hand labor employed in the building of the car. The operation begins with two, 9½-foot long steel tubes which form the basis of the chassis. The right-hand one of these is also, cleverly enough, the reservoir for the brake servo so don't drill into it later when installing an accessory. With the two tubes aligned, cross members are

Panic stops may be made in 141 feet from 60 mph without fade from the servo-assisted four-wheel Girling discs. Unlike the FF, this model does not have anti-skid.

Rear seats look comfortable enough but when the driver adjusts to normal position, you might as well forget sitting in back of him.

then hand welded with CO2 equipment, not electrically. Then the semi-finished body joins the frame.

The body itself, after being essentially hand hammered and constantly hand smoothed, goes through no less than 24 steps in the painting process, the color being anything you wish to order. Doors, hood and decklid are already attached so that their color is an identical match. After this, the car receives its engine, wiring, brakes and transmission, and finally, the Connolly hide trim which is hand sewn to each car's measure. The reason for this last extravagance may be the catalog writer's imagination, because certainly a body welded so securely beforehand couldn't change its dimensions. However, it's done that way and so be it. Over 100 different measurements are taken by those assigned to trim each car.

As a near to last check, each car is taken on a 150-mile test run and then it's re-polished and the speedometer replaced with a new, zero-mileage one. Finally, one of the Board of Directors drives it home and if he says it's okay, the car is released through the dealer to its customer. With human frailty in mind, try to order your Jensen so that the Director's inspection won't occur on the evening of the work's Christmas party or on any Director's birthday. Perhaps, even, the Director's drive could be made a delete option.

As if all the standard power assists were not enough, each Jensen is equipped with an electric fuel filler cover which pops open at the touch of a dash button. Then you have two sets of horns; the primary being the American variety and the other, again actuated by flipping a dash button, one piercing note from Maserati's "Colonel Bogey." Thankfully, it doesn't play the whole tune because while one note is enough to raise resentment, four more would cause the owner of the Cadillac ahead to turn around and ram you.

The brakes are servo assisted Girling discs on all four wheels with the reservoir being contained, as we've noted, in the right-hand chassis girder. These stop you impeccably, ours after 5,000 hard test miles in the hands of ourselves and others, doing it in 141 feet from 60 mph. Pedal pressures required are minimal so that wasteful lock-up may be easily avoided.

The other Jensen feature we kind of enjoyed was the two thermostatically controlled electric fans that cooled the radiator. You can't hear them while you're running, if indeed they operate under these conditions at all, but the minute you shut the engine off, the fans invariably turn on. Then you hide behind a bush and watch the reaction of pedestrians to the very audible roar. They come about as near to the car as they would a brown paper package on the sidewalk emitting a loud ticking noise.

Seriously, however, we question this obviously expensive installation because the thermostats can't tell whether you're climbing a desert hill at 90 mph in 90 degree heat or soaking the car in a Las Vegas parking lot afterward. If they start working on the hill, they'll only obstruct airflow through the radiator. In the parking lot, it's after the fact. We think the money would be better spent on a larger radiator and a viscous clutch type, feathering fan with a belt drive. This Jensen runs a little too hot even in cool weather for us to expect that there's much margin if any under tropic conditions.

Our subject Jensen Interceptor II, of course, is not the ultimate Jensen that Qvale expects to import. In a few more months, he'll start bringing in the rare FF model with its Ferguson four-wheel-drive and Dunlop Maxaret anti-skid braking system that acts on all four wheels. This one must be the world's safest automobile if all this stuff is working right. However, the type first hit the roads of England in 1967 and Jensen haven't seen fit as yet to sell them much outside a 60-mile radius of the factory service center. Qvale, though, has enough confidence to expect them in San Francisco shortly and if we understood him correctly, he doesn't plan to charge more than $2,500 extra for these two vital features.

Imperial already has the option of a four-wheel anti-skid feature. We're sure, though, that they don't plan to add four-wheel-drive. In any case, four-wheel anti-skid is infinitely better than a two-wheel system acting only on the rear wheels for the simple reason that you can still steer with the four-wheel kind. The two-wheel variety simply keeps your tail from slewing around. Then, when you combine it with modulated traction at all four wheels, you have the ultimate in bad-weather safety. Safety, in this sense, can mean either stopping or keeping going. Or, put another way, if the snowplow driver could afford $16,000 motor cars, he'd drive a Jensen to work instead of a Volkswagen.

This is the third month of our new rating system with a total now of about 18 cars in all price categories being graded. The Jensen Interceptor II, with an overall rating of 93, gets the highest mark so far. The only individual grade subject to question is giving it an 85 for room. However, this primarily concerns front seat room in a car of this category. If the Jensen laid claim to being more than a 2+2, that 85 would dwindle to 65 or so with a subsequent drop of the overall average from excellent to just good. That, really, is about the only serious fault we can find in this car. Vignale should be made to ride in the back seat of his 2+2 all the way from West Bromwich to Rome.

Don MacDonald

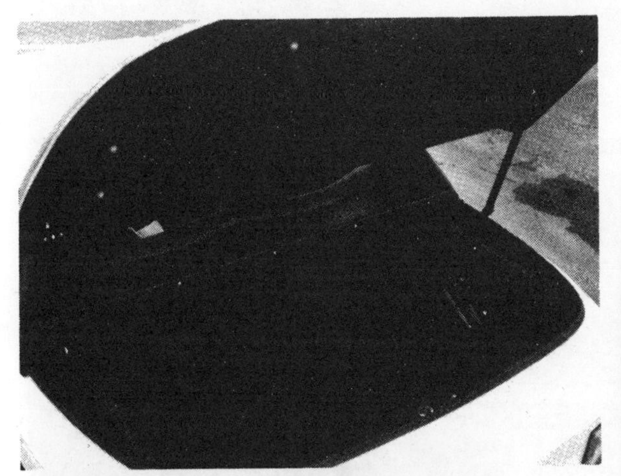

Trunk lid rises on counterbalanced hinges. Spare is under floor and is reached from under the car by lowering it. A complete set of tools is provided.

Jensen uses a Canadian Chrysler 383 with a 10 to one compression ratio that's rated at 330 horsepower. Engine is completely docile in traffic.

JENSEN INTERCEPTOR II COUPE

PERFORMANCE AND MAINTENANCE

Acceleration:	Gears:
0-30 mph	2.8 secs.— I
0-45 mph	4.4 secs.— I
0-60 mph	5.9 secs.— I, II
0-75 mph	9.4 secs.— I, II
0-1/4 mile	13.82 secs. @ 103.4 mph
Ideal cruise	100+ mph
Top speed (est)	140 mph
Stop from 60 mph*	141 ft.
Average economy (city)	12 mpg
Average economy (country)	19 mpg
Fuel required	Premium
Oil change (mos./ miles)	3/4000
Lubrication (mos./miles)	3/4000
Warranty (mos./miles)	12/12,000
Type tools required	SAE
U.S. dealers (plus Canada)	100 total

SPECIFICATIONS AS TESTED

Engine	383 cu. in. ov V-8 (Chrysler)
Bore & stroke	4.25 x 3.38 ins.
Compression ratio	10 to one
Horsepower	330 (SAE gross) @ 5000 rpm
Torque	410 lbs.-ft. @ 3400 rpm
Transmission	3-speed, automatic (Chrysler)
Steering*	3.4 turns, lock to lock 38.0 ft., curb to curb
Brakes*	Disc front, disc rear (Girling)
Suspension	coil front, leaf rear
Tires	ER 70 VR 15 SP Dunlop Radial

Dimensions (ins.):

Wheelbase	105.0	Front track	56.1
Length	186.0	Rear track	56.8
Width	69.0	Ground clearance	5.0
Height	53.0	Weight	3500 lbs.

Capacities: Fuel . . . 24.0 gals. Oil . . . 5.0 qts.
Coolant . . . . 16.8 qts. Trunk. . . . n/a cu. ft.

*Power assisted as tested

RATING

	Excellent (90-100)	Good (80-90)	Fair (70-80)	Poor (60-70)
Brakes	96			
Comfort	95			
Cornering	91			
Details	94			
Finish		88		
Instruments	95			
Luggage	91			
Performance	98			
Quietness	96			
Ride	94			
Room		85		
Steering	91			
Visibility	95			
Overall	93			

n/a — not available

BASE PRICE OF CAR

(Excludes state and local taxes, license, dealer preparation and domestic transportation: $13,500 at any P.O.E.

Plus desirable options:

Std. Air-conditioning
Std. AM/FM stereo radio
Std. 8-track stereo tape
Std. Radial tires
Std. Power steering
Std. Power disc brakes (4)

$13,500 TOTAL
$3.86 Per lb. (base price).

ANTICIPATED DEPRECIATION

(Based on current Kelley Blue Book, previous equivalent model): $ n/a 1st yr. + $ n/a 2nd yr.

N/A — not applicable

Gentleman's Express

Jensen Interceptor III — Rapid transit for gentry in a hurry/By John Christy

Thirty-odd years ago the British had an automotive term: "gentleman's express." It was used to describe an automobile combining the attributes of handling, stopping and performance of a sports car with the accommodation and sheer comfort of the most expensive luxury cars. Added to all this was the feature of practicality. In short, a blending of the best of all possible automotive worlds, a Grand Touring car in the classic rather than the current two-seats-with-a-fastback-roof sense of the word. With such a device a gentleman could commute from his ancestral home at Tottering-on-the-Brink to his offices in The City or his seat in The House, dash off for a weekend in Scotland on a grouse shoot or take a fortnight on the Continent *en famille.* The gentleman's express was, in short, a motor carriage for all seasons — rapid transit for gentry in a hurry.

A global war, partitioning of Empire and an era of austerity made such things irrelevant for some and an era of increasing specialization in automobiles made it all rather unnecessary for the more fortunate who could still afford to indulge themselves. For sport there were sports cars, for the sybarite there were luxury cars, for utility there were wagons and for the rest there was that form of transportation designated by the euphemism "volume car." That was it; you had mundane cars for mun-

Above: The Jensen is no small car but it doesn't feel big to the driver. Precise handling, excellent road-holding give it the feeling of true GT car. Left: Trunk is large and can be made even more so by unsnapping cover to allow tall objects to protrude up under backlight. Below: Vignale design is totally uncluttered.

MEMO

To: Eric Dahlquist
From: John Christy
Subject: Citation

Look, boss, I know it's policy to contest moving violation citations as a matter of principle, especially when (as usual) the ticket is a bummer. But in this case I will beg your indulgence in the matter. I am going to forfeit the bail. I am not going to try to expense account it even if the bean counters would accept the tab. And I am going to be both the poorer (by the amount of bail) and the richer (by both the lesson and the experience) for it all.

It's like this: I was motoring comfortably over the pass to the Valley the evening I picked up the test car under discussion. The Lear Jet Multiplex Stereo was laying the day's news on me through all four speakers. The road through the canyon felt as though some one Up There had transformed it into a silk surfaced slot track. I was tucked into the most sybaritic and snug leather form-fitting seat ever placed in a wheeled conveyance. I was, in a word, comfortable, as comfortable and secure as I've ever felt in an automobile. But I was bugged. I couldn't for the life of me figure out why everybody else was going so slow and still driving so raggedly. After all weren't they headed for hearth and home?

Well sir, when I got to the top and the road widened into four lanes I figured if all these other folks wanted to crawl along they bloody well could but not this kid. I toed the throttle a bit and started to motor around them--you know, the old through-the-traffic slalom number. As you are aware, that downhill stretch is a series of sweepers and a reasonably well-suspended coupe does well to stay in one lane at 50 mph and your ordinary large sedan is hard put to exceed 45 without raising the dead with tire squeal. Well, since I was doing this slalom number without paying any heed to taking a line--just sort of treating the stretch like any four-laner--I didn't think to look at the meter. Hell, I couldn't be going too fast. Here I was in a 4,000-lb. car moving through downhill turns making like I was in a Lotus, right? Now nothing does the Lotus act like a Lotus except another Lotus or, just possibly, a good Porsche 914-6. Not unless everything is in slow motion, right? Wrong. As I came out of the last left-hander I figured I'd best look at the meter. Sheesht! It said I was doing 65 miles-an-hour and change! Since they don't put shoddy speedos in cars like that, I quick grabbed for second range. Too late. But the officer was understanding about it--or something. Muttering something about "no court would buy what actually happened" he wrote the ducat up for 47 in a 35, after I explained the situation. He turned out to be sort of a specialist, too. Said he'd nailed a Citroën SM the other night in the same spot that was going slower and making more fuss about it than I was.

Now I ask you, could I go into court and plead "not guilty" with a straight face under those circumstances? NO WAY!

dane chores, sports cars for sport(s) and stately carriages for the stately, all for the most part with good, solid lines of demarcation between each category. And then, in the last few years, things began to change. The lines of demarcation began to blur, categories to blend, time to curve back on itself — all of which was hardly unabated by the propensity of marketing boffins to hang GT badges on anything with wheels. There are still stolidly mundane cars, there are still very sporting sports cars and there are still very luxurious stately carriages but in between, there are categories of machinery that defy the exact pigeonhole. You now have sedans that behave like sports cars, sporty cars that behave like sedans and utility vehicles that behave like limousines — and once again we have the "gentleman's express" which brings us to the Jensen Interceptor III.

The Roman numeral suffix indicates that there have been Interceptors I and II preceding the one under discussion. The first of these was hailed as the embodiment of the G's. E. concept. The second was described in *Sports Car Graphic* as ". . . the ideal and there is nowhere left to go." Wrong, both times, if only in point of time, because (insert discreet ruffles and flourishes) there is now the Interceptor III. So how do you improve the unimprovable?

Express

JENSEN INTERCEPTOR III SPECIFICATIONS

Engine	V8 — water cooled
Bore & Stroke — ins.	4.25 x 3.38
Displacement — cu. in.	383 (6276cc)
HP @ RPM (Gross)	330 @ 5000
Torque: lbs.-ft. @ rpm	425 @ 3200
Compression Ratio/Fuel	8.7:1/Premium
Carburetion	Holley 4v
Transmission	Torqueflite
Final Drive Ratio	2.88:1
Steering Type	Power
Steering Ratio	17.1:1
Turning Diameter (curb-to-curb-ft.)	38 ft.
Wheel Turns (lock-to-lock)	3.4
Tire Size	Pirelli GR 70 VR 15
Brakes	Disc/disc
Front Suspension	Double A-arm, coil springs, tube shocks, anti-roll bar
Rear Suspension	Live axle, leaf springs, tube shocks, Panhard rod
Body/Frame Construction	Unit steel plus longitudinal tubes
Wheelbase — ins.	105.3
Overall Length — ins.	187.0
Width — ins.	70.0
Height — ins.	53.0
Front Track — ins.	56.3
Rear Track — ins.	57.5
Curb Weight — lbs.	4,080
Fuel Capacity — gals.	24.0 (U.S.)
Oil Capacity — qts.	5.0

PERFORMANCE

Acceleration	
0-30 mph	3.7
0-45 mph	5.9
0-60 mph	8.8
0-75 mph	13.2
Standing Start ¼-mile	
Mph	87.0
Elapsed time	16.2
Passing speeds	
40-60 mph	4.3
50-70 mph	4.8
Speeds in gears*	
1st . . . mph @ rpm	45 @ 4000
2nd . . . mph @ rpm	75 @ 4000
3rd . . . mph @ rpm	142 @ 5600
Mph per 1000 rpm (in top gear)	27.2
Stopping distances	
From 30 mph	26 ft. 11 in. (2 sec., 1.1g)
From 60 mph	132 ft. 11 in. (3.2 sec., 1.1g)
Gas mileage range	10-12 mpg

Speedometer error						
Car speed	30	45	50	60	70	80
True speed	30	45	50	60	71	81

Base price	$14,700
Price as tested	$14,700
Car of the Year Score	**83.8**

*Speeds in gears are at shift points (limited by the length of track) and do not represent maximum speeds.

One of the more practical aspects of the Jensen is the Chrysler power train which allows the car to be serviced anywhere Chrysler products are sold — providing you can get the Service Manager convinced that it really is all Mopar. Brawny 383, coupled with Torqueflite, gives the car strong but totally smooth performance, even with all the accessories in operation.

First of all you start with a firm which has long specialized in building fine coachwork for the gentry. Then you have someone who has specialized for years in selling fine coachwork to the gentry to buy the heavy end of the firm and who, in turn, puts in someone who has spent a lifetime designing fine cars for gentry with a sporting bent to run the operation. At least that's for openers. Then the two latter gentlemen are set to work nitpicking the already fine product with the precision of a D.I. going over the effects of a "boot" who shows great promise but of whom he isn't very fond. The result by the time of the third generation has to be about as perfect as a product can be, especially when there is no quibbling by committees about "the market" or by the bean counters over costs. The gentlemen in question are Kjell Qvale who is probably the foremost purveyor of quality conveyances in the world and Donald Healey whose credentials as a designer/builder shouldn't need repeating to a car-conscious readership at all. Their connection with the Jensen firm came just prior to the introduction of the Interceptor II which was the result of some fine nitpicking on the part of the Jensen brothers on the Interceptor I which had been, in its turn, a replacement for the superbly built and wildly fast but incredibly unattractive looking Jensen C-V8, a car of such surpassing homeliness that most people failed to look beneath the surface to find out how truly good it was. Actually there isn't that much mechanical difference between the Interceptors and the C-V8. The initial fix came with the attractive Vignale body design and the rest has been detailing on what appears to be a cost-no-object basis. No detail on the car has been considered too small to be executed just right. Try as we might we couldn't find one crudity.

However, quality is as quality does and there are maybe three or four other marques in the world with equal quality control. You can come by that sort of thing in a number of ways. But the effect the Jensen seems to deliver is that nobody stood over the builders with a whip; they just *wanted* to build it that way. The result is that one feels that this is the sort of thing to which one would like to become accustomed rather than the feeling of awe that cars of this price range tend to engender. It might as well be pointed out right here that one *does* pay for all this quality, fourteen-point-seven big ones to put a bottom line on it. That's right, the price is $14,700 as it sits on the showroom floor without options since there are no options to be had. The interesting part of it is that it doesn't sit there very long since Jensens sell very well indeed now that those who have that sort of money to spend are not repelled by the exterior. Just the opposite, in fact. We have seldom driven a test car which drew as much favorable attention as the Interceptor III; wherever we took it, the car attracted a group of more than mildly interested questioners, even in gas stations and car-wash establishments. Most weren't even terribly put off at the price, the concensus being that if any wheeled conveyance was worth the price of a small house the Interceptor was that conveyance.

If mere inspection conveyed the opinion that the car was worth the asking price, the driving of it was the confirmation. No big car we've ever driven has felt more secure and at the same time more nimble. And go? It just sort of squats down and then takes off in one vast, silken rush. No fuss, no tire-squealing, fuzz-calling nonsense, just this long, insistent pull that will eventually end up somewhere in the neighborhood of 140 mph and change (142 at 5200 to be precise) if you let it. You have to watch it because it will quietly, oh, so quietly, ease on up to 90 mph or better without the driver ever really being aware of it. What is all the more deceptive is that it hangs on to the road to such effect that one isn't even mildly aware that what one is doing might

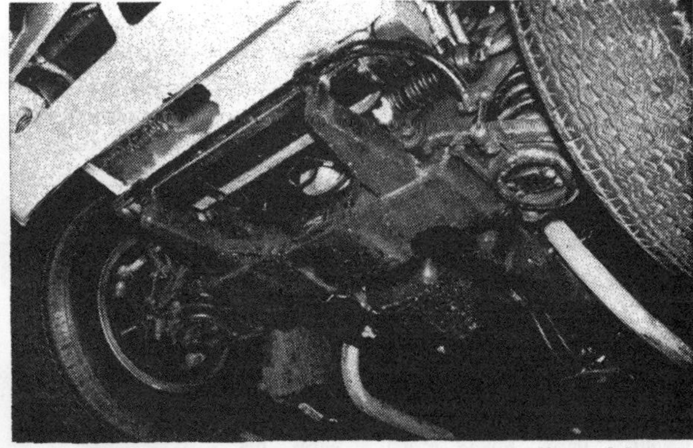

Left: Instrumented control area looks complicated but everything is quickly memorized, every motion natural. Above and below: Everything underneath is totally bullet-proof; ordinary-looking suspension is perfectly controlled.

be indecently illegal and please note that we said "illegal" not "unsafe." The car is capable of maneuvering safely and securely and even almost sedately at a rate of knots that would have a lesser car of comparable size writhing like a dory in a high sea. As a car goes, so should it stop and, oh Mother, does the thing haul down to a halt. This is one of the areas that differentiates the Interceptor III from the Interceptor II. The latter stopped well enough for a two-ton car at .8g and 150 feet from 60 but this one consistently pulled *better* than a full g (see specs) and came to a full stop from 60 in three seconds and 135 feet or less! This is the sort of thing one might expect from a good sports car but from a two-ton-plus luxury car? Awesome!

None of the foregoing really comes out and describes what is really one of the most outstanding features of the Jensen, i.e. that this thing is *fun* to drive. Not merely good for the ego or merely comfortable, safe and secure, though it's all of those, but actually fun like in sports car. If you can find the right sort of road you discover that you are doing all sorts of things just for the sheer joy of it that you wouldn't do in anything but a sports car because you'd have to work at it. What might be labor in any other heavy car the Jensen does with a sort of effortless ease that makes it all a sensuous pleasure. Part of it is the firm but silky suspension, part is the tremendously firm grip it gets on the ground thanks to the huge Pirelli GR-70 HR 15 tires, part is the fact that the car is as nearly perfectly balanced front to rear as a car can get — 50-50, give or take a pound or two for gas and passengers — and part is the never-ending torque put out by the smooth Chrysler 383 that makes it go.

Which brings up an element of practicality not found in your usual glamour car. You might not want to as a matter of course but in an emergency you can get service at any Chrysler products emporium, something you're not going to be able to do with a Rolls, Mercedes, Bentley, Ferrari, Maserati or what-have-you. As far as that goes, you're better off than the man with a Cadillac; there's a MoPar store of some type within shoutin' distance of almost any fencepost in the country. The Jensen driver hung up with engine or drive-line trouble somewhere in the hinterlands can at least get motoring again where the owner of something else might find himself taking up residence in the West Fencepost Hilton while he waited for parts and somebody who knows what to do with them to show up.

We actually did come up with one objection to the Jensen although it is one that could be considered irrelevant in a car of this type. It's a thirsty beggar, getting anywhere from 10 to 12 miles to the U.S. gallon of gas which gives it a cruising range of just a little over 200 miles. If you've the kind of money it takes to get into a Jensen you've probably got the wherewithal for a heavy fuel appetite but the car is so comfortable that stopping for gas every couple of hundred miles on a long trip could be a nuisance instead of a relief. And tripping, if you'll excuse the word, is what the Jensen is all about. You can commute happily with it and run errands to the store if you're so minded but where it really comes into its own is long-legging it over great distances, never mind what the road does. We also tended at first to boggle a bit at the back seats. It does give the impression that normal people couldn't live there but it is an exercise in efficient people packaging. There's no real room to squirm around but once situated one doesn't want to squirm. The seats are completely individual, completely form-fitting and completely comfortable. They were good in the II but they're superb in the III. And, like the front seats, each is equipped with an inertia operated seat belt that lets you move around either slowly or suddenly since it only cinches down when the vehicle, not the passenger, reaches a half g deceleration. These belts no one could object to or offer an excuse for not using.

There is really only one way to describe the latest Jensen Interceptor III — a quality motor carriage for all seasons, rapid transit for gentry in a hurry. A gentleman's express, if you will. /MT

JENSEN SP

FOR Exciting performance, very quiet high speed cruising, good roadholding and handling, well planned interior, good air conditioning

AGAINST Uncertain throttle response, heavy fuel consumption, indifferent low speed ride, noisy under power

The term sports car used to be fairly clear cut — two seats and wind in the hair — but now it embraces the GT brigade, still largely two-seaters or at best two plus twos; yet nobody would really think of a Jensen as a sports car. With its distinct boardroom appeal it isn't, but there are very few of the genuine article which can keep up with the Jensen SP either in a straight line or through the twisty bits. With its massive 7.2-litre engine, performance is instantly on tap up to a maximum of around 140 mph and the roadholding and handling are remarkable for such a large car with a relatively simple suspension layout — an excellent power steering system helps tremendously as do the low profile high speed Pirelli tyres.

SP stands for Six-pack which is the triple two-choke carburetter system on the bigger (7.2-litre) engine; the normal Interceptor III makes do with a mere 6.3-litres. In addition to the extra power, standard SP fittings include a very good air conditioning plant and the sporty louvred bonnet which plays its part in keeping the engine compartment cool.

At one time the bulk of Jensen revenue came from production of bodies for the big Healey and Sunbeam Alpine/Tiger. With the axing of both these from the respective ranges, Jensen have devoted their full efforts to the cars that bear their own name. Performance with four seats has been their theme and refinement has followed close behind, until with the SP the only criticism that can fairly be levelled at the £7000 vehicle is that the ride is over firm. Although this is a natural product of designing nearly two solid tons to behave like a middle weight sports car, the low speed firmness detracts from the overall high standard of comfort. Particularly good is the almost complete insulation from noise — the ride is quiet too; the harsh throb when all six chokes are sucking is more pleasurable than obtrusive, but you can cruise quite happily at 110-120 mph on the first pair of chokes with very little noise. Big seats are very comfortable and it requires little seating compromise to convey four adults for long distances.

Limit on the distance to be travelled at any one spell is set by the fuel consumption which at an average 11 mpg is heavy by any standards, and even a 20-gallon tank will only give you 1¾ hours of *autoroute* cruising; on 100-octane too.

But the Jensen's forte is its ability to cruise far and fast in comfort; it has its own combination of aggression and grace and no gimmicks. Whether it or any car can justify a £7000 price tag is up to the buyer, but there is a lot of car for the money and it is well put together.

Performance and economy

When they changed their 541 range to the CV-8, Jensen went Chrysler and they have remained faithful to the American company ever since. The big V8s have got bigger and the 440 (7.2-litres) is the biggest yet. In terms of specific output it isn't a particularly efficient unit with only 330 bhp from over 7 litres, but it develops this at only 4800 rpm and its maximum torque of 410 lb. ft. at 3600 rpm. If not efficient it is certainly effective with about 160 bhp per ton when fully laden; this gets it away from rest very smartly with 60 mph clocked up in only 7.6 seconds. Manual override of the Chrysler Torqueflite transmission doesn't affect this figure as the revs can be held to allow 60 mph in first gear, but to 100 mph holding second gear chops 0.3 seconds off for a best

You can see the heat haze rising through the SP's louvred bonnet when the engine's hot. The bonnet rigidity isn't improved by the slots

figure of 19.2 seconds. Such figures are less academic when they can be repeated at will with just a single foot movement; cars with manual transmissions may be faster in theory but no owner is going to treat every traffic light like a MIRA performance test.

The operation of the six-pack system isn't entirely satisfactory; most of the time you will probably be quite content to accelerate away, albeit still quickly, on part throttle which means just one carburetter until about 110 mph. The extra four chokes come in according to throttle position and engine load — a pressure compound system rather than mechanical. You soon know when they come in as the engine, which is hardly audible on part throttle, begins to emit a purposeful roar and you receive a firm push in the back. This sounds simple enough, but there are two side effects; one is that response to sudden demand for acceleration when cruising slowly is a bit slow as the torque converter winds up and the carburetters gulp air to compensate for the powerful accelerator pumps; it pays to select the lower gear manually. This is all relative but when you get used to the potential acceleration you expect response to match — driven intelligently the Jensen can be very quick through the traffic.

The second side effect is more obtrusive. With the extra chokes coming in with increase in engine load you can get a sudden excess of power with no noticeable throttle movement. This can happen when cruising at 110 mph and you start to climb a slight hill: the extra load on the engine is enough to open the chokes and it won't slow down until 130 mph unless you lift off first, in which case the shut-off is rather sudden. It can also happen when rounding a corner on constant throttle and the extra load provoked

Motor Road Test No. 14/72 Jensen SP

Maximum speed mph

100 110 120 130 140 150 160

Aston Martin DBS V-8 £8,749
Maserati Indy £10,089
Jensen SP £6,980
AC 428 £7,251
Citroen SM £4,689
Mercedes 350 SL £5,379

Acceleration sec

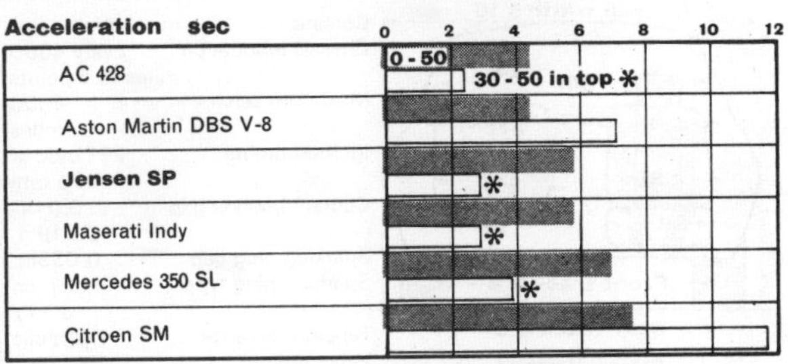

Fuel consumption mpg

0 5 10 15 20 25 30

Overall
Touring

Citroen SM
AC 428
Mercedes 350 SL
Aston Martin DBS V-8
Maserati Indy
Jensen SP

* Kickdown

Make: Jensen
Model: SP
Makers: Jensen Motors Ltd, Kelvin Way, West Bromwich, Staffs.
Price: £5580 plus £1396.87 purchase tax equals £6976.87

Conditions

Weather: Cloudy; Wind 11-19mph
Temperature: 40°F.
Barometer: 28.7 in. Hg.
Surface: Damp.
Fuel: 101 octane (RM) 5 Star rating.

Maximum Speeds

		mph	kph
Mean maximum (see text)		140	225
2nd gear	at 5100 rpm	94½	152
1st gear	at 5100 rpm	56	90

Acceleration Times

mph	Auto	Manual select sec
0- 30	3.1	3.1
0- 40	4.4	4.4
0- 50	5.9	5.9
0- 60	7.6	7.6
0- 70	9.8	9.7
0- 80	12.2	12.2
0- 90	15.4	15.0
0-100	19.2	18.9
0-110	24.3	23.9
0-120	31.5	30.8
Standing quarter mile	15.6	—
Standing Kilometre	28.5	—

mph	(kickdown) sec
10- 30	—
20- 40	—
30- 50	2.8
40- 60	3.2
50- 70	3.9
60- 80	4.6
70- 90	5.6
80-100	7.0
90-110	8.9
100-120	12.3
110-130	—

mpg 10 15 20
30 40 50 60 70 80 90 100 110 mph

Fuel Consumption

Touring (consumption midway between 30 mph and maximum less 5% allowance for acceleration) 15.2 mpg
Overall 11.0 mpg (=25.7 litres/100km)
Total test distance 3170 miles

Brakes

Pedal pressure, deceleration and equivalent stopping distance from 30 mph

lb.	g.	ft.
25	0.33	91
50	0.79	38
75	0.88	34
100	0.95	31½
140	1.00+	30

Fade Test

20 stops at ½g deceleration at 1 min. intervals from a speed midway between 40 mph and maximum speed (=93 mph)

	lb
Pedal force at beginning	29
Pedal force at 10th stop	40
Pedal force at 20th stop	40

Steering

Turning circle between kerbs:	ft
Left	33½
Right	37½
Turns of steering wheel from lock to lock	3.7
Steering wheel deflection for 50 ft. diameter circle	1.2 turns

Speedometer

Indicated	10	20	30	40	50
True	10	20	30	40	50
Indicated	60	70	80	90	
True	60	70	79	89	
Indicated	100	110			
True	97	106			

Distance recorder 1% fast

Weight

Kerb weight (unladen with fuel for approximately 50 miles) 35.1 cwt.
Front/rear distribution 52/48
Weight laden as tested 38.9 cwt.

Performance tests carried out by *Motor's* staff at the Motor Industry Research Association proving ground, Lindley.

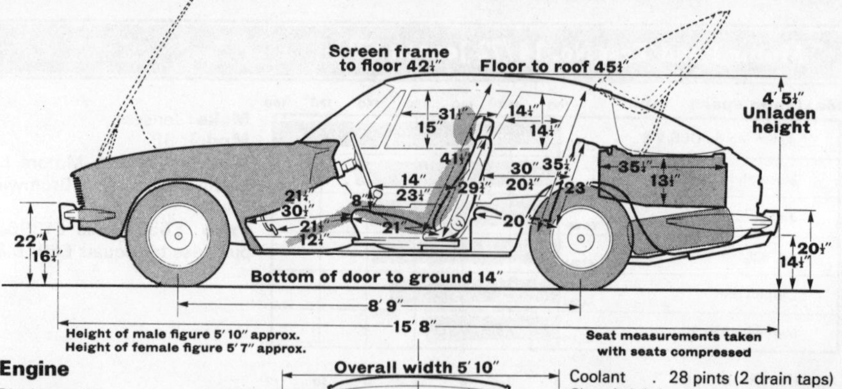

Overall width 5' 10"

Front track 4' 8"

Rear track 4' 9"

Ground clearances
Lowest point:–
(under exhaust system) 5½"
under front suspension 6½"
under engine 7"

Engine

Block material	Cast iron
Head material	Cast iron
Cylinders	V-8
Cooling system	Water pump, fan and thermostat
Bore and stroke	109.8mm (4.32in.) 95.3mm (3.75in.)
Cubic capacity	7212cc. (440 cu.in.)
Main bearings	5
Valves	Pushrod OHV
Compression ratio	10.3:1 (Octane rating:100)
Carburettors	Three 2-barrel Holleys
Fuel pump	Mechanical
Oil filter	Full flow
Max. power (net)	330 bhp at 4800 rpm
Max. torque (net)	410 lb.ft. at 3600 rpm

Transmission

Clutch	Chrysler Torqueflite with torque converter
Internal gear box ratios	
Top gear	1.00
2nd gear	1.45
1st gear	2.45
Reverse	2.20
Final drive	Hypoid bevel with Powr-Lok 2.88:1
Mph at 1000 rpm in:—	
top gear	26.3
second gear	18.1
first gear	10.7

Chassis and body

Construction	Tubular steel chassis with welded on steel body

Coachwork and equipment

Starting handle	None
Tool kit contents	Pressure gauge, 3 AF spanners, 1 adjustable spanner, 3 screwdrivers (1 Philips), 1 pr. pliers, 1 pr. gloves
Jack	Bevelift
Jacking points	4, adjacent to each wheel
Battery	12 volt negative earth 67 amp hrs capacity
Number of electrical fuses	12
Headlamps	4 tungsten-halogen Lucas
Indicators	Self cancelling flashers
Reversing lamp	Yes
Screen wipers	Two-speed electric
Screen washers	Electric
Sun visors	Two, padded
Locks:	
With ignition key	Steering column
With other keys	Boot and lockers, door key
Interior heater	Air conditioning
Upholstery	Leather
Floor covering	Carpet
Alternative body styles	None
Maximum load	800 lb.
Major extras available	None

Maintenance

Fuel tank capacity	20 galls
Sump	8½ pints SAE 20W/40
Gearbox	17 pints SAE ATF A
Rear axle	3 pints lsd oil
Steering gear	Power steering fluid
Coolant	28 pints (2 drain taps)
Chassis lubrication	Every 4000 miles to 5 points
Maximum service interval	4000 miles
Ignition timing	2½° btdc at 800 rpm
Contact breaker gap	0.014-0.019in.
Sparking plug gap	0.035in.
Sparking plug type	Champion J 11Y
Tappet clearance	Hydraulic
Valve timing:	
inlet opens	21°btdc
inlet closes	67°abdc
exhaust opens	79°bbdc
Exhaust closes	25°atdc
Rear wheel toe-in	None
Front wheel toe-in	1/16in.
Camber angle	0° ± 30′
Castor angle	2° ± 30′
King pin inclination	6°30′
Tyre pressures:	
Front	28 psi
Rear	32 psi
laden 32 psi / 36 psi	over 110 mph 36 / 40

Suspension and steering

Front	Independent double wishbones, coil springs, anti-roll bar
Rear	Live axle on dual rate semi-elliptic leaf springs, Panhard rod
Shock absorbers	
Front / Rear	Armstrong telescopic
Steering type	Adwest rack and pinion with power assistance
Tyres	Pirelli GR 70 VR 15
Wheels	Cast alloy
Rim size	6½ JK x 15

Brakes

Type	Girling ventilated discs, dual circuit with servo
Dimensions	10¾ in.dia. discs front and rear

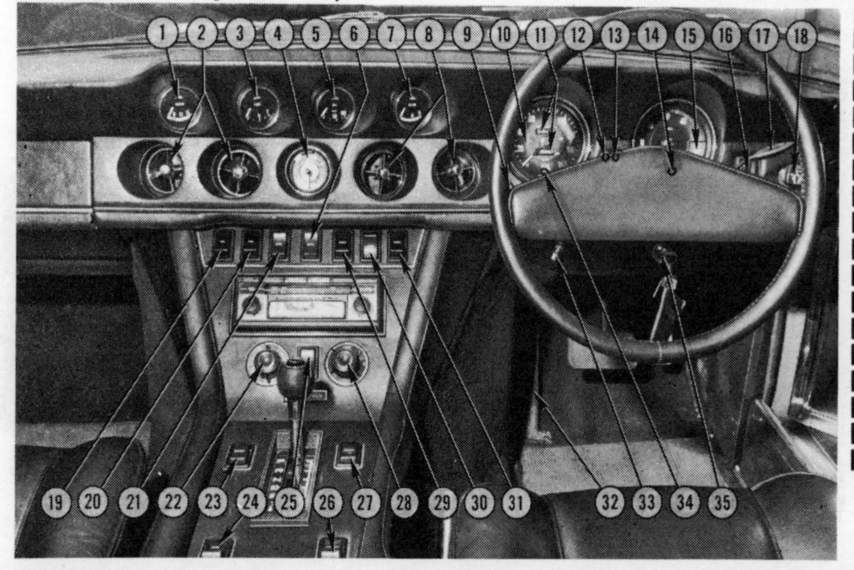

1 battery condition indicator. **2** fresh air vents. **3** fuel gauge. **4** clock. **5** oil pressure gauge. **6** aerial hoist. **7** water temperature. **8** fresh air vents. **9** indicator tell-tale. **10** speedometer. **11** trip and total mileage recorders. **12** oil pressure warning light. **13** fuel filler flap tell-tale. **14** low level fuel tell-tale. **15** rev counter. **16** handbrake/low fluid level warning light with check button. **17** flasher/indicator stalk. **18** washer/wiper switch. **19** fog light (spare). **20** fuel filler flap release. **21** horn selector switch. **22** air conditioning temperature control. **23** left window lift. **24** parking lights. **25** air conditioning. **26** hazard lights. **27** right window lift. **28** air conditioning fan. **29** rear window demister. **30** panel lights. **31** side/headlights. **32** dipswitch. **33** trip zero. **34** main beam tell-tale. **35** ignition/starter key

from tyre scrub etc can open the chokes in mid-corner which can be enough to dislodge the tail. When you are accustomed to these shortcomings it is easy enough to drive around them but we would still prefer an entirely mechanical linkage.

For our maximum speed we took the SP abroad; unfortunately an earlier test had involved the use of some substandard fuel which had caused a partial seizure of two pistons. This wasn't obvious until we came to check the figure which worked out at a mere 140 mph, compared with 143 mph recorded by another journal or nearer 150 mph expected by the manufacturers. With an engine delivering its full whack of horses we would expect faster acceleration and a top speed of 146 mph; this compares with the 6.3-litre Interceptor we tested with 330 bhp (gross), which is about 280 bhp (net), and that achieved 138 mph.

Starting is not instantaneous on the Jensen; it usually needs several turns of the engine before it fires with a little help on the accelerator, though warm up is rapid.

Fuel economy just doesn't really apply to the Jensen — it is thirsty at 11 mpg. At worst in France we recorded 10.2 mpg, at best in England it was 14 mpg. Even at 30 mph it only does 14.4 mpg although it gets less thirsty as you go faster until you get back to the same figure at around 98 mph. At 50, 60 and 70 mph, the figure was 17.7 mpg which suggests that the best you are likely to achieve is about 15 mpg. Our touring figure is 15.2 mpg.

Transmission

Chrysler's Torqueflite transmission has always been one of the smoothest of automatic transmissions and it works extremely well in the Jensen where the potential owner is more likely to use the manual override control than is the owner of the equivalent Chrysler. The changes are just about always smooth enough to be hardly perceptible to a passenger, and even a manual downchange slows the car smoothly. It is only when you kick the throttle to the floor that the combination of a dropped ratio and all the chokes opening gives an uncomfortable jerk. With a high final drive ratio the individual gears have a very useful span and you have to remember to change up again if you select second for a corner, as that gear is good for nearly 100 mph.

A limited slip differential is standard and it controls the grip very well; even wet standing starts on a clean surface only produce a few yards of wheelspin. In the dry there is a little spin, then a growl and slight shudder (possibly from the torque converter) as it speeds away. In normal circumstances though the transmission is quiet. Needless to say a start on a 1 in 3 hill presented no problems.

Handling and brakes

Most people could be forgiven for thinking that the Jensen used some form of independent rear suspension, so good is the traction and handling. In fact it has a live axle mounted in traditional form on two leaf springs with a Panhard rod and well placed telescopic dampers. The rear axle is pretty heavy but so is the car and the sprung/unsprung weight ratio remains favourable. With the power steering it is

We fitted 8.5 cu.ft. of our Revelation cases in the bootwell; this is all hidden underneath the lift-up canopy shelf. Toolkit is really useful

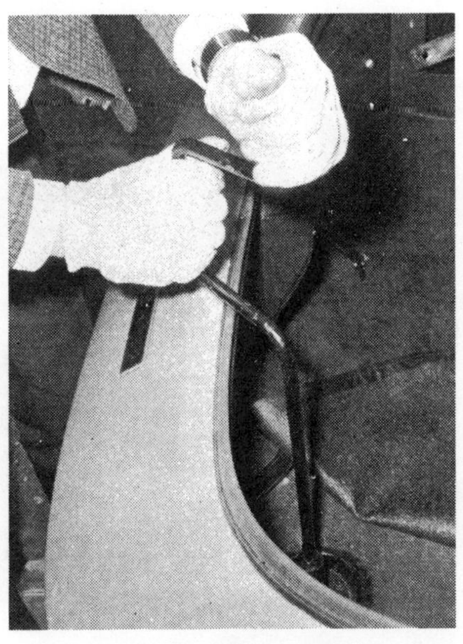

Included in the toolkit is a pair of gloves, very useful when changing a wheel on a wet night. The spare is under the floor

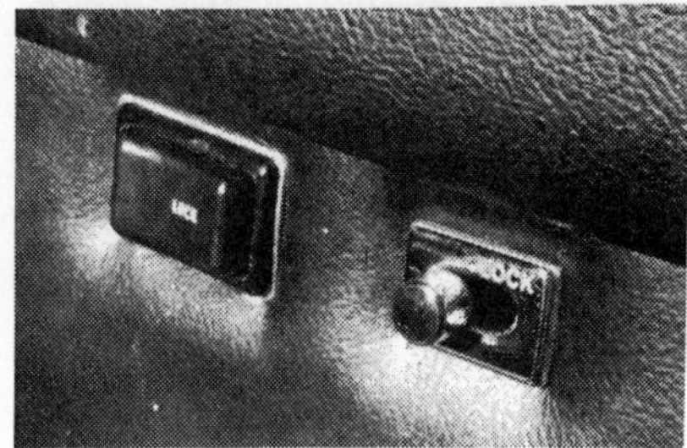

The toolroll is clipped neatly out of the way and the jack is held against the back. The switch below is for the driver to unlock the passenger's door

difficult to be certain how strong is the understeer, but the Adwest system is sufficiently sensitive to transmit the required messages from the front end in slippery conditions. Inevitably with all that power it is quite easy to flick the tail out of line if you have pre-chosen the right gear to do it. Mostly you will be in top and the absorptive qualities of a torque converter cushion the suddenness of power to the rear wheels, so the back end stays well in check. If you do get it sliding, lifting off lets the Pirellis grip almost too suddenly. In wet or dry these tyres grip very well but traction in snow is virtually non-existent.

In comparative terms the roadholding is good and you find that favourite corners taken fast in a Lotus Elan can be taken nearly as fast in the Jensen. There is very little roll.

With big ventilated discs, stopping power is excellent with a nice progressive feel to the pedal; the weight is on the firm side but this is no disadvantage. Our fade test had no effect after initial warming up, nor did the water splash. The handbrake just managed to hold the car on a 1 in 3 hill and provide the legal 25 per cent, although twin circuit braking is unlikely to force requirement of the handbrake as an emergency measure.

Comfort and controls

Most of the time the impressive quietness of the SP masks the slightly bobbly ride; comfortable seats ensure that this is no tummy jerker but at town speeds you sense the unevenness of the road with slight thumps and a little rocking. As speed rises the ride smooths out unless the undulations are large and the car movements correspondingly so, but at all times it feels well damped with none of the wallowy movements which one gets with large cars where handling is at less of a premium.

The seats adjust through a multitude of sliding and reclining positions which ensures a comfortable driving position for all sizes; the wheel is at a nice distance for a fairly straight arm driving position and the pedals are well related to it. The foot brake is large enough for either left or right foot braking although the fact that the brake pedal is rather nearer the driver than the accelerator tends to encourage left foot braking. This causes minor problems at night as there is a foot dipswitch controlling four powerful headlights; it is easy enough to use the right foot at that stage if you need to dip at the same time.

With the door angled back at the top you

have to stand clear when swinging it open as the point is very sharp. Access to the rear seats is easy for the agile but there isn't much room until you are installed in the comfortable buckets. Adult knees stick into the seat back but it is soft enough; less so is the rake adjuster bar which is potentially hard on the ankles of those behind. There is masses of width at the back and it is easy enough for rear passengers to look past the tall front seats. Visibility generally is good with large areas of glass, and the rear window keeps exceptionally clean even in heavy spray conditions; the heater element does a good job too.

Two particularly neat ideas are incorporated in the Jensen door-lock system; the first is an electric lock/unlock switch in the driver's door for the passenger's door, and the second is a time delay switch on the courtesy lights which keeps the interior light on for 20 seconds after the door has been closed. A seat belt tell-tale also stays on for the same time.

The standard air conditioning system has two controls, a temperature one which has a position for a full hot blast to the windscreen, and a three speed fan. There is no ram effect through the air conditioning but at first speed it is hardly noticeable and it is enough to maintain the atmosphere at a comfortable level. In addition there are four fresh air vents on the facia and another two at leg level. Altogether an effective and simple system.

As already mentioned the Jensen is very quiet with little engine noise and not much from the suspension; just a slight whoosh from the tyres and a faint rustle from wind at high speed. Turn on the standard stereo radio/tape player and you can be forgiven for feeling rather remote from the outside world. The VHF radio worked very well on AM, but FM reception was poor except in a few areas even out of town. We understand this is going to be changed.

Fittings and furniture

Unlike previous Jensens, the latest ones have nicely planned facias which are easily negotiated in the dark. The light switch is the nearest out of a battery of seven and the rest are for occasional use only; the washer/wipe switch is on the right. Inertia reel seat belts are easy to use with fixed clips in the centre.

With a release in the door jam, the rear screen canopy lifts upwards to reveal a usefully large boot capable of taking 8.6 cu.ft. of our Revelation cases. The toolkit is clipped out of the way and you don't have to unpack everything to get the spare wheel which is slung underneath. Inside the car there are two lockers, the one in the centre gets used for tapes which leaves the facia locker for maps etc. Ashtrays are fitted in each door and there are two on the transmission tunnel for those in the rear.

Servicing and maintenance

Servicing, including a spot of greasing, is required every 4000 miles or 3 months and is best left to one of the 30 or more Jensen servicing agents. With a high performance car (particularly one with such a bonnetful) professional service should be mandatory. Despite this there is a comprehensive toolkit including a pair of gloves.

Spacious interior gives comfort for four adults; the headrest pads are held by Velcro. Access to the rear is adequate but you need to move the seat a bit further forward than this to get your ankles under

With the air cleaner removed, the six-pack carburetter system is easily visible. Jensen rocker covers are used for the Chrysler engine. The dipstick is on this side, the oil filler cap is on the other

THE END OF THE JENSEN FF

Jensen FF: Born October 1965, production started autumn 1966. Last car built December 1971. A four-wheel-drive GT with anti-lock brakes and 6.3-litre Chrysler vee-8 engine

At the end of 1971, without ceremony, the last four-wheel-drive Jensen FF was built at West Bromwich. Thus an historic model has fallen under the safety legislation axe, its production volume being insufficient to justify full-scale crash testing and development. Ironically and in total ignorance, Ralph Nader has been responsible for killing the safest high performance car ever built.

When a modified Jensen C-V8 appeared at the 1965 London Motor Show, it was hailed as the most advanced high performance car in the world. Mated to its 6.3-litre Chrysler vee-8 engine was a sophisticated Ferguson four-wheel-drive system incorporating Dunlop Maxaret anti-lock braking. That model never reached production because the Vignale-styled Interceptor was already on the way and a year later two new models were announced.

This Mk.I version of the FF sold remarkably well, considering its 35 per cent price premium compared with the Interceptor. By October last year the Interceptor price had more than doubled, yet the additional cost for Ferguson four-wheel-drive and anti-lock brakes actually went down from £1,322 to £1,095. During the three-year production run of the Mk.I FF a total of 263 were built. This rate of about two per week was maintained until the end. By the time production ceased, only 387 Jensen FFs had been built. The most exclusive version of all was the Mk.III, of which there are only 15.

Our introduction to the FF started when a Mk.I came to us for road test in 1968 (test published 28 March). Apart from putting the car through its paces in this country and at MIRA, we despatched a team to the Swiss Alps to explore its unique four-wheel-drive properties on snow and ice. Apart from the remarkable handling, the incredible traction provided by the transmission system enabled the car to start on and climb a 1-in-5 ski slope on ordinary high-speed cross-ply tyres.

We were so impressed with its behaviour in these atrocious conditions that when the Mk.II was announced at the end of 1969, we took one into our long-term test fleet for a period of six months, but we never really encountered conditions which did it justice.

The passing of the FF from the scene makes the Land-Rover and Range Rover the only British four-wheel-drive vehicles now available and neither of these has the unequal front/rear torque split that gave so much to the FF's handling, nor do they have self-locking differentials. Ferguson four-wheel-drive development is continuing, both in the hands of GKN, who bought most of the manufacturing rights and FF Developments Ltd (a new company formed by Tony Rolt), who can carry out "FF" conversions to cars like the Ford Capri 3000 and Triumph 2.5 PI.

As far as Jensen are concerned, they have turned their attention to more commercial models. The new Jensen-Healey is now in production (our road test will be published on 31 August) and there are plans to add other models to the range in the future. In this connection, Kjell Qvale, the American who owns most of Jensen now, was seen recently in Turin having discussions with some of the leading stylists including Bertone. G.P.H.

Original Jensen FF on test at MIRA in 1968. We found it had extraordinary cornering power mainly by virtue of its four-wheel-drive with a front/rear torque split of 40/60

This version of the FF, based on the old C-V8 never went into production

When the road test car first arrived we published this picture to pave the way

This was the long-term staff car, a Mk.II version with improved facia and radial-ply tyres

TAKING STOCK

What it means to own a Jensen Interceptor III

By Edward Eves

Introduced:	**October 1971**
Price:	£6158.02
Delivery Charge:	£14.50
Plates:	£6.30
Year's Tax	£25.00
	£6203.82

IF you have it in mind to spend £6,000 to £9,000 on a British built GT Coupe with a big engine and around 150 mph performance, the choice is virtually restricted to the Aston Martin DBS vee-8 and the Jensen Interceptor III. The former is capable of 160 mph and costs £8,949, the latter just falls short of 140 mph and costs £6,158. Good reasons for choosing the Jensen, apart from the price difference and the fact that you don't often want to do 160 mph, are that the 6.3-litre engine from Chrysler is well developed and leads an easy life in typical UK motoring. And it is matched by the Chrysler Torqueflite transmission which most engineers — the dissenters work at Crewe — acknowledge to be one of the best available anywhere. The Anglo-American combination may not appeal to purists but it gets results in terms of performance and refinement.

What it Costs

The total cost on the road is detailed in the heading. It does include the cost of a tankful of petrol. And, of course, a lot of features which are usually extra are standard fittings. Notable among these are power steering, electric windows, a heated rear window and all the little luxuries one takes for granted in a high class motor car. Important options which I would take up if I were spending over £6,000 would be air conditioning — once you've had it you never want to be without it — at £217.50 and the Radiomobile Radio stereo tape player costing £90.63. Air horns cost £16.92 and would be next on the list ahead of Whitewall tyres £24.17, Sun-Dym glass £48.33 or a vinyl roof £24.17. The Interceptor falls into BIA Group 7 and insurance would be between £120 and £150 for a 30-year-old Midlander before deductions. Potential owners are likely to be a little older and to have good insurance records so this figure could be considerably reduced.

Living with the Jensen

The doors open not only wide but the openings are high enough between the edge of the seat and the top of the door opening to make getting in and out a pleasure. One learns to avoid the sharp corner of the window frame while doing so. Getting into the back is not so easy — a front seat squab has to be folded forward and ideally the seat should be slid forward on its very smooth runners. The only snag is that the seat slide release bar rests on the carpeted floor, and one has to dig one's fingers into the pile to lift it. The rear seats are well shaped, but the rather obtrusive wheel arches tend to push one shoulder forward. The front seats are similarly well shaped, giving good sideways location without the sides being too high. A nice touch is the provision of small padded cushions attached to the headrests with Velcro fastenings.

Seat adjustment is manual and there is no easy adjustment for height. However, there is ample fore and aft movement and Jensen would willingly raise the seat height. In combination with a telescopic steering column (2in. movement) most people can be accommodated.

In general, the instrument panel is well laid out but one needs to live with the car for a long time before one can touch-switch the services controlled by the row of switches placed below the angled minor instruments.

Internal stowage is adequate for keeping the car tidy. Apart from map pockets in the seat backs, there is a big locker beneath the centre armrest. In common with the cubby box in front of the passenger, it is lockable.

The boot, all 12 cu ft of it, is capacious by reason of its size rather than its shape. Being rounded to conform with the shape of the tail it takes a little unkindly to rectangular cases. And it is not quite high enough to take two large size cases on top of each other. However, they will go side by side with smaller ones on top and lots of soft bags to fill out the curved rear panel. If extra bulky objects have to be carried the "parcels shelf" can be detached by unscrewing about nine knurled nuts which retain it. In this configuration the shelf would normally be stowed beneath the luggage. The milled nuts tend to work loose and should be checked regularly when the panel is in position.

In-car entertainment is an extra. Early 1972 models featured a Learjet radio and combined eight track stereo player delivering its output through four speakers. This type of American radio suffers from not having the long wave band on which the Droitwich transmitter broadcasts throughout the land. On my car it was also rather crackly on the other bands. I was glad to learn that later cars are fitted with Radiomobile 108SR sets which are radio/stereo players. An electrically operated aerial is standard equipment.

Electric windows are another standard, and very essential, piece of gear on what is a wide motor car, too wide to reach over and wind a handle. For the same reason the electric door locks are a good idea. They are less noisy than those on the Silver Shadow but are equally effective and can be overridden manually. It is impossible to slam lock the doors from outside — they must be locked with a separate key. A further key is provided for the two glove boxes. A lever set into the driver's door pillar very conveniently opens the boot.

A "large-bore" ventilating and heating system ensures a good throughput of fresh air. Air is heated by a 4.5Kw heater matrix in the system. The whole thing is controlled by a pair of positive action knobs set in the console. The left-hand one controls temperature and the right-hand one the volume of air. Air conditioning is well worth while in a car of this class. It is really a necessity in hot weather because of the tendency for the relatively small volume interior to heat up. When it is fitted and switched on all incoming air is dehumidified. It can then be used cold or reheated when it does not cause the misting up which is inevitable with heated humid air.

A good took kit, apart from the wheel changing kit, is provided. It comprises a tool roll containing three open-ended spanners, a King Dick adjustable (for appearance rather than use) and no less than three screwdrivers, one of them a Phillips. A plated, universally jointed plug-spanner with T-handle lives in a big leather-cloth bag along with the jack, wheelbrace and a pair of white cotton gloves. The latter are a good idea because the spare wheel is slung unprotected in an open cradle under the boot floor and is bound to accumulate dirt. However, it *can* be wound down without having to disturb too much luggage if the boot is laden.

No difficulties are to be anticipated in keeping your Interceptor III clean. The only tricky bit is the panel under the bumper which requires either a long handled brush or a prayer mat. Full instructions for looking after the paint are given in the instruction book. The carpets come out easily and are retained by substantial brass fasteners properly attached to the carpets.

Fits and Finishes

It is difficult to fault the Jensen-built, Vignale designed body on the traditional points of paint, door fits and shut-lines. Going along a row of cars in the West Bromwich despatch bay I found the shut-lines to be equal round each car and equal from body to body indicating first class inspection. This is based on careful handwork and thorough painting. The body is rustproofed, slip-coated up to waistline and then given five coats of colour on top of a sealer-coat primer which is fully stoved before painting. After painting the underside of the body is sprayed all over with rubber-based sealer. Bumpers and door handles are plated to the top British Standard 1224 specification while all the rest of external brightwork is in stainless steel.

Only Connolly hide trim is available and the carpets throughout, including the whole boot lining, are Wilton pile, edged with leathercloth.

On the Forecourt

The only quibble one might have with the underbonnet layout is the arrangement of the dipstick and the oil filler on opposite sides of the engine. The forward hinged bonnet precludes working from the front of the car. Access to the oil filler is hampered by a pair of ignition leads which trail over the neat but inconspicuous oil filler cap. A good pourer is needed if oil is not to be spilt over the engine. All other fillers are quite accessible. The battery

Good Points

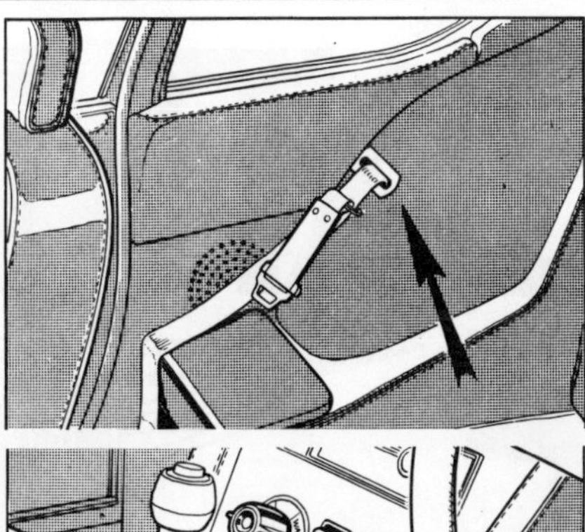

Apart from a fixed under-bonnet light, an extra light on a flexible extension is provided and reaches almost anywhere in the engine compartment.
The inertia-reel seat belts retract neatly into the wheel arches
The complex heating and air conditioning system is accurately regulated by these very simple controls which permit almost infinite variations of temperature and humidity

Bad Points

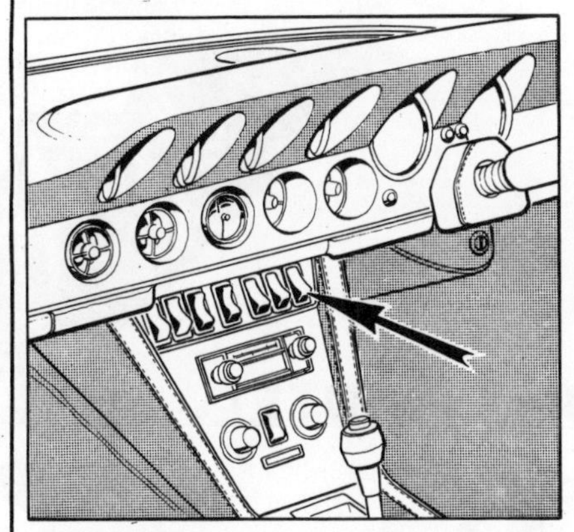

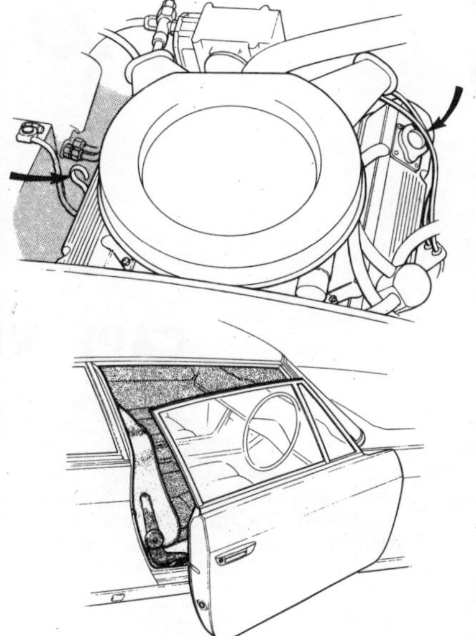

It is difficult to decide which switch is which without looking.
Having the dip stick on one side and the oil filler cap on the other side makes it difficult to check the oil without walking round the car. It is difficult to replenish oil without spilling it on the engine because of the inaccessible aperture.
Strangers to the car tend to catch their clothes on the top corner of the door frame.

is located high up on the side of the engine bay where it can be topped up or changed without fiddling. Incidentally, the aluminium foil heat shield appears to be susceptible to damage if the battery is removed.

Most forecourt stops are for petrol only. This is a slick operation, the petrol filler lid being spring loaded and electrically triggered so that one need not get out of the car if the attendant can be trusted to replace the filler properly. Moreover it can be filled from a can without a spout if you have the knack.

Doing it yourself

Keen owners might like to service their own Jensens. Twelve grease nipples require attention at 4,000 mile intervals. They are accessible by jacking up the side of the car without removing the wheels, but it is always best to have them off and make a good eyeball check for loose nuts and brake pad wear. Oil changes require a lift or a very slim owner since ground clearance is not excessive. A $\frac{7}{8}$in AF spanner to do the job will be found in the tool kit.

Girling disc brakes are fitted all round and pad changing is therefore an easy operation. Incidentally, one does not have to be afraid of the forged light alloy wheel nuts, they will take all the tightening loads that you are accustomed to apply to steel ones.

Topping up the radiator is another regular do-it-yourself chore because the level must be checked with the engine cold. Check alternator belt tension at the same time. It is important because you depend on it not only for electrical energy, of which a great deal is required, but also for steering power. It is easily adjusted or changed by slacking off the alternator adjustment. A spare is provided in the toolkit.

Fiddling with the engine should be unnecessary between major overhauls. When the time comes the work should only be tackled by experts.

Electrics

Full details of the complex electrical system are contained in the instruction book. A 60-watt alternator supplies the large amount of current required by extra equipment. All circuits are fused, the main fuse boxes being mounted accessibly on the panel on the right-hand edge of the engine bay. The function of each fuse is indicated on miniature etched labels. Headlamp adjustment and replacement are achieved by removing the lamp surrounds (three screws each); and access to the rear light bulbs is through little doors inside the boot. There is a delay built into the interior light switch which holds the light on after the door has been shut. This refinement is intended to help one find the ignition keyhole, but it holds the light on too long and one has to drive off fully illuminated.

Summing up

The Interceptor III is the kind of car one would dearly love to own. It has almost the refinement of a Rolls Royce Silver Shadow, attained with more mundane components, but it is a bit more dashing for the young executive. On its big, wide-rim Dunlop Sp sports tyres it is "Groundhog" personified. Handling and cornering ability are predictable and well up to the performance of the big engine. This helps build up a real affection for the car.

Fuel consumption worked out at 15.2 mpg of 4-star petrol with the 6.2-litre car tested. Later cars have low-compression, 7.2-litre, US emission engines which will consume more fuel. To make up for this they run quite happily on 2-star petrol so fuel costs should not be unduly affected. □

Service Interval	**4,000**	**8,000**	**12,000**	**24,000**	**36,000**
Time Allowed	$4\frac{1}{4}$ hours	$8\frac{1}{2}$ hours	$4\frac{1}{2}$ hours	10 hours	$4\frac{1}{4}$ hours
Cost @ £2 per hour	£8.50	£17.00	£9.00	£20.00	£8.50
Oil	£1.35	£1.35	£1.35	£1.35	£1.35
Oil Filter		£2.25		£2.25	
Breather Filter			£3.04		£3.04
Air Filter				£7.27	
Contact breaker points		£1.58 if nec.		£1.58	
Sparking plugs		£2.80 if nec.		£2.80	
Total cost:	£9.85	£24.98	£13.39	£35.25	£12.89

Routine Replacements:	**Time**	**Cost**	**Spares**	**Total:**
Brake Pads	3.0 hours	£6.00	£25.14	£31.14
Exhaust System Silencer, Tail Pipe & Trim	2.25	£4.50	£50.68	£55.18
Shock Absorbers — front	2.00	£4.00	£10.16	£14.16
Shock Absorbers — rear	3.00	£6.00	£20.48	£26.48
Generator	1.10	£2.20	£72.50	£74.70
Starter	1.50	£3.00	£71.60	£74.60

DEATH OF THE FF

FF in full cry — one of the safest cars ever made.

Rab Cook, leading English motoring writer now living in Australia, mourns the passing of the Jensen FF, a car he knew well.

THE NEWS from Up Over that the Jensen FF has sort of faded from production didn't actually come as a surprise. One can only sit quietly in a darkened corner, forcing back the beers — woops — tears and think of far-off things and bottles long ago.

Quite a car, quite a car. When it was first announced I made immediate steps to borrow one for a holiday trip but I was advised against it by a more technically minded colleague. "In the meantime," he said, "they are only selling them to people who live within a five-mile radius of the factory".

So instead I borrowed an Interceptor and waited until the FF had shown that it was reliable. A typical conversation about it at the time would go: "But what do you do if it breaks down?"

"Oh — no problem. You just take it to the nearest aircraft factory and get it fixed."

Unkind and, as it emerged, totally undeserved, because I never heard of anyone getting into trouble with an FF — any kind of trouble, mechanical or otherwise, apart from a PR man who took one home every evening and added a few mph each time he took a long sweeping bend. He upped the speed from the fast to the ridiculous, then to the Oh-my-gawd-what've-I-done stage and still it went round until the evening he ended up on the grass verge. But that was the only way an FF would go out of control, neatly and sedately sideways.

My chance came one December when I asked a friend, one Ken Laidlaw, what he was doing over Christmas. "Staring at the bloody ceiling, I expect," he said. So that settled it. We borrowed the FF and headed off through the snows for the extreme north-west tip of Scotland, Cape Wrath, with the avowed intention of having Christmas Eve lunch at the hotel there.

Sweet taste of success. Intrepid travellers made it to Cape Wrath, the extreme north-west tip of Scotland, for Christmas Eve.

The first thing we found was that the FF plus snow was the ideal recipe for travelling fast in a 70-mph-limited environment because the police were all tied up attending to cars which had gone into the ditches. The things that could be done with it were ridiculous by ordinary car standards and they were nearly all due to the four-wheel drive.

Let's get this into perspective. The anti-lock braking system is great but it is the lesser of the car's two attributes. It is the sort of thing that should be fitted to every car because it stops people from doing silly things, but with a driver experienced on slippery surfaces its major contribution is peace of mind. You know you can't lock the wheels so you are less tensed.

It is obvious that the electronic systems now being developed will be much cheaper and lighter than the Ferguson way of doing it; but they won't be better because they probably won't have the same interlinking. And as I understand it, they are still having problems with loose surfaces which they regard as slippery whereas really brutal braking will make the tyres cut through to the firm ground below the gravel and give a better result.

And the Ferguson system on the Jensen could be over-ridden with a really hard stab at the pedal. In other words, if you lost faith in it or even deliberately wanted to lock the wheels, you could push your way through it. The snag was the low cycling rate, which seemed to fit in too neatly with the periodicity of the suspension with the result that when you brought the anti-lock into action the whole car bounced on its springs and made a noise as though being struck by a very large padded hammer. The bouncing motion while this was going on was quite alarming the first time you tried it on black ice, but the results were so reassuring that you accepted the situation on future occasions.

It could be a mild nuisance, though, but it was also educational. Braking moderately on a wet road on what seemed a reasonably good surface you would get the occasional dum-dum-dum noise as the anti-lock dealt with an incipient slither. Educational, because this would often happen in places where you would never have dreamt that a wheel was likely to lock.

The system also got the early Jensens out of some trouble because the first Interceptors didn't have a very good tyre specification and braking in the wet needed thought and care. The quaint reason for this was that it would have been illegal to sell them in Britain with the correct tyres because then their headlamp centres would have been a fraction lower than the law stipulated. But once this was sorted out and the Interceptor had a good grip of the road, the need for the four-wheel anti-lock system became less and today's Jensen is as sure-footed as you'll get.

But the four-wheel drive was something else, and that was what really made the car the wonderful device it undoubtedly was — and still is. In fact, anyone who bought one had a real vintage car on his hands from the word go and I can't see the secondhand price ever falling much below what it stands at today. It may even start to rise in time, as is happening with the Interceptor's predecessor, the CV-8.

My first experience of the four wheel drive was in London's Tottenham Court Road. I was sitting at traffic lights in the FF when my attention was attracted by something going vroom-vroom, vroom-vroom beside me and there was an E-type with a young and eager driver determined to make it to Euston Road before me. The surface was wet, oily and really wicked looking and though I was new to the car I decided to chance it and have a go.

When the amber shone I floored the pedal and the FF just eased itself rapidly forwards. A glance in the mirror revealed that the E-type was in profile and being shouted at by a taxi. If you've ever been shouted at by a London taxi, you'll know what straits he was in.

That was only the start of the adventures. Ken and I went to visit one Hamish Cardno who was staying with his parents in Stonehaven, Scotland, during the holiday. The conditions were of the blizzard variety and as we sat in Chez Cardno sipping coffee, the FF was being slowly but surely buried in snow. Time to leave and we borrowed a brush to clear the windows and noted that the white stuff was more than two-thirds of the way up the big wheels, which meant it was around 15 to 18 inches deep.

With any other car it would have been a job for the shovels but not the FF. Snicked into first, it gave a slight shudder and a grunt and then heaved itself forwards accompanied by that lovely creaking noise that fresh snow makes when you squash it flat with two tons of machinery, and we were away.

Soon after, we took a wicked delight in rocketing past a brand new Aston Martin that was being driven at some dangerous pace like 35 miles an hour on the main road. We'd have been touching 80 in perfect safety.

Laidlaw is a very quiet chap who quite often uses actions to replace words. Frinstance, we were on the Aberdeen-Fraserburgh road in about two feet of wet, heavy slush and approaching a left hand bend. To understand this, you should know that the roads in north-east Scotland very often have banked corners, which is a splendid idea that few other parts of the world seem to cotton-on to. Wet snow was falling and the visibility was not good. I think I have a picture somewhere which was taken at the time.

Round the bend towards us came a three-ton truck laden with empty fish-boxes (how well the mind remembers the detail at such moments!) and it was clearly obvious to me, to Laidlaw and to the truck driver that he had lost directional stability in a big way. He was doing about 45 mph and while the nose of the truck was where it should have been, the rear end was slithering down the banked corner towards us in an alarming manner.

CONTINUED ON PAGE 163

Top right: Song of the Hills — a low moan from the FF, and teeth chattering from Laidlaw while Cook takes the picture.

Centre: Marathon within a marathon — the dear old lady had a hand-operated pump and it wasn't long before Cook was doing the work. Laidlaw grabbed the camera.

Right: The conditions on which the FF thrived. Most of the trip it was snowing, with treacherous black ice under the snow.

DEATH OF THE FF

SHELL

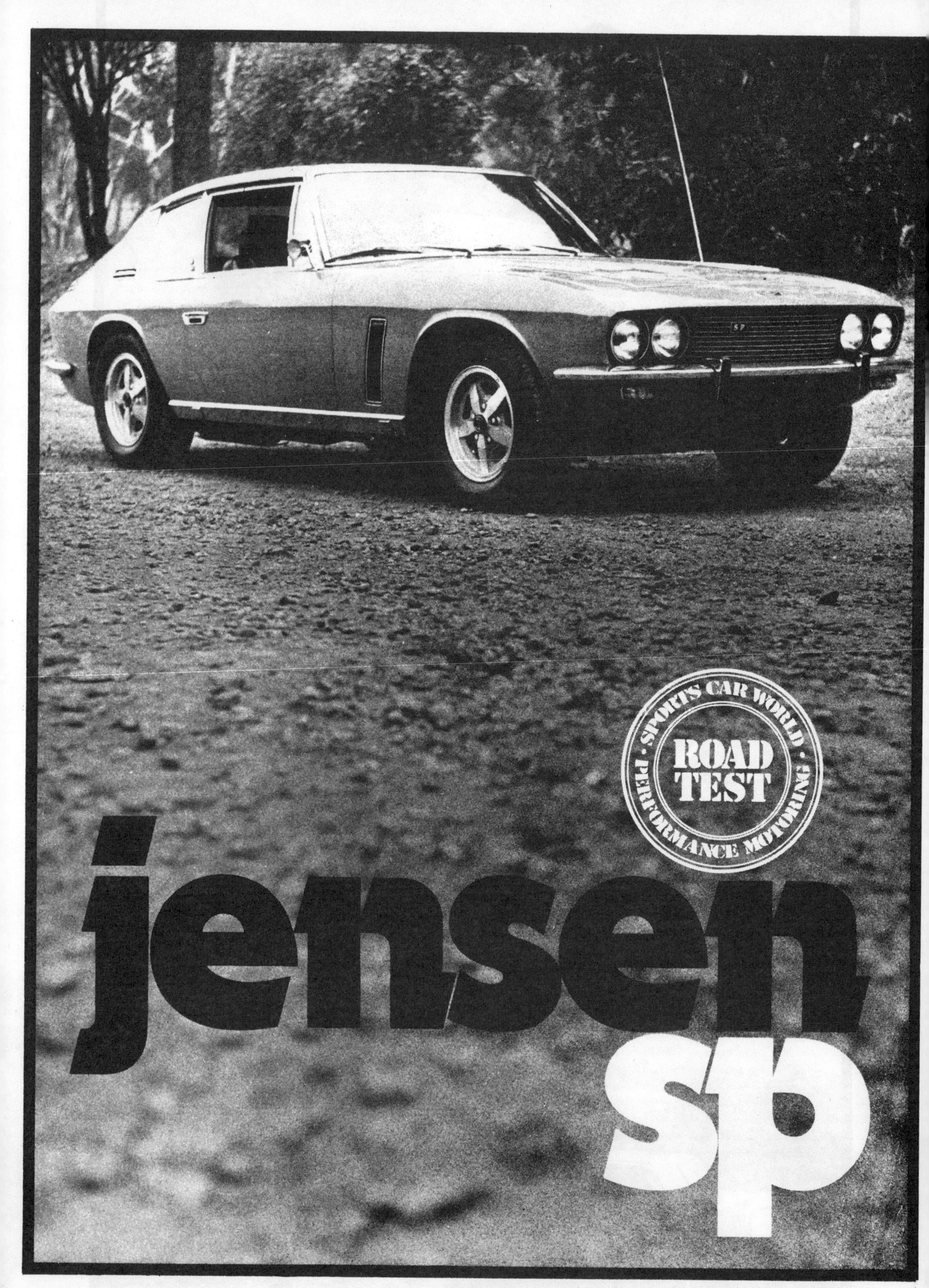
SP
SPORTS CAR WORLD
ROAD TEST
PERFORMANCE MOTORING
jensen
sp

To the Jensen fold, now comes Big Brother — complete with 7.2-litre V8 engine packing three dual-choke Holley jugs . . . and 410 lb/ft of torque. The result? Fantastic. RAB COOK reports from Melbourne . . .

IF THE JENSEN SP can be summed up in one word, then that word unquestionably is "relentless". This big, beautiful car seems to flatten hills, ignore bends, smooth out bumps and just keep pounding on and on.

Driving it is rather like being in a jet aircraft with a remote hum of expensive machinery somewhere beyond your ken and when a stretch of bad road passes below the wheels, the effect is exactly like a plane hitting bumpy air or flying through a rain cloud.

It is a car in which, as a passenger, you can be completely fooled into thinking that the speed is 40 mph less than what the speedometer shows on a straight road because of the detached, remote feeling and stable ride. Cruising at 120, you are quite liable to find that your passenger has lost interest and started to read a newspaper. Any minute, the air hostess will be round offering drinks . . .

All these things applied to previous Jensens, but they are even more true of the latest car, the SP (which stands for Six Pack and immediately lets you know where the motor comes from). It is even quieter than before (what is quieter than hush-power?) and the bigger engine, now at 7.2 litres in place of the Interceptor's 6.3, is so beautifully blended with the Chrysler Torqueflite automatic box that it is almost impossible to detect change points without looking at the rev-counter.

The torque, spread over a very wide band and peaking at 3600 rpm, feels sufficient to tip over Ayers Rock and it comes as something of an eye-opener when you tread some more on the throttle at speeds away above the hundred mark to discover that there is still more power to come when the second choke of the three Holley carburettors come into action. You feel that the acceleration is never going to stop. It does, but not until you are doing well over 140 mph.

Where the Jensen of today scores so heavily over ephemeral Continental exotica is that it is fully sorted out. There are many beautiful cars in the world which are almost impossible to enter or leave unless you are a pole-vaulter. Some have rotten ventilation, awkward driving positions, poor visibility, noisy, temperamental engines and a noteworthy but seldom admitted lack of reliability. It is easy to be blinded by a famous name, exciting coachwork or even an astronomical price tag, but experience shows that some of these cars are often far from being practical means of transport other than on the waterfront at Monte Carlo.

The Jensen, on the other hand, has years of experience behind it with the one chassis and engine because the CV-8 was mechanically the same — ignoring different engine sizes and detail improvements, that is — and the tubular chassis was made strong enough to carry that car's glass-fibre body which, naturally, carried no loads. When the stressed steel body of the Interceptor was introduced it was fitted to the same chassis, not by rubber mounting points, but by welding it on.

So it is hardly surprising that the result is outstandingly rigid and free from rattles, and that it is so acoustically dead.

And it is this rigidity which permits excellent use of a live rear axle with leaf springs. Properly located, such a system can play a big part in keeping a car level on fast bends but it can only work if it has a really solid base. Another thing that enables Jensen to "get away with" a live axle is the sheer weight of the car — 35 cwt plus — because although the unsprung weight is fairly considerable this in itself doesn't matter. What counts is the ratio of unsprung weight to total mass of the vehicle — the sheer inertia of the body.

Jensen just hasn't bothered to save weight, realising that weight is comfort and that when your petrol consumption is going to be in the 12 to 16 mpg range in any case, a few miles back and forth have ceased to matter. If you can afford nearly $26,000 for a car you're not going to burst into tears because the annual fuel bill is $20 over the odds.

Neither has it been snobbish about its engines. Too often one hears the comment: "It's got an ordinary Chrysler engine". That is far from being valid. For a start, you can hardly call a three-carb 7.2-litre V8, specially modified for Jensen, "ordinary", and in any case, Chrysler motor engineering has always been outstandingly good and its Torqueflite box still leads the field as it did from the day it was introduced.

The next point is that, for this type of car, getting "moderate" power from a big unit rather than the same amount from a double ohc of half the capacity has very many virtues. The results prove that — and bear in mind that Chrysler spares and know-how are readily available anywhere in the world that an SP is likely to go.

You may ask why Jensen doesn't make its own V8, and there are two answers to that. One is "Why on earth should it when this one is available?" and the other "Look what has happened to Aston Martin".

So let's get into the driving seat. It need hardly be said that it has a complete range of adjustment, gives good lateral support and, like all the other interior fittings, is beautifully made. The headrests are interesting because they pull off completely, being held in place only by Velcro "sticky burr" fasteners so you can set them at the height you want, or invert them, or put them sideways.

The pedals are a goodly stretch away and to get the driving position you want you set the seat for

pedal reach and then adjust the length of the steering column, Jaguar fashion, to get your arms comfortable.

You want to unlock the other door for a passenger to enter but it seems too far away? No problem, for there is an electric unlocking button for it on your own door. Electric windows, too, of course, electrically heated rear window, built-in stereo radio/tape, air conditioning, electric aerial, hazard lights, low or high-note horn selector switch, delay courtesy light that gives you time to find the ignition keyhole, a battery of four face-level vents, dipswitch by a large pedal, electric petrol tank lock release, brake fluid warning check-button light, and so on and on. You begin to understand why no options are offered, because there are none left unfitted. Even a pair of gloves to don if you have to change a wheel.

The air conditioning is delightfully simple to operate, with only two controls plus an on-off switch. The one on the left is turned to select cold, warm, hot or whatever you desire and it controls both the air conditioner and the normal heating/fresh air system. The other knob, close to the left hand, controls the speed of the blower fan and is handy for making a quick adjustment.

The four eyeball vents have separate flow controls and they can be angled to direct air through wide cones of adjustment. You can have one straight at your face, for example, and another either shut off or coping with sun beating through the window on to your chest while the heater is keeping your feet warm. So there are more permutations of control than even before but setting them is very ,much simpler and idiot-proof.

The engine is an easy but not immediate starter. It has to be churned over on the starter a few times before the mixture finds its way into the pots, and then it comes to life with the characteristic Jensen VROOM which is now less explosive than on the earlier models. After that you can forget the engine. It is out of sight, out of mind and out of earshot.

What you do notice, even though the figures may not flash through your mind, is that it gives the car a power/weight ratio of around 11 bhp/lb and when you tread on the pedal you're not so much concerned with the fact that the car does the standing quarter in 15.5 seconds but that it gets from zero to 120 in half a minute.

And even at that speed, if you think acceleration will be preferable to braking to get you out of an unhappy situation, it is there for the asking. At the other end of the scale (0 to 30 in 3.1 sec) you can operate the treadle as hard as you like and you won't make the back wheels spin unless the surface is really bad. Even so, nothing will get out of control and you can feed in a lot of power on something like wet, oily cobblestones.

Accelerating in Drive, the maximum change-up points are 48 in first and 82 in second. These can be changed to 56 and 95 by using the manual override and knocking off at the 5100 rpm line on the tacho, but there isn't a lot of point in doing so. Just let it happen.

On the other hand, should you want sudden acceleration from a low speed — say, to take advantage of a traffic opening — the delay while the torque converter winds itself up can be beaten by a quick snick down on the selector, rather than using kick-down. The selector is well placed and easy to use — it is brought into play quite a lot on twisting roads, not so much through necessity as for the sheer hell of it. Comfort-wagon, yes. And fun-wagon, yes, yes, yes.

Quite a few furrows on Jensen designer Kevin Beattie's brow were caused by thinking up some way of increasing the size of the Mk. I's 16-gallon petrol tank. Well, he managed to make it 20 on the Mks. II and III, but with the bigger engine the advantage is all but lost again and the SP has a terrible range of but 200 miles between fills.

At one time it was contemplated using the chassis tubes as petrol tanks but can you imagine the reaction of the safety campaigners to that one? The boot is so huge that a few gallons removed from its capacity would hardly be noticed and a 30-gallon tank would be much more satisfactory, particularly in Australia.

At around-town speeds the suspension is firm, no question about that, but the mass of the car ensures that there is no jolting. As the speed rises, the ride gets smoother and smoother but very well damped so that there is no trace of wallowing even on surfaces with widely spaced ripples which might be expected to cause this. Lean in corners is minimal and the grip taken on the road by the big fat Pirelli tyres is exceptional.

There are very few cars, and certainly fewer still of this weight, which can be hustled through the bends so rapidly as a modern Jensen and its performance in this respect could only be seriously criticised by someone who has been used to driving an FF — now unhappily defunct at the hands of the safety regulators, as I reported in SCW, July.

Cornering, the trend is towards understeer, masked by the Adwest power steering but not to such an extent that you cannot detect a front-wheel slide almost before it starts on a wet road. By changing down and tramping on the throttle you can make the tail slide outwards, and back in again by raising the foot. This is done fully under control and the result is that the driver, if so minded, can choose between long sweeping bends or going straight on and then cornering sharply at the last minute by balancing the car between throttle and steering.

There is no need for such party tricks but they do demonstrate that the SP can be tossed around, still completely under control. Though the steering is power assisted it has good feel.

In a straight line the car is extremely stable and the habit noticed in some earlier Jensens of giving a slight wriggle when power was suddenly shut off at speed on a wet road seems to have gone. The splendid quartz-iodine lights make night-time cruising at 100 perfectly safe.

JENSEN SP

Of the brakes, there is little need to say more than that they are progressive, not over-heavy, and pull the car up in a perfectly straight line even under crash-stop condition. It is difficult to lock the wheels completely except on a loose surface.

So far as noise is concerned I have already mentioned that the engine is completely remote. Considerable use of sound-deadening material — for example, inside the roof panel — has ensured that the body doesn't resonate. Wind noise is confined to a slight hiss at really high speeds and you can leave the radio volume constant between 30 and 100 mph. The tyres can be heard as a squelchy sound on granite chip surfaces, but only just.

There is a good selection of cubbyholes and boxes and the boot holds about 9 cu ft of suitcases in its 12 cu ft total capacity. More can be carried if you unscrew the huge shelf above it and let the luggage pop up into the car's interior. An unusual feature is that, when the shelf is in place and the boot lid (including the huge rear window) is open, items can be tossed into the boot from the car's interior. Although the natural reaction to this piece of information may well be "big deal", it is surprising how useful it is, especially on holiday trips.

There is plenty of room everywhere except in the back seats. With disarming honesty, the Jensen sales literature captions a picture of the rear seats: "With the front seats in mid-position, there is ample room for two passengers in the rear". Maybe. But with the seats back it's barely even a 2+2. And it's not a good car for slap-and-tickle because the occupants are sternly separated from each other by a padded wall which runs from the dashboard right back to the rear seat headrests. You can't even play footsie.

But this won't affect sales will it? Not when you remember that the SP is a fabulous car indeed, both as long-range transport and as a docile and easy to place town car because of the square corners.

And above all, it is outstandingly safe. *

JENSEN SP

SPECIFICATIONS AND PERFORMANCE DETAILS

MAKE	**JENSEN**
MODEL	**SP**
BODY TYPE	**Coupe**
PRICE	**$25,900**
COLOR	**Mustard**
MILEAGE START	**1660**
WEIGHT	**35 cwt, 14 lb**
DISTRIBUTION F to R	**52/48**

FUEL CONSUMPTION:

Overall	12 mpg
Cruising	15 mpg

SPEEDOMETER ERROR (mph):

Indicated	30	40	50	60	70	80	90	100
Actual	30	40	50	60	70	79	89	97

PERFORMANCE

MAXIMUM SPEEDS:

Fastest run	147 mph
Average of all runs	144 mph
Speedometer indication, fastest run	151 mph

IN GEARS:

	Drive	Held	
1st	48 mph	56 mph	(5100 rpm)
2nd	82 mph	95 mph	(5100 rpm)

ACCELERATION (through gears):

0-30 mph	3.1 sec
0-40 mph	4.3 sec
0-50 mph	5.7 sec
0-60 mph	7.4 sec
0-70 mph	9.4 sec
0-80 mph	12.0 sec
0-90 mph	14.7 sec
0-100 mph	18.5 sec
0-110 mph	23.5 sec
0-120 mph	30.2 sec
	Auto kickdown
20-40 mph	2.4 sec
30-50 mph	2.7 sec
40-60 mph	3.1 sec
50-70 mph	3.8 sec

STANDING QUARTER MILE:

Fastest run	15.4 sec
Average all runs	15.5 sec

BRAKING:

From 30 mph to 0	1.2 sec
From 60 mph to 0	2.9 sec

SPECIFICATIONS

ENGINE:

Cylinders	V8
Bore and stroke	(4.32 x 3.75 in.) 109.8 x 95.3 mm
Cubic capacity	(440 cu in.) 7212 cc
Compression ratio	8.2 to 1
Valves	Ohv
Carburettor	Three, 2-barrel, Holley
Fuel pump	Mechanical
Oil filter	Full flow
Power at rpm	385 bhp at 4700 rpm
Torque at rpm	410 lb/ft at 3600 rpm

TRANSMISSION:

Type	Chrysler Torqueflite
Gear lever location	Floor

OVERALL RATIO:

		mph per 100 rpm
1st	7.05:1	10.7
2nd	4.16:1	18.1
3rd	2.88:1	26.3
Final drive	2.88:1	

CHASSIS AND RUNNING GEAR:

Construction	Tubular chassis, welded-on steel body
Suspension front	Wishbones, coil springs
Suspension rear	Live axle, leaf springs
Shock absorbers	Telescopic
Steering type	Powered rack and pinion
Turns lock to lock	3.4
Turning circle	38 ft
Steering wheel diameter	16 in.
Brakes type	Girling ventilated discs
Dimensions	10¾ in.

DIMENSIONS:

Wheelbase	105 in.
Track front	56 in.
Track rear	57 in.
Length	15 ft 8 in.
Width	5 ft 10 in.
Height	4 ft 5½ in.
Fuel tank capacity	20 gallons

TYRES:

Size	GR 70 VR 15
Pressures	Normal 28 F, 32 R
	Over 110 mph — 36 F, 40 R
Make on test car	Pirelli

GROUND CLEARANCE:

Registered	5½ in.

USED CAR TEST

1970 JENSEN INTERCEPTOR II

PRICES

Car for sale at Beaconsfield at	£4,225
Typical trade cash value for same age and model in average condition	£3,300
Total cost of car when new including tax	£6,109
Depreciation over 3 years (to cash value)	£2,809
Annual depreciation as proportion of cost new	22 per cent

DATA

Date first registered	22 January 1970
Number of owners	1
Tax expires	30 April 1973
MOT expires	16 January 1974
Fuel consumption	13-15 mpg
Oil Consumption	Negligible
Mileometer reading	26,273

PERFORMANCE CHECK

(Figures in brackets are those of the original Road Test, published 4 September 1969).

0 to **30** mph	**2.8** sec (2.5)
0 to **40** mph	**3.9** sec (3.7)
0 to **50** mph	**5.2** sec (5.0)
0 to **60** mph	**7.3** sec (6.4)
0 to **70** mph	**9.4** sec (8.7)
0 to **80** mph	**12.2** sec (11.2)
0 to **90** mph	**15.2** sec (14.3)
0 to **100** mph	**18.7** sec (18.2)
0 to **110** mph	**23.7** sec (23.7)
0 to **120** mph	**29.5** sec (30.6)
In top gear:	
30 to **50** mph	**5.9** sec (3.5)
40 to **60** mph	**4.4** sec (4.1)
50 to **70** mph	**4.8** sec (5.0)
60 to **80** mph	**5.3** sec (6.0)
70 to **90** mph	**6.4** sec (6.8)
80 to **100** mph	**7.5** sec (7.8)
90 to **110** mph	**9.0** sec (9.9)
100 to **120** mph	**10.8** sec (12.4)

Standing $\frac{1}{4}$-mile **16.0** sec (15.0)
Standing Km **28.6** sec (27.7)

TYRES

Size: ER 70VR 15 Dunlop SP Sport on all wheels.
Approx. cost per replacement £17.50 (tubeless).
Depth of original tread 8.5 mm; remaining tread depth. 6mm right front and left rear; 8mm left front; 3mm right rear; $4\frac{1}{2}$mm on spare.

Tools

A few items missing from original and apparently little-used comprehensive toolkit. Jack and wheelbrace, and handbook with car.

CAR FOR SALE AT:

Hughes of Beaconsfield Ltd., Station Road, Beaconsfield, Buckinghamshire. Tel: Beaconsfield 2141.

ONE way of looking at the price of this used Jensen is to think that a figure of more than £4,000 is an awful amount to spend on a used car; but the other consideration is that nearly £1,000 a year represents a decidedly brisk rate of depreciation. Naturally inflation plays its part in the prices of top-rank cars such as this as well, and the fact that the cost of a new Interceptor has risen by some £650 despite two reductions in purchase tax makes the used example seem better value.

Price considerations fade into relative insignificance when one drives the Interceptor, experiencing again that superbly effortless acceleration, accompanied by very high standards of handling and comfort. The engine, never a very prompt starter, needs quite a lot of churning over on the battery before it will fire, but then it bursts into life giving that distinctive vee-8 exhaust beat and offering almost as good acceleration as the figures set by the original test car. Some ignition and carburettor attention may be needed to give a more even tickover when the engine is warm — at present it is tending to hunt slightly between 500-650 rpm. In examination of the underbody, we saw ample evidence of oil leakage along the chassis, but no definite source for it was identified, nor was there any significant drop in oil level during the test.

All Interceptors have Chrysler Torque-flite automatic transmission, providing very smooth changes. Most of the time the car does all its acceleration in top gear, but since there is so much torque available intermediate is seldom needed. The occasional kick-down change into intermediate, however, gives a great bound of acceleration and is a great safety factor to have in reserve when overtaking. In this gear the car can be held to 95 mph before reaching the 5,100 rpm rev limit. In top gear the effortless cruising pace, still with ample acceleration in hand, continues to at least 110 mph.

The power-assisted rack and pinion steering is still as delightfully positive as when new, but there is no doubt that the dampers have softened considerably, allowing a certain amount of wallow over undulations, which upsets the directional stability slightly. Apart from this floating tendency, the ride comfort is still excellent. From this weakening of the suspension and the accumulations of thick mud deposits underneath, it is considered that the car must have been driven a great deal on unmade roads.

It is the brakes, however, which give real cause for concern. They stop the car well enough but produce vibration, increasing in severity the harder they are applied. On checking this with Hughes of Beaconsfield it was learned that the disc faces have become slightly distorted, and that new discs are on order, to be fitted before the car is sold. The handbrake is also rather frail, and should be adjusted at the same time.

After these attentions, the Interceptor should be mechanically very fit. There is no doubt that the effortlessly smooth, swift and quiet travel which it provides, in a body of highly distinctive and purposeful styling, makes the high purchase and running costs seem very worth while indeed.

Condition Summary

Bodywork

It is felt that more is owed in the condition of the Jensen to thorough pre-sale preparation by Hughes of Beaconsfield, than to specially careful use of the car by its one owner. However, the car is now in quite smart condition, and its metallescent light blue paintwork looks very attractive. We spotted one or two signs of local respraying, and were told by the vendors that the car had, during its life, assaulted a gate post at the back end, and been assaulted by a horse at the front. Literally, it is understood that a horse bit the front corner. Otherwise the paintwork is original, and there are few blemishes. The chromium is unmarked apart from a dent in the bumper at the back on the right-hand corner.

The beige roof upholstery and door trim is in very clean condition, though the floor carpets show a lot of marks. The head lining and the black PVC facia have obviously been thoroughly cleaned. The stitching of the steering wheel has

(Below) The back window of the Jensen swings high into the air to provide access to the boot. It is a hefty lift to take heavy cases up and out over the high lip and care must be taken not to scratch the paint. The shelf comes out if a tall article needs to be carried.

come undone at the joint on the rim. The overall impression of the interior is fair enough in relation to age and mileage. Underneath the car we saw considerable evidence of impact with rough roads, and there are a number of dents in the front exhaust pipes. But the main exhaust systems are sound, and the general lack of corrosion is good. A good squirt round with a high pressure hose will remove lots of caked mud from the wings and underbody, and we found a lot of sand trapped in the front jacking point.

Equipment

The rev counter needle is prone to swing rather erratically; and the brake light on the left is not working. All other items in the car's comprehensive array of equipment are in good working order.

(Below left) As one would have expected at this price, everything inside worked. The instrument and control layout is ideal, and the four speaker radio superb. (Below) the Jensen is still an eye-catching car and excites interest and comment wherever one goes.

Accessories

A Radiomobile push-button radio is fitted, as standard. The Voxson cartridge player available at very high extra cost, was not fitted to this car. The extremely neat Tudor Webasto opening roof still slides easily and shows no signs of leakage. Britax fixed seat belts, instead of the inertia reel ones which might have been expected, are fitted. As well as such basic necessities as a heated rear window, vigorous but rather uncontrollable heater, and electrically operated window lifts, the Jenson comes with full air-conditioning, still in good order.

About the Interceptor

Following successful use of the Chrysler vee-8 5.9-litre engine in the C-V8, Jensen used the basically similar unit in its larger 6,276cc form for the new Interceptor launched in October 1966. The sleek new body was built in steel by Touring to Vignale patents and represented a breakaway from the glass fibre construction used for the C-V8. A sturdy tubular chassis was retained, welded to the steel body, and the car was available initially with either automatic or manual transmission. When we tested it in 1967 it gave a maximum speed of 133 mph. Power-assisted steering became first available, then standard, from January 1969.

In October 1969 the Series II Interceptor was introduced, having Dunlop SP Sport tyres, a larger radiator, and air-conditioning as an optional extra at £220. The fuel capacity was increased to 20 gallons and, externally, black headlamp surrounds, new bumpers, overriders and side grilles identified the new car. The example tested was one of the early Series II Interceptors produced.

In this form the Interceptor continued for two years, until replaced by the Interceptor III, having ventilated disc brakes, cast aluminium wheels, and remote locking for the passenger door. Finally, last year both the bore and stroke of the vee-8 engine were increased to give a capacity of 7,212 cc, and this was introduced on Interceptor production from chassis number 4643 in May 1972. □

(Below left) 6,276 cc's of smooth, unstressed power. Underbonnet condition was excellent. (Below right) The condition of the interior owes a lot to the pre sale cleaning carried out by the vendors.

NEA 7L

THE JENSEN SP really is the car for the man who has arrived in life. Not only has it got the sort of price tag that puts it into a small sector of the buying market, but it provides pretty near the ultimate in elegant, easy and luxurious motoring. Distinguished styling with just a hint of sporting overtones, a delightfully comfortable interior and a lazy great V8 that bowls the SP along very easily and very quickly, all combine to make the Jensen one of life's desirables.

JENSEN

The Jensen SP — a true Grand Touring car

FOR MANY YEARS, dating back to their origin at West Bromwich in 1935, Jensen Motors have specialized in producing large-engined luxury performance cars, not so much sports models, but GT cars in the true meaning of the word. Up to 1965 the curvaceous CV8 led the Jensen line-up, and that Chrysler-powered hybrid had been preceded by the 541 series, a similarly appealing two-plus-two which had started life with a great 4-litre Austin lump.

Then in 1966 came a major change with the introduction of the Interceptor series, a model highlighted by a deliciously-styled Fiore designed body. Chrysler power and the excellent Torqueflite Hi-Performance transmission provided the mechanicals, and pretty well instantly the package proved very successful. Gradual refinements followed to the Interceptor and also the technically superb four-wheel-drive FF, which was regrettably dropped in 1972. Late in 1971, along with the uprated Interceptor III, came along the SP. Fundamentally, the SP is an Interceptor with the 7.2-litre Chrysler V8 rather than the standard 6.3, a Vinyl-covered roof and certain items like the Radiomobile radio/stereo player, which comes as standard. But really it's the bigger motor and the louvred bonnet that make the difference in prices: the Interceptor III retails at a tax-paid £6744.06 and the SP works out at £7191.15.

It is fair to assume that the Rolls-Royce Corniche coupe, higher in prestige terms and price (£13,777), is the sort of car that might appeal to a Jensen buyer, but we tend to think that performance counts for a great deal with the Jensen. That makes the Jensen's closest rivals the Aston Martin V8 (£8949), the AC 428 Fastback (£7010) and the Bristol 411 (£7795). Bearing in mind that the considerably more expensive Aston's cost is mainly due to its pedigree four-cam engine and that the performance is considerably higher, the other three work out very evenly priced, and similar in performance, all with top speeds of around 140mph.

Power basis for the SP is the 90deg V8 7212cc Chrysler motor which is mated to the excellent three-speed Torqueflite automatic. With a high compression ratio of 10.3:1, five star fuel is required and it disappears dramatically through the three twin-barrel Holley carburettors. With a fuel tank capacity of a relatively measly 20 gallons, range is restricted to about 160-180 miles, as an average of about 8mpg resulted from general town and motorway driving.

Nevertheless few SP owners will worry unduly about the heavy fuel consumption, and the reward is exhilarating performance from such a heavy car. The kerb weight of the Jensen is only just under two tons and dimensionally it is pretty big, 15ft 8ins long and 5ft 9ins wide. Having said that, the 0-60mph is around 7secs, just over 1sec slower than the Aston and very much on par with the 6.3 Mercedes 300SEL.

Of course, with a car of the Jensen's sort, out-and-out performance is not the key to the car's character. The great advantage of the hulking great V8 is its immense torque. In the normal Drive position the SP eats up motorway miles very leisurely and quietly, and only on kickdown or manual override does its note change from a subdued rumble to a dragster-style growl.

Stability is a key note to the car. On motorways it will cruise very comfortably at 100-120mph, and taken to its red-line of 5500rpm the maximum speed is around 143mph.

The ride of the SP is superlative. Very pretty cast aluminium alloy wheels shod with Pirelli GR70 VR15 tyres cling firmly to the road. At the front, suspension is by coil-springs and wishbones with an anti-roll bar, while, believe it or not, rear suspension is by semi-elliptic (ie cart) springs and a Panhard rod. Nevertheless, with a 5½ins ground clearance, the Jensen laps up harsh surfaces with only a dull thud from the road wheels to let the occupants know.

The general handling qualities, as distinct from roadholding, are made excellent by the ease of all the controls, not least of all the steering. As power-assisted steering systems go, the feel of the Jensen fitting is medium, a factor which inspires confidence at speed in direct contrast to, say, the Jaguar systems. The Jensen does hold the road very well, but it is a great lump of motor car, something which must deter enthusiastic flinging into corners and roundabouts. In fact, the early braking, power-on technique works beautifully on the SP with its vast torque. When it comes to braking, the two tons are handled admirably by servo-assisted ventilated discs on all four wheels, and the only concern is in making panic stops in traffic when the automatic transmission is trying to drive the car on and can make locking-up possible. We didn't get any brake fade at all in a series of six consecutive panic stops from 60mph. The centrally-mounted handbrake also seemed quite effective.

The Jensen certainly is a safe car. For a start the body is of steel on a tubular frame. It has plenty of power for any conceivable overtaking situation, plenty of stopping ability and it holds on well so long as it isn't provoked into silly attitudes. It's certainly not a car that would take to a Ronnie Peterson driving style!

If the exterior styling is distinguished with its crisp, angular lines and acres of glass which ensure good all round visibility, then the interior really is out of this world. Our metallic blue test car had a beige interior, and Connolly leather is standard on all Jensens. The front seats really are the most comfortable we've ever sat in. They look rather like aircraft seats and provide comfort all round: they support the back and thighs; there are detachable head cushions which are Velcro-attached to the head rests; and, of course, they recline and move fore and aft adequately. Truly, the Jensen is a classic two-plus-two, for although the rear seats are comfortable too, their use dictates that the front passengers move their seats to at least mid-position, which can be restricting for a six-footer.

In the wide centre console between the front seats is located the excellent four-speaker Radiomobile radio/stereo player, a row of rocker switches, and the controls for the air conditioning, another standard fitting. Working in conjunction with this are four airflow vents, two each side of the silent clock *(sic!)*. The ventilation works out well: you can get a cool flow of air to the face and heat to the feet!

Primary instrumentation is of a 6000rpm rev counter and 160mph speedometer, ahead of the driver and behind the 15ins leather-covered steering wheel. Ranged towards the driver from the upper centre console are further instruments for water temperature, oil pressure, fuel and battery condition. All instruments are by Jaeger.

Naturally enough you don't have to use your hands much in the Jensen, other than to press buttons. Windows are electrically operated, as is the radio aerial. The rear window is electrically heated and automatically operated. The fuel filler opens from inside. The interior light stays on for 15secs after the car door has been closed. A nice touch. There are others. Red courtesy lights in the doors. A warning light for the seat belts, aricraft-style. Wipers are two-speed and self-cancelling, but it's a pity there's no wash-wipe control.

There are the usual plethora of warning lights, inertia reel belts and even a first aid kit. It's typical of the attention to detail that makes this £7000 plus investment worthwhile.

Overall the Jensen is a mighty impressive machine. It looks good. It feels good. Long distances really are effortless. In fact, during our test with the SP we drove many, many miles in the car purely for the fun of driving it. Its transatlantic power may not give it the pedigree of something like an Aston but the reliability is assured.

Jensen are only making two to three of the SP series a week and so they sell their entire production. Of its rivals we tend to think that both the AC and the Bristol appeal to very small groups of individualists, and when it comes to a whole concept of motoring, the Jensen provides the answer. In overall character the SP must be the best car we've ever driven for suitability to all sorts of conditions. A Ferrari Daytona may be the thing for the *Autoroute*, a Rolls-Royce for town, but all in all, if it has to be a one-car stable, we reckon the Jensen must come out on top. And that's praise indeed.

JUSTIN HALER

Road test

by John Bolster

If the design is conventional, the execution is superb. The body is beautifully made.

Improving the breed

There is a lot of pleasure in driving a car with a small, high-efficiency engine, keeping up the revs by using the gearlever with skill. Nevertheless, there is no sensation in motoring to equal a big, lazy engine doing most of its work on a fractional throttle opening, with hundreds of horsepower in reserve to out-drag the opposition with contemptuous ease on occasion.

For this sort of luxurious travel, the big American engines take a lot of beating. They have been developed over the years at vast expense, and provided they are left in standard condition they have a phenomenally long life with absolute reliability. Some American cars are totally unsuited to European conditions, while their unrestrained styling and juke-box interiors are not to everybody's taste. What is wanted is a craftsman-built coupé, with handling characteristics to suit British and Continental roads, but with lots of effortless American horsepower to push it along. Such a car is the Jensen.

The Jensen has been built to the same basic design for many years. Yet, for no obvious reason, the roadholding, handling and braking have undergone a steady improvement until they are incomparably better than they were. The disadvantages of a live rear axle are always obvious when one drives a light car, but with a larger and heavier vehicle the ratio of sprung to unsprung weight can be much more favourable. Though an independent or de Dion rear end would still have theoretical advantages, the Jensen designers have probably decided that the proved reliability of their existing axle, not to mention the reduction in the number of parts subject to wear, make this classical solution the best. When universally-jointed driveshafts become available which will transmit nearly 300 bhp for year after year without developing backlash, perhaps we shall be offered an all-independent Jensen.

If the design is conventional, the execution is superb. The body is beautifully made and the standard equipment includes all the extras available on other cars, such as refrigerated air-conditioning. Naturally, the windows are raised and lowered electrically, while a most useful thing is the electrical control on the driver's door to lock or unlock the passenger's door—with a wide car this saves a lot of stretching. A good point is the delay switch, which keeps the courtesy lights on for half a minute after the doors are closed, and the electric trap-door for the fuel filler saves waste of time fiddling with keys. These small but practical features make all the difference on a long, fast journey.

When Gethin Bradley proposed the road test of the Interceptor III, I at once suggested using it for the Geneva Show trip. I choose horses for courses and I wanted to perform this long and demanding journey in sinful luxury, as a contrast to the frenzied little Alpines which had provided such memorable transport in 1971 and '72. When I swept into Geneva in splendour and silence, some of my jealous friends immediately suggested that Bolster must be very rich to drive nearly 1500 miles in a 7.2-litre car.

In fact, I used less fuel than a friend with a considerably smaller engine, admittedly with four more cylinders, and the Jensen drinks the cheapest petrol you can get. If a man spends over £6,000 on his car, he probably does not have to worry over-much about fuel consumption and he knows that, to some extent, such effortless speed and acceleration must be paid for when refuelling. That the robust construction and the simplicity of the design ensure low maintenance costs is certain, but about 15 mpg is the best you can hope for if you drive fairly fast in England. Cruising at over 100 mph on the Continent, 12 or 13 mpg is more usual, and if you have a long burst at 130 to 140 mph, you had better call at the next filling station. Frankly, few people apart from test drivers do much travelling at such speeds, in spite of what they claim in the bars, and for me the tremendous performance more than justifies the consumption.

The performance figures are made possible by the quite exceptional traction. The big engine is set well back and, for some unknown reason, the rear axle never tramps or hops. Of course, the wheels spin on the getaway, even with automatic transmission, but thereafter all the power goes into the road, the up-changes being so smooth that they are literally imperceptible. The Jensen is a big, heavy car with lavish equipment but 0-60 mph in 6.4 s, or 0-100 mph in 17.6 s, show that one is unlikely to be challenged on the road, as does an easy 135 mph, with 140 mph just possible.

Indeed, on my trip to Geneva I found nobody who could match the Jensen, except when my conscience bade me lift my foot for economy reasons. My best fun was when I found two Citroëns, of the Maserati-engined variety, slipstreaming each other at a steady 130 mph. To leave them behind, I had quite a few kilometres at 140 mph, which is just below the start of the red mark on the rev-counter. The car goes through curves well at this speed and tough side wind can be felt, stability is outstanding for a rear-drive car. One does not feel inclined to fling a car of this weight into sharp corners, though its overall width is moderate for this class of luxury speed-model and it seems surprisingly compact in traffic. Understear and roll are both quite gentle and the acceleration out of sharp bends is most impressive.

The ventilated disc brakes cope admirably with their considerable task. There is some bump-thump at slow speeds but the level of road noise is low at more usual velocities. Some wind noise is evident around the rear quarters but this is strictly moderate. The great engine makes little sound, never seeming to be highly stressed, and that ultra-smooth transmission is totally silent. When the engine is idling, the two huge exhaust pipes make an aristocratic gurgle, rather like a duke's bath water going down the plug 'ole.

Although the ride is fairly firm, it is far better than one would expect of so classical a chassis design. Many people prefer a suspension which gives a feel of the road rather than a floating sensation. The power-assisted steering is light at all times but retains enough feel for full and certain control. The seats are most comfortable and of course one sits on the best Connolly hides, which have that expensive aroma. The interior treatment is impeccable and both the exterior and the upholstery of the test car were in

The Jensen: a craftsman-built coupé with lots of effortless power to push it along.

a discreet light green—immensely smart yet inconspicuous.

The pleasure of handling such a beautifully made machine cannot easily be put into words. Though the sheer performance is highly spectacular, it is the way the doors close, the lazy idling of the engine at 100 mph, and the refrigerated breathing air coming from four adjustable vents, that make this such a special car. If these are the things that appeal to you, then the Jensen is not expensive, for it has an air of quality about it that cannot be excelled at any price.

The long Geneva trip became even longer than expected because, on the way home, there was one of those international financial dramas and the French banks refused to change travellers cheques. Luckily, there was just enough petrol in the tank to make a return to Switzerland, driving carefully, where I changed the cheques and started all over again. After a memorable drive through France, the Jensen reached the Townsend Ferry at Calais in perfect condition. Not so a large German car with pneumatic suspension, which had evidently found the rough roads of Northern France too much for it and collapsed drunkenly on the floor with its rear wheels akimbo. There's nothing to be said for a good old axle and semi-elliptic springs, after all!

Car tested: Jensen Interceptor III 2-door, 4-seater coupé, price £6,744.06 including tax.

Engine: Eight-cylinders 109.6 mm x 95.2 mm (7212 cc). Compression ratio 8.2 to 1. 284 b.h.p. at 4800 r.p.h. Pushrod-operated overhead-valves with hydraulic tappets, 4-choke Carter downdraught carburetter.

Transmission: Hydraulic torque converter and 3-speed automatic gearbox, ratios 1.0, 1.45 and 2.45 to 1. Hypoid rear axle with limited-slip differential, ratio 2.88 to 1.

Chassis: Steel body on tubular chassis. Independent front suspension by wishbones, coil springs, and anti-roll bar. Power-assisted rack and pinion steering. Live rear axle on semi-elliptic springs with Panhard rod. Telescopic dampers all round. Ventilated disc brakes on all four wheels with power assistance. Bolt-on aluminium-alloy wheels, fitted GR 70 VR 15 radial ply tyres.

Equipment: 12-volt lighting and starting. Speedometer. rev-counter, oil pressure, water temperature, and fuel gauges. Voltmeter, clock, heating, demisting and ventilation system with heated rear window. Refrigerated air conditioning. Electrically-raised windows. Electrically-operated fuel filler cap. Electric passenger door lock. Radio with four speakers. Electrically operated radio aerial. Hazard warning. Windscreen wipers and washers. Flashing direction indicators, reversing lights, fire extinguisher. First aid kit. Parking lights. Red door lights. Cigar lighter. Hazard warning.

Dimensions: Wheelbase 8ft 9in. Track (front) 4ft 8½in (rear) 4ft 9⅝in. Overall length 15ft 8in. Width 5ft 9in. Weight 1 ton 11 cwt 1 gr.

Performance: Maximum speed 140 mph. Standing quarter-mile 14.9 s. Acceleration 0-30 m.p.h. 2.5 s. 0-50 m.p.h. 4.5 s. 0-60 m.p.h. 6.4 s. 0-80 m.p.h. 10.7 s. 0-100 m.p.h. 17.6 s.

Fuel consumption: 12 to 15 m.p.g.

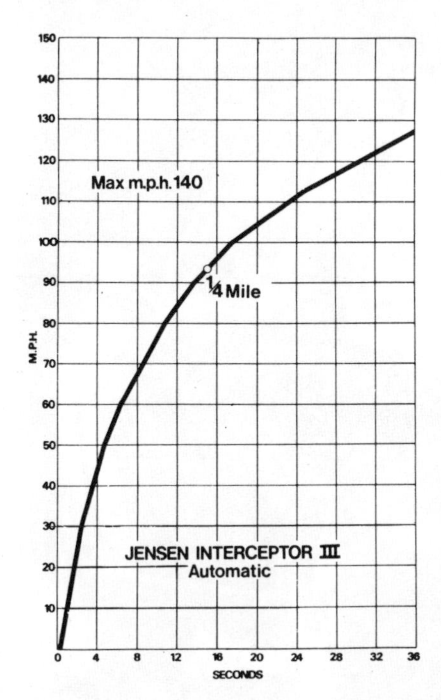

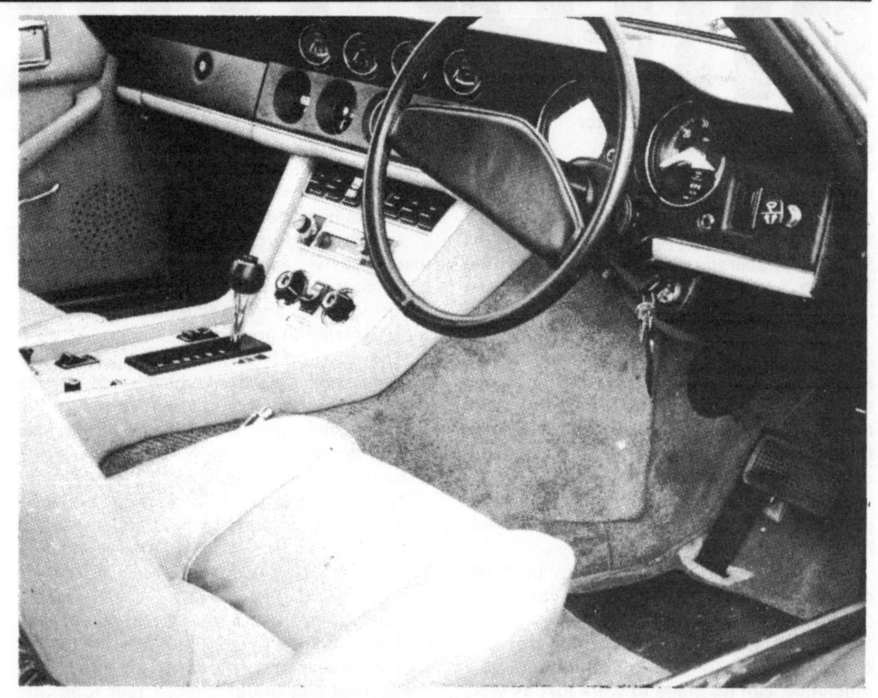

The interior treatment is impeccable. Below, the two huge exhaust pipes make an artistocratic gurgle like a duke's bath water going down the plug 'ole.

The great engine makes little sound, never seeming to be highly stressed.

INTERCEPTOR III: RUGGED

THE JENSEN Interceptor is an extraordinarily ordinary car.

It sells in the most exclusive world markets against the most exotic automotive creations known to man. It ranks equally with cars bearing such proud titles as Ferrari, Maserati, Lamborghini and de Tomaso — ownership of a Jensen Interceptor is a sure mark of one's having "arrived".

Yet despite the car's acceptance by the international jet-set and the fact that it can comfortably rubs shoulders with the most delicate and high-priced of European thoroughbreds, its basic engineering and design concepts are pure Detroit.

But the Jensen continues to thrive and grow, spreading its gospel to the most well-heeled corners of the earth.

The fact that many people probably overlook, however, is that the car's very ordinariness is its secret of success.

It proves that good, solid, straightforward design, refined to give maximum possible efficiency, can be made to work just as well, and a lot more reliably, than designs which are over-complicated, fragile and frighteningly expensive to produce.

The Jensen philosophy has changed over the years since the first prototype was built in 1934, but the present accent on mechanical reliability, coupled with exceptional standards of comfort and roadability, has produced a very workable formula.

The methods by which most of these ideals are achieved are extremely orthodox, yet the final result is a car which looks and feels totally modern.

In the Interceptor, sound-deadening insulation is applied extensively, adding significantly to the car's weight, but reducing road and mechanical noise to a mere whisper at any speed.

The steel body is mounted on a tubular chassis similar to that which once carried the lightweight fibreglass Jensen CV8. Torsional strength, understandably, is said to be exceptionally high, but once again there is a weight penalty.

Suspension layout is perfectly straightforward, with wishbones, coils and anti-roll bar up front and live axle with semi-elliptic springs, telescopic shock absorbers and Panhard rod at the rear. Rubber separators are used to reduce noise level and ride harshness.

The Interceptor is not a small car, measuring just under sixteen feet long and slightly less than six feet wide. With standard equipment like air conditioning, power steering, power braking and automatic transmission, it's not hard to understand why it weighs in at 4000 lbs.

But Jensen's use of big, lazy V8 engines from Chrysler U.S. sees to the problem of maintaining an adequate power/weight ratio.

The Interceptor III uses a 7.2 litre V8 of undisclosed horsepower driving through "Tourqueflite" three speed automatic transmission to a limited slip 2.88:1 differential. This is enough to propel the car at 140 mph and provide standing quarter mile acceleration times in the low 15 second bracket.

The fuel consumption penalty, considering the car's weight and performance, is fairly reasonable. Highway cruising at legal speeds will return around 15 mpg, while even the hardest driver would be pushing to manage less than 10 mpg.

The Interceptor's weight is an important factor in it's ride and handling characteristics.

Because the unsprung weight ratio is brought up to a favourable level by the bulk

of the body and because Jensen has done a compctont job in designing the suspension, the car's behaviour on all types of roads is comparable to that of one with a good fully independent system.

The ride tends towards firm and there is very little body roll on fast corners.

The effective damping provides both comfort and stability on rough roads.

The braking system is an interesting exercise in fail-safe design. Four-wheel ventilated discs, with a rear proportioning valve, separate front and rear systems and anti-dive front suspension provide a pretty good formula for a start, but Jensen has gone one clever step further. In the event of engine failure and the loss of power assistance, the Jensen has the extra back-up of an additional servo cylinder incorporated into the off-side chassis tube, more than doubling the number of brake applications available. With over 36 hundredweight of car to stop, that's a very comforting safety margin to have!

The Interceptor's power assisted rack and pinion steering is the same as that used in the XJ6 Jaguar and the Leyland P76, but Jensen has put more feel into the system so that it doesn't become over-sensitive at speed.

It is a variable-effort system that leaves plenty of road feel in the straight-ahead position, but becomes lighter as lock is applied to allow easy parking. It is, in fact, hard to believe that the steering is assisted when the car is cruising on the open highway.

So with all these factors working for it, the Interceptor is ready-made for long interstate hauls.

The next item of consideration is the passenger environment. Once again, Jensen has tackled the design in a straightforward fashion. The interior is trimmed entirely in leather (the company claims it uses six complete hides in every car) and the seats are shaped to perfection. Accommodation in the rear is not exactly all that the company would have you believe, but it is still a more likely proposition than in other super-status 2 plus 2.

The backrest adjustment for the front seats uses a re-setting device that returns to the original angle of inclination after the seat has been tipped forward to allow access to the rear.

Driver familiarisation takes a relatively short time, as the most-used controls are placed logically and well away from those used only occasionally. The wiper/washer switch is located to the right of the steering column where it can be found instantly at night and uses a logical twist-for-wipers, push-for-washers action.

A Jaguar-style lineup of rocker switches controls items like horn tone selection, rear window demister, fuel flap opener (there is an emergency manual over-ride in the boot should this fail) and instrument lighting. The only criticism here is that the master switch for the lights is incorporated into, and is sometimes difficult to find in the array of other switches.

Headlight dipping is by a switch under the footrest by the brake pedal, but a flasher is incorporated into the indicator stalk on the steering column.

A wide central console houses penthouse-style creature comforts like the powerful air-conditioning system (which incorporates an automatic climate control for maintaining steady interior temperatures) and the four speaker radio/cassette tape player. There are also controls for the (naturally) power operated windows.

The driver gets a full complement of Smiths-copy Jaeger instruments with glass faces that sometimes glare when the light hits them at the wrong angle, an adjustable steering column and, as mentioned before, a rest for his left foot in the somewhat cramped space between the brake pedal and the transmission hump.

The climate control system is extremely effective — once you learn how to use it properly.

On cold nights, the heating/demisting system is not able to keep the Jensen's

MORE ▶

THOROUGHBRED

INTERCEPTOR III:

considerable glass area un-fogged. Bringing the air conditioner into action, however, takes the humidity out of the air and keeps all windows clear. The electric rear window demister is only used during the initial warm up.

One must keep in mind, however, that the four adjustable eyeball vents strung out along the centre of the instrument panel can pass only cold, refrigerated air when the compressor is switched on. Heated, conditioned air is passed into the interior via ducts under the instrument panel.

The Interceptor rates exceptionally well when it comes to driver vision.

The huge rear window drops right down to a level where one can judge the car's rearmost extremities within inches. Blind spots are minimised to as great an extent as possible so the driver has every assistance to preserve the beautifully shaped panels. Even the long nose presents few problems when the car is being inched through close-packed traffic lanes or manoeuvred into tight parking spots.

But above all else, the Jensen is a highway car in the very best tradition.

With its inherent road handling qualities, its easy, relaxed performance and hushed interior, it's the next best thing, for putting away the miles, to flying.

Part of our test comprised a 200-mile trip on both open highways and unsealed secondary roads into Victoria's snow country. In the Interceptor, arriving at our destination was an anti-climax.

Cruising on the Princes highway at legal speeds, the car just loafed along comfortably — only a fraction of its potential being used and almost eerily quiet. Absolutely no wind noise and only a distant thudding from the two giant exhaust pipes as we accelerated past slower traffic.

Onto less well-paved secondary roads and the car sat faithfully on line through every corner, regardless of how rough or corrugated. The steering felt beautifully precise and the car responded in a fashion that made you forget that you were driving such heavyweight machinery.

The braking system behaved as it should on a 140 mph car, bringing the Jensen to seatbelt-straining stops without a waver or any suggestion of lock up — whether it be from 40 or 100 mph.

The overriding impression was one of complete sympathy between car and driver — the car responding to all commands and the driver confident that there were no hidden behaviour quirks to be discovered.

And that's the whole secret of the Interceptor.

It's honest, straightforward design inspires confidence in its durability and one feels that the car is so solid and well put together that he need have no fear of using it. The engine is so under-stressed and flexible that it can slog away at low speeds without overheating, falling off the cam or loading up the carburettor, then open up for a hole-shot down the highway without any suggestion of faltering. The suspension feels almost truck-like in its ability to take punishment, yet provides a comfortable ride in all conditions.

Buying a $20,000 car is one thing. Buying a $20,000 car that you know you can use is another . . .

Below: Interior has the unmistakable tang of real leather; seats are perfectly shaped and superbly comfortable. Note speakers built into doors.

SPECIFICATIONS

CAR FROM: Peter Manton Motors, 683 Elizabeth St., Melbourne.

PRICE AS TESTED: $23,250.
OPTIONS FITTED: Nil.

INSURANCE: NA.

ENGINE

Type	V8 OHV
Bore & stroke	110 mm x 95.3 mm
Capacity	7212 cc
Comp. ratio	8.2:1
Power	325 bhp @4600 rpm
Torque	Not available

TRANSMISSION:

Type: 3 speed automatic with torque convertor

Ratios:

1st	2.44:1
2nd	1.44:1
3rd	1.00:1
Final drive	2.88:1

CHASSIS

Wheelbase	105 inches
Length	188 inches
Track F	56.3 inches
Track R	57.5 inches
Width	69 inches
Height	53 inches
Clearance (minimum)	5.5 inches
Weight	4000 lbs
Fuel capacity	20 gallons

SUSPENSION:
Front: Independent, coil springs.
Rear: Live axle, leaf springs, panhard rod.

BRAKES: Servo assisted, dual circuit.
Front: 11⅜ in. disc.
Rear: 10¾ in. disc.

STEERING: Power assisted.
Rack and pinion 3.5
Turns lock to lock: 38 ft.

WHEELS/ TYRES: Magnesium cast alloy 15" x 7" wheels with ER 70X15 Dunlop aquajet tyres.

★ Australian Associated Motor Insurers Ltd., 365 Little Collins St., Melbourne. Tel. 60 0751.

PERFORMANCE

Zero to

30 mph	2.7 seconds
40 mph	4.0 seconds
50 mph	5.6 seconds
60 mph	7.5 seconds
70 mph	9.7 seconds
80 mph	NA.
90 mph	NA.

Standing quarter mile 15.4 seconds.
Fuel consumption on test 13 mpg on super fuel.
Fuel consumption (expected) 13-18 mpg.
Cruising range approx. 300 miles.
Speedometer error:

Indicated	30	40	50	60	70	80	90	100
Actual	30	39	48	59	67	76	86	95

MAXIMUM SPEEDS IN GEARS:

1st	48 mph
2nd	78 mph
3rd	NA

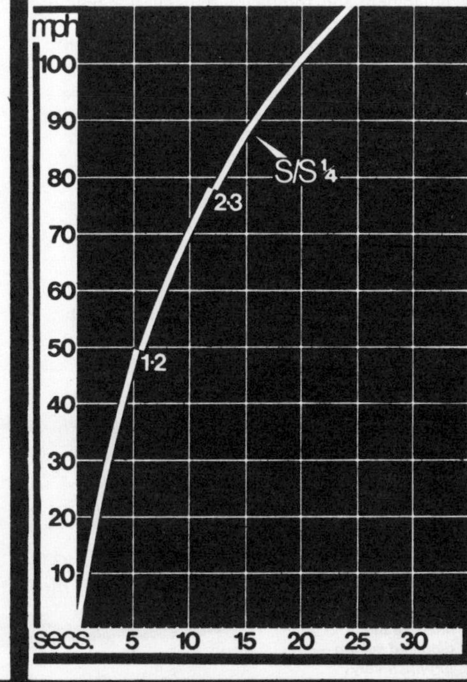

COMMENTS

ENGINE:

Response	Excellent
Vibration	Minimal
Noise	Low

STEERING:

Effort	Light
Road feel	Very Good
Kickback	None

SUSPENSION:

Ride comfort	Firm
Roll resistance	Very Good
Pitch control	Very Good

HANDLING:

Directional control	Excellent
Predictability	Excellent

BRAKES:

Pedal pressure	Medium
Response	Excellent
Fade resistance	Excellent
Directional stability	Excellent

CONTROLS:

Wheel position	Very Good
Pedal position	Good
Gearshift position	Very Good

INTERIOR:

Front seat comfort	Excellent
Front leg room	Very Good
Front head room	Very Good
Rear seat comfort	Very Good
Rear leg room	Poor
Rear head room	Good
Instrument legibility	Very Good

VISION:

Forward	Very Good
Front quarter	Very Good
Rear	Excellent

CONSTRUCTION QUALITY:

Paint	Excellent
Chrome	Excellent
Trim	Excellent

GENERAL:

Headlights — high beam	Very Good
Headlights — low beam	Very Good
Parking/signal lights	Very Good
Wiper coverage	Very Good
Wipers at speed	Very Good
Maintenance accessibility	Fair

The very first Jensen used British Ford parts under a beautiful body style. The latest cars have American Chrysler components, and another beautiful — though Italian styled — body. For 38 years Jensen have relied on other people's mechanical parts but built their own bodies. We chronicle the successes, surprises — and failures too.

A Jensen history

NEARLY 40 YEARS OF EXCLUSIVE SMALL PRODUCTION CARS

by Graham Robson

JENSENS have always been impressive cars. They were always scarce, usually as fast as their competitors, but never achieved the glamour of Ferrari or Aston Martin. Perhaps that's because they never indulged in racing, or never made their own engines and transmission, but at least they have survived. Yet, even after 38 years, their life and times are not as well chronicled as other specialist firms. Apart from the cars, there has usually been other activity in the West Bromwich factory — first on van bodies, and later on sub-contract work for BMC and Rootes — and now the plushy Interceptors and SPs have been joined by the Jensen-Healey. Survival seemed unlikely at times — particularly after the Healey 3000 and Tiger had gone — but after several changes of ownership the company's future looks secure enough.

Until recently, there have been Jensen names in the firm, but its original base can really be traced back to the West Bromwich Carriage Works of 1863. This eventually became W. S. Smith and Sons, who made a good living building commercial and coach bodies. The Jensen brothers — Alan and Richard — joined the company in 1931, took it over in 1934, and produced a prototype Jensen car soon afterwards. There was always a Jensen among the directors until 1967, though financial control had passed into the hands of the Norcros conglomerate in 1959. Norcros put in "company doctor" Carl Duerr in 1968 to sort things out after the loss of the Healey and Tiger business, later selling out to a merchant bank, William Brandt's. Brandt's persevered — with the company making not more than 12 cars a week — until spring 1970, when American Kjell Qvale took a controlling interest, became president, installed Donald Healey as chairman and ex-Rolls-Royce man Alfred Vickers as managing director. At the same time he said that a new sports car would be made, and this was duly announced last year. Qvale, a wealthy sports-car distributor from California, now has complete control at Jensen, and Donald Healey is no longer chairman.

In all these eventful years, Jensens have been body building specialists. Originally that was the West Bromwich plant's trade, though chassis building was added at a later stage. Like many small concerns before them, or since, Jensen have always had to rely on bought-out power trains. The early cars relied on modified versions of the ubiquitous side-valve 3.6-litre Ford V8, while other pre-war examples used V12 Lincoln Zephyrs or straight-eight 4.2 litre Nashes. A 2.2-litre version of the Ford V8 car was shown at Earls Court in 1938, but it is doubtful if any were actually sold.

Car production re-started in 1945, but the true post-war model (aptly coded the PW) came in 1946. This time a special engine was chosen, an ohv 3.9-litre straight-eight designed and built by Henry Meadows, but this only lasted until 1949. Jensen then turned to Longbridge, choosing a 4-litre Austin Sheerline (and Morris Commercial truck) engine which they used until 1962. Ten years ago the American invasion was sweeping Europe, with many small concerns opting for V8 power; Jensen soon joined this fashion, choosing a 5.9-litre Chrysler. Since then the engine has grown a bit, to 7.2 litres, but still arrives from Detroit complete with anti-pollution equipment and Torqueflite transmission bolted onto the back. The 2-litre Jensen-Healey engine comes from Lotus, of course, and will be used by Lotus in their own new car soon.

Jensen strategy now seems clear, with the Jensen-Healey intended to be the volume seller, and the Interceptor as the "flagship". Things have not always been as clear cut as this, as a study of their history shows.

It's important to realize that production has always been low, at first very low. The first 1,000 Jensen cars took 32 years to build — 1935 to 1967 — though the first 1,000 Interceptors of the current shape then took only 33 months. Big Jensens left West Bromwich at a rate of 25 every week in 1972, with 30 a week at the moment. Jensen-Healey production is building up all the time; 50 a week was current late last year, with 110 a week in summer 1973. The highest throughput so far was probably in the mid-sixties, when 160 Austin-Healey 3000s, and 100 Sunbeam Tigers completely overshadowed the tiny output of CV8s.

It all really started in the late 1920s, when the Jensens re-built a 1925 Austin Seven given to them by their parents as a joint birthday present. The new body was strikingly styled and low slung for the time, and attracted the attention of Standard, who invited them to perform similar miracles on a Standard chassis. Standard liked the result, farming it out to Avon Bodies as the Standard Avon; later Alan Jensen (at 20 years old) left his pupil's job at Serck Radiators to join Avon and develop further special styles. Meanwhile Richard Jensen, then 17, stayed with Lucas where he was a trainee, but both of them were, by now, itching to strike out on their own.

Their artistic reputation with these early cars eventually helped them both to join the West Bromwich coachbuilding company of W. S. Smith and Sons in 1931, and it took only three years before they took financial control of the company. Almost at once they began to build the very first car to be called Jensen;

Right: From 1946 to 1949 Jensen tried to get a Meadows-engined car into production, but eventually substituted an Austin Princess engine instead. This was the massive but dignified saloon — of which very few remain

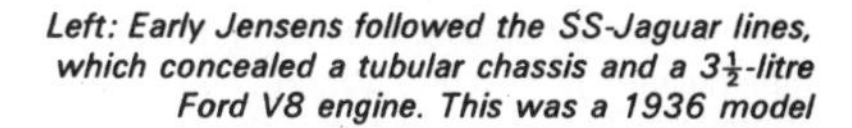

Left: Early Jensens followed the SS-Jaguar lines, which concealed a tubular chassis and a 3½-litre Ford V8 engine. This was a 1936 model

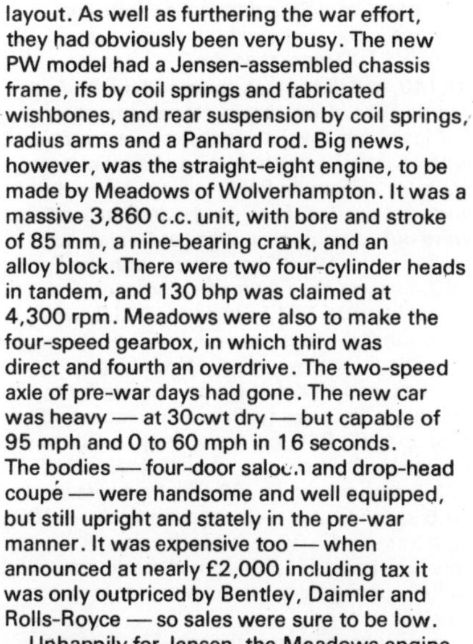

Below left: The Interceptor, first shown in 1966, was the first Jensen not styled by the Jensen family. Vignale did the job and made the tools — seven years later the car is as popular as ever and selling at the rate of 30 cars every week

meanwhile bodies for commercial vehicles and coaches, and other sub-contract work, continued unabated.

The prototype chassis were Jensen-designed, but made by Rubery Owen. Where and how to obtain suitable power trains was a big worry at first, but Lord Brabazon eventually used his influence to bring the Jensens together with Edsel Ford. Ford eventually allowed them to use the 3.6-litre side-valve V8 engine and gearbox that was just starting production at Dagenham. The prototypes were beautifully styled — perhaps finer than the Derby-built Bentleys which had just appeared or the Jaguar SS100s which followed — but production cars were toned down somewhat and were very much in the mainstream of styling practice. One interesting feature was the overdrive axle, which could be brought in, or cut out, by a pre-selector and movement of the clutch pedal; this was intended as a pure overdrive, with effective axle ratio jumping from 4.11 to 2.9, but could be used on all gears and gave, with a bit of juggling, a six-speed gearbox. Overdrive gearing was very high — 32 mph per 1,000 rpm — so acceleration was negligible, even though the Ford engine was extensively modified. Maximum speed was over 80 mph, and with acceleration to 60 mph in only 20 seconds the car was no sluggard. Then, as now, equipment was lavish, with built-in jacks, adjustable dampers and a radio; the cost of the four-door saloon was £695 — competitive with the Alvis Speed 25, Brough Superior, Talbot 3½-litre and Railtons.

Early cars were all individually built, being either four-door saloons, four-seater tourers or drop head coupés; there was no two-seater.

It didn't take long for the few, and selective, Jensen customers to indicate that Ford V8 power wasn't all that they wanted, so the next production cars used the same basic chassis, but adopted a more powerful straight-eight Nash engine and transmission. Some 120 bhp at 3,500 rpm was guaranteed to improve the performance, while independent front suspension by a transverse leaf spring improved the ride, if not the roadholding. Maximum speed went up to nearly 90 mph, quite enough to be competitive. The rear suspension was modified to coil springs in 1939, and the V8-engined version dropped.

The war-time hiatus was spent making aircraft components, bombs and special versions of armoured vehicles for amphibious landings.

A few cars to the pre-war HC design were assembled as soon as possible in 1945, but the Jensens were more interested in their post-war layout. As well as furthering the war effort, they had obviously been very busy. The new PW model had a Jensen-assembled chassis frame, ifs by coil springs and fabricated wishbones, and rear suspension by coil springs, radius arms and a Panhard rod. Big news, however, was the straight-eight engine, to be made by Meadows of Wolverhampton. It was a massive 3,860 c.c. unit, with bore and stroke of 85 mm, a nine-bearing crank, and an alloy block. There were two four-cylinder heads in tandem, and 130 bhp was claimed at 4,300 rpm. Meadows were also to make the four-speed gearbox, in which third was direct and fourth an overdrive. The two-speed axle of pre-war days had gone. The new car was heavy — at 30cwt dry — but capable of 95 mph and 0 to 60 mph in 16 seconds. The bodies — four-door saloon and drop-head coupé — were handsome and well equipped, but still upright and stately in the pre-war manner. It was expensive too — when announced at nearly £2,000 including tax it was only outpriced by Bentley, Daimler and Rolls-Royce — so sales were sure to be low.

Unhappily for Jensen, the Meadows engine never worked out, because Meadows were simply not interested in supplying tiny quantities of expensive engines and also because they could not sell the design to any other concern. By 1949, with very few examples built, Jensen and Meadows had decided to pack it in, so Jensen had to find alternative sources, and quickly! An alliance was struck, just down the road at Longbridge with Austin, which was to last for 13 years. A 4-litre six-cylinder engine already fitted to the A125 and A135 Sheerlines (and Morris Commercial trucks too!) was suitable, and when tuned to 130 bhp equalled the Meadows unit's performance.

Most important in 1949, though, was the decision to move away from town carriages to sporting vehicles. First evidence of this was the Interceptor cabriolet, followed later by the hardtop version. Compared with the 4-litre saloon it had a 12in. shorter wheelbase, narrow tracks and much less passenger space. Half-elliptic springs replaced coils in the rear suspension. It was heavy, but quick — 29cwt of car could be hauled up to 60 mph in less than 14 seconds, and on to a 102 mph maximum. Fuel economy was often 24 mpg, perhaps even more with the optional overdrive.

It's worth remembering that the Austin A40 Sports of the same period looked very similar to the Interceptor — probably because both bodies were styled and erected by Jensen!

It wasn't until 1953 that the next sporting model appeared — and it certainly caused a stir. The 541, as it was christened, used existing Jensen mechanicals in a yet shorter wheelbase (8ft 9in.), with narrower tracks, but had a sleekly windcheating fastback body described as a two / four seater saloon; in fact there was much more rear seat space than in the Astons and Jaguars of the day. The combined bonnet and wings hinged upwards from the scuttle (incidentally pre-dating the Austin-Healey Sprite by five years), and a blanking panel in the nose could be swivelled to regulate airflow into the radiator. Prototype shells were in aluminium, but the car was tooled in glassfibre — a material Jensen were to stay with until 1966.

Left: When the Qvale-Healey consortium took over in 1970 they set about designing a quantity-production sports car. The Jensen-Healey arrived in 1972, and more than 100 a week are being made, mainly for U.S. This is the 1974 version

Overdrive was optional, and the most powerful engine developed 140 bhp. When *The Autocar* eventually tested a 541, in 1955, they recorded a maximum of no less than 112 mph in overdrive, acceleration to 60 mph in 12.1 seconds, and overall fuel consumption of 20 mpg. Caustic comments were made about slow gearbox synchro-mesh and poor rear wheel adhesion; but nevertheless the testers thought it " . . . a thoroughly desirable car, combining the comfort of a luxury touring saloon with many of the virtues of high performance sports car practice". The price, without extras, was £1,822 — only £100 more than the 2+2 Jaguar XK140, and very much cheaper than the Aston Martin DB2/4 which was also a competitor.

Meanwhile the Jensen factory was crammed with chassis/body production of Austin-Healey 100s for delivery to BMC, so large 541 sales were not needed. Even so, the Jensen brothers were not content, giving the car Dunlop disc brakes at the 1956 Show; along with the Triumph TR3, this was the first road car so equipped. A year later the 541 became the 541R, which meant that the most powerful DS7 Austin engine was fitted, there was a new Moss (Jaguar-type) gearbox, and rack-and-pinion steering for the first time. The price (with overdrive standard) shot up to £2,866, but fortunately so did the performance. The new car, when tested, recorded 123.5 mph maximum, 60 mph from rest in 10.6 seconds, and — more remarkably — 100 mph from rest in 30 seconds. It was still very high geared (4,100 rpm at maximum speed) so fuel consumption stayed reasonable at 18 mpg.

It must have been in the mid-50s that the Jensen brothers' styling touch started to desert them. Each succeeding version of the 541 shell was less attractive, and in the end an all-new car had to be styled by Vignale. Certainly the 1960 541S was a step back from the 541R, probably because a wider body was achieved simply by splitting the chassis and body tooling and adding four inches down the middle. The front track, however, only increased by 2.75in., because obsolete Austin A95 bits were replaced by A99 components. The other innovation was standardization of Rolls-Royce automatic transmission, though the older manual box could still be ordered. Among the styling changes were a conventional grille in place of the swivelling panel, and a new facia. The fact that the DS7 engine had been dropped was not publicized, because Jensen had stopped quoting power figures. The Austin engine used was much less powerful than before, this and automatic transmission losses dragging down maximum speed to 108 mph, and putting up fuel consumption to 15.5 mpg. The price was up too — £3,196 with automatic.

Meanwhile, the company's energies were turning to more important things, for they undertook final assembly of the new Volvo P1800 sports car from 1961 to 1964. This was a unique Anglo-Swedish venture, where Pressed Steel in Scotland (now Chrysler's body factory) built bodyshells, Volvo supplied mechanical parts, and Jensen did the rest. It was a satisfactory deal, beset apparently by some quality problems, which Volvo finally terminated by taking back assembly themselves for 1964.

By 1962, the reduced performance and eccentric styling of the 541S was causing customer resistance, and drastic action was needed. Jensen, like Bristol at about the same time, looked across the Atlantic for more power, and slotted a 5.9-litre V8 Chrysler engine and transmission into a much-modified structure and body. The re-styled body, compared with early 541s (and those luscious prototypes of 1934) was a beast, for it had grown a slant-eyed four-headlamp arrangement, notch-back roof style, and more slots and bulges than ever before. Living space

A Jensen history . . .

The Jensen family tree

Years Produced	Model	Description	Engine/transmission
1935-39	S	4-seater saloon, drophead coupe, tourer, hard-top coupe. Wheelbase 126in.	Ford 3.6-litre V8 + Lincoln V12 to special order
1938-39 & '45-46	H and HC	Bodies as above Wheelbase 131in.	Nash 4.2-litre Straight-8
1946-49	PW	4-door saloon and drophead coupé Wheelbase 126in.	Meadows 3.9-litre Straight-8
1949-52	4-litre	4-door saloon and drophead coupé Wheelbase 126in.	Austin 4-litre 6-cylinder and gearbox
1949-58	Interceptor	2-door convertible and (from 1951) hard-top. Wheelbase 114in.	Austin 4-litre 6-cylinder and gearbox
1953-59	541	2-door hardtop Wheelbase 105in.	Austin 4-litre 6-cylinder and gearbox
1957-60	541R	2-door hardtop Wheelbase 105in.	Austin 4-litre DS7 6-cylinder, and Moss gearbox
1960-62	541S	2-door hardtop Wheelbase 105in.	Austin 4-litre 6-cylinder, and Rolls-Royce automatic transmission
1962-66	CV8	2-door saloon Wheelbase 105in.	Chrysler 5.9-litre V8 and automatic transmission (6.3 litres from 1964)
1965	FF	CV8 saloon shape, prototype only Wheelbase 109in.	Chrysler 6.3-litre V8 and automatic, and 4-wheel-drive
1965	Interceptor	Prototype 4-seater tourer. 102in. Wheelbase. Prototype only	Chrysler 4.5-litre V8, and automatic
1966-71	FF Marks I, II and III	Vignale-style 2-door saloon body. Wheelbases 109in.	Chrysler 6.3-litre V8, automatic, and Ferguson 4-wheel-drive
1966 to date	Interceptor, Marks I, II and III	Vignale-style 2-door saloon body. Wheelbase 105in.	Chrysler 6.3-litre V8, and automatic (7.2-litres from end 1972)
1971 to date	SP	Vignale Interceptor body. Wheelbase 105in.	Chrysler "Six-pack" 7.2-litre V8 and automatic

NB: Alongside Jensen car production, body construction and/or final assembly has taken place for several volume production cars including:

1960-63	Volvo P1800	2-door coupé, body built initially by Pressed Steel, Scotland, and final assembly at Jensen. Production transferred to Sweden during 1964
1953-67	Austin Healey 100/100-6/3000	2 or 2/4 seat open sports car. Bodies and chassis built at Jensen, then sent to Longbridge or Abingdon for final assembly. Production ceased at end of 1967
1964-67	Sunbeam Tiger Marks I and II	2-seater open sports car. Bodies converted from Alpine specification, followed by final assembly. Production ceased at end 1967
1972-	Jensen-Healey	2-seater open sports car. Complete assembly at Jensen. Production began mid-1972

In addition body construction has been carried out for cars as varied as the Austin A40 Sports of the early '50s, Lea Francis (1940s) and the Invicta Black Prince (1940s).

Above: In 1960 the 541 grew corpulent — the body being widened, and Rolls-Royce automatic transmission standardized. This was known as the 541S

Right: The nose of the original 541 had a movable flap over the radiator, which could be left closed in normal motoring without adverse effect on the cooling

Below: Jensen bravely introduced the world's first four-wheel-drive production car — the FF — in 1966. It used the Ferguson Formula layout, yet the basic chassis and styling was identical with other Jensens. The engine unit is a 6.3-litre Chrysler Vee-8

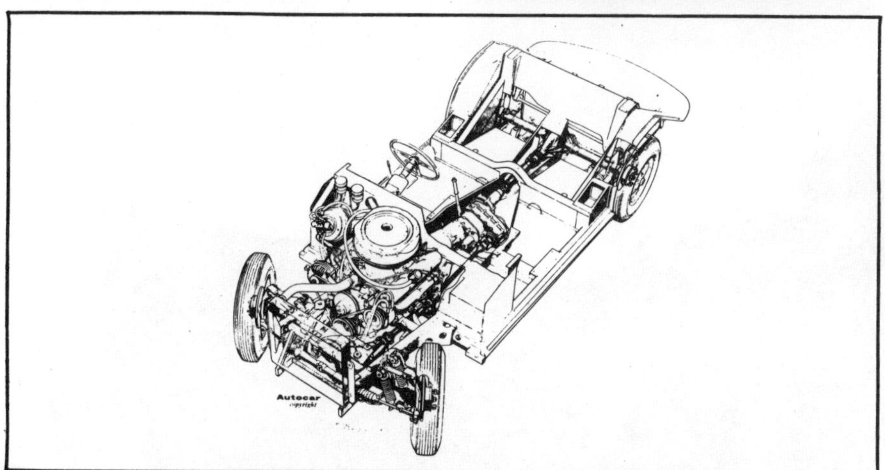

was not improved, and the driver was faced by a huge 18.25in. steering wheel. Chassis development had improved the balance and the new car's road behaviour was excellent. Power steering was needed, but no one had yet invented assistance for a rack and pinion.

With 305 gross bhp on command, the new CV8, as it was called, was sure to be ferociously rapid. *The Autocar* testers clocked a 131.5 mph maximum, acceleration to 60 mph in 8.4 seconds, and to 100 mph in only 22.4 seconds. Fuel consumption had risen to 14.4 mpg overall, perhaps reasonable in view of the performance and engine size. But the testers didn't like the styling, prefacing their test with the remark that "... it seems only fair to Jensen chassis engineers to suggest that the CV8 is less distinguished in appearance than in behaviour ...". Certainly, at £3,392, the customer could demand more, especially as this new price was within £120 of the Aston Martin DB4, and more than twice that of a Jaguar 3.8 Mk II saloon.

A few details were smoothed out in 1963, and in 1964 the engine size crept up to 6.3-litres, but by now Jensen were interested in new and exciting engineering. An unofficial statement at the 1964 Show suggested that Jensen were working with Ferguson on four-wheel-drive cars, but nothing more was said. Meanwhile the building of Healey 3000s was joined by Sunbeam Tiger production, and the only further attention given to the CV8 was in 1965, when a few more rough edges were smoothed off and the windscreen enlarged. The price, too, was enlarged — to £3,679.

Later in 1965 the secret was out — Jensen, through chief engineer Kevin Beattie, had been working with Ferguson, and the result was the prototype FF, based on the CV8. A four-wheel-drive system meant a 4in. longer wheelbase so that the front differential could live ahead of the engine, and completely new front suspension to accommodate drive shafts. The chassis was basically unchanged (incidentally, continuing to use the tubular side-members as vacuum reservoirs for the brakes) though power-assisted rack and pinion was fitted. Full anti-skid Maxaret braking was specified. The car was given a price — £5,249 — but imminent policy changes were to stop this particular car.

Another blind-alley pursued at the same time was a new convertible, confusingly called the Interceptor, with 4.5-litre Chrysler engine, de Dion rear suspension, and an aluminium body. It was provisionally priced at £2,394 — which would surely have been a loss-maker — and never got further than the first prototype.

However, it was now clear that radical styling changes were needed; further, tooling would have to be finished before the following winter. This could only be achieved by going to Italy, and after a brisk survey of the offerings, the Vignale style (tooled by Superleggera-Touring) was chosen. In October 1966 the car was announced, with Italian-built shells delivered to West Bromwich soon afterwards. Tooling then transferred to Jensen, where body erection has proceeded ever since. The new body style was undoubtedly sleek and attractive, with a two-door saloon shape and a huge opening rear window/boot lid. Panelling was in aluminium and steel, the only real difference between two- and four-wheel-drive cars being 4in. between front wheels and scuttle; the twin air outlet grilles on the flanks of the FF, compared with one on the Interceptor, was the recognition point.

Chassis changes were minimal. The CV8 became the Interceptor, the FF having the chassis shown previously as a prototype. Prices on announcement were £3,743 and £5,340 respectively, although these have increased with monotonous regularity in the past six years.

Interceptor production got under way quickly, but FFs, virtually hand built then (as they were to remain), took time. Later Jensen developments are basically financial and commercial, as the Interceptor has soldiered on to Mk II and Mk III guises, culminating in the release of the "hotter" 7.2-litre SP version in 1971, and standardization of the basic 7.2-litre engine a few months ago. FF production was never more than two cars a week, and closed down in December 1971 after 387 cars had been built. Apart from the cost premium — FFs cost £1,095 more than Interceptors at the end — there were ticklish adjustments to be made to every car before it could be released, and the effort was hardly worthwhile. One feature of the car — Maxaret anti-skid braking — was no better than conventional systems when used by skilled drivers, and was never fully appreciated by the Jensen clientele.

The Interceptor became Mk II in 1969, when revised front suspension, new facia styling optional air conditioning and — at last — radial ply tyres plus power-assisted steering were added. The price leapt again — to £5,838. Performance was more than adequate, with a top speed of 137 mph and 14 mpg available. A Mk III followed in 1971, due to the inclusion of cast-alloy wheels, ventilated discs, and yet more engine modifications to suit American emission requirements. The SP variant arrived at the same time.

But somehow, the beautiful Interceptors have always been overshadowed by financial problems. When the Healey 3000 was killed by American safety regulations, and the Ford-engined Sunbeam Tiger by Chrysler, Jensen were suddenly down to 12 cars a week to keep them solvent. Carl Duerr was brought in by Norcros to sort things out, but they tired of the problem and sold out in 1968. Production crept up to a maximum of 20 cars a week, before the demise of Austin-Healeys at BLMC allowed Donald Healey, Kjell Qvale and Jensen to get together. The Jensen-Healey, which takes no part in this story, was the eventual result, and production is now building up so strongly to make it seem safe for the big-engined cars to carry on. At a selling-price of £6,744 the Interceptor buying queue is never likely to be long.

Perhaps, like the dinosaurs, the Interceptor will find the future climate unfriendly, and become extinct. Perhaps there will be son-of-Interceptor one day, cheaper, smaller and more suited to more people's pockets. One thing seems certain; with 38 years of sometimes precarious existence behind it, the Jensen name ought to be with us for many more years. □

BY JENSEN TO FRANKFURT

How we travelled to this season's first motor show

by Geoffrey Howard

WHEN IT COMES to making a trip across Europe these days, few methods of travel are more exhilarating than a fast car. Jet planes are pretty commonplace, and what with all the messing about at airports, air traffic delays and the cost of taxis at the other end, there is a lot in favour of the private car—and few can be better suited to a "Grand Tour" than the Jensen Interceptor. So when it came to choosing our transport to last month's Frankfurt Show, I hesitated no more than two seconds before accepting the offer of the latest Series III model.

I somehow thought that this car was big enough to take four of us plus luggage, and it might have—just—if I had remembered to warn the others to travel light. As it happened we met hurriedly at Dover with very little preparation and one man short due to unavoidable work problems at the office. Three suitcases, two typewriters, a professional tripod, flashgun and a briefcase filled the boot. Peter Cramer's Hasselblad case just fitted in the spare back seat.

We crossed the Channel on a fully-laden Seaspeed hovercraft in 50 min, arriving at Boulogne just before noon. For the fastest route to Frankfurt we would have done better to arrive at Calais and head for the motorway from Ostend to Brussels, but that route out of Dover had been fully booked. With time on our side we decided to head due east to St. Omer, then to Lille and Brussels.

Before long we all felt the effects of an early breakfast and nothing *en route*, so we started looking for somewhere to eat. As is the way in France, an inviting sign for a *Relais* appeared immediately and we duly turned off the main road following the directions it gave.

We threaded our way through a small village and under an arch to find a typical French country-house restaurant where the rough *pâté* came free "with the compliments of the house" and the choice of main course (escallop of veal braised with cheese and ham in a mustard sauce) was a *fait accompli*. We better than we expected and paid £10 for three, all-found.

The Interceptor outside the Hotel du Grand Cerf at Spa in Belgium, where we spent a very tranquil night and ate delicious fresh partridge

With half the afternoon gone, we set off again with a strong determination to reach Germany that night. We were soon on an excellent motorway to Lille, cruising at a steady 110–120 mph and covering the ground very fast indeed. Lille passed as we swept on towards Brussels, but then suddenly the motorway ended and we were stuck in the evening rush-hour traffic. We asked directions from the driver of an adjacent car and he volunteered to lead us to the E5. Within 20 minutes we were headed for Liège at 120 mph again, but as the fuel gauge visibly dropped towards zero we were eventually forced to turn off and look for a filling station. There are no signs for the service areas on the E5 from Brussels to Liège until you get within 3 km. We found a welcome Shell sign in a village and replenished the tank with great relief all round.

It was already getting dusk as we skirted Liège and decided to stop the night at Spa. This home of the Belgian Grand Prix and other important motor races is but 15 minutes from the main motorway system into Germany and well worth a visit if your journey brings you to this region at lunch or dinner time. We chose the *Hotel du Grand Cerf* on the hill up towards the circuit. The *patron* served us with delicious fresh partridge, after which we slept well.

The next day we rejoined the E5, turned south-east at Cologne and turned off the *autobahn* just after Koblenz to Montabaur. With a couple of hours in hand we decided to run down the Riesling route on the east bank of the Rhine. After the deep green forests around Bad Ems we broke out to join the Rhine at Lahnstein. Mediaeval castles sprouted from almost every hill top as the river twisted and turned, sometimes dividing into two before sweeping down another straight reach. Each little village struck memories of a bottle of white wine, an evening in good company, a picturesque label or just a fruity taste. After the rocks of Loreley where, as legend has it, the maidens lured the sailors to their death we spotted the steep slopes of Liebfrauen on the opposite bank and passed the fairytale island castle at Kaub.

On the hills south-east of here the grapes for the many Rheingau wines are grown and although we would have liked to stay longer and take the signposted route away from the river, business in Frankfurt was our prime objective and time was running out. We took the *autobahn* to Wiesbaden and on to Frankfurt.

As we had expected, the Jensen proved an admirable choice for this journey, having the potential to stack 100 motorway miles easily into each hour and doing it with such contemptuous ease. With air-conditioning and tinted glass we were able to shut out all trace of wind noise and avoid buffetting—particularly unpleasant for the chap in the back. Our only criticism of this excellent system was that the fan had to be switched on to get

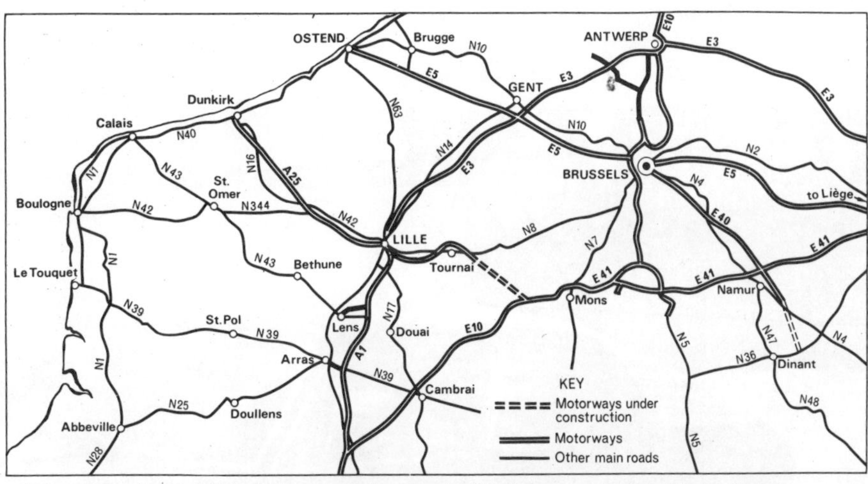

Although we had published this map twice already (18 January and 19 July), we forgot to take it with us and did not realise how near we were to the Mons motorway, now open right through to Lille, which would have avoided our time-wasting diversion to Brussels

sufficient flow, and even on its slowest setting it was noisy enough to be annoying. Stability was very good up to 120 mph, but above this speed with three-up, a full boot and a load of fuel on board it seemed to get light at the front end. The addition of a fashionable "bib" spoiler would probably improve this no end.

Overall for a return journey of 1,160 miles the car used 92.2 gallons of regular 2-star fuel, giving a consumption of 12.6 mpg. With such astronomical costs for the British traveller throughout Germany, the saving achieved by this modest octane requirement is very worthwhile.

On the way back from the Show there was more urgency to our pace, so we kept to the motorways all the way, heading round Brussels to Ghent for an overnight stop after leaving Frankfurt in the late afternoon. With more determined drivers behind the wheel we could have covered much greater distances in quicker times, but we wanted to make this a journey in the grand style without the stress of too many hours at the wheel and with time to pause here and there to enjoy the view. That's where a car with a big, lazy American engine sets you in the right frame of mind. You don't have to be keyed-up at fever pitch to overtake at the first opportunity; anytime you are ready, the car will hurtle past with a hard shove in the back and in no time at all.

Driving a car like the Jensen around the UK one often wonders what the point is of all that power. As soon as you get across the water and shed the speed limits, it really comes into its own and makes the greatest sense in the world. This is what motoring is all about. □

Right: On the banks of the Rhine with the Riesling vines growing opposite, the author gets back behind the wheel for another stage in the riverside tour

PHOTOS BY JOE RUSZ

JENSEN INTERCEPTOR III

It now ranks among the world's best cars

IN 1931 THE two Jensen brothers Richard and Alan joined W. J. Smith Ltd, a coachbuilder in Britain, and within three years they had taken over the company and given it their name. Their first production car, the S-Type, appeared in 1935 and was a big open touring car with a V-8 engine.

Jensens have been available in the U.S. sporadically during the 26 years R&T has been published, but the purchase of Jensen Motors Ltd by the pioneer car importer Kjell Qvale brought the marque firmly back to the U.S. market with new financial backing and considerable sophistication about what is needed to entice well-heeled Americans into an unusual imported car. Qvale's takeover has worked wonders for Jensen Motors and improved the Jensen Interceptor considerably. When Qvale purchased the company it was building seven to nine of the Interceptor and its 4-wheel-drive variant the FF per week; now the FF is gone and Jensen is building about 30 Interceptors a week, about half of which are exported to the U.S. Jensen also created a new make, the Jensen-Healey, and this open sports car in the $5500 class is being produced at the rate of about 130 a week.

Qvale must have known that in the Jensen Interceptor he had a car basically well suited to the American prestige market—a large, heavy GT coupe with smooth styling and a practical, powerful American V-8 engine coupled with an excellent American automatic transmission. With this base it was mainly a matter of improving certain details of the car and getting the company ready to produce more of them as he developed the demand for them.

We tested the Interceptor II, the version current at the time of the takeover, when Qvale began importing them here in early 1971 and found it an altogether pleasant car: something like a Thunderbird, we thought, but more compact, more tastefully styled and, totally unlike the Ford product, a serious road car. We found fault with its utilization of space; Jensen placed the big Chrysler engine well back in the chassis for good weight distribution and this left a very small rear seating space in a rather large car. And there were some flaws in detail design like heat from the engine getting into the interior, some old-fashioned and not very durable upholstery work around the dash, look-alike switches for most controls, and considerable torque-steer under acceleration.

In the 2½ years since we tested the II the big Interceptor has become the III, showing several changes ordered by Qvale to improve its appearance as well as some significant mechanical alterations. The 6-in.-wide styled steel wheels have been replaced by 7-in.-wide cast alloy ones that look much better, the leather interior has been redesigned and the seatbelts have been improved. On the mechanical side the 383-cu-in. Chrysler engine has been replaced by a low-compression 440-cu-in. unit that develops less power (no surprise these days), ventilated discs have replaced the solid disc brakes and both the air conditioning and engine cooling have been improved.

The effect of all this, if our Interceptor III test car was an

indication of what's coming off the Jensen assembly line these days, is a good car perfected. Nearly all the positive qualities we noted in that 1971 test are still there, most of the negative ones have been eliminated or minimized and despite the greater quantity of production at Jensen the assembly quality and finish are even better.

We usually take a skeptical view of the term "handmade" in that it doesn't always mean high quality. In the Interceptor III it most emphatically does. We were impressed by the smoothness of the bodywork, in which seams where various panels join each other are filled and smoothed before painting, and the quality of the paintwork. Likewise the interior, which is almost entirely done in supple leather, is fitted and finished beautifully and any trace of shabbiness we found in the Interceptor II is gone. There are no body rattles on rough roads, although there was a slight wind leak around the driver's door in the test car. The standard equipment is such that those who delight in ordering "all the extras" will be frustrated: an elaborate AM/FM-stereo-tape (8-track) system; most of the power assists Americans expect in a luxury car; remote outside mirror adjustment, a rarity on imported cars; air conditioning; and delightful little touches like a hardbound (and very detailed) owner's manual, white gloves in the toolkit for dignified tire changes, a time-delay switch that leaves the interior lights on for a few seconds after you get in or out of the car, and a console pushbutton for the fuel filler door.

Naturally the front seatbacks are adjustable for angle, and the steering column telescopes for additional accommodation of differing physiques. The front seats have been re-contoured in the III and are altogether more comfortable now. The rear seating is still extremely tight, but if the front seats are halfway forward or more rear passengers of moderate size can make themselves comfortable. Instrumentation is complete and nicely arranged for reading, but the Jensen lacks some of the better control ideas of contemporary cars like a steering-column wiper and washer switch. In all the Interceptor is a very comfortable car for two long-distance travelers–its interior noise level at highway speeds is as low as that of any GT car we've tested–and can take four people short distances in reasonable comfort: in other words, a true 2+2, albeit a rather large one.

Though the Interceptor is a fairly large, heavy car and one that sounds and performs pretty much like an American car, it lacks the cumbersome feel of a domestic luxury barge in traffic. The power steering is quick and has good feel, the front body corners are well defined and vision to the rear is reasonably good. On the road, straight or winding, the Interceptor is a car that's at ease going fast. If the winding road is smooth one finds stable, near-neutral response to the steering wheel; that torque-steer problem of the Interceptor II test car wasn't evident in this car. Our III had Dunlop SP tires rather than the Pirelli Cinturatos of the 1971 car and they neither respond as well as the Pirellis nor give the Jensen as much cornering power. These are the same tires Dunlop developed for the Jaguar XJ and it may be that they were designed for vari-

able-ratio steering; the Jensen doesn't have this and the Dunlops' response to steering inputs is decidedly squishy.

The Jensen's one serious deficiency emerges when it's driven with a full passenger load or cornered briskly on an uneven road surface. There's not much room for the live rear axle to move up and down, so it's snubbed quickly and sharply on bumps under either of these conditions. The result is a poor ride when it's loaded, or skittery cornering on rough surfaces. We're sure the Interceptor would benefit from irs.

Other elements of the Interceptor's road behavior are better. Braking dive is at a minimum, the pedal effort required for braking is now just right (it was too light in the II), the brakes pull evenly in normal-to-hard use and there's very little squeal from the discs and pads. On an anchors-out stop we got some locking at the rear wheels, though, so it took conscious modulation of the pedal to get the Interceptor stopped within 300 ft from 80 mph. Interestingly, the fade indicated by our 6-stop brake fade test is almost exactly what it was with the II despite the change to vented discs.

Engine performance with the low-compression 440 engine isn't what it used to be with the high-compression 383; in fact we were surprised at just how much it has dropped since our 1971 test. That car did 0-60 mph in 7.4 sec and the standing ¼ mile in 16.0; the current Interceptor takes over 10 sec to get to 60 and over 17 sec to cover the ¼ mi. But the III runs smoothly; we couldn't detect any hesitation or surge in normal driving, and that's rare these days. Cold starts were something else, however—it took 10-15 pumps of the accelerator pedal to get the III going in the morning. Fuel consumption was little heavier for the III than for the II, probably because the engine engineers decided not to try to maintain performance, but it's still heavy and could be a serious problem in the period of gasoline shortage just ahead.

The Chrysler automatic transmission is a near-perfect adjunct to the huge V-8 engine; it simply lets the engine get on with its smooth, unfussy delivery of torque and all the driver needs to do is mash the pedal and go. If one wants to downshift manually for braking or cornering the Chrysler automatic doesn't respond as quickly as, say, the Mercedes 3-speed automatic; otherwise it's a wholly satisfactory piece of machinery.

The stereo system installed in our test car wasn't the normal Jensen equipment, which is a super-elaborate Learjet affair; rather, this car had a Boman system the Jensen people were testing. It had provision for simulated quadraphonic sound on the FM stereo band and this certainly surrounded us with good sound when the broadcasting station was strong and included the quadraphonic signal. Reception on weaker stations, however, wasn't very good. It's likely that this or some other system will be used in future Interceptors as the Learjet system seems to be going out of production.

We think Jensen has a unique and highly attractive car in the Interceptor, if only the owner can find enough fuel to keep it going. It's put together about as well as any car we've ever tested and its virtues include comfort, reasonably good handling and braking, automation, adequate performance and the sort of detail finish that can give an affluent, demanding car enthusiast lasting pleasure. All things considered, the Jensen Interceptor III ranks among the world's best cars.

PRICE

List price, west coast	$15,500
Price as tested, west coast	$15,750

Price as tested includes std equip (auto trans, air cond, power steering, stereo system, elec windows, lim-slip diff, etc), dealer prep ($250)

IMPORTER

Jensen Motors Inc.
1200 Van Ness Ave
San Francisco, Calif. 94109

GENERAL

Curb weight, lb	4020
Test weight	4340
Weight distribution (with driver), front/rear, %	50/50
Wheelbase, in.	105.0
Track, front/rear	56.1/56.9
Length	186.0
Width	69.0
Height	53.0
Ground clearance	5.0
Overhang, front/rear	32.0/49.0
Usable trunk space, cu ft	16.0
Fuel capacity, U.S. gal.	24.0

ENGINE

Type	ohv V-8
Bore x stroke, mm	109.7 x 95.3
Equivalent in.	4.32 x 3.75
Displacement, cc/cu in.	7212/440
Compression ratio	8.2:1
Bhp @ rpm, net	220 @ 3600
Equivalent mph	96
Torque @ rpm, lb-ft	350 @ 2400
Equivalent mph	64
Carburetion	one Holley 4V
Fuel requirement	regular, 91-oct
Emissions, gram/mile:	
Hydrocarbons	3.0
Carbon Monoxide	32
Nitrogen Oxides	2.6

DRIVE TRAIN

Transmission	automatic; torque converter with 3-sp planetary gearbox
Gear ratios: 3rd (1.00)	2.88:1
2nd (1.45)	4.17:1
1st (2.45)	7.05:1
1st (2.45 x 2.0)	14.10:1
Final drive ratio	2.88:1

CHASSIS & BODY

Layout	front engine/rear drive
Body/frame	tube frame with integral steel body
Brake system	10.8-in. vented disc front & rear, vacuum assisted
Swept area, sq in.	417
Wheels	cast alloy, 15 x 7
Tires	Dunlop SP 205/70 VR-15
Steering type	rack & pinion, power assisted
Overall ratio	17.1:1
Turns, lock-to-lock	3.4
Turning circle, ft	38.0
Front suspension	unequal-length A-arms, coil springs, tube shocks, anti-roll bar
Rear suspension	live axle on leaf springs, Panhard rod, tube shocks

INSTRUMENTATION

Instruments: 160-mph speedo, 6000-rpm tach, 99,999 odo, 999.9 trip odo, oil press, coolant temp, ammeter, fuel level, clock

Warning lights: oil press, brake system, hand brake, alternator, low fuel, rear window heat, seatbelts, high beam, directionals

ACCOMMODATION

Seating capacity, persons	2+2
Seat width, f/r	2x19.0/2x16.0
Head room, f/r	37.5/35.0
Seat back adjustment, deg	45

MAINTENANCE

Service intervals, mi:	
Oil change	6000
Filter change	6000
Chassis lube	4000
Tuneup	12,000
Sparkplugs	18,000
Warranty, mo/mi	12/12,000

CALCULATED DATA

Lb/bhp (test weight)	19.7
Mph/1000 rpm (3rd gear)	26.6
Engine revs/mi (60 mph)	2250
Piston travel, ft/mi	1405
R&T steering index	1.29
Brake swept area, sq in./ton	193

ROAD TEST RESULTS

ACCELERATION

Time to distance, sec:	
0-100 ft	3.7
0-500 ft	9.3
0-1320 ft (¼ mi)	17.3
Speed at end of ¼ mi, mph	78
Time to speed, sec:	
0-30 mph	3.8
0-40 mph	5.4
0-50 mph	7.6
0-60 mph	10.4
0-70 mph	13.6
0-80 mph	18.0
0-100 mph	31.8

SPEEDS IN GEARS

3rd gear (5100)	133
2nd (4500)	83
1st (4500)	50

FUEL ECONOMY

Normal driving, mpg	11.5
Cruising range, mi (1-gal. res.)	265

HANDLING

Speed on 100-ft radius, mph	32.7
Lateral acceleration, g	0.714

BRAKES

Minimum stopping distances, ft:	
From 60 mph	158
From 80 mph	300
Control in panic stop	fair
Pedal effort for 0.5g stop, lb	30
Fade: percent increase in pedal effort to maintain 0.5g deceleration in 6 stops from 60 mph	26
Parking: hold 30% grade?	no
Overall brake rating	good

INTERIOR NOISE

All noise readings in dBA:	
Idle in neutral	65
Maximum, 1st gear	79
Constant 30 mph	65
50 mph	72
70 mph	73
90 mph	76

SPEEDOMETER ERROR

30 mph indicated is actually	33.0
50 mph	53.0
60 mph	64.0
70 mph	74.0
80 mph	84.0
Odometer, 10.0 mi	10.2

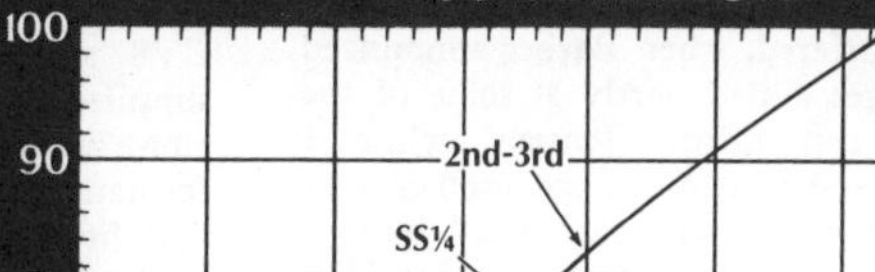

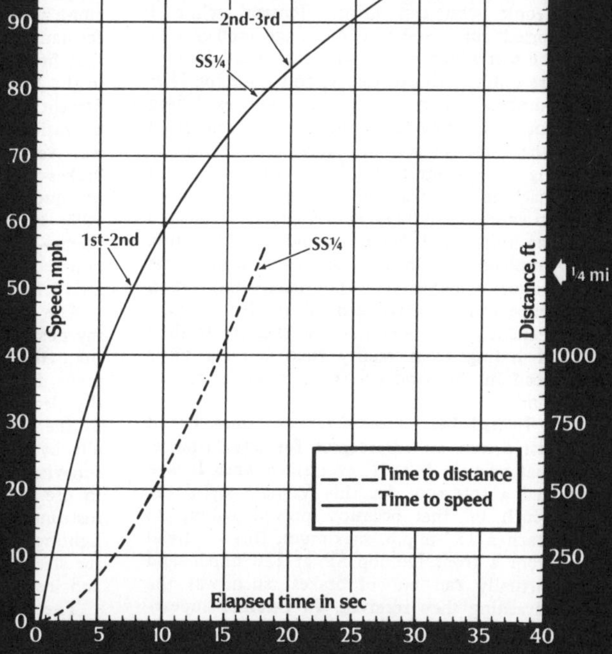

ROAD TEST

Jensen Interceptor III

A relaxing experience

LIKE THE Aston Martin DBS V8 tested last month, the Jensen Interceptor III, with 7.2-litres in eight vee-formation cylinders to feed through its four-barrel Carter carburetter, is hardly the appropriate car to be using in the midst of a fuel crisis, but when the test was arranged with Gethin Bradley, of Jensen's PR consultants, Good Relations, at Motor Show time, imminent petrol starvation was far from our minds. On the basis that MOTOR SPORT failed to give in to the Germans in the last war, so why should we give in to the Arabs, we decided to proceed with the test, 50-m.p.h. limit notwithstanding.

In a week when Joe Gormless was enjoying his Christmas holidays while the rest of the country suffered, when Barber announced his mini-budget aimed partly at some of the people who can afford Jensens, while I sorted out first-house mortgage problems of the sort which people who can afford Jensens are unlikely to experience, and while the IRA bombed London, one such bomb exploding not much more than a quarter-of-a-mile from where the Jensen was parked, merely driving this magnificent West Bromwich-built machine at a fraction of its potential proved an enormously therapeutic exercise. It soothed the mind and body, shrinking surrounding problems into insignificance, which made me wonder whether some politicians and Union leaders must drive around in Jensens permanently, a much more satisfactory method of hiding from reality than burying one's head in the sand or living in cloud cuckoo land.

It had been some 2½ years since I had last driven an Interceptor for any distance, that being a Mk. II, ever since when I have had a soft spot for this Vignale styled car which on that occasion proved willing to reach a 137-m.p.h. maximum, threw a tread from a front Dunlop SP at 120 m.p.h. and virtually ran out of brakes, such was the thrashing they received. In external appearance the Interceptor, updated to Mk. III in October '71, has changed little since then, other than in the much enhanced looks of the wheels, changed from Rostyle steel to five-spoke alloy. However, rather more than a wheel change had gone into the Interceptor when a revised version of the Mk III was introduced in May 1972. The earlier 6,267 c.c. (383 cu. in.), 300-b.h.p. engine was superseded by a 7,212 c.c. (440 cu. in.), 284-b.h.p. unit of the same 109.72 mm. bore x 95.25 mm. stroke dimensions used in the Interceptor SP, the high-performance, 385-b.h.p. option of the 6.3-litre Mk. II and III which has been dropped because of emission problems.

Like all the Jensen engines since the CV8 appeared in 1962, the Mk. III's is supplied by Chrysler from the United States, along with the Chrysler Torqueflite Hi-Performance 3-speed automatic box, similar to that fitted as an option to the DBS V8, but in the Jensen's case a standard, no-alternative fitment. Interior appointments received detail alterations in Mk. III form, though there was very little to improve upon, but the brakes were left alone—few can be ill-treated as much as those were 2½ years ago, and 99% of owners will find little fault with them—and Dunlop ER70, VR15, SPs retained for RHD cars with Pirelli GR70, VR15 for LHD models, of 205 section.

The RHD Dunlop-shod test car, still in my possession as I write, is to 1973 specification, though few modifications have been made for 1974, all of them advantageous: the electric aerial is automatically controlled by the radio on-off switch instead of manually by a separate switch, the surface of the sun visors facing the occupants when they're in use is now black to avoid reflection, the instruments are given rheostat-controlled lighting instead of three fixed positions and the steering wheel has been restyled for looks and instrument visibility.

The Interceptor's shape may not have changed since its introduction at the 1966 Motor Show, but like anything else its price certainly has—£3,473 was the original tag and £5,340 bought the brilliant four-wheel drive FF, no longer available. Today a cheque for £7,179 is necessary to command ownership of one of the 30 cars per week rolling ever more rapidly (not long ago the figure was 10) off the West Bromwich lines, most of them destined for the States where they are marketed by Kjell Qvale, Jensen's major shareholder and controller of the purse-strings. By current standards of prices for luxury cars, £7,000 makes the Jensen almost the best value for money on the market, excelled only by Jaguar's unbeatable value. It is almost £2,500 cheaper than the DBS V8, partly justified by the Aston's coachwork, more sophisticated suspension and racing specification, hand-built, complex V8, offering superior performance, but not really by its overall impression from behind the wheel in automatic guise, and is roughly £1,400 cheaper than a BMW CSi or CSA if equipped with the options which are standard on the Jensen, a price differential which isn't justified at all in relative terms. It is capable of more than 135 m.p.h., will accelerate from 0-60 m.p.h. in not much more than 8 sec. and drinks fuel slightly more heavily than the Aston, at 10 to 14 m.p.g. All this is in spite of the massive engine being hampered by the fitment of US emission equipment, even for the British market, although one benefit is that the 8.2-to-1 compression ratio V8 will absorb happily almost any rubbish that the mechanical fuel pump will throw at it, right down to 88 octane two-star, which can mean quite a saving every time the 20-gallon tank is filled. The main drawback to the emission equipment is a severe restriction on power output, more obvious on paper than from behind the wheel, 16 b.h.p. less than the old 6.3-litre engine and 101 less than the SP whose engine was somewhat different in design and carried three twin-barrel Holley carburetters. I confess to not having driven an SP, but imagine that the performance difference between that and the current Interceptor must be quite marked. The difference between the latter and the old 6.3 if anything is one of improvement in spite of the power loss: it is quieter, smoother and obviously has more torque, which would seem to have required different settings in the gearbox, for change-down speeds appear to be lower. I had been warned by an acquaintance that this emission controlled engine had poor throttle response, or at least the car he had driven had. The test car's pickup is beyond criticism, smooth and progressive with no lag and certainly none of that run-on sensation after the throttle is closed from which some emission controlled engines suffer. Overall, my impression is that the new engine's effect has been to make the latest Jensen much more obviously a relaxed and effortless luxury car rather than a sports car. It has simply made the performance a little more subtle by removing some of the bark without interfering with the bite.

For many years Jensen relied on glassfibre coachwork for the 541 and CV8, but today the Nordic wing symbol graces an all-steel construction, which at least is less prone to damage by careless hands and leaners than is that rather more delicate aluminium panelling of the Aston. Rust-preventative treatment is obviously first class, for early examples appear to remain free of the need for body-filler. The body is gas and CO_2 arc-welded to a massive tubular and boxed pressing chassis structure, which ensures strength and rigidity. After rust-proofing the body receives two coats of primer and three coats of final finish, all rubbed down by hand, followed by undersealing. It is a far cry from the multitudinous coats of paint applied to the Aston, but still, one gets what one pays for and while it does not have the Aston's mirror-like effect, nevertheless the finish is excellent enough to deter a self-respecting owner from feeding it into the barbarous tentacles of a car-wash, rather to set the gardener or chauffeur to work with a chamois.

Four quartz-halogen headlights grace the familiar front-end and at the other extremity is the unique "glasshouse" boot-lid, the curved Sundym heated screen opening to reveal a long, wide, flat, but fairly shallow, impeccably carpeted, 12 cu. ft. boot and an unobstructed view through into the interior. To enable more luggage to be carried, the rear parcel shelf within the boot lid can be removed by unscrewing a few knurled nuts. The lid is opened by means of a lockable lever in the driver's door shut-face and many an owner has doubtless cursed himself and Jensen when he has shut the door with the key remaining in the lock, with disastrous consequences to the head of the key. On the test car the lid requires a superhuman effort to release it from its catch. The spare wheel is carried in a wind-down tray beneath the boot, open to the elements, and it doesn't take much imagination to realise what road salt might do to the alloy spare. Winding-down mechanism is operated from within the boot by an adapter placed on the wheel brace, this, the Bevelift jack, spare fan belt and tin of paint being stowed in the centre rear of the boot while a comprehensive tool roll is carried in a compartment on the left-hand side of the boot. At last Jensen have moved the fire-extinguisher from its mounting in the boot, where it would have been accessible *after* the car had burnt out, to a clip below the front of the driver's seat. Another detail safety aid is a first-aid kit stowed in the capacious lockable locker between the two front seats.

Wide doors have automatic red warning lights on their rear edges when open, their quarterlights are fixed, but their main windows motivated rapidly by electricity only when the ignition is on, the passenger door can be locked electrically and remotely by a switch on the driver's door, though there is an over-riding manual lock too, and though the handbook and a hand-out photograph give evidence of door-pockets, the test car is bereft of them. There are generous full-length door armrests with door-pull apertures, large ash-trays are fitted, and the bottom front corner of each door contains a radio speaker, a further two being fitted one on either side of the rear passenger seats. The four speakers are activated by the standard specification push-button Radiomobile radio, or, for an extra £89.38, by the Radiomobile 108SR combined stereo radio and eight-track stereo, as fitted to the test car, or, for £161.05, a Philips RN712 stereo/radio/cassette player/recorder.

Six separate Connolly leather hides are used in each Interceptor, boast Jensen, and they're certainly put to good and beautiful use. The front seats are exquisitely comfortable, have reclining back-rests and built-in head-rests, each with a cloth-covered cushion attached by Velcro and have map-pockets in their rears. Rear seats are deeply and separately shaped, split by a wide arm-rest containing two ash-trays and continuous with the front console, and after travelling in the rear of a Mk. II for a couple of hundred miles I can vouch for their comfort. However, leg room in the rear is severely restricted when the front seats are in a normal position, meaning that the driver would have to suffer discomfort should he wish to carry a passenger behind him. To help him, the steering column is adjustable in and out by two inches. To one side of each rear seat is a traditional Jensen lidded locker, and there is an opening quarterlight (fixed on 1974 US market cars) alongside each seat. Apart from the moulded facia cowl, virtually everything that isn't upholstered in Connolly leather is treated to Wilton carpet, each front floor well being protected by a rubber heel mat.

The facia is excellently laid out to the advantage of the six Smiths instruments and Kienzle clock. In the centre of the facia, raised as close to eye-level as possible and angled in the moulding towards the driver are voltmeter, fuel gauge for the 20-gallon tank, oil pressure gauge and temperature gauge. Below them are four eyeball fresh-air outlets, in the centre of which is mounted the Kienzle clock, which the eyes, used to the ideally-positioned auxiliary instruments, are slow to locate. Directly in front of the driver lie the 160-m.p.h. speedometer with trip and 6,000-r.p.m. tachometer, red-lined at, would-you-believe, 5,100 r.p.m., the give-away to an extraordinarily lazy and under-stressed engine. To the right of that are a brake warning light with a switch to check whether the warning light is working or not, a typically American compulsory fitment—unless you happen to check the light at just the right time, if it doesn't work it probably means you're dead anyway—which usefully doubles up as handbrake and worn pad warning light as well as low, or non-existent fluid level warning. Further right is the disappointing control for the otherwise excellent two-speed wipers and four-jet electric washers: it is an identical Lucas switch to that fitted to my TR6, featuring clockwise turns for the wipers and push-in action for the washers. Whilst it works, it is not the sort of detail I would expect on a car of this class and I would hope that Jensen have plans to mount a finger-tip stalk on the vacant left-hand side of the steering column. The stalk on the right controls winkers and headlamp flasher only, the dip-switch being an organ pedal for the left foot to operate, an old-fashioned feature which I wouldn't

Sumptuous fittings and exceptionally well-positioned secondary instrumentation.

mind if it weren't for the fact that I use my left foot to operate the wide pendant brake pedal in this automatic car, and on occasions I have had to transfer my right foot to that pedal part way through braking in order to dip the lights.

The central transmission tunnel is a massive structure which effectively isolates the driver from passenger, yet adds to the feeling of comfort while leaving adequate foot room. The console on top of the tunnel is trimmed entirely in leather, though American market cars feature a polished wood inset. A row of rocker switches lies at the top edge of the console where it meets the facia, controlling from the left the optional fog lamps, the electrically-operated fuel-filler lid on the car's nearside (operable only when the engine is switched off), selector switch for the town and country horns, aerial switch (not fitted on the 1974 cars, with automatic operation), heated rear screen switch (without a warning light on the test car—or certainly not one that works), panel light switch (again redundant in 1974) and the lights switch. The radio lies below them and below that the rotary air-conditioning control switches, between which is a rocker switch to activate the air-conditioning pump. An aircraft-type sign below that screams "Fasten Seat Belts" if you haven't. Electric window switches flank the conventional automatic gear-lever at the front of the flat part of the console and at the rear are a hazard warning switch, parking light switch to override the main lights to operate the driver's side sidelights only, surely illegal now, a balance knob for the speakers and a cigar lighter. On the left of the facia is a lockable cubby hole, and underneath the facia a point for charging the battery. Naturally the 15 inch steering wheel, controlling a reasonable, for the car's size, 38 ft. turning circle at 3.4 turns lock-to-lock, has a hide rim.

Inertia reel seat-belts should retreat into the sidewall on either side of the rear seats, but prove loth to do so and are confoundedly difficult to grab hold of from the front seats. Push-buttons to release the buckles from the fixed centre mountings are on the bottoms of the mountings, awkward to get at because of the centre console and seats and would be better switched to the tops. Belts are comfortable enough once they are on, but like most other installations their design is far from perfect.

Frequent reminders from passing pedestrians when walking away from the car after locking it have been invoked by the unusual feature of a thermo-switch connected to the interior courtesy lights, so that after the doors are closed the lights stay on for anything up to 30 sec., depending upon the temperature, before extinguishing themselves automatically. These two lights, each with a self-contained switch (a remote switch on the console would be far better) are situated above each door and aren't really bright enough to allow a London A to Z to be read.

General impressions of driving the Interceptor belie the old-fashioned and almost primitive design by current sophisticated standards, of the suspension, not too far removed from that of the old Austin Westminster. The live rear axle is suspended by semi-elliptic, dual rate cart springs with rubber button interleaved separators. The only other location is by a Panhard rod and Armstrong telescopic dampers. Independent wishbone-type front suspension has coil springs, telescopic shock absorbers and an anti-roll bar. The arrangement couldn't be much less sophisticated yet it works admirably and has the added attraction of being relatively cheap and easy to maintain. Indeed the whole car requires very little more routine maintenance than an ordinary family saloon: service intervals are restricted to every 4,000 miles, when attention is required to, among other things, the good old-fashioned chassis grease points. This compares with every 2,500 miles for the DBS V8!

Adwest power steering is fitted as standard, and while it is fractionally inferior in feel to that fitted to the Aston Martin, it is slightly lighter without being too light. In other respects the Jensen feels a much easier car to drive, particularly with regard to parking and driving through narrow gaps, though this is no scarecrow at 5 ft. 9 in. wide, the Interceptor being 3 in. narrower than the DBS.

Girling ventilated disc brakes are fitted to all four wheels, 11⅜ in. diameter at the front and 10¾ in. at the rear. There are separate systems for front and rear brakes with a tandem master cylinder, direct-acting servo, aided by a vacuum reservoir in the main chassis tubes, and with a load-conscious valve to prevent rear-wheel lock-up. Like the Aston, the brakes become quite rough while driving around London, once again a fair amount of gearbox creep and high tick-over speed needing their frequent, light application. The pedal isn't firm enough for my liking, but they stop the 35.7 cwt. car effectively from the speeds used in this test, if not inspiring the same confidence as those of the Aston. A hand-brake lever of non-fly-off type nestles between the driver's seat and the console, from where it operates self-adjusting pads on the rear discs and seems to have no problems holding the heavy car.

In general the Interceptor's handling is reasonable, its ride comfortable, while remaining firm enough to give good control without reverting to the sogginess of a Rolls-Royce system. However, it is far from being as sure-footed as the Aston, once again, and needs delicate control in the wet, particularly under power, when the rear end, in spite of a Salisbury Powr-Lok differential, can soon lose traction and sideways adhesion—and it is not an easy car to regain control of. This is very much a car to treat with respect when cornering at speed and really it is much more at home travelling flat out down motorways and autoroutes, when I recall that the Mk.II I referred to earlier was no noisier and no less stable at over 130 m.p.h. than it was at 80. Apart from a distant hum, wind-noise is non-existent at any speed and the big V8 behaves as though insulated in a sound-proof box. The Mk. II gave quite a marked V8 warble when opened up, while the Mk.III's 7.2-litre engine is almost completely unobtrusive. When the throttle is floored the gearbox changes up at 40 m.p.h. and 76 m.p.h. or on a light throttle at 11 m.p.h. and 15 m.p.h. with the engine at not much more than tickover speed. Maximum speeds in low and intermediate gears available by using the manual hold are 48 m.p.h. and 82 m.p.h., but this is purely academic, for this super-smooth engine can be left in Drive more happily than any other automatic car I can recall. Progress is lazy, effortless and utterly relaxed, it is a tremendously easy car to drive when not trying to break any records, yet when overtaking performance is required, kickdown gives a tremendous thump in the back, the start of impressive and safe acceleration which keeps this Jensen well up in the league of the World's high-performance cars—certainly of the automatic variety. On the other hand, the current 50 m.p.h. limit is no real problem the V8 burbling happily (and quietly —tappets are hydraulic) at less than 1,500 r.p.m. with the occupants surrounded by almost absolute silence, breathing dehumidified air through the standard air-conditioning equipment, which is less satisfactory at maintaining suitable constant heat than it is at demisting the interior. For this last trick the air-conditioner itself must be switched on—using just the heater causes a worse fog than ever. The rotary knobs are convenient to operate and usefully illuminated at night.

Starting those eight cylinders from cold is equally drama-free: the throttle is depressed fully and slowly to activate the automatic choke, after which the pedal is left well alone, the key is turned and the engine invariably fires and can be driven away smoothly and cleanly immediately. The hand-book warns that a small amount of throttle should be applied when starting a warm engine and that 15 sec. of churning is not unusual—the test car starts instantly with no throttle. Twin thermostatically-controlled electric fans and a 28-pint cooling-system keep the engine cool when it is warm and for customers who may use their cars regularly in hot climates —standard for the States—a louvred bonnet is available as a no-cost option as an aid to removing unwanted underbonnet heat.

After more than seven years, the almost futuristic Vignale body style is almost undated and the Jensen Interceptor remains the epitome of the high-speed executive express. It would benefit from a more sophisticated chassis design to improve its high speed cornering behaviour (not that it does a great deal wrong—it just feels that it might) and beyond that this hand-built West Bromwich product rivals that product from Crewe in terms of comfort and silence, is more relaxing to drive because it is more compact and has far more precise handling and is faster. What more could a man require who doesn't want an out-and-out sports car, but wants something more individual that an XJ12.—C.R.

Plumber's nightmare and driver's aream — the 7.2-litre, emission-controlled, Chrysler V8

NEW OPEN JENSEN

Power-operated hood for luxury Interceptor convertible. By Philip Turner

A new sister car for the Jensen Interceptor III is the Interceptor Convertible with power-operated hood, full air conditioning and a luxury specification. The new car is based on the saloon but the rear has been restyled with more square-cut lines and with a new boot lid. These modifications have been made to provide sufficient space for the hood when lowered.

As the body is mounted on the very strong tubular chassis of the saloon, an open car presented few of the usual stiffness problems. None the less the body sills have been stiffened by using thicker metal. The screen pillars have also been strengthened by the insertion of an additional 12 SWG member inside the A posts.

With the hood raised, the new convertible has all the snug comfort of a normal saloon. To lower the hood, the two snap-action clamps securing the hood to the top of the screen are released and the rocker switch on the instrument panel pressed. This starts the electric motor which, with its shaft-driven rotary hydraulic pump, is carried transversely in a special compartment at the front of the boot. The hydraulic pump feeds two massive rams mounted at an angle just ahead of the rear wheel arches and connected to the hood irons. The rams pull the front of the hood off the two locating pins at the top of the screen and draw the hood back until it reaches the folded position, when they cut out automatically.

Continued pressure on the " hood " switch brings into action the electric motors for the rear quarter lights which are lowered into the body sides. A hood cover can then be secured in place by pop fasteners to conceal the furled hood. The cover must be removed before the hood can be raised. A wire built into the hood cover earths current via two of the pop fasteners to prevent the hood mechanism from operating with the cover still in place. Thermal cut-out switches are also incorporated in both the quarter light motor circuits to protect the quarter light motors from damage should the raising or the lowering of the quarter lights be blocked by odd items dropped into their cavities. Similarly, a manually set thermal switch mounted on the steering column protects the hood operating mechanism should some absent minded owner attempt to lower the hood with the screen clamps still in position.

The hood cannot be raised or lowered except when the gear selector for the Torqueflite automatic transmission is in neutral or park, though the rear quarter lights may be raised or lowered with the car in motion.

The hood rear window is retained in place by zip fasteners and may be removed completely to increase the flow of air through the car in a very hot climate, or to protect the rear window from damage if the hood is to be stowed for a long period.

The new convertible is expected to account for 50 per cent of all Interceptor production before long. Initially about seven out of every ten convertibles will be shipped to the United States and three will be sold on the home market, but by the autumn it is expected the convertible will also be exported to important Jensen markets in Australia, New Zealand, Hong Kong, and Japan.

The usual test of good looks in a convertible is when the hood is in place and the new Jensen is no less pleasing than the familiar closed model. Square-cut lines round the boot are the only alterations below the waistline—the purpose being to allow plenty space for the folded hood in the front of the boot. Electric hood operation is by a switch on the facia

JENSEN CONVERTIBLE— DROPTOP LUXURY

THE CONCEPT of the Interceptor saloon has been a successful marketing exercise for the British Jensen company and now comes the Interceptor convertible. The drophead drops into the luxury sector at high point in the firm's history and seems set to carve out its own market niche . . .

SINCE 1966 Jensen Motors have sold more than 5000 Interceptor Saloons. World exports of Jensen cars are at an all time high, boosted partly by the release of the Jensen-Healey. Jensen's performance in the market place is about to be boosted again, this time by a new Interceptor Convertible.

At present the life span of the convertible concept appears to be in some doubt but the design, performance, safety and features of the Interceptor drophead will assure *its* success.

Instigated mainly at the insistence of North American buyers, the convertible is a fully hand-built vehicle and initial production is expected to run at about five vehicles a week. However, the new convertible will eventually account for half of total Interceptor production. Despite the extra rigidity required for open cars, there were very few modifications required (to the basic Interceptor saloon shell) to give the convertible the required strength.

Six weeks after the tubular chassis is placed in the jigs, the car is being finished for delivery. The production schedule which Jensen have set is quite conservative. Built as a completely exclusive vehicle the Jensen features hide-covered seats, electric windows and power-operated hood. Jensen boast luxurious accommodation for four but it is still a squeeze in the back seat. Designers have shaped the rear quarters to give a new wing line which incorporates a new boot lid.

The new car will be shown for the first time at the New York Motor Show this month. Its price in Britain will be £stg9862 ($A15,882). Obviously aimed at the super luxury areas, Jensen has spared no expense (the customer's expense) on detail finish items.

The power-operated hood is fully wool-lined with a zip-out rear window. The convertible uses similar mechanics to the Interceptor Saloon — 7.2litre Chrysler V8 engine and automatic transmission, fully integrated air conditioning, electric control over windows, passenger door lock, fuel filler cover and radio aerial. The rear quarter windows are also power-operated, but can only be lowered when the hood is down.

ABOVE: Basically the same as the saloon, the convertible features new rear end styling and a very useful luggage boot. The hood stows in a shallow well, leaving luggage area unrestricted. RIGHT: Getting it all together. Jensen say it takes just over six weeks to produce one convertible. The quality of the finish is excellent and the final presentation of the vehicle is immaculate. BELOW: The heart of the hood-work. The pic at right shows the cross-bar which helps stiffen the upper body after the roof is removed. The pic at left shows the hood folding mechanism. Both the convertible top and side windows are power-operated.

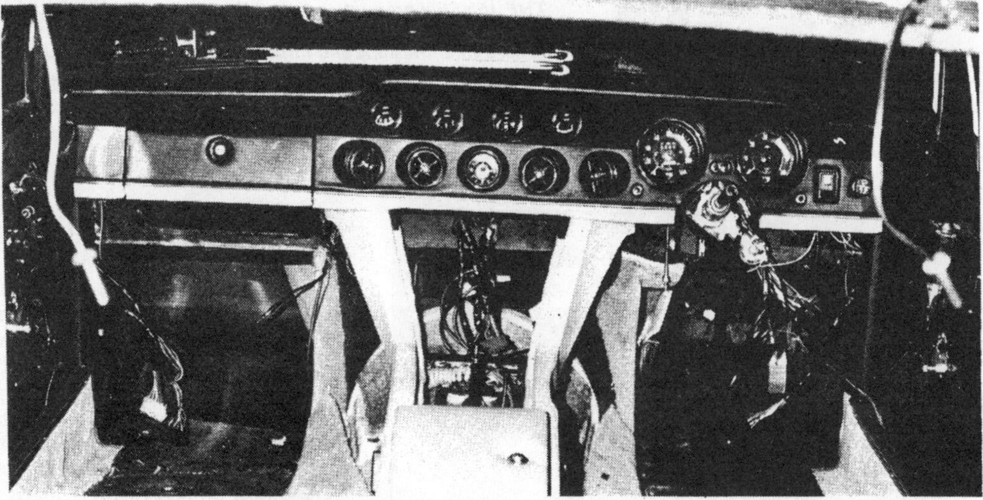

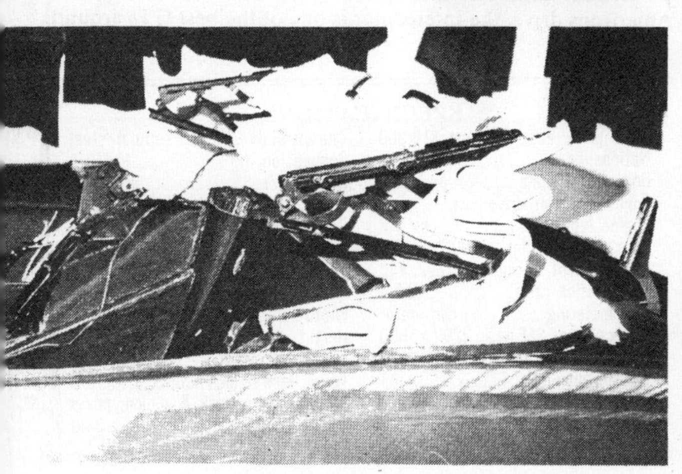

JENSEN CONVERTIBLE–

Like the Interceptor, the Convertible gets alloy sports wheels and massive ventilated disc brakes and limited slip differential.

The luxurious appearance of the car is very stunning and its effect cannot be underestimated. The quality of the finish is an important reason why the Interceptor range has grown in popularity.

Performance is impressive without being brain-snapping. 0-60mph runs up in 8.2seconds. It accelerates from 40-60 in 3.6seconds, and top speed is a shade under 133mph. However the *torque* makes the Interceptor a great town and touring car.

Power output of the 7.2 litre engine is 383bhp and the relatively low compression ratio of 8.2 to one allows the car to be run on standard-grade fuel. Consumption would probably average out between 11 and 12mpg.

The Interceptor saloon was known for its quietness at speed. It will be interesting to see what effect Jensen's efforts in the insulation department have on convertible noise levels.

At first glance, the Interceptor convertible concept appears to be a simple *slip-the-roof-off* job, in practice it is almost as simple. The only strengthening which was carried out was across the floor pan, behind the front seats, and in the body-sides between the trailing edge of the door and the rear of the passenger compartment — this says much for the basic structural rigidity of the chassis.

In profile the convertible is very handsome, more so with the hood raised. The excellent re-styling job on the rear quarters makes the convertible sleek and smooth. With the top down there is naturally some buffeting at the back of the head when travelling at speed but at normal town speeds it is extremely comfortable open-top motoring.

Australia should see the Interceptor convertible in November of this year — most of the early production being syphoned off for the British and American markets. (The US bought more than 2500 Jensen-Healeys and almost 300 Interceptor saloons during 1973).

Jensen Motors are anticipating a sales increase in Australia, for 1974, of three times the 1973 figures. This means a target of 100 Interceptors and 300 Jensen-Healeys. The Interceptor convertible is truly a sophisticated motor car completely in sympathy with the luxury concept established by the marque on a world-wide basis, and if concern over fuel shortages does not play too big a role in buyer choice it is doubtful Jensen will have any trouble selling their production quota.

THE JENSEN production line at West Bromwich. Here Jensen-Healeys roll down toward final finishing and inspection.

Jensen Interceptor III

THE OTHER side of Jensen's West Bromwich, England operation is the low-volume production of their big car, the Interceptor. In its current III form this hefty 2+2 coupe is a highly refined version of an old design and exhibits the best characteristics of that sort of package: it's well built, well thought-out in detail and most likely quite reliable, though not absolutely up to date in some aspects of engineering.

The most noticeable deficiency of the Interceptor is its simple, cheap rear suspension—a live axle on leaf springs, stabilized laterally by a Panhard rod. An arrangement like this provides neither the best rough-road adhesion nor the best ride possible, and in a low car like the Jensen it usually requires a compromise in vertical wheel-travel space. The Interceptor shows the expected traits, with a poor ride when loaded with four passengers and skittery cornering on rough surfaces whether loaded or not. And we're sure the rear seating—very tight for the car's size—could be improved with a fixed differential rather than one that has to move with the wheels.

The positive aspects of the big coupe are smooth, effortless performance from a Chrysler engine and transmission (with heavy fuel consumption, however), the way it's put together and finished, the complete equipment it comes with, and the expected reliability and ease of servicing that go with the American powertrain units. For the American market and the way most Americans drive, the Interceptor is one of the best GTs around.

SPECIFICATIONS

Basic price, east	est $16,000	Chassis-body	tubular/steel
Nationality	Britain	Suspension, f/r	ind/live
Body types/seats	coupe; 2+2	Brakes, f/r	disc/disc
Engine position/drive	F/R	Tires	radial 205/70VR-15
Engine type	ohv V-8	Curb weight, lb	4020
Bore x stroke, mm	109.7 x 95.3	Wheelbase, in.	105.0
Displacement, cc/cu in.	7212/440	Track, f/r	56.1/56.9
Compression ratio	8.2:1	Length	186.0
Fuel metering	carburetor	Width	69.0
Power @ rpm, SAE net	220 @ 3600	Height	53.0
Torque @ rpm, lb-ft	350 @ 2400	Turning circle, ft	38.0
Transmission	A3	Turns, lock-to-lock	3.4
Final drive ratio	2.88:1	Steering type	rack & pinion, power
mph/1000 rpm	26.6	Fuel capacity, gal.	24.0

BELOW: In a truly sophisticated setting – the Jensen Interceptor Drophead. The new convertible is beautifully appointed and handles exactly like the successful fixed head version. The hood is power-operated and wool-lined! The rear end styling has been re-worked to give a new boot lid shape. INSET: Seats are sumptuous and the driving position is excellent. Export versions get sheepskin seat inserts.

Part of the Jensen-Healey production line.

JENSEN FACTORY VISIT

Impressive Jensen production

By JOHN BOLSTER

Well before the war, I knew Richard and Alan Jensen, first as builders of bodies on other people's chassis and then as motor manufacturers in their own right. At that time, they used traditional coachbuilding methods, but after the conflict they became outstandingly adept at the construction of glassfibre bodies, such as that of the Jensen CV8. They also proved their mastery of the modern pressed-steel monocoque by various design exercises for the big manufacturers, as well as the complete construction of the big Healey and the Sunbeam Tiger, for BMC and Rootes respectively.

Of recent years, the brothers have taken a less active part and have now both retired. It is no secret that the company has had its ups and downs. When Leyland took over BMC, they soon cancelled the Healey 3000 contract, and a similar blow was sustained through Chrysler killing the Tiger, because it had a Ford V8 engine. The CV8 was hard to sell, having a somewhat Chinese look instead of the Italian line, which is now almost obligatory for costly cars.

First stage in the recovery was to take what was virtually the CV8 tubular chassis and get a body designed in Italy—indeed the first steel shells of the new Interceptor were made in that country. It was decided that the Interceptor should be built to a higher standard of quality than any previous Jensen, with price a secondary consideration. In addition, a less costly model, to fill the place in the market—and on the assembly line—of the Healey 3000 should be undertaken. The Americans were still shouting for the big Healey and British Leyland's MGC was a total flop, so it was natural for Donald Healey and Jensens to get together and produce the Jensen-Healey.

A Jensen Interceptor takes shape on the jig.

All this has not been done without blood, toil, tears and sweat. There have been several changes of management and of the financial structure but now there is a team which really believes in the company and its products. Leading the team is Kjell Qvale, who has the inestimable advantage of possessing a vast sales network for European cars in the United States, where most of the cars are sold.

I recently visited the Jensen factory at West Bromwich, which has been greatly expanded and employs more than three times as many people as only four or five years ago, if one includes the new factory lately opened in Wales. Production has now risen to 25 Interceptors and 105 to 110 Jensen-Healeys per week. Of the Interceptors, about half will be the new convertibles of which eight or nine will go to the North American market, including Canada, and a goodly portion of the saloons, too. At least 80 Jensen-Healeys per week will go to the same market. The demand in Australia is rising and in the nine-month period ending in December, 30 Interceptors and 75 Jensen-Healeys will have been sold to Japan.

There has been a bottleneck in the supply of Healey hard-tops, due to an outside supplier failing to meet the demand, so Jensens have gone back into the glassfibre game. In addition to rushing hard-tops to impatient purchasers, they now make their own transmission covers and instrument panels for the Interceptor.

Though the cars are built side by side, different methods are employed; while both bodies are of steel, the Interceptor has a twin-tube chassis but the Healey is of monocoque construction. The outer wing panels of the Healey are not part of the structure but bolt on, for ease of repair and reduced insurance premiums. The Healey is built on a normal assembly line but the Interceptor requires more craftsmanship and only moves on a chain when it is going through the priming-dip and painting booths. The body pressings for the Interceptor come from Motor Panels of Coventry and those for the Healey from Dowty, Boulton, and Paul.

The Jensen-Healey is of relatively simple shape but the Interceptor is more complex and requires a great many pressings. These are received straight from the press and undergo much trimming and hand-finishing. The two large tubes are welded to the body, the floor pan and front and rear diaphragms being secured first. Then the rear and side panels go on—different pressings for the convertible here—followed by the front wings, front panel to carry the grille, scuttle and roof. Bonnets and doors are fed in from the side as needed.

The amount of electrical wiring on a modern luxury car is enormous. All Interceptors have air conditioning and the doors contain window motors, locks and speakers. A very heavy jig is bolted in place, allowing the front of the body to be hammered into shape to take the screen accurately. A somewhat similar arrangement ensures the perfect opening and closing of the rear glass panel and the hoods for convertibles are built up on a jig and are completely interchangeable. There's a vast amount of undersealing on an Interceptor, applied while the body is mounted on pivots and turned over, while a lot of sound-proofing is applied before trimming. The trimming of a car of the Interceptor's class is a long and painstaking task, performed by craftsmen; only Connolly's best hides are used.

Construction is far advanced before the car meets its Chrysler engine with automatic transmission, Salisbury axle and Girling brakes with ventilated discs all round. Construction of an Interceptor, from the moment when the tubes are placed on the jig to the end of the 120 miles road test, takes six weeks. Options include sheepskin centre panels for the leather seats and louvred bonnets for the saloon—standard on the convertible.

The Jensen-Healey also meets its engine and suspension late in the game. The body—painted, trimmed, fully equipped and glazed—arrives on an overhead conveyor and finds its mechanical components laid out underneath it. Gently lowered with a hoist, it lands accurately on the front crossmember, which already carries the engine and suspension parts, and the rear springs and axle. Suspension and axle are by Vauxhall, gearbox is Sunbeam Rapier, and the engine is the 2-litre Lotus 16-valve slant-four. The assembly only takes a matter of seconds and wheels and tyres are fitted at the end of the line.

As I knew that a few teething troubles had been experienced with the Lotus engine, I interviewed Roy Marshall, the technical service supervisor.

Oil leaks were at first a problem, that from the cam cover being cured by a gasket of later specification. A leakage between the cam housing and head was remedied by the use of a latex-dip gasket positively located by a hollow dowel. Excessive oil level was traced to owners, who did not wait for the oil to drain back from the top of the engine to the sump before reading the dipstick—a job much better done with a cold engine. Actual oil burning with new engines was experienced and has been overcome by fitting different piston rings, including 3-piece oil-control rings. There was a tendency for oil to be drawn through the breathing system, which has been prevented by improving the crank case ventilation.

More serious was a delay in building up oil pressure after a cold start. This was due to air on the pressure side of the pump and was cured by drilling a .05 inch hole—the leakage of oil through this back to the sump is of no consequence and does not affect the pressure as the relief valve is working at all times anyway. It was this oil delay that was the primary cause of some camshaft seizures, forcing the drive belt to jump a cog or two, but this has been eliminated by increasing the bearing clearance by .001 of an inch and re-shaping the oil drillings.

If the car was parked all night facing downhill, petrol could siphon out of the tank and, overcoming the needle valves of the Dellorto carburetters, could flood into the engine. A little anti-siphon valve has overcome this problem, which never occurred on engines fitted with Stromberg carburetters to US specification. The back axles have been blameless and a tendency to slip out of gear was cured by replacing the rubber gearlever gaiter with a leather one. Complaints about the paint job on early cars have been avoided by improved finishing techniques and a new insulating strip between mudguard and body has greatly reduced fretting at this point. Some improvements to the hood have also taken place.

A Healey body is lowered on to the running gear.

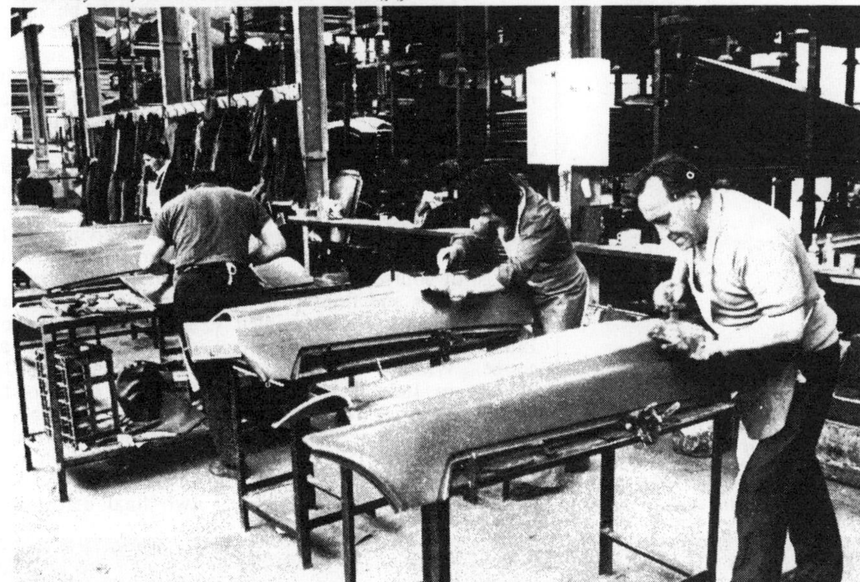

Above: Hand smoothing Interceptor panels. Below: Healey body comes out of the primer bath.

Unfortunately, the first owners of a new model are apt to get loaded with such unexpected annoyances and it is at least a blessing that the troubles were really quite trivial. Colin Chapman should be grateful to Jensens for getting the bugs out of his engine before he started selling new Elites. The Jensen-Healey is now a sound and reliable car, with a lot more performance than the old big Healey in spite of having only 2-litres instead of 3.

I was very impressed with all I saw at the Jensen factory. There is a cheerful spirit among the men on the shop floor, most of whom seem to be avid darts players, indulging in their sport at every tea break. They are certainly receiving dynamic leadership from the top and, against all predictions, the sale of powerful and expensive cars has recovered amazingly since the fuel crisis, regardless of the rising price of petrol.

To appreciate the materials and craftsmanship in a costly car, it is profitable to spend a few hours seeing how it is made. The ordinary car of commerce provides effective transportation, but for real pride of possession the hand-built job wins in a canter. The ownership of a Jensen Interceptor is something to which few can aspire, but for the man who has made his pile it can be a fitting reward for years of endeavour and toil.

AUTO TEST

Jensen Interceptor III Convertible

7,212 c.c.

Convertible version of Jensen's familiar Interceptor. Excellent performance, steering and brakes as before; thirsty. Rather noisy. Most pleasing with hood down. Expensive.

CONTRARY TO what, seemingly, every American and some British car manufacturers appear to have assumed, the convertible-top car is neither outlawed by safety regulations, nor unwanted by customers. There are, of course, a number of open sports-cars, mostly British, but nowadays very few open four-seaters of medium size, and only two luxury open tourers with room for four (now that there are no big American convertibles). One of these is the Rolls-Royce (or Bentley) Corniche convertible (£16,343), and the other the subject of this **Road Test**, Jensen's Interceptor convertible, announced early this year, and priced at the figure of £9,863.

It is, of course, based on the running gear and floor pan of the familiar Vignale-bodied Interceptor III fixed-head coupé. Without recourse to anyone in Italy, Jensen have re-bodied the car (to most eyes) very elegantly indeed, with an attractive slim tail, and a traditional fabric folding roof, with power raising and lowering – and traditionally bad over-the-shoulder vision.

The engine and three-speed automatic transmission are both Chrysler as before, except that the engine is equipped with most (not all) of the modifications introduced in its native country to meet exhaust and evaporative emission regulations.

Remembering that, it is pleasant to be able to say that on the test car there were few of the usual signs of an emission-controlled engine in driveability, apart from a reluctance to fire on automatic choke when cold.

The V8 power unit is markedly over-square at 109·72mm × 95·25mm bore and stroke, giving a total swept volume of 7,212 c.c. It has hydraulic tappets, a central camshaft, a five-bearing crankshaft, a four-choke Carter carburettor, and an 8·2-to-1 compression ratio. It runs satisfactorily on two-star fuel, of which it uses plenty (see below). To some extent the test car's thirst must be due to the fact that it used the lower of the two final drive ratios offered, 3·07-to-1 instead of 2·88-to-1, corresponding (assuming no torque converter slip) to maximum overall gearing of only 24·8 mph per 1,000 rpm, instead of the more preferable 26·4 mph per 1,000 rpm. The unit's claimed peak power of 280 bhp (net) occurs at 4,400 rpm, so that the car as delivered proved to be geared down, top speed being limited by the maximum allowed engine speed of 5,100 rpm. Observing the red line at 5,100 rpm on the rev-counter corresponded to 123 mph, though if, as is usually the case at maximum, torque converter slip is negligible, top speed is actually 126 mph (the rev-counter over-reading by 2¾ per cent).

The test car was rather short of mileage when delivered, and performance figures had to be taken with only 2,300 miles on the distance recorder. This only partly explains the performance figures, which, though more than adequate for most people, are not quite as good as any previous Interceptor we have tested. No doubt measures taken to meet American regulations are another reason why

Seven litres of relaxed open-air motoring – the Jensen Interceptor III convertible in its best guise, with the top down

this 7·2-litre Interceptor takes over 1sec more to reach 60 mph, and 2sec longer to reach 100 mph, than the 6·3-litre tested in 1969 – though that car did not have air-conditioning. Weight is also in the earlier car's favour, the convertible turning the scales at 35·7cwt in kerb condition, compared with 33cwt of the former.

Nevertheless, acceleration is pretty vivid for the size of car. The Chrysler Torqueflite transmission is ideally ratioed for the job, changing up flat-out at 4,400 rpm, and road speeds of 44 and 74 mph. We tried holding the changes to higher speeds, but only at 4,700 rpm indicated was there a tiny improvement (0·2sec in the 100 mph time). Holding the car momentarily on the brakes against full throttle, then letting go, there was a brief flurry of wheelspin before it swept up to 50 mph in 5·5sec, 60 in 7·6, 80 in 12·5, the quarter-mile in 15·8, 100 in 20·2, and 120 in 35sec, all comfortably within the mile. Gearchanges are noticeable when driven thus, but with gentler driving are fairly unobtrusive. Kick-down response is good, so that one is not dependent on the selector lever for that extra bit of urge which makes overtaking so much safer in this sort of car; such changes are on the jerky side by the standards of a competent and sensitive manual gearbox driver, but not excessively so by automatic standards. Maximum kick-down speed from top to intermediate is 65 mph, and from intermediate to low is 30 mph; interestingly the handbook claims higher speeds, respectively 78 and 32 mph.

Throttle control is smooth and progressive, and the same goes for the engine's delivery of its power. Starting has been mentioned already; there was never any complete failure to start, but a surprising amount of starter cranking was needed when cold. In fact we found it helped to make use of the accelerator pump, prodding the accelerator three or four times to help obtain a rich mixture.

We have always held up Jensen as an example of the opposite school of thought in Grand Touring cars to that of the Italians – the latter with the accent on performance regardless of noise, the former striving towards performance with refinement. For mechanical refinement, one can do little better than start with a big American V8 (except to employ either a familiar double-ohc six or a vee-12 from a notable Coventry firm). There is very little mechanical noise from the engine when hot. We were not so happy this time about exhaust noise – not so much when the engine is working hard, when it is acceptable, but, surprisingly, on tickover in traffic, which is the one time when one expects any car to be most quiet. On the Interceptor convertible one is immediately conscious of a pronounced boom from the exhaust at standstill; winding down a window makes little difference to the volume, showing that it is heard through the hood. Nevertheless we do not recall anything similar on the earlier cars. Gentle acceleration in town produces a little more noise from the same source than one expects from a luxurious and refined GT like this.

Whilst on the subject of noise, we thought that wind noise from the front of the hood was higher than we would expect from this type and price of car. From 70 mph onwards there is a noticeable roar which means that one must raise one's voice in order to converse. Bump-thump is slightly better than average.

The fuel tank holds a claimed 20 gallons, which the engine empties at an impressive rate, even for 2-star petrol. The best figure we achieved was 14 mpg, compared with 12·5 mpg overall, which includes a fair amount of fairly gentle driving in the early stages, since we had to complete the running-in. Oil consumption worked out at 500 miles per pint, a figure which was improving towards the end of the test period.

There is a noticeable momentary increase in engine mechanical noise on cold starts, accentuated by the somewhat high idling speed (2,500 rpm) on automatic choke; we preferred to give the accelerator pedal a "kick", which dropped the idle to a more reasonable 1,200 rpm.

Handling, ride and brakes

The power-assisted rack and pinion steering received warm praise from all our drivers. It is light as an assisted system should be, yet unlike some other set-ups has a most pleasing degree of feel, and even a little kick-back, though not by any means too much. It is also accurate, and combined with the excellent roadholding of the car on the Dunlop ER70 VR15 radial-ply tyres, it responds well to the driver's wishes. Straight-stability is good, on all types of surface and in side-winds. There is naturally a degree of understeer, but it was never too much. Thanks to the Salisbury Powr-Lok limited-slip differential, traction is very good indeed, even in the wet, giving one great confidence considering the amount of power there is at one's disposal. A minus point on this particular car was the noisiness of the limited-slip diff., which, especially on turning tightly but unhurriedly into a main road, produced alarming grunts – a not unfamiliar feature of this type of unit.

For all normal purposes the handling of the car is all that might be desired; only at track speeds does one have to be ready for a quite rapid ultimate rear-end breakaway, which needs quick correction. The ride was a little more firm than we recall, with a distinctive pitching movement, amplified visually by the handsome bonnet. It is nearer the sports-car than the luxury car in this respect, but not too much so.

The Girling ventilated disc brakes on all four wheels have vacuum-servo assistance, and a load-conscious pressure regulator in the rear circuit (with separate hydraulic circuits front and rear). In the condition tested (two-up, with a half-full tank), there was slightly too much front-end braking, front-wheel locking limiting the retardation to a maximum of just fractionally below 1g. Brake response is excellent for normal use, light and powerful, inspiring confidence. Fade resistance is good too, only a very hard stop from over 100 mph to a standstill producing any noticeable increase in pedal effort, plus the usual rumble which seems to accompany hard use of ventilated discs.

The handbrake is just capable of locking the back wheels with a two-handed pull, producing a maximum before locking of 0·35g. It did not shine on the test hills, just holding on 1-in-4 if one held the lever pulled up beyond the final ratchet position.

Driving position and controls

In most respects the Jensen is a comfortable and convenient car to drive. There is just enough leg room for the majority of drivers, with space for the left foot to rest on the organ-pedal dip-switch when not used for left-foot braking. People who like to left-foot brake will wish that the dip-switch was on a stalk, not the floor, for obvious reasons. The steering wheel can be adjusted fore-and-aft over a useful range, but not for rake.

Seat adjustment is easily achieved, thanks to a wide

Car's external appearance is not spoiled when hood is erected, but over-the-shoulder vision is very poor. There is a refreshing lack of unnecessary decoration

Jensen Interceptor III Convertible

release bar, and a slide which is spring-loaded forwards. To the right of the rev-counter is combined handbrake, pad-wear, and hydraulic-fluid-level warning lamp mounted in a rocker switch, which enables one to check that the bulb is functioning. Beyond that is the somewhat old-fashioned combined two-speed wiper and wash switch, which is not awkward to get at, though we would prefer a stalk switch beside the steering column at fingertip reach. The wipers, incidentally, are the Lucas type which do a sort of double-take when switched off. There is no hesitation or flick wipe provision. The single stalk controls signalling and flashing only.

Comparisons

MAXIMUM SPEED MPH

Aston Martin V8 auto	(£11,349)	146
Mercedes 350SL auto	(£6,868)	140
BMW 3·0CSi manual	(£7,657)	139
Jensen Interceptor conv.	**(£9,863)**	**126**
Rolls-Royce Corniche conv.	(£16,343)	120

0–60 MPH, SEC

Aston Martin V8 auto	6·2
BMW 3·0CSi	7·5
Jensen Interceptor conv.	**7·6**
Mercedes 350SL	9·3
Rolls-Royce Corniche conv.	9·6

STANDING ¼-MILE, SEC

Aston Martin V8 auto	14·7
BMW 3·0CSi	15·4
Jensen Interceptor conv.	**15·8**
Mercedes 350SL	17·0
Rolls-Royce Corniche conv.	17·1

OVERALL MPG

BMW 3·0CSi	20·7
Mercedes 350SL	14·7
Jensen Interceptor conv.	**12·5**
Aston Martin V8 auto	12·4
Rolls-Royce Corniche conv.	11·9

Performance

ACCELERATION

True speed mph	Time in Secs	Car Speedo mph
30	2·7	30
40	4·0	40
50	5·5	49
60	7·6	59
70	9·8	69
80	12·5	79
90	15·8	89
100	20·2	99
110	26·0	111
120	35·0	123

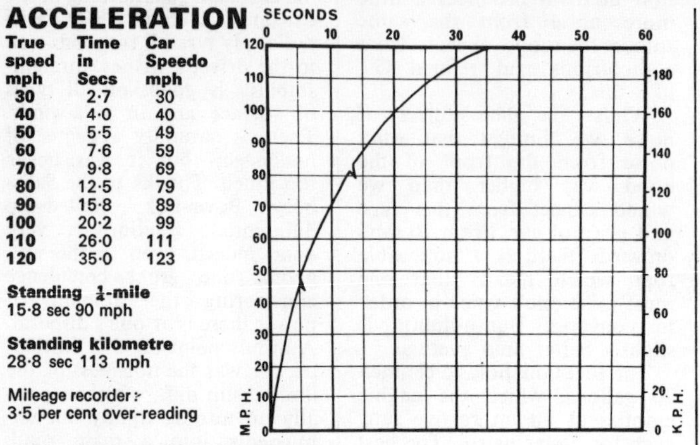

Standing ¼-mile
15·8 sec 90 mph

Standing kilometre
28·8 sec 113 mph

Mileage recorder:
3·5 per cent over-reading

GEAR RATIOS AND TIME IN SEC

mph	Top (3·07–6·14)	2nd (4·44–8·88)	1st (7·50–15·0)
0–20	—	—	1·7
10–30	—	—	1·9
20–40	—	—	2·4
30–50	—	—	2·7
40–60	—	3·6	—
50–70	—	4·3	—
60–80	—	5·1	—
70–90	6·9	—	—
80–100	7·4	—	—
90–110	10·1	—	—
100–120	14·6	—	—

GEARING
(with ER70 VR15in. tyres)

Top 24·8 mph per 1,000 rpm
2nd 17·13 mph per 1,000 rpm
1st 10·14 mph per 1,000 rpm

MAXIMUM SPEEDS

Gear	mph	kph	rpm
Top (mean)	126	203	5,100
(best)	126	203	5,100
2nd	87	140	5,100
1st	52	84	5,100

BRAKES

FADE (from 70 mph in neutral)
Pedal load for 0·5g stops in lb

1	30	6	30–25
2	30–25	7	30–25
3	30–25	8	30–25
4	30–25	9	30–25
5	30–25	10	30–25

RESPONSE (from 30 mph in neutral)

Load	g	Distance
20lb	0·22	137ft
40lb	0·65	46ft
60lb	0·85	35ft
80lb	0·91	33ft
100lb	0·96	31·4ft
Handbrake	0·35	86ft
Max. gradient	1 in 4	

Consumption

FUEL
Typical mpg 14 (20·2 litres/100km)
Overall mpg 12·5 (22·6 litres/100km)
Grade of fuel Regular, 2-star (min. 91RM)

OIL
Consumption (SAE 20W/50) 500 mpp

TEST CONDITIONS:
Weather: Fine
Wind: 8–15 mph
Temperature: 10 deg C (50 deg F)
Barometer: 29·2in. Hg
Humidity: 80 per cent
Surface: Dry concrete and asphalt
Test distance: 2,032 miles

Figures taken at 2,300 miles by our own staff at the Motor Industry Research Association proving ground at Nuneaton.

Dimensions

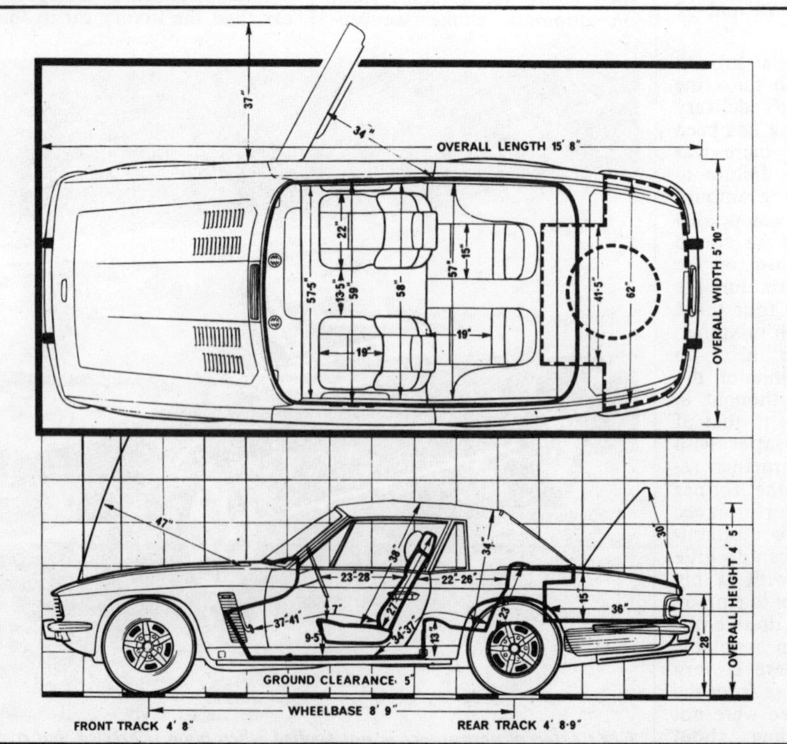

STANDARD GARAGE
16ft×8ft 6in.

TURNING CIRCLES:
Between kerbs
L, 37ft 7in.; R, 37ft 2 in.
Between walls
L, 30ft 4in.; R, 38ft 11in
Steering wheel turns, lock to lock 3·6

WEIGHT:
Kerb Weight 35·7cwt (3,997lb–1,813kg) (with oil, water and half full fuel tank).
Distribution per cent F, 51·8; R, 48·2.
Laden as tested: 39·0cwt (4,372lb–1,983kg).

One has no trouble finding the ignition - cum - steering lock, which faces one and has no awkward additional locks to release before you pull the key out.

The speedometer and rev-counter are straight in front of the driver, with an old-fashioned trip zero, easily reached. To the left, all except the clock angled towards the driver, are the subsidiary instruments – temperature, oil pressure, fuel, and voltmeter. On the centre console are switches for foglamps, the fuel filler flap (working only when the ignition is off), town and country horn selector, hazard flashers, power roof raising or lowering, parking lamps, and lamps proper.

Each side of the selector lever are the electric window switches, which raise or lower the side glasses pleasingly fast, though a little noisily; the glasses however will not wind down completely into the door. Just in front of the driver's door lock is a switch which saves one leaning across to lock the passenger's door; a solenoid device, it works quietly. The boot-lid has no external release, but a remote handle in the driver's door jamb, with a separate key to lock it; pulling the lever allows the boot-lid to rise on its counterbalance springs.

Heating and ventilation is dependent on a combined heating and air-conditioning cooling unit, which works best on either of the two fan speed settings rather than on ram air

Specification

Jensen Interceptor III Convertible

FRONT ENGINE, REAR-WHEEL DRIVE

ENGINE	
Cylinders	8, in 90 deg vee
Main bearings	5
Cooling system	Water; pump, thermostat and electric fans
Bore	109·72mm (4·32in.)
Stroke	95·25mm (3·75in.)
Displacement	7,212 c.c. (440 cu. in.)
Valve gear	Overhead, hydraulic tappets
Compression ratio	8·2 to 1. Min. octane rating: 91RM
Carburettors	One Carter four choke
Fuel pump	Carter mechanical
Oil filter	Full flow, renewable element
Max. power	280 bhp (net) at 4,800 rpm
Max. torque	380 lb. ft. (net) at 3,200 rpm
TRANSMISSION	
Gearbox	Chrysler Torqueflite 3-speed epicyclic with torque converter
Gear ratios	Top (Auto) 1·0–2·0 Inter 1·45–2·90 Low 2·45–4·90 Reverse 2·2–4·4
Final drive	Salisbury hypoid bevel with Powr-Lok differential
Mph at 1,000 rpm in top gear	24·8
CHASSIS and BODY	
Construction	Steel body welded to tubular steel frame
SUSPENSION	
Front	Independent; coil springs, double wishbones, telescopic dampers, anti-roll bar
Rear	Live axle; half-elliptic leaf springs. Panhard rod, telescopic dampers
STEERING	
Type	Adwest rack and pinion, with power assistance
Wheel dia.	15in.
BRAKES	
Make and type	Girling ventilated discs front and rear. Divided hydraulic circuits
Servo	Girling vacuum
Dimensions	F, 10·75in. dia. R, 10·75in. dia.
Swept area	F, 208·5 sq. in., R, 208·5 sq. in. Total 417 sq. in. (216 sq. in./ton laden)
WHEELS	
Type	Cast aluminium alloy 6·5in. wide rim
Tyres – make	Dunlop
– type	Radial ply tubed
– size	ER70VR 15in.
EQUIPMENT	
Battery	12 volt 66 Ah.
Alternator	60 amp a.c.
Headlamps	Lucas 4-lamp 110/220 watt (total)
Reversing lamp	Standard
Electric fuses	12 + 10 in-line
Screen wipers	Two-speed, self-parking
Screen washer	Standard electric
Interior heater	Standard, air conditioning
Heated backlight	Not applicable
Safety belts	Standard, inertia reel
Interior trim	Leather seats, pvc headlining
Floor covering	Carpet
Jack	Bevel lift screw pillar
Jacking points	Two each side under sills
Windscreen	Laminated
Underbody protection	Bitumastic compound on surfaces exposed to road
MAINTENANCE	
Fuel tank	20 Imp. gallons (91 litres)
Cooling system	32 pints (inc. heater)
Engine sump	8·5 pints (4·7 litres) SAE 20W/50. Change oil every 4,000 miles. Change filter every 8,000 miles
Gearbox	17 pints. ATF type A. No change
Final drive	3 pints. Shell l.s.d. oil S6721A Change every 8,000 miles
Grease	4 points every 4,000 miles
Valve clearance	Hydraulic (non-adjustable)
Ignition timing	10 deg. BTDC (static)
Spark plug	Type: Champion J11Y. Gap 0·035in.
Compression pressure	100 psi.
Tyre pressures	F 28; R, 32 psi (normal driving) F, 36; R, 40 psi (over 110 mph)
Max. payload	800lb (363kg)

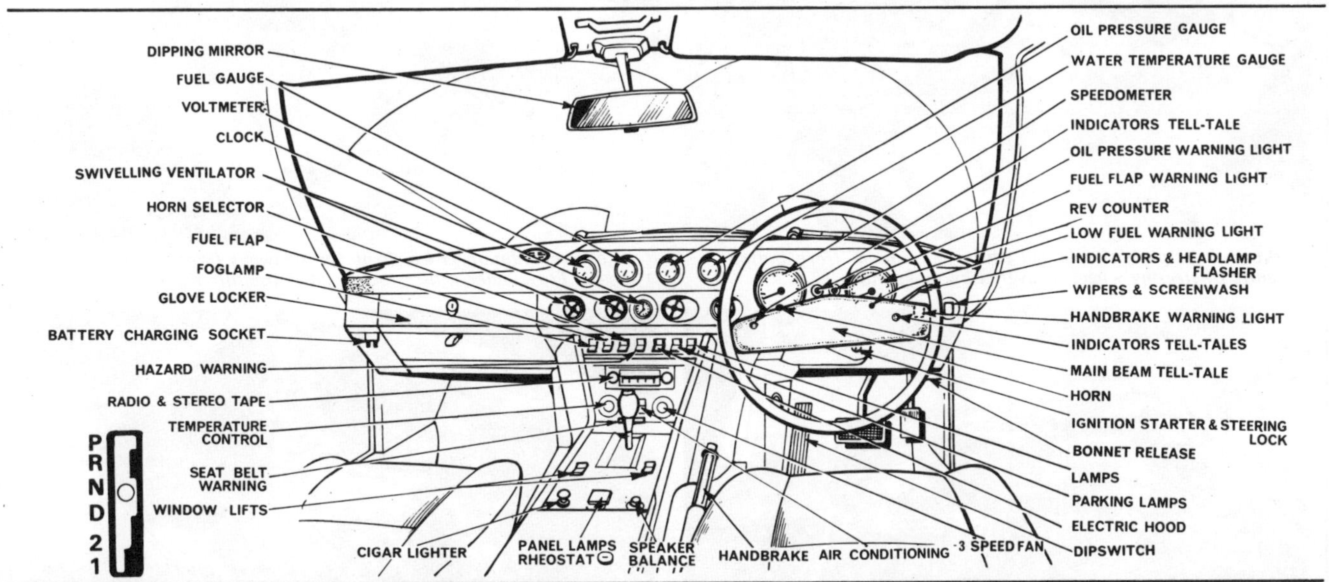

DIPPING MIRROR
FUEL GAUGE
VOLTMETER
CLOCK
SWIVELLING VENTILATOR
HORN SELECTOR
FUEL FLAP
FOGLAMP
GLOVE LOCKER
BATTERY CHARGING SOCKET
HAZARD WARNING
RADIO & STEREO TAPE
TEMPERATURE CONTROL
SEAT BELT WARNING
WINDOW LIFTS
P R N D 2 1
CIGAR LIGHTER
PANEL LAMPS RHEOSTAT
SPEAKER BALANCE
HANDBRAKE
AIR CONDITIONING
3 SPEED FAN
OIL PRESSURE GAUGE
WATER TEMPERATURE GAUGE
SPEEDOMETER
INDICATORS TELL-TALE
OIL PRESSURE WARNING LIGHT
FUEL FLAP WARNING LIGHT
REV COUNTER
LOW FUEL WARNING LIGHT
INDICATORS & HEADLAMP FLASHER
WIPERS & SCREENWASH
HANDBRAKE WARNING LIGHT
INDICATORS TELL-TALES
MAIN BEAM TELL-TALE
HORN
IGNITION STARTER & STEERING LOCK
BONNET RELEASE
LAMPS
PARKING LAMPS
ELECTRIC HOOD
DIPSWITCH

Servicing

	4,000 miles	8,000 miles	18,000 miles
Time Allowed (hours)	4	7	2·25
Cost at £3.30 per hour	£13.2	£23.1	£7.43
Engine oil	£2.72	£2.72	—
Oil Filter	—	£2.27	—
Sparking Plugs	—	—	£5.84
Total Cost:	£15.92	£28.09	£13.27

Routine Replacements:	Time hours	Labour	Spares	TOTAL
Brake pads – front (2 wheels)	0·75	£2.48	£8.61	£11.09
Brake pads – rear (2 wheels)	0·75	£2.48	£7.32	£9.80
Exhaust system complete (one side)	3·0	£9.90	£37.25	£47.15
Dampers – front (pair)	1·0	£3.30	£10.24	£13.54
Dampers – rear (pair)	1·5	£4.95	£10.24	£15.19
Replace half shaft	4·0	£13.20	£16.32	£29.52
Replace alternator (exchange)	1·1	£3.63	£62.0	£65.63
Replace starter (exchange)	1·5	£4.95	£59.10	£64.05

Hood under its cover sits on rather than in the neat tail

A driver's door mirror is standard; a nearside wing mirror would be welcome for use when the hood is up

Dashboard design is simple and easily understood. Horn button in centre of steering wheel is covered by spoke material

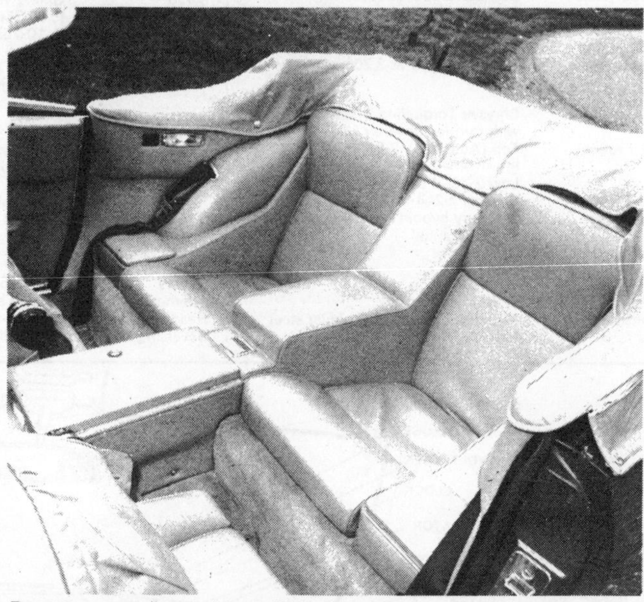

Rear accommodation is excellent for sideways location, but cramped. Tray under centre locker lid is usefully-sized

Engine accessibility is less daunting with the carburettor air cleaner removed

Spring-loaded lid opens to reveal quite roomy boot. Toolkit is generous

Jensen Interceptor III Convertible

Headrests obstruct rear passenger vision to some extent. Pockets are provided in seat backs

flow, of which there is too little. The slow speed setting is fairly quiet, yet adequate for most purposes once one has achieved the state one wants; the high speed is noisy but pretty effective. You can also with the same switch close the car to incoming air, which is welcome in unpleasant atmospheres, Between the two rotary switches is the compressor isolating switch, marked A/C (switched off for the performance-testing runs). The left-hand rotary switch selects temperature and distribution of air-flow, having five basic positions, defrost, cold, cool, warm and hot. In cold conditions the arrangement works satisfactorily, giving as much hot air as one wishes, with tolerable heat variation; the same applies if one wishes to cool the interior on a hot day, although every time that we used the cool setting, we noted an unpleasant smell from the air-conditioning. On average English autumn days when one wants a little flow of cool (not cold) air, we found it difficult to achieve that, in spite of the four generous facia vents. One small disadvantage of the flexible back window in the hood is, of course, that it cannot be fitted with any form of heater, so that it tends to mist up sometimes.

Since rear vision anywhere other than directly aft with the hood up is bad, one has to be very careful of Y junctions, trying to treat them like a van driver, approaching as nearly at right angles to the road joined as possible. Front and direct side vision is quite good, with no great blind spots even in rain, since the wiper arcs are satisfactory. The same cannot be said of side vision for anyone in either of the two back seats, who are somewhat blinkered unless they lean forward, which the careful – and very comfortable – shaping of the seats does not encourage one to do.

Living with the Interceptor convertible

Back seat passengers declared themselves pleased with the way they were held in place sideways by the cup-like recesses of the rear squab. If adult passengers are carried in the back it is necessary for the front seats to be adjusted forwards noticeably – to the slight discomfort of any tall driver and the insecurity of a front passenger of more than slim figure, who could not buckle the seat belt, since it was not long enough on the test car used here.

As with most open cars, the Interceptor convertible comes into its own with the hood down. Lowering the top is simple enough initially – just release the two hood rail clamps, unzip the back window and fold that on to the rear shelf, and press the hood switch. The top then slowly winds back, with a pause in mid-stride, folding on to rather than into the back, the rear quarter windows then tilting backwards into the side if one continues to work the switch; the windows can be left up if wished.

The not-so-convenient part of the operation is fitting the hood cover, for which no power is available other than your own weight, which may be needed to compress the hood frame enough to allow all of the numerous press studs on the cover to be done up. As mentioned before, the hood sits on top of the back, and not in a well, so that to some eyes it does not look tidy or neat. One can see over it in the inside mirror, however, and of course vision generally is vastly improved. There are various safety drop-out switches to prevent overloading, which can be reset; they live in a panel in front of the driver under the dashboard.

We were surprised by the doors, which lack enough restraint in the door-holding straps; even on a slight camber, they will not hold their door open. When one shuts the driver's door, there is a tendency for its ingenious American-style internally adjustable mirror to lose its setting. There are releases to allow the seat backs to be pushed out of the way of rear passengers – one release on either side of each seat. Their position at the base of the back means that one needs two hands to move the seat; also it is kinder if the driver or front passenger moves the back for anyone behind who wants to get out, since it is a big stretch forward from the back seat to release either lever.

A pleasantly thoughtful feature is the thermal delay switch for the four courtesy lamps. As on the Rolls-Royce Silver Shadow, the lamps do not extinguish themselves immediately one shuts both doors, so that you have light to don seat belts and find the ignition keyhole and so on. Another item that works when everything is supposedly off, is the pair of radiator electric fans. They will switch on and run for a little while after one has got out of the car and locked up, dealing with the heat that soaks out of the cooling engine. Their sudden whirr – one can feel them as a vibration in the steering wheel and floor inside the car incidentally – and the brilliantly lit interior both evident in a car which you have clearly already left prompts thoughtful bystanders to suggest that you have forgotten to switch off.

Another thoughtful point, once not so unfamiliar, is the provision of a battery charging socket on the passenger's side, complete with plug. Ground clearance is adequate, the silencers being the lowest point and therefore having small skid-plates welded underneath. Boot space is fairly generous, though not quite as big as one might wish on some occasions. The nicely produced handbook provides an unusually thorough amount of information for the owner-driver on how to look after the car himself. The tool kit is quite comprehensive too, with various screwdrivers, three open-ended AF spanners, an adjustable spanner, a pair of pliers and a tyre pressure gauge. There is also a jack, wheel-brace, plug spanner and a pair of spare fan belts, all stored separately. The test car was fitted with a Radiomobile cartridge player/radio whose performance was spoiled by unduly resonant door-mountings for the front speakers. The Philips RN 712 cassette machine is also offered. Smaller cassettes would more easily be stored in the Jensen, which has only a limited amount of oddment space – a quite useful centre locker, and a much smaller one in the dashboard.

Remembering its price, and the company it is therefore among, one must be strict about the Jensen Interceptor convertible. There are points which we have felt deserve criticism, but it must be stressed that for the man with a comfortable-enough wallet (both to buy it and to pay the fuel bill), it is a highly enjoyable car. We certainly enjoyed driving it – and, even remembering the price, it has very little competition. □

MANUFACTURER:
Jensen Motors Ltd., Kelvin Way, West Bromwich, Staffordshire

PRICES			
Basic	£8,276.00	Licence	£25
Special Car Tax	£689.67	Delivery charge (London)	Not quoted
VAT	£717.25	Number plates (approx.)	£10
Total (in GB)	**£9,682.92**	**Total on the Road (exc. insurance)**	**£9,717.92**
Seat Belts	Standard	Insurance	Group 7

The English make such things as the Wilkinson blade, Spode china and the Purdey shotgun—art objects as much as commodities. In this company must be included

THE JENSEN INTERCEPTOR CONVERTIBLE

By John Christy

When, on Friday, March 22, 1974, Mr. Kjell Qvale, the nation's if not the world's foremost purveyor of motor cars to the gentry, announced the latest confection from his British Jensen works, he stated that there would be a mere 750 to 800 of them, comma, *ever,* period. Introducing the Jensen Interceptor convertible as a rational alternative to Rolls-Royce's cost-spiraling (50-odd thousand dollars) Corniche, Qvale stated that the edition would be strictly limited.

Now that the cars are arriving in the U.S. that limit must obviously be raised. With their clientele putting down non-returnable deposits of up to $5000 on the car sight-unseen, Jensen dealers are justifiably clamoring for more production. In the face of such demand, in a country the size of the United States, limiting a success such as this by the purveyor would be an insanity. Nobody who is himself quite all there has ever suggested that Kjell Qvale does not pack a full seabag in the good sense department so it is inevitable that the limit will be raised to supply the demand.

What is this paragon that draws people to commit themselves well ahead of delivery to laying down the price of a small house for a mere automobile? It is, quite simply, the convertible version of that other paragon of automotive virtues, the Jensen Interceptor III, an Interceptor III with a cloth roof, if you will. If that sounds like an oversimplification it is not. To understand why one really has to have watched the Interceptors being put together at the small plant in West Bromwich, in England's Midlands.

Your traditionally assembled car consists of a chassis frame built in one area of a plant onto which is grafted a body assembled in another area. Each is roughly three quarters complete by the time they are introduced to each other and only from that point on is the car treated as one entity. The other traditional method is to build the body and frame together from a number of steel pressings and stampings welded together as the pieces move along an automated or semi-automated line, adding the running gear and interior after the whole business is assembled and painted.

The Jensen Interceptor is built more like a house or other building, being constructed from a foundation with each piece of the construction going up and outward from there. Each piece is welded, not bolted, to the structure that precedes it in the building process. By the time the process is half completed there is no way the layman or even a knowledgeable mechanic can point to one part or another and say "that is the frame and that is the body." They are one structural entity. It would take an engineer familiar with the construction to say where the chassis structure ends and the body support structure begins and even then he would be hard put to find the ex-

The changeover from hard to soft top has altered the original design by Touring of Italy for the better. The addition of a proper deck ties it all together.

The engine that now powers the Jensen is the Chrysler 440 wih cast rocker covers and detail changes. Emissions regs have weakened it but it is still a brute.

act line of demarcation because no such line exists by the time the outer panels are being added. The result is a structure so solid that when you walk along the line you could be forgiven for wondering whether the end result was going to be equipped with tracks or wheels.

The result of this method of construction is that there need be no difference in the basic structure between the hard top version and the convertible. As a matter of fact it is next to impossible to tell until the rear outer panels and windshield structure are being added whether a given structure is to be a convertible or a hard top version. The only clue prior to that point is that the unit destined to become a convertible has some very minor structural details added to the rear cockpit area to take the top mechanism. All this, of course, is in complete distinction from the normal convertible which requires a heavily strengthened frame and often added torque boxes in the body structure to provide added rigidity and offset the lack of the support normally provided by a steel top. In the Jensen the top is a roof, nothing more, and it makes no difference in torsional rigidity whether it is steel or cloth.

When this steel body-chassis structure is complete and as smooth as the hands of the craftsmen on the line can make it, the whole assembly including doors—and in the case of the convertible the deck lid—is totally immersed in a combination rust-proofing and primer bath until every part is coated against corrosion. Every surface including those that will never again see the light of day is thus protected. After a thorough drying the structure is then given its color painting, each structure being sent through the paint booths on a giant rotisserie-type carriage like a huge steel roast so that nothing is missed. This is one of the differences between Jensen and Rolls-Royce finishing—the Interceptor is painted before other components are added and the Rolls, any Rolls, does not get its final paint until the entire car is otherwise finished and tested. Which is the better way is difficult to say. On the one hand all metal surfaces are finish-color painted and on the other there is no chance of a mar in the final finish during assembly.

From here the Interceptor begins to take on the look of the quality motor carriage it is destined to become rather than some futuristic combat vehicle. All of the interior appointments other than proprietary hardware are manufactured on the premises. In a loft over a building adjacent to the main assembly building craftsmen and women put together the upholstery, trim, carpeting, seats and the convertible tops from the finest available materials. Each piece of material, unblemished hides, cloth and lambs wool trim pieces are laid out on tables and cut to patterns with the precision of Savile Row suiting, then stitched with the same care. The redolence of the combination of leather and wool is almost intoxicating.

These pieces are carried down to the final assembly area where they are installed by more craftsmen, the appropriate color combinations each going to the proper body structure. There, along with a host of proprietary hardware, including some 30 items that on lesser cars would be optional, the bits and pieces are assembled into one of the best ergonomic exercises in interior design in the business. The totality is both body coddling and, to anyone used to lesser equipage, mind boggling. When the final assembly is completed it is impossible to find a single crudity either in the material or the execution. Cheap plastic and other expedients are totally eschewed. There are no unfinished ends, no crude tuck-unders, no "Irish pennants"; all is finished by-seam, welt or the finest polished chrome trim.

Between the wiring and the final assembly of the interior trim each car is lifted onto the only bit of machinery or equipment that resembles the normal production line, a long platform on which the car gets its running gear, engine, transmission and driveline. From there it is lowered back down to the floor level and given its final finishing as explained above. The running gear is of quite conventional design but it is conventionality superbly executed. It is also seemingly stout enough to go under something designed to carry quarried rock. Up front is a normal but strongly built double A-arm, coil sprung suspension with massive tubular shock absorbers and tied together with a heavy sway

SPECIFICATIONS	JENSEN INTERCEPTOR CONVERTIBLE		
Engine	V-8 OHV		
Bore & Stroke-ins.	4.32/3.75		
Displacement—cu. in./cc.	440/7212		
HP @ RPM	215 @ 6200		
Torque—(lbs. @ RPM)	330 @ 3200		
Compression Ratio	8.2:1		
Carburetion	4 bbl.		
Transmission	3-speed automatic		
Rear Axle Ratio	2.88:1		
Steering Type	Rack & pinion		
Steering Ratio	17.8:1		
Turning Circle—ft.	38		
Wheel Turns (lock-to-lock)	3.4		
Tires	Dunlop ER70-VR 15-SP		
Brakes	Disc—disc		
Front Suspension	Independent coil springs Armstrong shocks Sway bar		
Rear Suspension	Live axle Semi-elliptic springs Armstrong shocks		
Body/Frame Construction	Monocoque		
Wheelbase—in./mm	105/267		
Overall Length—in./mm	184.5/4686		
Width—in./mm	69/1754		
Front Track—in./mm	56.25/1420		
Rear Track—in./mm	57.5/1440		
Height—in./mm	54.4/1381		
Weight as Tested—lbs.	4215		
Storage Capacity cu. ft/cm³	12/4200		
Fuel Capacity gals./liters	24/91		
Oil Capacity—qts./liters	6/ 4.7		
Base Price	$22,500		
Price as Tested	$22,805		
PERFORMANCE			
Acceleration			
0-30 mph	3.2 sec		
0-40 mph	4.6 sec		
0-50 mph	6.6 sec		
0-60 mph	8.8 sec		
Standing Start (¼-mile) Elapsed Time (sec.)	15.8		
Speed (mph)	82.0		
Passing Speeds 40-60 mph	4.7		
50-70 mph	4.9		
Stopping Distance (ft.) 30-0 mph	28 ft. 10 in.		
60-0 mph	134 ft. 8 in.		
Fuel Mileage	11.2 mpg		
Speedometer Error Indicated Speed	40	50	60
True Speed	40	50	60

Look as you might, you won't find a single crudity in the interior. With the exception of the hardware it is all done on the premises of the West Bromwich plant.

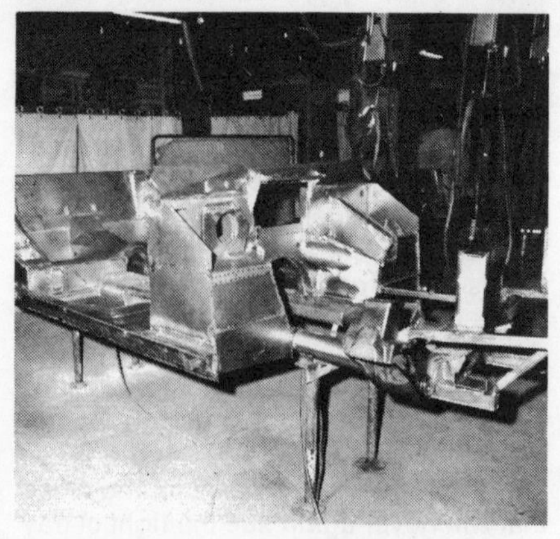

The chassis and body frame are all one integral structure with the result that there is no real structural difference between the hard top and the convertible.

Every seam and weld in the body is hand finished by craftmen for a flawless paint base. Seams are undetectable.

bar and a massive rack and pinion power steering system.

At the rear, hung on semi-elliptic springs is a conventional but massive live axle, again controlled by large Armstrong tubular shock absorbers and located securely by a Panhard rod to eliminate any unwanted lateral movement. On all four corners are massive Girling ventilated disc brakes with separate systems for the front and rear and power assistance. The rear system is equipped with a load-conscious valve to prevent rear wheel lock-up. Given the proper tires these brakes are capable of pulling the 4000-pound car to successive stops at over one g from 30 miles per hour and very nearly that from 60 mph, braking on the order of such things as Panteras, Ferrari Dinos, Porsche 911 Carreras and the like.

The engine, transmission and drive-train that motivates the whole assemblage is all Chrysler, a special version of the 440 4-barrel V-8 coupled to a Torque-Flite transmission operated by a floor shift. This is one of the things that makes such an exotic car practical for the United States, more so, possibly, than a Cadillac. If engine or driveline trouble occurs in some rural area far from home there is almost always a Chrysler products dealer within reasonable calling distance. The troubled Jensen owner can most likely be gotten back on the road without waiting for some exotic part and someone who knows what to do with it. There is, of course, a fly in this particular ointment. Like all other American V-8 engines the Chryslers have suffered from the results of the ever more strictured emissions requirements. The Interceptor III was originally introduced with a strong 383 that belted out 330 bhp and 425 lbs/ft. of torque which was sufficient to propel the car ever so smoothly up to 140 honest miles per hour. As 1972 turned into 1973 and controls became tighter the 440 was substituted for the 383 in an effort to hold the original power through more, though weaker, inches. Performance for 1973 didn't suffer as a result though neutral handling turned into a certain amount of understeer due to the added weight. Now it is 1975 and not even the added cubic inches can offset the added controls. The car is still no slouch but it does lack the brilliant snap of the earlier Interceptors. However, since everything else has suffered in the same proportion, the Interceptor is still in the same comparative performance category which is to say high for a '75 car.

Quality, luxury, strength, integrity and ergonomic *tours de force* are all very well but what else has Mr. Qvale's Jensen works wrought in the car to command sight-unseen commitments on the part of customers to part with $23,000 for the convertible Jensen as opposed to the $17,000 hard top version?

I first met the convertible one rainy night outside of the West Bromwich plant after spending a day seeing how it was put together. It was one of those rainy nights that only England can come up with—rain that seemed wetter than mere water, the sort of cold that seeps into the bones, a darkness that was almost tangible and large raindrops that rattled like hail. I dove out of the plant and into the waiting Interceptor convertible and at first thought I'd gotten into the hardtop by mistake. There was none of the usual rattle of rain on a convertible top and it was only when I looked around that we could see that the car was indeed a soft-top. In fact, if anything it was quieter, the heavy rain being barely audible through the muffling wool inner liner. Our destination was dinner at an inn in the Cotswold hills and eventually the hotel in which we were to stay in Warwick. The route lay over typical English secondary roads, high crowned, twisting, narrow, almost too narrow for the massive Jensen, and glistening with water. Driving the car was no less a personage than Mr. Kevin Beatty, formerly chief engineer, now Managing Director of the Jensen works, i.e., in the absence of owner Qvale, the senior officer pre-

sent. Mr. Beatty takes his driving seriously in the English manner which is to say he drives very well and very fast. Like many people for whom driving is prerequisite to making a living, I am a poor passenger, nervous, watchful and a bit paranoid when someone else is driving in other than the normal urban/suburban situation. But the combination of Jensen and Beatty, even on those narrow roads in that awful weather, left me totally at ease. The big car glided rapidly, smoothly and quietly over the thin, wet macadam ribbons without a single indication of approaching the edge of control. Mr. Beatty's skill notwithstanding, a car with the mass of a Jensen driven at those speeds and under those conditions could be expected to exhibit some signs of nearing or being on the ragged edge unless it was very, very good. The only conclusion, since there were no such signs perceptible even to a paranoid passenger, is that the car is very, very good indeed.

This was borne out later when we received our test car in the U.S. There *is* a difference between the coupe and the convertible. The understeer effect brought about in the coupe by the addition of the 440 engine is not nearly as apparent for one thing. For another, though the specs on paper for the coupe and the convertible are to all intents and purposes identical, the convertible feels more "sporting", somehow more responsive and, if anything, more stable. Just why this should be would be most difficult to explain since the weight of the convertible is within 100 lbs. of the latest coupes and roughly the same as that of the earlier 383-equipped version. Possibly the fact that the weight is concentrated below the belt line has something to do with it and very likely motoring in the open air has its own psychological effect. Whatever it is, the convertible feels subtly different from the hard roofed version. Not that it's any less pleasant or less anything, mind; if anything it's a feeling of more of something or a number of somethings that you can't quite put your finger on. There is one obvious aspect; with the top down it isn't quite as deceptive as is the coupe in its unobtrusive tendency to creep up to illegal speeds before you notice what it's doing. The effect of top down, open air motoring lets you know when you are starting to motor too fast unlike the coupe which will with total lack of obtrusion increase its speed in such a way that one is totally unaware that what the car is doing might be wildly illegal. Mind that the term is "illegal" not "unsafe," because the car, either the convertible or the coupe, is capable of maneuvering safely, securely and from an inside standpoint even sedately at a rate of knots that would create motion sickness in lesser conveyances. What to an outsider might look to border on the suicidal is to the insider, driver or passenger, mere motoring. What might be labor in any other heavy car is, to the Jensen driver, an effortless process that makes the progress a sort of sensuous pleasure. Part of this is the solid but silk-smooth suspension, part the tenacious grip it gets on the ground and part is due to the fine balance – 50-50 give or take a pound or two depending on load. I was once snookered by all this with an earlier version (I know better now) into committing an illegality for which the penalty was a well-deserved citation. I was motoring comfortably homeward bound the evening of the day I picked up the car. All four speakers of the Lear Jet stereo unit (standard equipment) were laying the day's news on me and the road up through the twisting canyon pass felt like a well-oiled slot into which the car was firmly attached. What I couldn't figure out was why everybody else was going so slowly. As you crest that particular pass the road turns into four lanes so I started doing the traffic slalom number through the traffic. This section is one of sweeping turns through which a sports car does well to maintain 50 mph and a heavy sedan feels distinctly edgy at anything over 40. As the car neared the bottom I glanced at the meter, thinking I might be doing maybe 45 mph. The thing informed me that I was doing 65 and change! I grabbed for second gear but too late; the inside of the car turned all nasty red and I was shortly signing the resultant ticket. The officer was kind, though; since he hadn't been able to clock the Jensen through the turn he wrote the cite for 47. Painful but instructive.

All the above aside, quality is as quality does and there are possibly two other convertibles in the world with quality control and finish equal to the Jensen Interceptor. You can come by this sort of ultimate finish in several ways: you can stand over the work force with a whip, you can station an inspector every few yards or you can use some sort of bonus system. The message the Jensen delivers is that it is built that way because the builders, from the managing director down to the sweeper *wanted* to build it that way. A visit to the Jensen works bears the message out – everybody looks as though they really *like* what they're doing and are proud of the results.

That and the result of the labor of love goes a long way to explaining why the cognoscenti are knocking on the dealer's doors for Mr. Qvale's latest offering at $22,000 the copy. Looked at one way, that is a lot of money but looked at another it's 30 thousand dollars less than the price of admission to a Corniche. ■

BRIEF TEST

Jensen Interceptor III

FOR: very fast ; quiet and refined ; well equipped

AGAINST: untidy handling at speed on bumpy roads ; poor rear-seat legroom ; heavy fuel consumption

Over the years we have been lucky enough to become very familiar with Jensen's current luxury car since it was first introduced in October 1966, having presently tried no fewer than five examples of it. But until now only the first of these was an Interceptor, two being the discontinued but pioneering FF with its four-wheel drive and anti-lock brakes, while a third was the high-performance SP version, also discontinued.

Each of these tests created or renewed our affection and respect for the car including this fifth one, which concerns the Interceptor III. It largely confirms our appreciation of the virtues which have made the Jensen one of the more successful of the high-priced luxury cars. The most obvious of these, of course, is the car's body—with its "gold-fish bowl" rear window—which was styled by Touring of Milan and which most of our staff still regard as being both strikingly handsome and modern in treatment, despite its age—eight years. The Interceptor's performance hasn't changed much over the years, either, but remains another important asset: its 7-litre Chrysler V8 engine gets it to 60 mph from a standstill in under 8 seconds with no more fuss than a gentle woosh; 20 mph can be added to 30 mph in less time than it takes to light a cigarette and the top speed is nearly 130 mph.

Under most circumstances the Interceptor also displays a very high cornering power and is even more impressive in the tautness and precision of its handling, which are unusually good for a large, luxury car. It was, we sometimes felt, the simple, mechanically unsophisticated car at its best. But not quite at its best—for the live rear axle is located only by leaf springs and a Panhard rod—and only sometimes, because our test car became distinctly untidy when driven really hard on bumpy roads. On such surfaces its handling is significantly outclassed by the handling of a number of rivals with more advanced suspension systems such as the Aston Martin V8 or the Porsche Carrera.

Although the Jensen is very quiet at all speeds, it is similarly outclassed by the Jaguar XJ 12 in refinement and noise suppression. This isn't a major fault, however, the Interceptor's big defect being its lack of rear-seat legroom which reduces virtually to nothing when all of the admittedly large range of front-seat fore-and-aft adjustment has been used up. And like so many cars of its type, it is inordinately heavy for its carrying capacity. The new Lotus Elite, for example, with a smaller boot but sensible rear seats, weighs over 11 cwt less.

But it takes more than a bit of weight to put a noticeable dent in the performance provided by the big Chrysler V8 which has powered the car from the beginning. The first Interceptors were fitted with a 6276 cc version of the engine, but three years ago the capacity was increased to 7212 cc, mostly to offset the losses created by exhaust emission controls. (For European models these are confined to thermostatically controlled inlet air temperature, timing and combination modifications plus crankcase vapour and evaporative loss control.) Fitted with a four-barrel Carter carburetter, this pushrod unit with hydraulic tappets now develops 287 (DIN) bhp at 4700 rpm and 383 lb ft of torque at 3600 rpm.

Judged by the 0-60 mph and 30-50 mph acceleration times, it gives the Interceptor III virtually the same (but highly satisfactory) performance as all its predecessors (of this series; the name was used before the war). Thus the quickest car to 60 mph was the original Interceptor of 1967—not the SP which came later—with a time of 7.3 sec and no car was slower than 7.7 sec. Similarly, the slowest in 30-50 mph acceleration was also the original Interceptor with a time of 3.4 sec, while the fastest is the current car with a time of 2.7 sec. Due to changes in gearing the maximum speeds attained have varied rather more: from an estimated 140 mph to the 129 mph which today's car will comfortably reach but to which it is limited by the red line on the tachometer. Strictly speaking this means that the gearing is a little low, but the engine is always very quiet, completely smooth and utterly unfussed so it doesn't really matter, and the car will still cruise at 110-120 mph on Continental motorways in a very relaxed way. Thanks to an efficient automatic choke, primed by a couple of pumps of the accelerator pedal, the engine was always quick to start and to warm up, pulling without hesitation.

The exhaust emission regulations may not have caused the performance to deteriorate over the years, but they haven't done the fuel consumption much good, though the Jensen's thirst has always been so gargantuan that it's doubtful if this will concern prospective owners very much—even with petrol at its present price. However, the overall consumption of our Interceptor III was a distinctly poor 10.0 mpg, compared to the 11 or more mpg obtained from earlier cars. With gentler driving than ours, this might improve to 11-13 mpg, but few owners are likely to be able to match the 15.6 mpg touring consumption which would give a range of over 300 miles from the 20-gallon tank.

We've always regarded the Chrysler Torqueflite automatic transmission as being the best in the world, better even than the Rolls-improved GM system fitted to the Silver Shadow, and our experience with the Jensen fully confirm our judgment. Under virtually all conditions the unit slurs imperceptibly from one gear to the next. The full-throttle changes of our standing-start tests were no more noticeable—and left no detectable kinks on the traces of our chart recorder. And if a manual change were called for, to hold a gear in a corner, the change remained almost as smooth. But manual selection to improve the acceleration times proved quite unnecessary on our test car, since full throttle automatic changes from first took place at 4800 rpm—the maximum power revs and only 400 rpm off the overall limit—while the unit changed from second at exactly that 5200 rpm limit, equivalent to 89 mph. There was sometimes a delay when selecting kickdown, however, and some of our drivers

Emission control systems involve maze of pipes which crowd engine compartment

didn't like the selector pattern, with a detent to be overcome—by pressing a button in the knob of the floor lever—before second could be obtained from drive, but no protection against the inadvertent selection of neutral on the move.

In the past we have been almost lyrical in our praise of the feel provided by the power steering systems fitted to the Jensen, but those fitted to the more recent cars don't seem to us to be as good as the ones used for the original models, though most cars have been equipped with the same Adwest rack and pinion system. The steering of the Interceptor III, for example, is precise and reasonably direct (though the lock is very poor) but has weight or resistance rather than the sort of feel which helps the driver to detect the presence of greasy patches. Nevertheless the car as a whole is so responsive and rolls so little that it is nearly always a great pleasure to drive, being magnificent on fast, sweeping bends if the road surfaces are tolerably smooth. The cornering power in the dry is high and the behaviour pleasantly neutral, the limited-slip differential making it possible to put down plenty of power without getting the tail out of line, even in the wet, when the cornering power was also high. Push the car hard on a bumpy road, though, and it will hop, lurch and generally become a bit of a handful. The limited-slip differential, too, would occasionally let the car snake under quite moderate acceleration when a slippery patch was encountered.

But the brakes had a firm, progressive action, and the four ventilated discs proved capable of repeatedly clawing the car down from high speeds without effort.

Unfortunately the ride doesn't reach the same high standards: it is not as good as in other luxury cars, nor even, we feel, as good as ought to be possible with a live-axled layout. Although it is firm and well damped, and although it tends to smooth out at high speeds, it becomes jerky and disturbed on rough or broken surfaces at low speeds. Even so, it was seldom really uncomfortable on the worst of the poorly surfaced French roads that we encountered during our test.

The Jensen's back seats, separated by a fixed division-cum-armrest, are well shaped and the headroom above them, if modest, is acceptable—the rear problem is legroom. The front seats must be moved forward several notches to provide enough legroom even for smallish children, and there is no legroom at all if these seats are in their rearmost positions. Unfortunately the necessary sharing of space is not pleasant for the driver and front passenger as their seats are close to the floor making a straight-legged sitting position the most comfortable — but impossible to achieve when passengers are in the rear of the car.

Beneath the huge, lift-up rear window is the boot, the largish size of which is partly the cause of the poor rear-seat legroom. The hinged cover beneath the window, however, makes a large rear parcel shelf, and there is quite a lot of additional space for oddments in pockets built into the front-seat backrests, in a lidded tray at the rear of the central console and in the lockable glove compartment.

The straight-legged driving position is extremely comfortable, the range of fore-and-aft seat adjustment ample (rear passengers permitting) for the tallest drivers and the steering wheel is adjustable for reach. The seat cushion is rather flat, though, creating a tendency, in conjunction with the slipperiness of the leather upholstery, for passengers to slide forward. More lumbar and lateral support is also needed, though sideways location is helped by the old-fashioned floor dipswitch which makes an ideal bracing pad for the left foot; we would like to see it adapted to that purpose alone.

Although the horn button is located where we feel it should be—in the centre of the steering wheel—and although there is an indicator/flasher stalk, the remaining controls, like the dipswitch already mentioned, are rather scattered, the washers and

Top: Front seats are quite comfortable but need more lumbar and lateral support. Flat cushion and leather upholstery promotes a tendency to slide forward. Above: rear seats are well shaped but lack legroom

Above: four eyeball vents admit heated or cooled air according to the setting of the control knob on the central console. Switches and minor controls are rather scattered

Left: despite hooding, speedometer and rev-counter glasses create unwanted reflections

wipers being controlled by a knob on the right-hand side of the fascia and the lights by a switch on the central console. The glasses of the speedometer and rev-counter, too, create unwanted reflections, but these instruments are well located and of good size and appearance, though the speedometer is calibrated only at 5 mph intervals. A clock and four additional gauges are mounted in the centre of the fascia above the central console. Short drivers might find it slightly difficult to look over this fascia, but the lack of bulge in the car's flanks makes it easy to thread through small gaps, the wiper pattern is good and there are no significant blind spots.

Jensen have shown a commendable if slightly over-enthusiastic desire to simplify the heating controls — over-enthusiastic because distribution control has been largely eliminated. There are merely two knobs, one of which controls temperature (but has a "defrost" position for heated air to the screen) and automatically brings in the standard-equipment air conditioner at the cool end of the scale, its output of refrigerated air being admitted through a battery of fascia vents with the help of the second knob which controls the booster fan; there is very little throughput without it. This system works well on the whole, the ability of the air conditioner to cool the car being particularly impressive, but the lack of distribution control does become apparent when the feet get cooled more than the face under certain conditions.

The Jensen's engine and transmission are always extremely quiet and there is little wind noise, even at high speeds, though the refinement of our test car was spoilt a little by a noticeable vibration at 100 mph or more. There is also quite a lot of bump-thump on rough surfaces—the road noise insulation is poor by Jaguar or Peugeot standards.

There aren't many fittings of any importance that the Jensen doesn't have. Air conditioning, electric window lifters, Sundym glass, a heated backlight, reversing lights, a fire extinguisher, a first-aid kit and warning lights in the door edges are all standard equipment. A four-speaker radio with an irritatingly noisy and ostentatious automatic aerial is another standard fitting, but we liked the remote switch for the passenger's doorlock and the delay-action interior light which saves a lot of fumbling in the dark.

In sum, we find the Interceptor III an admirable luxury car with excellent performance and a slightly sporting bias. It is not quite as quiet and refined as some of its rivals, nor does it ride so comfortably, but by the same token it handles more responsively than many of them. It does not transcend the limitations of its excessive weight or space-wasting design, but neither do many of its competitors transcend theirs.

MOTOR ROAD TEST No. 4/75 • Jensen Interceptor III

PERFORMANCE

CONDITIONS

Weather	Cool and dry
Temperature	46-54° F
Barometer	29.1 in Hg
Surface	Dry tarmacadam

MAXIMUM SPEEDS

	mph	kph
At max revs	129	207
Terminal Speeds:		
at ¼ mile	91	146
at kilometer	114	184
Speed in gears (at 5200 rpm):		
1st	53	85
2nd	89	143

ACCELERATION FROM REST

mph	sec	kph	sec
0-30	3.0	0-40	2.3
0-40	4.2	0-60	3.8
0-50	5.7	0-80	5.6
0-60	7.7	0-100	8.0
0-70	9.8	0-120	10.8
0-80	12.5	0-140	14.5
0-90	16.0	0.160	19.6
0-100	20.0	0-180	26.5
0-110	25.5	Stand'g km	33.5
0-120	34.0		
Stand'g ¼	15.9		

ACCELERATION IN KICKDOWN

mph	sec	kph	sec
20-40	2.5	40-60	1.5
30-50	2.7	60-80	1.8
40-60	3.5	80-100	2.4
50-70	4.1	100-120	2.8
60-80	4.8	120-140	3.3
70-90	6.2	140-160	5.1
80-100	7.5	160-180	6.9
90-110	9.5		
100-120	14.0		

FUEL CONSUMPTION

Touring*	15.6 mpg
	18.1 litres/100 km

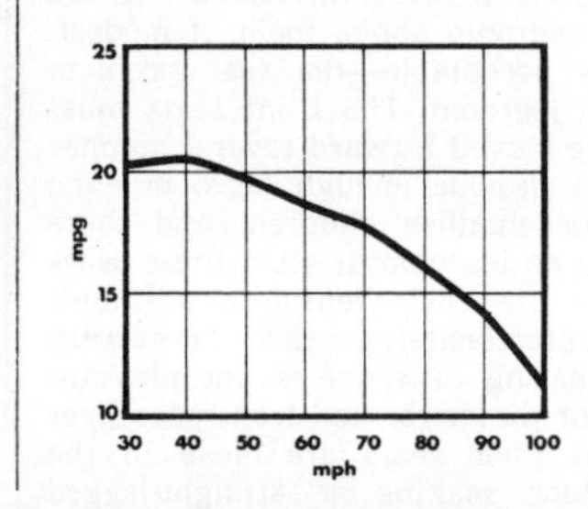

Overall	10.0 mpg
	28.3 litres/100 km
Fuel grade	91 octane
	Two star rating
Tank capacity	20 galls
	91 litres
Max range	312 miles
	502 km
Test distance	1420 miles
	2410 km

* Consumption midway between 30 mph and maximum less 5 per cent for acceleration.

SPEEDOMETER (mph)

Speedo	30	40	50	60	70	80	90	100
True mph	30	40	50	59	69	78	87½	96

Distance recorder: 1.5 per cent fast

WEIGHT

	cwt	kg
Unladen weight*	34.8	1765
Weight as tested	38.6	1960
Distribution front/rear	52/48	

* With fuel for approx 50 miles

Performance tests carried out by Motor's staff at the Motor Industry Research Association proving ground, Lindley.

GENERAL SPECIFICATION

ENGINE

Cylinders	8 in V
Capacity	7212 cc (440 cu in)
Bore/stroke	109.8 x 95.3 mm (4.32 x 3.75 in)
Cooling	Water
Block	Cast iron
Head	Cast iron
Valves	Pushrod ohv, hydraulic tappets
Valve timing	
inlet opens	21 btdc
inlet closes	67 abdc
ex opens	79 bbdc
ex closes	25 atdc
Compression	8.2 : 1
Carburetter	4-barrel Carter
Bearings	5 main
Fuel pump	Mechanical
Max power	287 bhp (DIN) at 4800 rpm
Max torque	383 lb ft (DIN) at 3200 rpm

TRANSMISSION

Type	Chrysler Torqueflite 3-speed automatic with torque converter

Internal ratios and mph/1000 rpm

Top	1.00 :	1/24.8
2nd	1.45 :	1/17.1
1st	2.45 :	1/10.1
Rev	2.20 :	1
Final drive	3.07 :	1

BODY/CHASSIS

Construction	Integral steel body and tubular steel chassis
Protection	Bitumen underseal-ant

SUSPENSION

Front	Unequal length wishbones with coil springs and anti-roll bar
Rear	Live axle on leaf springs with Panhard rod

STEERING

Type	Adwest rack and pinion
Assistance	Yes

Toe-out	1/16 in
Camber	+ 1°
Castor	2°
King pin	7°

BRAKES

Type	Ventilated discs
Servo	Yes
Circuits	Two: front/rear
Rear valve	Yes
Adjustment	Yes

WHEELS

Type	Alloy, 6.5 in. rim
Tyres	ER 70 VR 15 Dunlop SP
Pressures	28 F, 32 R (normal) 36 F, 40 R (max speeds and loads)

ELECTRICAL

Battery	12V 67 Ah
Polarity	Negative
Generator	60A alternator
Fuses	12
Headlights	4 x 5¾ in. 55W halogen

COMPARISONS

	Capacity cc	Price £	Max mph	0-60 sec	30-50* sec	Overall mpg	Touring mpg	Length ft in	Width ft in	Weight cwt	Boot cu ft
Jensen Interceptor III	7212	8334	129.0†	7.7	2.7	10.0	15.6	15 8	5 10	34.8	8.5
Aston Martin V8	5340	11,349	154.8	5.7	7.0	13.2	14.7	15 1.3	6 0	34.7	8.9
Citroen SM	2670	6691	—	8.3	12.9	14.9	—	16 0.5	6 0.5	29.5	9.0
Fiat 130 Coupe	3253	7100	115.6	10.6	3.9	18.8	—	15 10	6 0	31.7	12.3
Iso Lele	5762	10,669	132.0	7.3	2.7	11.3	15.7	15 4.5	5 9	33.1	9.1
Lotus Elite 503	1973	6674	125.0†	8.1	11.6	18.6	26.9	14 7.5	5 11.5	23.0	6.6
Porsche Carrera Coupe	2687	9000	150.0†	5.5	—	16.7	—	13 7	5 3	21.2	2.9‡
Jaguar XJ12C	5343	6009	135.7	7.4	2.6	11.5	13.5	15 10	4 11	34.8	11.8

*in kickdown ; 5th for Aston, SM and Lotus †estimated ‡measured with boxes

Make: Jensen
Model: Interceptor III
Maker: Jensen Motors Ltd, Kelvin Way, West Bromwich, Staffs.
Price: £7123 plus £593.58 car tax plus £617.33 VAT equals £8333.91

JENSEN INTERCEPTOR III CONVERTIBLE

One of the world's few convertibles is luxurious and comfortable

PHOTOS BY JOHN LAMM

OUR LAST EXPERIENCE with a Jensen Interceptor III was in October 1973 and we concluded, "All things considered, the Jensen Interceptor ranks among the world's best cars." That judgment remains true today and can be extended to the convertible version as well. First, it's one of the only true convertibles you can still buy, which is worth something in itself. Second, the Jensen is characterized by superior attention to detail and finish, comfort, reasonable performance and handling that is sufficiently good for impressing passengers, keeping in mind that one does not often take a $20,000+ luxury car out on the back roads and flog it around twisty turns.

Although the Interceptor's styling is undistinguished, we do like the looks of the convertible version. It's neater and simpler than the hardtop version with its large rear glass area. The convertible top is fully as elegant as the leather interior appointments and our single complaint is that the top on our test car did not fit as well as it should. We discovered a rather sizable opening at the top of the driver's door that is just not in keeping with the quality of the car. In addition to the leather seats, which have an unmistakable and rich aroma, the Jensen has a polished wood dash and console and a leather-wrapped steering wheel.

The instrument layout and arrangement of switches is reminiscent of the early Jaguar XJ sedans: twin dials for speedometer and tachometer directly in front of the driver, smaller gauges centered between those two and seven identical rocker switches to the driver's right. The telescoping steering wheel is also very Jag-like. The turn indicator lever is positioned high on the steering column but the headlights are not dipped and raised by means of this lever. A movable dead pedal to the left of the brake, an arrangement we don't find sensible, serves for this function.

Many small touches set the Jensen apart from ordinary cars: a switch for changing the horn from a relatively mild city sound to a harsh country noise and an electrically actuated switch for opening the fuel filler flap on the rear deck, for example.

The ventilation system is effective, with four eyeball vents in the center of the dash (these do, however, allow engine noise in when opened) and efficient air conditioning. The rear seats

are not very wide because the wheel wells intrude, but they are adequate for average-size people for short periods of time. Also, the rear seats are deeply contoured which helps make up for the lack of legroom. There are map pockets in the backs of the front seats, small compartments outboard of the two rear seats, a small locking glovebox and a huge locking center console compartment. The trunk is fairly deep but not terribly long and is opened by means of a lever on the driver's door post.

The Jensen Interceptor III is powered by the Chrysler 440-cu-in. V-8 which offers an abundance of smooth performance.

The 440 is coupled to a TorqueFlite automatic transmission, also from Chrysler, which makes an effective combination of good torque, smooth performance and no-fuss driving. It's a remarkable example of Anglo-American cooperation, producing as simple and pleasant a car as we can recall. However, the 440 engine has dual catalytic converters and is hampered by the loping idle and flat throttle response of a lean-running, retarded engine. Our test Jensen did not downshift with either part or hard throttle application as we expected it to but this was a minor matter of maladjusted linkage.

We were disappointed with the steering characteristics of the convertible as it was plagued by vagueness and a light feeling that required rather constant inputs to maintain a straight line. The steering is non-linear in effort, being heavier on center and getting lighter during turning but then becoming heavier again as the wheel returns to center.

The suspension design is not especially sophisticated: A-arms,

coil springs and an anti-roll bar in the front and a live rear axle located by leaf springs and a Panhard rod. The lack of independent rear suspension necessitates a good deal of snubbing of the rear axle, limiting travel over dips and bumps. The Jensen feels skittery over uneven surfaces while cornering, but the ride is not bad at all in most situations. We did find considerably more thumping over highway dots than we care for, which in turn leads to some drumming inside the car, but this is a characteristic of VR-rated tires.

Our on-track testing of the convertible gave us few surprises; it's actually little different from the hardtop model. The convertible weighs some 200 lb more than the hardtop but the added weight does not adversely affect acceleration. In fact, the convertible goes from 0–60 mph a full second quicker than the 1973 Jensen Interceptor: 9.3 vs 10.4 sec. Conversely, we found the convertible does not stop as well as the hardtop version in terms of distance, taking 25 feet more for a stop from 60 mph and 16 ft more from 80. However, the control during braking was much better with the latest Jensen than with the 1973 car.

The use of dual catalytic converters has enabled the Jensen factory to make a small improvement in fuel consumption with this latest model. We measured 12.5 miles per gallon with the convertible whereas the 1973 Jensen turned in a figure of 11.5 mpg. It's not a drastic difference but these days every little bit helps, especially in the under-20 mpg cars.

The Jensen Interceptor III convertible is a luxurious, comfortable touring car for two adults and two small children but not for four adults. It encompasses many of the good features of its hardtop stablemate with the added attraction of a top that goes down to let the sun shine in. And the convertible top works as smoothly and easily as any we have used. With the top down, there is little wind noise or drumming, and even at highway speeds it is pleasant and unruffling. The Jensen is an exotic car tempered with sensible running gear and understated styling. The quality of the workmanship is high and the driving characteristics are sure to satisfy the most discriminating enthusiast.

PRICE

List price, all POE	$24,812
Price as tested	$24,812

GENERAL

Curb weight, lb	4225
Weight distribution (with driver), front/rear, %	51/49
Wheelbase, in.	105.0
Track, front/rear	56.1/56.9
Length	186.0
Width	69.0
Height	53.0
Fuel capacity, U.S. gal.	24.0

CHASSIS & BODY

Body/frame	tube frame with integral steel body
Brake system	10.8-in. vented discs front & rear, vacuum assisted
Wheels	cast alloy, 15 x 7
Tires	Pirelli Cinturato HS CN73, 225/70VR-15
Steering type	rack & pinion, power assisted
Turns, lock-to-lock	3.4
Suspension, front/rear:	unequal-length A-arms, coil springs, tube shocks, anti-roll bar/live axle on leaf springs, Panhard rod, tube shocks

ENGINE & DRIVETRAIN

Type	ohv V-8
Bore x stroke, mm	109.7 x 95.3
Displacement, cc/cu in.	7212/440
Compression ratio	8.2:1
Bhp @ rpm, net	215 @ 6200
Torque @ rpm, lb-ft.	330 @ 3200
Fuel requirement	unleaded, 91-oct
Transmission	automatic; torque converter with 3-sp planetary gearset
Gear ratios: 3rd (1.00)	2.88:1
2nd (1.45)	4.18:1
1st (2.45)	7.06:1
1st (2.45 x 2.10)	14.82:1
Final drive ratio	2.88:1

CALCULATED DATA

Lb/bhp (test weight)	21.3
Mph/1000 rpm (3rd gear)	23.5
Engine revs/mi (60 mph)	2550
R&T steering index	1.29
Brake swept area, sq in./ton	182

ROAD TEST RESULTS

ACCELERATION

Time to distance, sec:	
0–100 ft	3.8
0–500 ft	9.7
0–1320 ft (¼ mi)	17.2
Speed at end of ¼ mi, mph	83.0
Time to speed, sec:	
0–30 mph	3.4
0–50 mph	6.8
0–60 mph	9.3
0–80 mph	15.8
0–100 mph	27.0

SPEEDS IN GEARS

3rd gear (4800 rpm)	120
2nd (5100)	89
1st (5100)	53

FUEL ECONOMY

Normal driving, mpg	12.5

BRAKES

Minimum stopping distances, ft:	
From 60 mph	183
From 80 mph	316
Control in panic stop	very good
Pedal effort for 0.5g stop, lb	28
Fade: percent increase in pedal effort to maintain 0.5g deceleration in 6 stops from 60 mph	25
Overall brake rating	good

HANDLING

Speed on 100-ft radius, mph	32.8
Lateral acceleration, g	0.720

INTERIOR NOISE

All noise readings in dBA:	
Constant 30 mph	66
50 mph	70
70 mph	76

SPEEDOMETER ERROR

30 mph indicated is actually	29.0
60 mph	60.0
70 mph	70.0

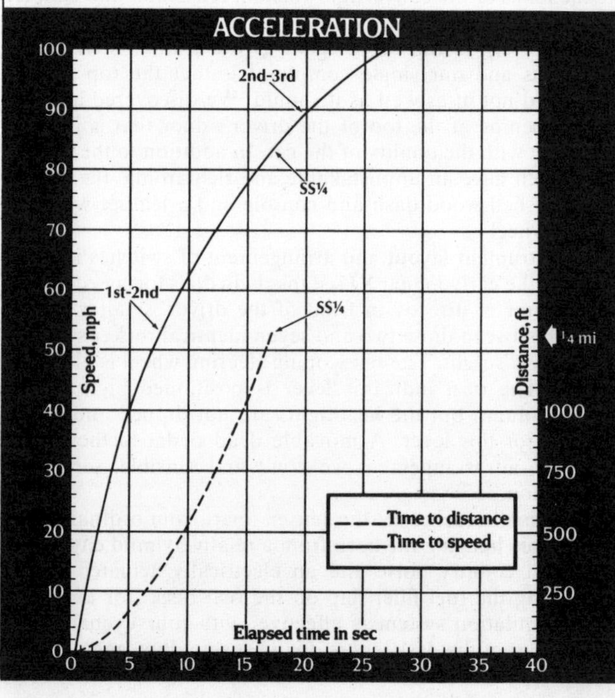

Jensen Interceptor

Above: A famous Autocar road test shot with the original FF in 1968. We proved that the FF would tear its tyres off the rims before it let go
Left: The original Interceptor at the 1966 launch of the car. Note the Ro-style wheels and cross-ply tyres
Below: The Convertible version is a rare bird, but one well worth seeking out for its outstanding lines
Right: The Interceptor trade-mark, that huge opening rear window. The rear window shelf can be removed for the storage of bulky items in the boot, making the Interceptor a sort of super-luxury hatchback

THE Interceptor is now nearly ten years old, having made its first appearance at the London Motor Show in October 1966. The steel body, built by Superleggera to Vignale patents took the Show by storm, and has lasted perhaps best of all the luxury high performance designs; so far as looks go. Today, when the future of the company is in such jeopardy, an Interceptor can still turn heads, and has immense appeal for the man wanting style, comfort and performance.

The building of a steel-bodied car presented no problems for Jensen, who had constructed the 541 and CV-8 cars from glass-fibre reinforced plastic, as they had been building the Volvo P1800, the Austin-Healey 3000 and were soon to build the Sunbeam Tiger in steel. For the new Interceptor, they retained the massive chassis of the V-8 in modified form. It uses very large diameter steel tubes with fabricated extensions to carry the engine, and front and rear suspensions. The body is welded to the chassis, and the resulting structure is extremely strong.

The car has always been powered by Chrysler, in different V8 forms. The original unit was a Chrysler 383 unit (6,276 c.c.) developing a rather optimistic 325 bhp in gross SAE figures. Jensen have always opted for a special specification engine from Chrysler, and have had remarkably little trouble with it. A "hot" specification Chrysler 440 (not the famed Hemi, but nevertheless a very powerful unit) of 7,212 cc was introduced in 1971 for the Jensen SP, fitted with the "six pack" carburation system consisting of three twin-choke Holley carburettors, and following considerable experience with this engine, the standard Interceptor was given the 440 unit in 1972, although without the Holley carburettors.

There have been nine different models of the car over the years, the Interceptors Mark I, II, and III, the FF, FF Mk II and FF Mk III, the SP, the Convertible, and most recent of all, the Coupé.

The Interceptor FF story would occupy a book, and since there are very few on the secondhand market, and the cars are eagerly sought after when a private owner does decide to sell, there is little point in going too deeply into their history here. Suffice to say that the FF was introduced at the same time as the Interceptor, and differed from the standard car externally with a bonnet some 4 inches longer, ahead of the windscreen, double ventilation grilles behind the front wheels, instead of a single one, a stainless steel roof panel, and FF badges. Underneath the skin, there were radical differences; the FF was, of course, the first production car to feature the Ferguson Formula four-wheel-drive system. At the back of the gearbox is a power take-off differential which splits the power 37:63 between the front and rear wheels. The FF has power steering, where the original Interceptor had none, and the brakes are the jointly-developed Dunlop/Girling Maxaret non-skid system.

The car is truly revolutionary in roadholding and braking performance, and has a devoted band of owners. Production ceased with spiralling costs at the end of 1971. During the three-year production run of the Mk I FF, a total of 263 cars were built, 110 Mk II cars were completed and only 15 Mk III cars were built before the decision was taken to stop production.

The convertible version of the Interceptor was introduced at the Geneva Show in 1974, and featured an attractive slim tail with separate boot lid, and power-operated hood. The Coupé was launched at the 1975 Motor Show, a brave move for a company which had appointed an Official Receiver, and was really a hardtop version of the Convertible. Both Coupé and Convertible are identical in all mechanical details to the Mk III cars.

As one might expect with a model that is ten years old there have been a vast number of specification changes in the Interceptor range. Basically, the Mk I ran from October 66 to October 69, the Mk II from October 69 to October 1971, and the Mk III from that date.

The Mk I car was fitted with cross ply tyres, usually Dunlop RS 5 or Avon Roadspeed and power steering was not standard, but was brought in as a much needed option in 1968, to become standard in 1969. The Mk II car featured a change to radial tyres and wider wheels, and had its 16-gallon tank increased to 20 gallons capacity. A larger radiator was fitted, and air conditioning was introduced as an optional extra. Black headlamp surrounds, new bumpers, overriders and side grilles identify the Mk II car. The Mk III brought in ventilated disc brakes, cast alloy wheels, remote locking for the passenger door, and after 1972, the bigger capacity engine.

Late in the life of the Mk I, the original Austin Westminster front suspension units, with lower wishbones and upper lever-arm dampers with bushed king pins gave way to a revised ball-jointed double wishbone and telescopic damper layout, which much improved the front end, giving better damping and easier adjustment.

It was possible during the first few years of the Interceptor's life to order a car with a manual gearbox, but few were in fact made, and virtually every used Jensen on the market today will have the Chrysler Torqueflite automatic transmission, a unit which is famed for quietness and the smoothness of its changes.

What to look for

Buying a secondhand Jensen Interceptor, according to the people who know them, can be a risky business. There are two sorts of Interceptor, the ones that have been run by wealthy and enthusiastic owners, who have had the cars regularly serviced and repaired by a Jensen specialist, and the other sort, which have been owned by people concerned about their "image" but unable or unwilling to meet the high maintenance costs of such a car.

Thus it is vitally important to have a thorough history with any car that you are contemplating, showing that the 4,000-mile services have been carried out, and that any body damage has been properly repaired.

Most of the Mk I and Mk II Interceptors will have been resprayed by now, an understandable condition since they were painted in cellulose that did not last well, and started to bloom and fade after about three years. The Jensen method of construction means that there are virtually no panels accessible from the inside for a panel beater to restore after accident damage, and the odds are that many cars without proven histories will be "full of filler." Interceptors do seem to pick up more than their share of bumps and scrapes, mainly because of their size and shape, and the only way to repair them properly is to cut the panel, re-shape, and then lead the welds and spray up. Incidentally, respraying a cellulose car is a time-consuming business since the paint has to be stripped off down to bare metal. Any heavy body damage which results in chassis repairs being necessary must mean a return to the factory, since they have the only chassis jig. Beware any major chassis repairs without evidence of such a visit.

Corrosion is non-existent so far as the chassis is concerned — the massive structure is coated in such thick sealant that it is difficult to see where it begins under the car. However, the Mk I and Mk II bodies are a different story, with rust creeping along the top of the doors at the window edges, round the edges of the bonnet and in the front apron. The rusting problems are quite serious, and require a great deal of very expensive bodywork repair if the damage is to be properly eradicated. Mk III cars are very much better in this respect, with most of the problem areas sorted out.

As with any car with power steering, it is worth checking the reservoir and the seals very carefully for any sign of leaks; repairs here are likely to be very expensive on a neglected car. The engine, gearbox and rear axle can be expected to be very reliable and long-lived. Jensen do not run an exchange engine scheme, since there is so little demand for new engines. If the limited slip differential is going to give any trouble, it usually does so in the first months of ownership, but once the plates have settled in and bedded down properly, the axles are quiet and reliable.

Any Mk I cars should still be on their crossply tyres and original wheels, unless they have had the Dunlop discs changed for Girlings, for the radial tyres and wide wheels on the original suspension result in fouling of the calipers, and overloading of suspension and steering.

Brakes are another expensive area for an Interceptor on the secondhand market. It could cost well over £200 to sort out the brakes on a car with scored discs and seized caliper pistons. The car is heavy and suspension and steering joints must be meticulously serviced if they are to last.

The leather trim of the Jensen stands up well to wear, and it is worth remembering that Connollys can re-chrome leather that has becomed rubbed and creased to make it look like new a a very reasonable price.

There is occasionally some trouble with rain water leaks around the edges of the big rear window, but the problem has largely been eliminated in later cars.

On the subject of water — early cars in the Mk I and Mk II series did have trouble with coolant leaks from burst water hoses. The problem here was really a function of the very high under-bonnet temperatures that the big V8 develops. The clips on the hoses are done up tight, the under bonnet temperature climbs and the hose rubber becomes soft and leaks develop. The hoses are tightened, and then the rubber cools the clips are too tight and failure of the hose wall results. The answer was to louvre the bonnet to get rid of excess heat, and change the specification of the hose material to withstand the wide temperature variations.

Incidentally the Chrysler engine is notoriously intolerant of non-standard parts. Belts are a notable example — the proper Chrysler belts give no trouble, but Interceptors fitted with proprietary fan, alternator and air conditioning pump belts are always in trouble with slip and breakages.

The electrical components of the car tend to give no more trouble than any other manufacturer's products, but there are occasionally problems with the relays in the cooling system which control the huge twin electric fans in front of the radiator.

The exhaust system should be carefully examined. On a secondhand car, it's an area where a less than conscientious owner might be tempted to save money, and replacement systems run into over £100 plus VAT and a hefty fitting charge.

Performance data

	Mk I	Mk II	SP	FF	FF Mk II	Convertible
Road Tested in Autocar **of**	5/1/67	4/9/69	7/10/71	28/3/68	22/10/70	26/10/74
Mean maximum speed (mph)	133	137	143	130	137	126
Acceleration (sec)						
0-30 mph	3.3	2.5	2.9	3.1	3.5	2.7
0-40 mph	4.3	3.7	4.1	4.4	4.8	4.0
0-50 mph	5.9	5.0	5.4	6.2	6.2	5.5
0-60 mph	7.3	6.4	6.9	8.4	8.1	7.6
0-70 mph	9.5	8.7	8.9	10.8	10.6	9.8
0-80 mph	12.1	11.2	11.1	13.8	13.4	12.5
0-90 mph	15.4	14.3	13.5	17.5	16.7	15.8
0-100 mph	19.0	18.2	16.8	22.5	21.5	20.2
0-110 mph	24.9	23.7	20.9	28.2	27.5	26.0
Standing ¼-mile (sec)	15.7	15.0	14.8	15.9	15.8	15.8
Top gear						
10-30 mph						
20-40 mph	—	—	—	—	—	—
30-50 mph	4.5	3.5	5.0	4.8	—	—
40-60 mph	5.1	4.1	4.8	5.6	5 4	—
50-70 mph	5.9	5.0	5.8	6.3	6.0	—
60-80 mph	6.1	6.0	6.4	6.9	7.0	—
70-90 mph	6.4	6.8	6.3	7.3	7.9	6.9
80-100 mph	8.0	7.8	6.6	8.3	9.0	7.4
Overall fuel consumption (mpg)	13.6	12.9	13.0	13.6	11.9	12.5
Typical fuel consumption (mpg)	14.2	14.0	14.0	14.0	14.0	12.0
Dimensions						
Length	15ft 8in.	5ft 8in.	5ft 8in.	5ft 11in.	15ft 11in.	15ft 8in.
Width	5ft 9in.	5ft 9in.	5ft 9in.	5ft 9in	5ft 9in.	5ft 9in.
Height	4ft 5in.	4ft 5in.	4ft 5in.	4ft 5in.	4ft 5in.	4ft 5in.
Kerb weight (cwt)	33.0	33.0	35.1	35.7	37.8	35.7

Milestones and chassis identification

	series	chassis no.
October 1966: Mk I introduced at London Motor Show, power assisted steering available	115	2497
by October 1968	115	5330
October 1969: Mk II car introduced	123	3551
October 1971: SP announced	131	
October 1971: Mk III car introduced	128	4249
July 1972: Sundym glass, air conditioning and air horns standard	128	4786
July 72-Jan 73: 7.2 litre engine introduced	136	8000
March 74: Convertible introduced		
January 75: New chassis numbers commence	2240	1001
October 75: Coupé introduced		
FF		
October 1966: Mk I FF four-wheel drive car announced	119	001
September 1969: Mk I production ceases	119	195
October 1969: Mark II FF production starts	127	201
October 1971: Mark II FF production ends	127	310
October 1971: Mark III FF production starts	130	315
FF production ends	130	328

Approximate selling prices

Price range	Mk I	Mk II	Mk III	FF	FF Mk II	SP	Convertible
£1,000-£1,250	1966						
£1,500-£2,000	1968			1967			
£2,000-£2,500	1969	1969		1969			
£2,500-£3,000		1970			1970		
£3,000-£3,500		1971			1971		
£3,500-£4,000			1972			1972	
£4,000-£4,500			1972 (big engine)			1973	
£4,500-£5,000			1973				
£5,000-£6,000			1974				
£6,000-£7,000			1975				1974

Spares prices

Part	Price	Part	Price
Engine (exch)	not available	Starter (exch)	£73.50
Gearbox (exch)	£285.50	Front wing panel	£73.56
Differential (exch)	£178.00	Front bumper	£73.72
Brake pads (front)	£8.45	Rear bumper	£100.00
Brake pads (rear)	£9.93	Windscreen	£75.00
Dampers (front)	£30.63	Rear window	£74.00 (clear)
Dampers (rear)	£27.00		£108 (Sundym)
Radiator assembly (exch)	£70.58	Exhaust system	£105
Alternator (exch)	£72.50	Exhaust pipe trims	£24 each

To sum up, the decision to buy a used Interceptor should only be taken after the buyer has established the cost of servicing and maintaining the car to the standards required by the factory, and has decided he can meet them. That groundwork having been laid, the buying of the car must be done with the utmost care. A bad choice can involve the fastidious buyer in enormous bills to put the car right, and there can be no question of short cuts with a vehicle capable or nearly 140 mph, and weighing over 1¾ tons. A proven service history with no gaps, and sight of bills for the work showing the name of the garage who did it is most important, and it is well worth asking a Jensen specialist to look over a car being bought privately — even if it means paying a stiff fee. The money saved in the long run will be considerable. The Jensen is such a good-looking car that it is easy to be carried away by gleaming paint and a brief and intoxicatingly exciting demonstration of the immense performance. The wary buyer must dig deeper. All that glitters. . . .

Which model?

The quickest of all the cars was undoubtedly the SP. Capable of a best top speed of 145 mph this car could bound from 0-60 in 6.9 seconds, and to 100 mph in 16.8 seconds. All this it offered — and 14 mpg, too. The infamous "six pack" could cause problems — the car normally ran on one carburettor, manifold depression and throttle travel bringing in the other two. The "snap" as the extra carburettors came in was sometimes difficult to predict, and would occasionally occur as the car was cruising at 100 mph to the consternation of the driver — at least it kept you on your toes!

There was resistance to the SP — some owners had trouble starting, especially when hot, but more enthusiastic owners who understood the intricacies of the system, and who had the wit to avoid flooding the engine had few problems, and stoutly maintain that the SP was the best Interceptor ever. A few SPs were fitted with standard carburettors on the 440 engine and this seems to be a good compromise for the owner who does not require the ultimate in performance. Of the standard Interceptors, there are now very few decent Mk Is around, and the low trade prices — as little as £800 for a 1967 model — reflect the anticipated condition that too many of the cars may be in. However, in the Interceptor class, price is very much a question of condition, so a really good, well maintained and cared for Mk II can often be on sale for more than a rather poorer example of an early Mk III — and incidentally might well be a better buy. Mk III cars are heavier than the Mk I and II cars, and with the emission controlled engines are slower. "Slower" here is, of course, relative — the Mk III will still top 125 mph, and 0-60 takes only 7.6 seconds, about a second slower than the '69 car, and is about two seconds slower from rest to 100 mph.

Left: One of the first Interceptors, a 1966 FF, was really rather fussy in design and layout, especially when compared to the Mk. III interior. It is interesting to note how the march of safety engineering has affected the design and layout of a car facia in a 10-year period

Interior trim and seating reflect the swing away from pleated leather panels on the 1966 car to the smooth unpleated expanses of the Mk. III. Rear seats have received a great deal of attention, but the switch to individually tailored rear seats has meant that tall people can no longer sit cross-wise in the rear. Leg and head room in the rear have never been an Interceptor forte, but standards of trim and leatherwork have always been to the highest standards

Below: The SP introduced the attractive alloy wheels and the multi-louvred bonnet concealing the "Six-Pack" engine

The FFs are a different proposition; no one is quite sure whether or not the car is a "classic" yet — there is nothing to replace it, so many owners are hanging on to their FFs, and the true value of the car won't be known till these owners start selling. Certainly the few that come on the market at the moment are eagerly sought after, and usually cherished and perfectly maintained by former loving owners. If you can find one, you will be buying a piece of automotive history. There appear to be no real problems at this stage with replacement parts for the four-wheel-drive system, but it is likely that brake parts for the Maxaret system may become difficult to obtain in the future. At the moment factory and distributors are still enthusiastically proud of the FF and the advances it represented, and owners are unlikely to be short of full, though expensive — co-operation in keeping these wonderful machines on the road. The convertible and Coupé are as yet too recent to be widely obtainable on the second-hand market. □

Jensen Interceptor

BOB VEZE

You see them often—but only if you go to the right places. Westchester, Greenwich, Grosse Pointe, Palos Verdes, yes, and maybe even Beverly Hills. More a social accessory than any other sportscar, the Jensen Interceptor is to the Beautiful Person's automotive wardrobe what his/her Cardin jacket or Gucci loafers or Von Furstenberg dress is to the clothes wardrobe.

Correction. The Jensen Interceptor *was* a social accessory; the company—bought recently by Kjell Qvale and kept going in the last year at a much reduced rate—is being sold, bit by bit, in a huge auction at its headquarters in England. So it is fitting that the last Jensen we test—the Interceptor Coupé—is the least sportscar and the most accessory of them all. The ultimate automotive Gucci.

It's no accident, either. Jensen officials bluntly admit that the Coupé was styled specifically for the buyer who liked the Interceptor but who didn't like the lack of adequate seating for four people, whether a golf foursome, business acquaintances or harem. Thus the famous shape of the "hatchback" Interceptor was altered to give the wealthy patrons from Grosse Pointe their rear-seat room, and in the process a roof straight out of Buck Rogers was grafted on. In a unique combination of both the vinyl top and opera window, the stylists split the top by a narrow band of smoked glass placed just where, in a serious go-fast car, you'd find a rollbar. They then wedded the top and convertible body, and the effect, to judge from the continual stares we got while driving the car, is exactly what they wanted: you get noticed. *All* the time.

Understandably, the Coupé provokes Corvette owners into a

Coupé

The last Jensen: less sportscar for more money than any before, it is a bargain for the Beautiful People.

reasonable facsimile of rage. Understandably, because underneath its fiberglass, the Jensen is an antique among sportscars, a hybrid Anglo-American device which actually performs only slightly better than the big Chrysler sedans its 440 cid V-8 pushrod engine normally powers. Weighing in at an astounding 4340 lbs. (the Jaguar XJ-S, no lightweight itself, tips the scales at 3845), the Coupé delivers its 215 horsepower through a three-speed automatic (also from Mopar) to a live rear axle hung on leaf springs, and it is amazing to note, given the design, that the Jensen designers have managed to give the car 50–50 weight distribution. Although, once on the road, the theoretical value of the perfect balance is lost by the incredibly vague power steering and strange suspension, which seemed to combine the worst elements of too-stiff springs and too-soft shocks. It all worked to give the car a lowish 0.70g on the skidpad and the driver a sincere desire to avoid racing those enraged Corvette drivers.

The big Mopar motor managed to propel the Coupé through the quarter-mile in a respectable 17.1 seconds at an equally respectable 83 mph, displaying the brawn of the famous engine in no uncertain terms. Even smog-freed and converter-equipped, the 440 is a potent powerplant, and should you be brave enough and the road long enough, the Jensen will see 130 mph.

Braking, with vented discs all the way around, was hampered by poor servo action and tires (Pirelli Cinturato CN73s), and thus resulted in a sliding 170-foot stopping distance from 60 mph. It was obvious that both the behavior of the car and the actual distance would have improved dramatically with every hundred pounds of weight you could remove from the car, an improvement which would be reflected by the fuel economy, which, at 11 mpg, wasn't exactly the big selling point.

The Coupé's shortcomings as a sportscar do not reflect its value as an accessory at the country club. When you're out to impress the Executive Sales Vice-President (or his wife), only the *feel* of the car counts—and there the Jensen scores highly. The incongruous massive look of the exterior is mirrored by the traditional wood-and-leather English interior. Gathering together all the strands of the Fighter Pilot Syndrome and the Manor House Syndrome, the interior designers molded an atmosphere guaranteed to convince whoever's riding with you that, not only do you know your woods, but you can also flick rocker switches like a hero of the Battle of Britain.

Unfortunately (if it's hot), the designers didn't make provision for air conditioning vents anywhere but in the center of the dash, so the Coupé heats up and stays hot if the temperature creeps much over 90° outside, somewhat marring the cool elegance of the interior atmosphere . . . as, indeed, the swearing of the passenger as he seeks to adjust his seat will mar it. Both front seats have a wealth of adjustment, but each requires careful study before action, or you will not only not adjust your seat, but will also break a fingernail on the fore/aft lever, which rides flat against the floor. The seats themselves are comfortable enough, with huge padded head restraints more like pillows than part of a restraint system meeting DOT Standard 208, but on a long trip they come in handy. Rear-seat room is, despite the Coupé's purpose, very limited, and with any kind of rake on the front seats at all, the rear-seat occupants instantly acquire sore knees, despite the deep-set molding around their seat bottoms.

The other ergonomics all fall into the same category as the dashboard and seats: traditional English. And whether or not you like that depends on how you reacted to the Jaguar Mk IX Saloon or the '56 Rolls.

But Jensens are—or *were*—English from the word go, so you'd expect all that. But what you might not expect would be the bill for all your hand-built elegance, which, in this case, came out to $25,650 . . . including $1200 for the trick Blaupunkt remote-control radio. Now, whether or not staggering price tags like that had anything to do with the demise of the company we don't know, but we do know that few car enthusiasts would put up with a price like that for a car like the Coupé we had to test. Which, considering that we haven't seen a lot of Jensens sitting around Honest Harry's Used Cars, must mean that most people who buy—or bought—Jensens were not measuring the effectiveness of the car against its price . . . and here we run smack into the Gucci Factor once again. Because to people with so much money that nothing counts but the impression, what does it matter if the car steers like an overweight camel? And who cares if any Porsche running on anything better than three bald El Cheapos and one good tire could thoroughly put it away? Not, clearly, the man who will write a $25,650 check for an Interceptor Coupé.

But right now it's all academic anyway, because no more Interceptors will roll out the factory doors. Jensen is as close to being finished as it can be, and unless something happens in the crazy, convoluted world of automotive manufacturing, it will stay finished. Which will probably not pain the Beautiful People too much (they need new accessories every season anyway), but may give rise to a thoughtful silence or two wherever enthusiasts gather. Because whatever its shortcomings—and there are a whole slew of them—the car and its company were at least different, and their extinction raises the grim image of a future devoid of differences, run by and for huge corporations cranking out billions of faceless automobiles.

But the best guarantees we have against such a future are the Beautiful People themselves; after all, whoever heard of a Gucci Urbocar? ■

ROAD TEST DATA

JENSEN INTERCEPTOR COUPE

SPECIFICATIONS

ENGINE

Type	OHV V-8
Displacement, cu in	440
Displacement, cc	7212
Bore x stroke, in	4.32 x 3.75
Bore x stroke, mm	109.6 x 95.2
Compression ratio	8.2:1
Hp at rpm, net	215@5200
Torque at rpm, lb/ft, net	330@3200
Carburetion	1 4-V

DRIVELINE

Transmission	3-spd auto
Gear ratios:	
1st	2.45:1
2nd	1.45:1
3rd	1.00:1
Final drive ratio	3.07:1
Driving wheels	rear

GENERAL

Wheelbase, ins	105.0
Overall length, ins	188.0
Width, ins	69.0
Height, ins	53.0
Front track, ins	56.3
Rear track, ins	57.3
Trunk capacity, cu ft	NA
Curb weight, lbs	4340
Distribution, % front/rear	50/50
Power-to-weight ratio, lbs/hp	20.2

BODY AND CHASSIS

Body/frame construction	separate
Brakes, front/rear	vented disc/vented disc
Swept area, sq in	417.0
Swept area, sq in/1000 lb	96.1
Steering	rack & pinion
Ratio	17.1:1
Turns, lock-to-lock	3.4
Turning circle, ft	38.0

Front suspension: Independent, upper and lower control arms, coil springs, tubular shocks, anti-roll bar
Rear suspension: Live axle, leaf springs, tubular shocks

WHEELS AND TIRES

Wheels	15-inch
Tires, front/rear	225/70 VR 15 Pirelli Cinturato HS CN73
Reserve load, front/rear, lb	1140/1180

INSTRUMENTATION

Instruments: 0–160 mph speedo, trip odo, 0-6000 rpm tach, coolant temp, oil press, volts, fuel level, clock
Warning lights: directionals, high beam, oil, brakes EGR service, rear defog, fuel lid, seat belts

PRICE

Factory list, as tested: $25,650
Options included in price: radio—$1200

TEST RESULTS

ACCELERATION, SEC.

0–30 mph	3.6
0–40 mph	4.9
0–50 mph	7.0
0–60 mph	9.6
0–70 mph	12.2
0–80 mph	16.2
Standing start, ¼ mile	17.1
Speed at end ¼ mile, mph	83.6
Avg accel over ¼ mile, g	0.22

SPEEDS IN GEARS, MPH

1st (3600 rpm)	38
2nd (4000 rpm)	73
3rd (5000 rpm) (calc.)	130
Engine revs at 70 mph	2700

SPEEDOMETER ERROR

Indicated speed	True speed
40 mph	39 mph
50 mph	49 mph
60 mph	59 mph
70 mph	69 mph
80 mph	79 mph

INTERIOR NOISE, dBA

Idle	59
Max 1st gear	78
Steady 40 mph	65
50 mph	69
60 mph	71
70 mph	73

BRAKES

Min stopping distance from 60 mph, ft	170
Avg deceleration rate, g	0.71

HANDLING

Max speed on 100-ft rad, mph	32.3
Lateral acceleration, g	0.70
Transient response, avg spd, mph	23.4

FUEL ECONOMY

Overall avg, RT cycle	11 mpg
Range on 26.0 gal tank	264 miles
Fuel required	unleaded

RATING

Graph Of Recorded Data Expressed in Percentage of 100 (100 = best possible rating)*

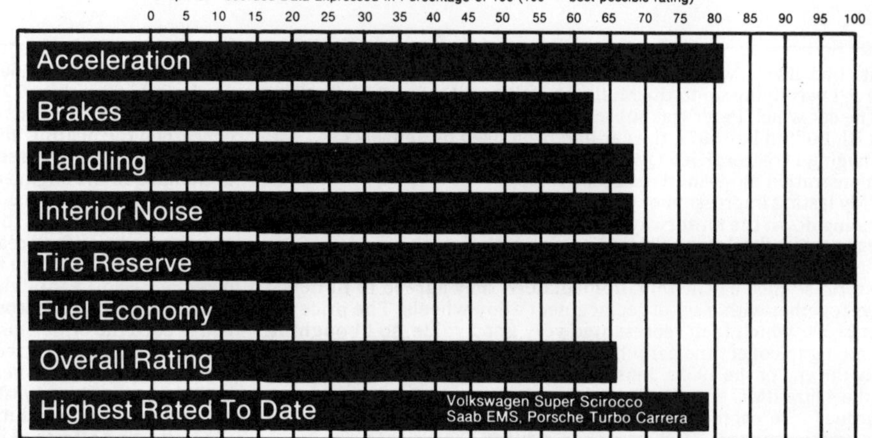

*Acceleration (0–60 mph): 0% = 34.0 secs., 100% = 4.0 secs.; Brakes (60–0) mph: 0% = 220.0 ft., 100% = 140.0 ft.; Handling: skidpad lateral accel., 0% = 0.3 g, 100% = 0.9 g, transient response, 0% = 20 mph, 100% = 25 mph (average skid pad and transient response for overall handling percentage); Interior Noise (70 mph): 0% = 90.0 dBA, 100% = 65.0 dBA; Tire Reserve (with passengers): 0% = 0.0 lbs., 100% = 1500 lbs. or more; Fuel Economy: 0% = 5 mpg, 100% = 45 mpg or more. Test Equipment Used: Testron Fifth Wheel and Pulse Totalizer, Lamar Data Recording System, Esterline-Angus Recorder, Sun Tachometer, EDL Pocket-Probe Pyrometer, General Radio Sound Level Meter.

Continuing with our series on post-war classics and those who own and love them

"THE OPPOSITION MUST have thought I looked fairly dangerous," reflected Peter Adams, present owner of the only Jensen Interceptor to have passed from Jensen Motors Ltd. to Jensen Parts and Service when the company was put into the hands of the Receiver in May 1976.

"I had always admired the Interceptor," he continued. "However, just when I could afford to buy one the company crashed. But I was extremely lucky. I had taken my XK 150 to a concours event at Biggin Hill in Kent, where I found myself parked opposite a group of Jensen C-V8s. Their owners obviously felt my Jaguar presented sufficient competition to warrant a closer look and we got talking I mentioned

Engaging Interceptor

A car that will still turn heads, Mike Taylor *looks at the elegant Jensen Interceptor*

that I had always wanted an Interceptor, and the next thing I knew, I was flying up to the Midlands to buy a Jensen."

The car which Peter was subsequently to buy was an Interceptor Mk III. Built in late 1972, the car had been used by Jensen's Managing Director, Kjell Qvale, before being taken as a work's demonstration model and road test vehicle.

"My lasting impression of the test run," recalled Peter Adams, "is of riding down the motorway at 120 mph in almost complete silence, while the Jensen Sales Director explained the car to me. When we arrived back at the factory, my only comment was that the tyres seemed a little thin. Immediately, they agreed to fit new tyres together with a set of replacement alloy wheels. The price was £5,500, which I felt represented very good value, so I bought it, arranging to collect the car when the work had been completed."

By the end of the 1950s, Jensen's 541 series, which were powered by the 4 litre BMC engine coupled to a manual gearbox, were long overdue for re-engineering. The trend towards automatic transmissions in this category of car induced Jensen into investigating the range of large American V8 power units, and in particular, the Chrysler engine with its Torqueflite automatic gearbox. Chrysler were happy to supply Jensen with engines, and so the C-V8 was born. Fitted with the Chrysler 5.9 litre engine developing 305 bhp at 4,800 rpm, the C-V8 was launched in late 1962. *Autocar* was enthusiastic, and said "To sum up the Jensen C-V8 in one brief sentence — here, indeed, is a car that more than fulfils great expectations."

Indeed, all the ingredients seemed to be there: 0-60 mph in 8.4 secs.; a top speed of 133 mph, and a very stable ride. Only its outward appearance remained a point for debate. Once described as a good design cleverly disguised as the ugliest car in the world, its distinctive glass-fibre bodyshell was clearly a matter of personal taste, and in the event was to last a mere four years.

Jensen's Chief Engineer, Kevin Beattie, was anxious that the bulbous C-V8 body should be replaced by a more graceful, Italian design. The result was a Superleggera-constructed body by Touring to Vignale design, of ideal proportions and dateless elegance. The steel body was welded to a tubular framework which, in turn, was attached to a chassis fabricated from sheet and welded into box sections, forming a very rigid structure.

The new car was called the Interceptor, and Beattie was proven entirely right in his decision to re-body the C-V8. *Autocar*, for instance, found that during their test the Interceptor was "an eye-catcher everywhere and its looks a clever combination of practicalities and an efficient shape."

The Interceptor was fitted with the Chrysler 6,276 c.c. engine, which had been introduced into the C-V8 in 1965. This power unit developed 325 bhp at 4,600 rpm and was capable of propelling the car from 0 - 60 mph in 6.7 secs. Maximum speed remained unaltered at 133 mph. The only adverse comments of the Interceptor concerned the heating and ventilation.

In 1969, the Mk II Interceptor was introduced. Modifications had been made to the engine (better torque and clean air combustion package); front suspension (ball-jointed wishbones and telescopic dampers); refinements to the gearbox (cushioned clutch to reduce snatch); and a revised rear-axle ratio (to suit new radial-ply tyres). However, it was still the heating and ventilation which let the car down.

In 1971, the Interceptor Mk III was introduced. At last, Jensen had heeded the criticisms concerning poor ventilation and fitted air-conditioning and a redesigned facia. This successfully overcame the problem of engine-heat entering the cockpit in hot weather. Unfortunately, *Autocar* found that the system lacked sufficient control. The engine, which had been enlarged mainly to overcome the restricting effects of the exhaust emission equipment, was now 7,212 c.c. and developed 280 bhp (net) at 4,800 rpm.

Of his Interceptor Mk III, Peter Adams continued, "After buying the car I ran it as a business vehicle for approximately five months,

19

Autocar ROAD TEST NUMBER 2113

Jensen Interceptor 6,276 c.c.

AT A GLANCE: New Italian body for Jensen C-V8 in steel. Top speed higher, but acceleration reduced slightly up to 100 m.p.h. Powerful brakes fade-free. Superb, smooth and quiet American engine with well-matched automatic transmission. Ride more comfortable and road-holding well balanced. Luxurious interior, but heating and ventilating could be better. Very satisfying high-performance touring car with practical seating for four plus luggage.

MANUFACTURER
Jensen Motors Ltd., West Bromwich, Staffordshire.

PRICES		
Basic	..	£3,043 7s 11d
Purchase Tax	..	£699 3s 3d
Total (in G.B.)	..	£3,742 11s 2d

PERFORMANCE SUMMARY	
Mean maximum speed	133 m.p.h.
Standing start ¼-mile	15·7 sec
0-60 m.p.h.	7·3 sec
30-70 m.p.h. (through gears	6·2 sec
Fuel consumption	14·2 m.p.g.
Miles per tankful	225

IT was entirely logical for Jensen to rationalize their production programme into just two almost identical looking models. The bulbous shape of the C-V8 was never very pretty and that kind of styling is now on the wane. The convertible Interceptor introduced at the 1965 Motor Show would have taken valuable production capacity and with the acute interest in four-wheel drive to the Ferguson formula, Jensen settled for just one body with the most sleek and graceful lines to come from Italy for some time. Superleggera construction by Touring to Vignale patents is used and although the first few cars have been built in Milan, the tools will soon be installed in the West Bromwich plant.

In order to keep costs low the ordinary (if that word can be applied to such a car) two-wheel-drive Jensen is identical with the FF (Ferguson Formula) except for an extra 4in. length ahead of the windscreen to accommodate the transfer gears for the front-wheel-drive take-off. Differentation is by name plates (JFF on the four-wheel-drive) and a double ventilation grille just behind the front wheels each side. The FF also has a stainless steel roof.

Price difference between the two versions is high, almost £600, but this includes power steering and, of course, Dunlop Maxaret anti-lock braking. This test concerns the two-wheel-drive Interceptor only, but we hope to add a supplementary portion on the FF in the near future.

The Interceptor is a direct replacement for the C-V8 and in its mechanical specification is much the same. There is a massive steel chassis fabricated from sheet steel welded into box sections, but instead of a separate composite body made up from glass-fibre and aluminium panels, an ali-steel body is welded to a tubular framework which all forms a structural part of the main hull. The result is tremendous strength and stiffness at the expense of an 11 per cent increase in weight, the Interceptor being nearly 3¼cwt heavier than the C-V8.

Such an increase, fortunately, is not much of a problem, as the 6·3-litre Chrysler vee-8 engine develops more than enough horse-power to give dynamic performance still. To say that the acceleration is electrifying is something of an understatement. The TorqueFlite automatic transmission is standard and really cannot be faulted at all; for those who ▶

Above: From the 1967 Autotest *of the Interceptor, featuring the Italian-designed steel bodywork*
Below left: Well-equipped dashboard of Interceptor Mk II
Below right: Earlier Interceptors were fitted with this 6,276 c.c. engine which produced 325 bhp
Bottom left: Interceptor III in convertible guise
Bottom right: Snug rear seats provide excellent sideways location. Note neat hood cover

covering some 5,000 miles. During that time I had no mechanical failures at all, however, I began to find that the two doors and the limited rear seat space were considerable disadvantages when I wanted to carry business colleagues."

Surprisingly, the rear seat accommodation of the Interceptor, while lavishly upholstered, is restricted, and *Autocar* commented that the front seats had to be moved forward "noticeably" when carrying adults in the back.

"The first thing to give trouble was the thermostatically controlled cooling fans, which caused the car to overheat in traffic, and a bad blow in the exhaust system. I telephoned Jensen Parts and Service, and they told me to put the car on a trailer and send it directly to them at West Bromwich. Three days later, I flew up to Birmingham, where I was met by a courtesy car and driven to the factory. On my arrival, I was told that the car was not quite finished, as they had yet to give it a wash, but was invited to have lunch with the Managing Director in the meantime. I was extremely impressed by their service. Not long after, I decided to use the car for concours shows only, and took the car back to Jensen for a routine maintenance, where the work and attention was of the same high standard."

Left: Later Interceptors have 7,212 c.c. engines, producing only 280 bhp because of emission control demands

Colour page opposite: Peter Adams' 1972 prizewinning Interceptor Mk III

While Jensen had been coachbuilders since 1875, it is probable that, before 1966, and the introduction of the Interceptor, little money had been made directly as a result of Jensen's own models. The company relied heavily on sub-contract agreements with Volvo, Rootes and BMC for its financial stability. It came, therefore, as a devastating blow when the latter two withdrew their support in 1967. Norcross, the holding company resigned their interests and Jensen found themselves in the hands of Brandt's the merchant bankers. In 1970, Kjell Qvale, an American, bought the controlling interest in Jensen, and had great plans for the Company's future. During 1971, 1972 and 1973 Jensen had made a profit. The trouble really began in 1974. Firstly, with the Jensen Healey, which got off to a bad start through teething troubles on the engine, and as a result of the oil crisis. With a financial straightjacket growing tighter as charges on investments spiralled, and dealers cut back on orders, Jensen's future looked grim and Qvale's investment shakey. There was no way the Company could proceed under such conditions, and on 21 May, 1976 Jensens built their last car.

Determined that Jensen had a future, despite its financial problems, a consortium called Britcar Holdings purchased Jensen from the Receiver, splitting the Company to form two separate and independent units. The first, Jensen Special Products, responsible for specialised engineering work most suited to the Jensen engineers still employed. The second, Jensen Parts and Service, responsible for the servicing and maintaining of Jensen cars, and the production of spare parts for many of the Jensen models. However, unable to continue financially buoyant on this work alone, in 1978 Jensen Parts and Service became the headquarters for Subaru UK.

Tales of extremely high mileages with American V8 engines are legion. Spares, servicing, and maintenance, on the Chrysler engine and transmission pose few problems as the power units fitted to all Interceptors are off-the-shelf items. Additionally, body panels and those parts special to Jensen are still available.

The Chrysler Torqueflite automatic transmission, under most conditions, behaves with impeccable taste. Changes, even under fierce acceleration, are only just perceptible. The ride, too, under most conditions is good, although Peter Adams, like most Jensen owners, treats his car with respect. The Salisbury Powr-Lok limited-slip differential ensures positive traction even in the wet. It is only when driving over uneven surfaces that there is a hint of instability from the solid rear axle. *Autocar* commented on the limits at which the Jensen Interceptor begins to break away, that only an idiot would try it on the open road.

Under normal driving conditions, the Interceptor's performance is effortless. This smooth delivery of power is a celebrated feature of all American V8s, and is achieved by mechanical refinement – excellent vibration damping to eliminate crankshaft whip and hydraulic tappets for quiet running.

The Interceptor has always been an expensive car to run: 13-15 mpg the norm throughout the changes in engine capacity, giving a range of some 300 or so miles. Indeed, the fuel tank capacity was increased from 16 to 20 gallons on the Mk III, perhaps suggesting an admission on the part of Jensen of the car's restricted range.

It is a point in Jensen's favour that the majority of Interceptors today are in such good condition. In Peter Adams' opinion, rust does not seem to be an Interceptor problem.

"If someone was looking for a secondhand Interceptor," he says, "I would advise them to check the electrics. That, and the air conditioning (only on Mk III cars) seem to be the weak spots."

Perhaps partly due to a general acceptance of the price of petrol, and partly due to the Interceptor becoming increasingly popular as a "classic," prices are gradually increasing. Assuming the car to be in good condition, an early Interceptor will probably sell for £2,000-£2,500, whereas a later model in pristine condition (such as Peter Adams' Mk III) will probably fetch between £6,000 and £7,000.

Since using his car for concours events, Peter Adams has done well. In 1977, he took second prize at the Jensen Owners' Club Concours, being beaten by an Interceptor Convertible. In 1978, at the Brighton and Hove Concours, where Jensens finished 1st, 2nd and 3rd, he took third place. However, later in the year at Woburn, he was awarded the Jensen Owners' Club Rose Bowl, the highest accolade, and the Interceptor Trophy. After winning the coveted Rose Bowl Award, Peter received a letter from Bob Edmiston, managing director of Subaru UK, congratulating him on his success.

"It only goes to further illustrate how much interest the Company still has in Jensen," said Peter Adams. □

Luggage space on a modern Jensen can be increased by removing the panel which normally forms a shelf under the back window.

CONTINUED FROM PAGE 37

liberties to be taken. I did all the fast driving of the Interceptor on dry roads—perhaps fortunately. In these conditions, sliding the car round corners is great fun, but there is always the uncomfortable feeling that front-wheel adhesion is low. This is especially so when sudden movements of the steering wheel have to be made. Initial mild understeer changes to lurchy oversteer, and in neither case does the steering, which becomes light as adhesion is lost, give much confidence in correcting these cornering tendencies. From the straight-ahead position the steering suffers from "stickiness", but the gentle castor return is satisfactory. The steering is free from kick-back and vibration, but is too low-geared for quick control of incipient understeer.

The 11 in. Girling disc brakes of the Interceptor are adequate and progressive for normal driving but could with advantage give more powerful retardation for really fast motoring. The hand brake nestles close to the driver's side of the wide transmission tunnel, being angled on the FF.

The ride tends to be choppy, although a four-position Armstrong Selectaride for the ½-elliptic back springs, with its control on the console, does enable suspension hardness to be varied. Front suspension is independent, using upper and lower wish-bones and coil springs. On the FF there is considerable "wump" as road gulleys and humps are taken with the ride on "hard", this being rather less apparent on the Interceptor. The doors incorporate red warning lights but lack

This picture of the fibreglass transmission tunnels used by Jensen Motors shows how much wider that for the FF is (right of picture) than the Interceptor's transmission tunnel.

effective "keeps".

These Jensens will do 100 to 110 m.p.h. almost anywhere, with ample reserves of power for getting quickly beyond "the ton" and on to 130 m.p.h. or more on the Motorways of civilised countries. The FF is one of the World's most sophisticated approaches to safe control of a fast, powerful car. Both are high-performance, high-quality British luxury cars, literally hand-assembled. Whereas the FF is for really ambitious drivers, the Interceptor has far lower limits of safe handling in slippery conditions. The former costs £7,007; the latter £4,728, or £4,258 with a normal gearbox, inclusive of p.t.

Next month I will describe how these cars are constructed with care and fine workmanship, at the average rate of 15 a week (three FFs and 12 Interceptors) at Jensen's West Bromwich factory.—W. B.

DEATH OF THE FF

CONTINUED FROM PAGE 102

The truck driver was doing the only thing possible in the circumstances — keeping his foot on the throttle. He was a Good Lad.

Having given the matter my very careful consideration for a full thousandth of a second at F2.5 I slammed my foot on the accelerator and we shot forward, literally under the tail of the truck just about the moment when the driver lost it completely and did a small spin. Laidlaw's reaction to this was to say not a word but to fasten his seat belt.

"What've you done up your belt for?"

"We nearly hit that lorry."

"Yes, but we didn't."

"Hm— I suppose you're right," whereupon he undid the belt again and went to sleep. Some people are ideal passengers.

There was the trip from Wick to Thurso, which is worth a mention. At dead on 6 pm we were in Wick where a signpost said "Thurso 20 miles". The roads now were of gleaming, polished snow, packed hard like ice, and occasional flakes were falling. It was pitch dark and the road was far from straight.

"Kenneth!" I said, "We're going to be in the Sinclair Arms Hotel in Thurso at 6.20." And we were.

But most astonishing of all was the moment on the return trip when we came over the brow of a hill somewhere in Kincardineshire and there before our very eyes was a scene that seemed to come straight from one of those Russian films that show Napoleon's army straggling through the snow. In a dip, a lorry had got itself sideways right across the road, and about 40 cars were queuing up at each side, many of them at odd angles and obviously stuck.

We climbed up on top of a nearby truck to survey the scene and it seemed to me that there was a path through via the verge, a brief sortee into a field and so on. To howls of derision from nearby drivers we set off and before we had got to the end of the quarter-mile road block we were touching 40 and people were looking at us in complete disbelief. Laidlaw permitted himself a few words: "That was absolutely incredible". It was, too.

The secret of the FF system as opposed to ordinary four-wheel-drive is that each wheel knows what the others are up to and you can't spin one unless you spin the lot — which is a great over-simplification but it will serve. I am convinced that it should be gone ahead with, forgetting about the brakes, and, as it happens, Australia has the ideal car for the job — the Austin X6, as has already been shown by an experimental 1800 in England.

This car has a fantastically stiff body and it is a very simple matter to take a drive from the front to the rear wheels. Leyland Australia has it in its power to produce one of the best cars in the world, even if it means going back to the 1800 engine to use bits which already exist.

But the FF is gone . . . pax vobiscum. Or to put it another way:

Parting is such sweet sorrow
FF today and FA tomorrow.

*

PROFILE

Jensen Interceptor and FF

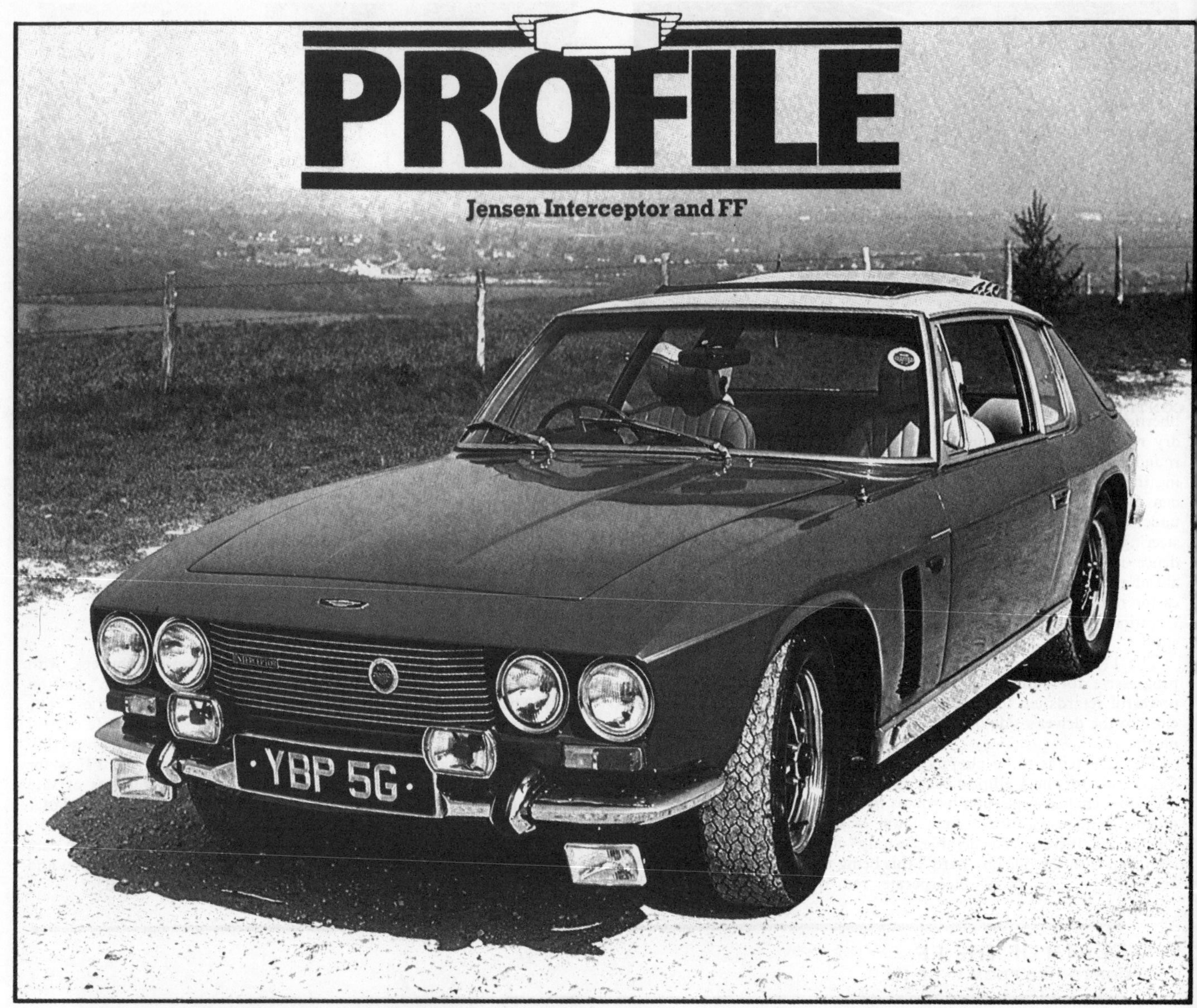

Unashamedly luxurious the Jensen Interceptor was aimed at the wealthy. It was, however, a well-engineered and inherently safe car, too

GENTLEMAN'S CARRIAGE

The Jensen Interceptor was an image car. Styled in Italy, powered by an American V8, it was hand built by British craftsmen. Mike Taylor and Peter Nunn look at the legend

The four-wheel drive Jensen FF, a rare and desirable variant. Only 320 were made so survivors are expensive

'Jensens are for gentlemen' ran the advertising theme used by Jensen Motors Ltd in the thirties to publicise their product, yet never was this slogan more apt than to describe the Interceptor. For this car more than any other firmly established Jensen as manufacturers of elegant, high performance motor cars.

As low volume specialist motor manufacturers, it is impossible not to think of Jensen, Bristol and Aston Martin in the same category, yet in reality they are poles apart. Aston Martin, particularly in latter years, always underline their thoroughbred engineering, not to mention their racing heritage. Bristol, it is true to say, utilise a 'foreign' power unit, but their attraction relies on rarity through availability. Jensen's *raison d'être* was its image, well honed over the years, for cars of style.

Jensen Motors was set up by two brothers, Richard and Alan Jensen who created a company whose strength lay in specialist coachbuilding. Taking chassis and engines from other manufacturers, they designed and built high quality bodies to fit on them. In the pre-war years it was the Singer and Wolseley, and even the American Ford

V8, while in the early post-war period they relied on the Meadows, and then – to a much larger extent – on the 4-litre, six-cylinder Austin unit.

As a management force, the two Jensens could not have been less alike. Alan was the administrator, while Richard was clearly the engineer. Neither could aspire to being a stylist of any note, but then in the thirties and forties, this was no hardship and their cars sold to wealthy people who desired something different.

But with World War II over and manufacturers unveiling their new models, car styling was becoming more important, particularly with the influx of designs coming from Italy. In the specialist world of high performance luxury tourers, looks were equally as important as maximum speed. A rift was appearing between British and Italian styles which some might say has never closed.

The first Jensen Interceptor was launched in 1949. It was a two-door coupé powered by the six-cylinder Austin engine. It was hardly sleek, but it possessed a certain elegance which, together with its 100 plus mph top speed, gave it appeal.

The next car to emerge from Jensen Motors was a classic of its type. Called the 541, this car was also powered by the 4-litre Austin power unit. But it was its sleek fastback appearance which turned people's heads. Also, significantly, it was the first four-seater production car to be made from glass-fibre.

541 no longer competitive

Despite facelifts and development, by the early sixties the 541 was no longer competitive in the Grand Touring market. Jensen customers were demanding even greater performance allied to automatic transmission and to satisfy these demands the C-V8 was launched in 1962. The Austin engine gave way to the 5.9-litre Chrysler V8 and the bodyshell was restyled. Unfortunately, this restyling was a disaster, for the C-V8 was bulbous and gross – reflecting not only Jensen's lack of styling flair but their inability to judge the mood of the market.

During 1965, Richard Jensen and Chief Engineer, Eric Neale, began work on a new model based on the C-V8. Called 'Interceptor' after the earlier 1949 model, the project was code named P66 and was a soft-top, two-seater with a third seat across the rear. The car was based on a perimeter-type chassis with an alloy body and was trimmed in PVC. There were to be two engine options: the 4.5 or the 6.3-litre Chrysler engines. Despite the fact that – at a time when the market trend was definitely towards coupés – this new car was a convertible, it created considerable interest when it was displayed at the 1965 Earls Court Show. And, priced at £2394 (some £1285 less than the C-V8) it did nothing to help potential sales of the C-V8. Clearly, Jensen had a problem.

After the Show it was decided to build another prototype using the same P66 styling but with cleaner lines and a fixed hard-top. But, by this time, opinions within the company as to the best course of action were split.

The man responsible for solving the situation was Jensen's Deputy Chief Engineer, Kevin Beattie. He argued that, because of the P66, the C-V8 was effectively dead, but that equally the P66 was not the car to carry the company into the seventies. What was needed, he said, was a car which had all the comfort and performance of the C-V8, but which had elegant lines: in other words, a car which was styled in Italy.

The Jensens were appalled. The very thought of a Jensen model carrying foreign lines was completely out of the question. But Beattie was very persuasive. Moreover, he had one strong ally – the Managing Director of Jensen's Holding Company, Norcros. However, having talked his way into going to Italy, Beattie now had another difficulty: time. There was just 10 months until the next London Motor Show.

After visiting Ghia and Vignale, Beattie finally decided on a styling proposal from Touring but, since Touring was not in a position to develop the proposal, the design was to be built in Vignale's far superior workshops. A C-V8 was sent to Italy in February 1966, and, within three months, Vignale

Right: in October 1965, Jensen produced this CV-8 and exhibited it at the Earls Court Motor Show. The four-wheel drive, anti-lock braking set up was later to feature on the FF. Note the car's characteristic wing vent. Below: the Jensen Nova existed as a one-off machine. Vignale's styling managed to incorporate Interceptor lines to the car's front end. It is said to be for sale; ring Cropredy 266 if interested

Impressive Mk I Interceptor interior

Powerhouse Mk I V8 delivers 325bhp with ease

had removed the GRP body and the first bare metal prototype had been assembled and was ready of inspection. By June 1966, the prototype was a road-going machine and Beattie returned to Italy to give the car an extensive four-day road test.

October saw the arrival in Britain of the first few bodies which had been made in Italy. The impossible had been achieved, largely by Beattie's hard work acting as both Development and Production Engineer, co-ordinating all the many facets which turned a paper styling exercise into a production motor car.

The Interceptor was unveiled at the London Motor Show in October 1966, where it received a rapturous reception. Fitted with Chrysler's 6.3-litre V8 engine and Torqueflite automatic transmission, the car retailed at £3743. The interior was trimmed in hide and accommodation was for four people with a 16 cu ft luggage area.

But that was not the complete picture for, in fact, Beattie and Jensen had achieved even more. Alongside the Interceptor was a four-wheel-drive version, known as the FF, and together the two cars made an impressive display – the FF winning the 'Car of the Year' Award.

The FF programme had, in fact, started in 1962 with the C-V8. Ever enthusiastic to introduce new ideas, the Jensen brothers knew that a four-wheel-drive system with anti-skid braking was being developed by Ferguson in conjunction with Dunlop. They were impressed, and the result was a modified C-V8 featuring the complete set-up which was exhibited at the 1965 Motor Show. The four-wheel-drive system centred around a special differential which split the power in the proportion 37/63 between front and rear wheels. The anti-skid device simply detected any locking on the shafts, restoring power, thereby overcoming the skid.

But with the introduction of the Interceptor, this arrangement was transferred to the new model. The FF version (known as the Jensen FF, incidentally, *not* Interceptor FF) could be distinguished by the fact that its bonnet was some 4ins longer and it had two air vents in the front wings. It cost some £5340. Expensive? Yes, but a car which was extremely safe and brought substantial publicity.

Rushed into production

If the Interceptor was rushed into production (and some might argue that the car's interior was functional rather than elegant because of it) then this might have attributed to the lack of quality on earlier models. It was clear in the early days that the quality of the Italian-built bodies was not up to standard and, since they had to be transported all the way from Milan, they were expensive. The solution was to transfer the manufacture of the bodies to Jensen's workshops where quality control could be applied. Also, Jensen instigated a continual development programme which ensured that the Interceptor improved drastically over the next four years so that, by 1970, it stood comparision with the world's best in this market.

In 1969, the Mk II Interceptor was introduced,

with the Mk II FF alongside. Although Jensen had relied very little on the American market for the sales of their cars, the safety and emission control regulations were having a profound effect on every motor manufacturer. To comply with these regulations, Jensen introduced the Mk III Interceptor in 1971 which featured a revised interior. At the same time an SP version was launched which featured a highly-tuned 7.2-litre engine producing 330bhp and most Interceptor 'extras' fitted as standard equipment.

The same year saw the demise of the FF. While not a great seller, the car had attracted much attention but the cost of clearing this car, as well as the standard Interceptor, through the American Safety Regulations was considered financially prohibitive. The SP lasted another two years until it, too, succumbed to the American legislation, its powerful triple carburettor engine unable to comply with the emission control specifications.

The Interceptor Convertible was launched at the Geneva Motor Show in 1974. Maintaining that, despite all the signs in motoring trends (shades of the P66?) there was still a market for a soft-top motor car, Jensen had slightly restyled the rear, giving the car a conventional boot and power-operated hood.

Finally, in 1975, came the Coupé. Introduced at the following year's Earls Court Show in an attempt to rejuvenate the *marque*, the Coupé shared the same hindquarters as the Convertible, but with a fixed hard-top. Arguably, it was the best-looking Interceptor of all. It was a brave attempt, but one doomed to failure since by this time the Company was in the hands of the Receiver and seven months later Jensen closed its doors.

The Mk III Convertible is arguably the most sought-after Interceptor variant. Expect to pay handsomely for a good example

Interceptor coupés, however, are rarer still. This late-model car is one of only 60 built by the factory before production ended

John Bolster tested this Mk I Interceptor for Autosport *in 1968. He recorded 133mph and a 0-60mph time of 7.4secs. His report described the car's acceleration as 'very vivid'*

SPECIFICATION

	Interceptor 1, 11	**Interceptor 111, SP**
Engine	90° Vee-eight	90° Vee-eight
Construction	Cast iron block and heads	Cast iron block and heads
Main Bearings	Five	Five
Capacity	6276cc	7212cc
Bore/Stroke	108mm × 86mm	109.8mm × 95.5mm
Valves	Overhead (pushrod)	Overhead (pushrod)
Compression	10:1	8.2:1 (10.3:1, SP)
Power	325bhp (SAE) at 4600rpm	284bhp (DIN) at 4800rpm 330bhp (DIN) at 4700rpm, (SP)
Torque	425lb.ft (SAE) at 2800rpm	383bhp (DIN) at 3200rpm (490bhp (DIN) at 3200rpm, (SP)
Transmission	Three-speed Chrysler Auto with torque convertor (manual option)	Three-speed Chrysler Auto with torque convertor
Top Gear	25.6mph per 1000rpm	24.8mph per 1000 (26.7mph per 1000rpm, SP)
Final Drive	Hypoid, 3.07:1 ratio	Hypoid, 3.07:1 (2.88:1, SP)
Brakes	Discs/discs with servo	Ventilated discs/discs with servo
Suspension F.	Ind. by coils, wishbones, lever dampers, anti-roll bar	Ind. by coils, wishbones, telescopic dampers, anti-roll bar
Suspension R.	Live axle, leaf springs, Panhard Rod, telescopic dampers	Live axle, leaf springs, Panhard Rod, telescopic dampers
Steering	Rack and pinion (power assistance standard from Oct '68)	Rack and pinion (assisted)
Body	All-steel body welded to tubular chassis	All-steel body welded to tubular chassis
Tyres	6.70 - 15	ER70VR15 (GR70 15, SP)
DIMENSIONS		
Length	15ft 8in	15ft 8in
Width	5ft 9in	5ft 9in
Height	4ft 5in	4ft 5in
Wheelbase	8ft 9in	8ft 9in
Weight	33cwt	34cwt (35cwt, SP)
PERFORMANCE		
Top Speed	133mph	130mph (142mph, SP)
0-60mph	7.4sec	7.7sec (6.9sec, SP)
30-50mph (kickdown)	2.7sec	2.9sec (2.4sec, SP)
Standing ¼ mile	15.5sec	15.8sec (14.7sec, SP)
Fuel cons	13/17mpg	12/15mpg (13/15mpg, SP)

FF: specification as Interceptor Mk 1/2 with following differences – **Transmission:** Three-speed automatic transmission and torque convertor coupled with Ferguson Formula four-wheel-drive system. Three differentials. Power steering standard. Girling braking system fitted with Maxaret anti-lock set up. **Length:** 15ft 11in. **Wheelbase:** 9ft 1in. **Weight:** 35¾cwt. **Performance: Top speed** – 132mph; **0-60mph** – 7.9sec; **Standing ¼ mile** – 15.7sec. **Fuel consumption**: 12/15mpg

The Mk III Interceptor was powered by a 7.2-litre V8 Chrysler engine

Interceptor interiors and facias were regularly updated. The Mk IIIs were very luxurious

Strictly speaking, louvred bonnets should only be fitted to SPs

Still more luxury: the contoured Mk III rear seats were finished in top quality Connolly hide

Production History

In total, nine different Interceptors were made during a production run which lasted from late 1966 until May 1976. These were: the Mk I, II and III Interceptors, with corresponding FF types which ran alongside until the FF was withdrawn from production in December 1971. The high performance SP, with its luxury interior, was launched in October the same year, only to be withdrawn in January 1973. At this point, the 7212cc 'J' series engine, which produced 284bhp at 4800rpm, was fitted to the Interceptor together with a letter 'J' on the car's hindquarters. This replaced the 6276cc unit which developed an optimistic 325bhp at 4600rpm. The Convertible was launched in March 1974, with the Coupé coming in October 1975 – both models sharing the mechanical specification of the Saloon, and remaining in production until 1976.

The first batch of Mk I Interceptors had Italian-built bodies until production was moved to West Bromwich. Mk Is had radial-ply tyres. In 1968, power-assisted steering became standard equipment, and by August the following year the 1000th Interceptor had been delivered. In October the same year, the Mk II was launched which had a larger fuel tank, radial tyres and optional air conditioning. The Mk III appeared in October 1971 and ran uninterrupted until 1976. It boasted ventilated disc brakes, alloy wheels, and a restyled interior trim.

In all, 1033 Interceptor Mk Is, 693 Mk IIs and 3419 Mk IIIs were made together with 105 SPs, 196 Mk I FFs, 109 Mk II FFs, 15 Mk III FFs, 267 Convertibles and 60 Coupés. Our thanks to Jensen Parts and Services for their help in compiling these figures although they do stress that the surviving records are not complete.

Rivals when new

There's no denying that these Jensens – be they Interceptors, FFs, Convertibles of SPs – were very much up-market, hand-built performance cars, and as such had to compete with similar Anglo-American hybrids of substantial size such as the AC 428 and post 409 series Bristols. It's open to argument whether the AC and Bristol were more in the Aston Martin/Bentley bracket than the Jensen whose somewhat unfashionable West Midlands background, lack of competition history and humble proprietary parts construction might have deterred some of the more traditional 'Twickers and Tweeds' customers but the fact remains that Jensen could compete strongly with the ACs and Bristols of this world, not to mention rival exotica of the Iso Grifo/Maserati Mistrale/Ferrari 330 variety, and still come out on top on a value for money basis.

Graceful Vignale styling and effortless Chrysler power coupled with a high-quality interior certainly made the Interceptor a desirable luxury express for four people; the short-lived Gordon Keeble GT could match most of these criteria but wasn't the FF with its Ferguson four-wheel-drive system and Maxaret anti-lock braking an even more attractive proposition? Perhaps only the Citroën SM, Mercedes-Benz 350/450SLs and present-day Audi Quattro can equal this rare combination of safety, performance, build quality, technical complexity – and good looks.

The hefty V8 under the Jensen bonnet meant that, in theory, the Oldsmobile Toronado, Cadillac Eldorado and Pontiac Tempest GTO were contemporary rivals to the newly-introduced Interceptor but it's probably fairer to say that the Aston Martin DBS V8 provided the early seventies Interceptors with closer competition. Either way, Aston or Jensen, they were both fine cars . . .

Clubs, specialists and books

Anyone with an interest in Interceptors/FFs, or Jensens in general, might like to join the 1000-strong Jensen Owners Club, an enthusiastic organisation formed in 1971. Spares discounts and technical advice from the club's own Interceptor Registrar, Clifford Oakes-Jones (address: The Bungalow, White Hall Road, Darwen, Lancs) are just two of the benefits of being a member; six copies a year of the club's high-quality magazine are more reasons to spend £12 on a year's subscription. New members are asked to pay an extra £2 joining fee but anyone who decides to enroll after the club's June AGM may have to pay an increased subscription, so be warned! The JOC's committee is also due to undergo a change of format at the AGM – a new secretary and membership secretary are to be elected along with several other appointments; in the meantime, however, all membership enquiries should be directed towards Doug Mason at 'Glendale', Broad St. Green Road, Heybridge, nr Maldon, Essex, while all general club matters should be addressed to Clifford Oakes-Jones at the address, below.

Although the club have an active concours d'elegance team and arrange a regular series of local pub meetings each month, the main event in the JOC calendar is the International Weekend, an event that will be held over the weekend of June 11/13 this year. A full weekend's activity will centre on the Penns Hall Hotel, Sutton Coldfield, nr Birmingham and it's just possible that you will be reading this before the festivities start on the Friday night . . .

Heading the list of outlets specialising in the defunct Jensen marque must be Jensen Parts and Services Ltd, a company set up in June 1976 following the untimely demise of Jensen Motors Ltd. JP & S, who are still based at the firm's old Kelvin Way, West Bromwich address (tel: 021 553 6741) can deal with anything Jensen, be it general restoration, spares or even a complete rebuild. Then there's the Jensen Owners Club's own Spares Department, run by Roy Goodrum at 40 Millfields, Danbury, Essex (tel: Danbury 5303); this flourishing organisation was set up in 1977 with just a few spares and £35 capital. Its assets now exceed £30,000. Of JP & S's recognised dealers, we must mention Charles Follet Ltd, 6 Hall Road, St. John's Wood, London NW8 9PA (tel: 01 289 2211), Sturdy & Lowe Ltd, 95 High Street, Grimethorpe, Barnsley, Yorks (tel: 0226 759128) and Mist's Garage Ltd, Hamstead and Soho Hill, Hansworth, Birmingham 19 (tel: 021 554 6311). Most Jensen OC members will tell you, incidentally, that Mist's are in the unique position of possessing an

Interceptor that's covered a mere 70 miles from new. A party of JOC enthusiasts make a point of travelling down to see the car at each International Weekend . . . Finally, Cropredy Bridge Garage of Cropredy, Banbury, Oxon (tel: Cropredy 266) have considerable Jensen expertise and can supply a full range of Interceptor parts but are not an official JP & S dealer.

On the reading matter front, the Jensen Owners Club can provide technical manuals and a full membership list for interested parties. Even though it only goes up until 1974 and is now sadly out of print (but still available from specialist book sellers), *The Jensen Healey Stories* (MRP) by Peter Browning and John Blunsden is the only hardback history of the marque published to date. Reasonably-priced and well-illustrated, the book is highly recommended and is well worth hunting down. Other Interceptor reading material includes Mike Taylor's *Jensen – A Glimpse of Perfection* which is a brief, soft-cover review of the company, and two Brooklands Books titles *Jensen Interceptor 1966-1976* and *Jensen Cars 1967-1979*.

The keen Jensen enthusiast will, of course, have all these titles on his bookshelf, along with *Management Kinetics* a book written by Jensen's 'Turn-around Man' Carl Duerr. This last title is essentially a guide to successful business management but one of the chapters provides an absolutely fascinating insight into the goings on at Jensen while Duerr was at the helm. It's understood that copies of the book are still available from ASO Management Centre, Brook Lane, Aldereley Edge, Cheshire; £7.50 might sound quite a lot to pay for one chapter of a text book yet the JOC tell us each copy of *Management Kinetics* is signed by the author himself prior to dispatch . . .

Buyers spot check

Never forget that Interceptors, and especially FFs, are large, heavy and expensive cars. Therefore, unless you are aiming for the tail end of the market, a documented service history profile detailing body and mechanical work carried out would seem an essential prerequisite. Early bangers needing the full restoration treatment can be good news, though, if you possess the time, inclination and capital to have the work carried out properly, so cheap Interceptors (and some, in relation to marque rivals, are very cheap) needn't be avoided if the car in question is complete and your wallet can take the strain. In the top bracket, we have heard that vast sums have been spent on late-model Interceptors, Convertibles and the like to keep them in tip-top shape although thanks to the Chrysler engine/transmission unit and the cars' significantly proprietary construction – Ford, Chrysler and BMC parts are used, among others – running costs on lesser examples can be kept down to sub-Aston levels without too much difficulty. Whereas this last statement is generally true of pre 1971 versions, later (Mk III/SP) versions tend to be more complicated and costly to maintain.

Corrosion problems are usually more acute with the Mk I and II models, the Mk IIIs having a good overall record against the tinworm. Rust invariably manifests itself around the sill area on either side, at the top and bottom of each door skin and around the front and rear aprons (below the bumpers). Watch out also for rust at the bottom of the front wings, around the porous tail gate area and in the fuel filler cap. Examine the bonnet closely then take a look at the engine bay inner wing panels as these have been known to suffer from corrosion damage in the past. Chassis rust is very, very rare but, alas, bodged crash repairs and 'cheapo' glass-fibre renovations can still be found in the rougher species; thus if you're contemplating a complete restoration of a 'poor' Interceptor (the parts are mostly available, the work is fairly straightforward and the finished result should make a profit), choose carefully, take specialist advice and you shouldn't go far wrong.

With regards to the big V8 engine, many problems in the past have involved temperamental emission control equipment, poor-quality, non-original ancilliaries (radiator hose, fanbelts and so on) and minor electrical faults. Properly serviced and cared for, the cast-iron motor should last for years despite its propensity for hot-running during all weathers and overheating if neglected. The Interceptor transmission system, along with the FF's Ferguson four-wheel-drive set-up, similarly should be trouble-free but check all is well on your road test and make sure all the oil changes have been carried out at regular intervals. Listen in particular for extraneous noises from the transmission while ensuring the automatic changes are precise and properly-timed. Repairs are possible, of course, but can be expensive. Although front hub wear was once a problem on FFs, one specialist we spoke to reckoned the FF design to be reliable and 'not much to worry about', which must be encouraging.

The Mk III Interceptors with their ventilated brakes are acknowledged to be a great improvement over the earlier Girling and Dunlop systems but watch for heavy disc pad wear and poor handbrake adjustment, the latter feature being among the model's weaker points. Not surprisingly, brakes (like the suspension) take quite a pounding and a full professional overhaul of the running gear will not come cheap; as for the renowned Maxaret anchors fitted to the FF, these last well so expect few serious problems in that department apart from spares availability and possible service costs. Power steering faults should be confined to high-pressure leaks and general wear and tear.

Finally, a tatty interior can be renovated quite easily even though the dashboard/facia/seating configurations of the various Interceptors and FFs chopped and changed as time went on. Post '71 interiors are especially luxurious.

Part of the Interceptor line at Jensen's West Bromwich factory. Quality control was commendably high

Mk III Interceptors wore stylish aluminium alloy wheels. Earlier cars were fitted with Rostyle equivalents

Every year the Jensen OC hold an International Weekend in the Midlands. These Interceptors were pictured at the 1981 event

Prices

Although it may be possible to pick up a Mk I Interceptor for less than £500, the chances are that you'll have to pay at least £1800 for a sound car with an MoT and traceable service history. Should you want a pristine early Interceptor, expect to part with £3000 upwards. The 1969/71 Mk IIs are slightly pricier but not, generally, quite so popular as the other versions; even so, rough ones start at around the £600/£700 mark and 'average' cars range between £1250 and £2250. The top limit for Mk IIs is reckoned to be set at around £3500.

Values really start to head skywards with Interceptor III prices. By all accounts, you'll be hard pushed to track down any kind of roadworthy Mk III for under £2000 while £4000 will buy you a good (but not A1) example of the marque. Superb, near faultless Mk IIIs are now fetching £9000 plus, we're told, with concours-winners nudging the 'silly money' league. Surprisingly, the potent 330bhp SP has yet to match Mk III prices; 3-condition machines can still be found for £1000 though 'average' SPs start at £2000 and mint examples at £4500.

Turning now to FFs, we understand that Mk Is range from £1500 upwards with fair specimens following on at £2250. Due to the model's overall scarcity (officially only 320 were built), FF prices are obviously pretty keen – a really top class Mk II could fetch £10,000, for example, although further down the scale, middle-of-the-road Mk IIs are usually priced in the £3000/£5000 bracket.

We are grateful to John Pellowe of the Jensen Owners Club for the above evaluations.

OWNER'S VIEW

The Interceptor Mk I of Jensen OC official Peter Williams

Peter with his coveted *Jensen*

It's probably fair to say that, sooner or later, most Jensen Owners Club members will come into contact with Peter Williams. To start with, he's the club's Regalia Secretary and thus keeps busy by selling official JOC merchandise – sweat shirts, cloth badges, ties and so on – in his spare time. His other claim to fame rests with a remarkable 1968 Mk I Interceptor that, in recent years, has won three class awards and one second place at successive Owners Club concours d'elegance contests.

It was at the 1966 Earls Court Motor Show that Peter, a self-employed building constructor from Sussex, first became aware of Jensen's new Interceptor model. In true fairytale tradition, he decided there and then that, one day, he would like to own one. However, it wasn't until 1972 and the purchase of YBP 5G, a 48,000-mile, two-owner example to replace a succession of Fords that this ambition was fulfilled. Although, by then, the Mks I and II Interceptor had been superseded by the Mk III/SP models, Peter went for a Mk I for reasons of economy, ease of maintenance and because the Mk I looked to be the best all-round buy. Furthermore, it had been the Mk I that, six years previously, had fuelled his interest in the breed.

Spares not a problem

To date, YBP's renovation job card includes, among other things, a new rack and pinion assembly, stainless steel exhaust system and a new set of road springs front and back. Thinking that spares might be a problem, in later years, Peter had all four spring units changed when one rear leaf snapped but it seems Interceptor parts are still available and plentiful due to the first-class efforts of the club's own spares outlet and other specialists. In fact compared to other exotica, keeping a Mk I Interceptor on the road can be a relatively cheap business according to Peter, due to the car's simple construction and number of patent parts in its make-up. To underline this welcome trait, Peter manages to keep costs down by having his Mk I serviced by his local Ford garage! "They do a good job," he said, "and are reasonably priced, but you couldn't do that with an Aston Martin, could you?"

YBP was resprayed seven years ago by this same Ford garage, the paint finish being good enough over the years for the car to drive away with the four Jensen Owners Club concours d'elegance prizes including three outright wins. Peter would be the first to admit, though, that these awards were gained for the most part by virtue of the car's outstanding originality and the fact that there are now very few Mk I Interceptors of any kind registered with the club.

Interestingly Peter hasn't gone quite as far as some of the keener members of the professional concours d'elegance fraternity; concours contests, he feels, should be enjoyable and competitive, but not *that* competitive. Having said that, he did take the Chrysler V8 engine out of his Interceptor last year to clean up the bay in readiness for another season's competition. Unfortunately in doing this he came up against more than he had anticipated for he found the inner front wings to be badly corroded and the job itself, which involved checking over the engine, spraying the block and polishing the bay area in general, gradually assumed nightmare proportions. All, however, is now well in that department although rust is breaking through in some other areas of body work so a spell of cosmetic metalwork surgery could be on the cards in the near future.

Other modifications? Peter had a sunroof fitted to try to reduce the greenhouse-type atmosphere of the Jensen's admittedly sumptuous interior. The additional driving lights at the front are also there for a purpose ("I found it hard to see where I was going at night") and the leather seats have been Connollised When the large rear window was damaged by vandals one night, two local garages broke three replacement windows before the job was successfully carried out by Jensen Parts & Services in West Bromwich. "Fitting that window must be a very difficult job," mused Peter, "but JP&S wouldn't let me see how they did it; apparently it involves a certain amount of immoral brute force!" On another occasion, the Interceptor's front nearside wheel blew while Peter was travelling at 110mph on the M1. "I can honestly say that I didn't know it had happened" he stated. "I looked in the mirror and saw smoke pouring out the back so I pulled over to the hard shoulder where I found the tyre to be torn to shreds. I rang up Jensen to say what a marvellous car they had designed – I was really impressed with the way it saved my life – but I got the impression from them that this safety aspect was nothing out of the ordinary. I was told they used to carry out tyre-blowing sessions on Interceptors at 120mph quite often . . ."

YBP 5G on the road: 'You'd be amazed at the attention it causes when I take it out for a spin. I think it's a fantastic car'

Speedo now reading 115,000

Following ten years of virtual everyday use, YBP 5G's speedo is now reading 115,000 miles. In an effort to preserve his concours winner (that's now valued at £10,000 by the way) Peter has decided to take the Interceptor off the road during the winter and use a company Vauxhall Viceroy as day-to-day transport. That's not to say that the Jensen, when it is ready for the road, will cease to be able to carry out hair-raising feats such as a frantic return dash between Brighton and Exeter in seven hours that once occurred. On that epic occasion, 22 gallons of petrol were consumed at a rate of 18 miles per gallon.

It's also unlikely that the Jensen will ever fail to satisfy Peter. "I've tested Turbo Porsches and a Ferrari Daytona but I've never experienced such a thrill in any car as I do with this Jensen. I wouldn't mind an FF, a 541 or even a CV8 if I had the money and I must admit an XJS HE is rather a nice car – but this Interceptor . . .! It's a car I've always wanted to own; it's never let me down or failed to live up to my expectations. When I feel depressed, a blast in the Interceptor often restores the status quo with no trouble at all. You'd be amazed at the attention it causes when I take it out for a spin, people keep asking me about it and what it's like to drive. I think it's a fantastic car and I'm never going to sell it – never!

Footnote: Peter organises a regular noggin 'n' natter at The Wheatsheaf, Woodmancote, West Sussex on the first Monday of each month. Call him on 0273 890740 for more details.

Interceptor and Beyond

Mike Taylor pays tribute to Kevin Beattie, the man behind the Jensen Interceptor, who in his tragically shortened life achieved so much. This is the story of his life, the Interceptor, and the cars that might have followed it. We are grateful to the Jensen Owners Club and William Towns for their help in the production of this article

FEW people who stopped to admire the new Interceptor on the Jensen stand during the hectic days of the 1966 Motor Show could have realised just how important this car would become to the company's future. Its striking lines had a dateless appearance, making it a worthy successor to the CV-8 which, though it had earned Jensen a reputation as a manufacturer of high-quality performance cars, had an appearance that was decidedly contentious. The CV-8 is better-loved now than it was in its day.

Within 12 months of the Interceptor's launch, Jensen's contracts with BMC (for the assembly of the Austin Healey), and Rootes (for their part in the manufacture of the Sunbeam Tiger) were to be cancelled, placing Jensen's sole survival prospects on the Interceptor alone. Ironically, the Interceptor itself had come about largely *against* the wishes of the Jensen Board and through the efforts of one man: Kevin Beattie. His story, and that of the two prototypes (the F and G types) which were developed under his guidance make fascinating reading.

Well-liked and respected by all who knew him, Kevin's story starts in South Africa. He was born there in 1927 and at a very early age his parents returned to the UK where he attended Kingsmead Preparatory School. He then went on to Gresham's School in Norfolk where he gained the necessary qualifications to apply for entry to Cambridge. But the unfortunate death of his father led to a change of plans and, through Bernard Winter — who was Rootes' engineering director, and whose son also went to Greshams — Kevin joined Rootes under their Pupilage Scheme (a scheme, incidentally, which was to produce many talented people, among them a certain William Towns).

Despite these changes in plans, Kevin was to gain a sound engineering background as well as having the opportunity of taking an HNC in Engineering. Then, it was on to London University as an external student to take a BSc.

Meanwhile, the Rootes Pupilage was to last three years after which he then moved into their Design Studio, under the leadership of Ted White. This was the late Forties and Rootes were busily engaged on shedding their pre-war styles, replacing them with new models equipped with modern engineering.

Then, quite by chance, Kevin was offered a place on the Rootes design team in Melbourne, Australia. The offer seemed to hold possibilities, so he accepted, but Kevin's fortunes were to change again just as dramatically when, on his voyage out, he contracted a serious disease. Had it not been for the quick and expert attention of his wife's sister (who was a doctor working in Australia) he might well have died. As it was, he made an almost total recovery and began his new life with relish.

Kevin's love of sport and his ability to communicate meant that he was readily accepted by the Australians. He was a keen golfer, and also played cricket, rugby and hockey. Off the field, the Australians' natural aggressive enthusiasm plus the demands of his new job inspired Kevin and he was soon deeply involved in his new life. Significantly, while he was in Australia he was approached by both BMC and General Motors with offers to join their teams.

Yet, despite a very promising future, Kevin decided, because of family pressures and responsibilities, to return to the UK. Once again, he was back in Rootes headquarters in Coventry where, to his dismay, he found that the old family atmosphere, which had abounded during his Pupilage, had gone. Despite an absence of only four years there was now, in his opinion, a sense of insecurity and no matter how he tried to shrug off these feelings, he was nevertheless aware that he no longer belonged there.

However, an opportunity presented itself for Kevin to leave Rootes when an advertisement appeared in the local Coventry newspaper. The well-respected company of Jensen Motors Limited at West Bromwich required a deputy chief engineer — a responsible job with a much smaller company, promising more opportunity for individual expression. Encouraged by his wife, Eileen, Kevin applied. It was now over 12 months since his return from Australia and he was anxious to get away from the atmopshere at Rootes.

In fact, he was to wait several agonising months before finally he received an invitation to attend an interview at the company's headquarters, where he met Alan Jensen. As it turned out, Alan Jensen was so impressed by Kevin that he hired him on the spot.

Kevin joined Jensen on January 1, 1960. At the time, the company was still very much a family concern with Alan Jensen the administrator and brother Richard remaining essentially the car enthusiast. A somewhat parochial environment, perhaps, but nevertheless one in which Kevin felt he could extend his engineering talents to the full. In fact, within a short time he was happily immersed in the company's activities and, despite the everyday traumas experienced by a small company like JML, Kevin's future looked very much brighter.

The company's two major projects during this period were the assembly of the Austin Healey sports car (which involved the total construction of the car except for the installation of the drivetrain), and the manufacture of a stylish glassfibre GT called the Jensen 541, which was powered by a 4·0-litre Austin engine. Trends in the high performance luxury car market were changing, however, and it was decided to make a complete break and fit an American Chrysler V8 power unit coupled to a Torque-flite automatic transmission, while at the same time re-styling

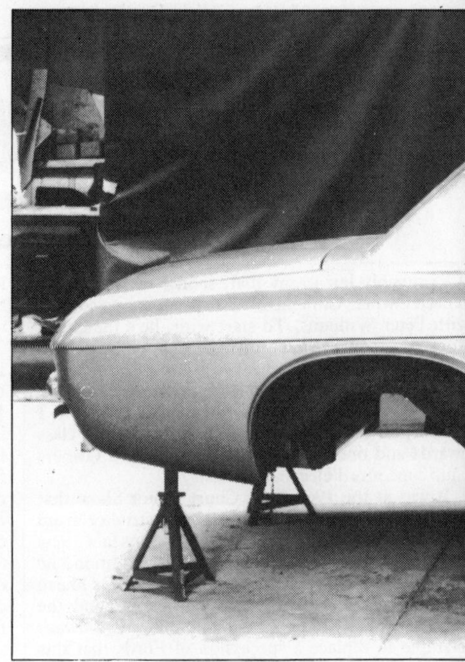

Above, by April, 1966, the Jensen P66 was in this form, having lost the ornate wheel arch treatment of its predecessor. At this point, Beattie made a stand for a new model — the successful Interceptor was on the way. Right, first new Interceptor in the Kent dealership showroom of Sundridge Park Motors

Above, 'Big Bertha', a widened and lengthened Interceptor, was the prototype for the Jensen F-Type's running gear. This picture shows part of the final drive layout and inboard rear discs. A de Dion axle was used and self-levelling gas struts were built into the design

Above, rare picture of Beattie (left) and Towns with G-type mock-up. Left, Kevin Beattie. Right, F-type scale model on Industor's computerised section drawing machine in Italy

the body in an attempt to update it.

Called the CV-8, the result — in Kevin's opinion — was a styling disaster. For whereas the 541 had been sleek and unpretentious, the CV-8 was bulbous and somewhat cluttered in appearance. As a result, it was to herald the beginning of a split in opinions between Kevin and the Jensen brothers as to who would style their next model. As it was, a new proposal was developed within the company, called the P66, and launched at the 1965 Earls Court Show. It too was powered by a Chrysler V8 engine, and featured a soft top body with slightly cleaner lines. But its retail price was set well below that of the CV-8, which automatically killed off a large proportion of the CV-8's potential market. Clearly, something had to be done — and quickly.

At this point Kevin made a stand, maintaining that the company's future lay in neither the CV-8 nor the P66, but in an entirely new car. A car styled not by Jensen themselves, but by one of the Italian styling houses.

Immediately, this suggestion brought about considerable resentment since the Jensen brothers were proud of the company's in-house facilities, despite the fact that these facilities were somewhat limited. In reality, Jensen's strength lay in their high quality craftsmanship not in their artistic capabilities. Indeed, it must be assumed that the combination of the Jensen brothers and their chief engineer constituted considerable opposition to Kevin's proposals. But, luckily, he had allies. The company was now in the hands of a holding company called Norcros and its managing director, John Sheffield, was in favour of an Italian-designed car, as was Jensen's own managing director, Brian Owen. So, still very much against the wishes of the Jensen family, Kevin went to Italy to seek a suitable design for the next Jensen model. What he ended up with was a styling proposal from Touring and, since their production facilities were somewhat limited, an agreement from Vignale to put the proposal into production.

Inevitably, this posed Kevin with a serious problem: that of time. As the P66 was a non-starter, and the CV-8 was effectively dead, the company had to exhibit a new model at the 1966 Earls Court Show — just eleven months away. The way in which Kevin achieved this surprising feat was to assume the dual role of development *and* production engineer for the new car.

Called *Interceptor* after one of Jensen's earlier models, the car reached Earls Court in time and aroused considerable interest. In fact, Kevin had every reason to be pleased for not only had he got the Interceptor into production, but on the same stand was the four-wheel-drive FF. It was the styling of the car which drew such admiring glances for, clearly, the Interceptor was not only strong in the areas where the CV-8 had appeal (interior comfort and effortless performance) but it was also strong in the areas where the CV-8 was weak: in its overall appearance. Kevin's ideas had been vindicated, although the continual strain of the past months — that of co-ordinating the many facets which resulted in the Interceptor reaching the Show — was beginning to take its toll and was probably a contributing factor in the deterioration of his health.

Above, sales of Interceptors to celebrities like Henry Cooper, seen here at the Jensen factory in 1968 after taking delivery of a new car, did nothing but good for the marque. Cooper was British and European heavyweight champion at the time

Interceptor and beyond

Tony Good, who was responsible for all Jensen's public relations, said of Kevin, "He had a monumental task in getting the Interceptor into production and he did an amazing job. Kevin was one of the most straightforward, nicest people — although in no way commercial. He also had an insatiable appetite for choc ices!'

Unfortunately, after the excitement of the previous year, 1967 was to mark the start of Jensen's fight for survival. The American safety regulations were just beginning to take effect and at a stroke BMC withdrew the Austin Healey contract. In addition, Chrysler's takeover of the Rootes Group meant that the Ford-powered V8 Sunbeam Tiger would be an embarrassment, so this too was dropped. As a result, Jensen suffered a considerable loss of revenue, the Austin Healey contract alone being worth an estimated £300,000 per year.

With Jensen's buoyancy beginning to fail, John Sheffield and Norcros, the holding company, began looking closely at Jensen and called in a company investigator to evaluate the situation. The man they called was Norwegian-American Karl Duerr. His interpretation of the situation was to increase output while trimming the workforce, thereby making the company more attractive to investors. His byword was 'public relations' and he set about finding ways to bring Jensen and its product closer to the public's eye.

Meanwhile, Kevin was ensuring continued production, maintaining a buffer zone between Duerr and the men on the shop floor. Inevitably, this was an unenviable position and Kevin was kept busy trying to improve quality control while at the same time fighting the feeling of apathy which was running through the workforce. However, as Duerr's plans took effect, so the position began to improve and in 1969 Norcros sold their interests to William Brandts, the Merchant Bankers. But they, too, became sceptical about Jensen's finances and Duerr's position was taken by company 'doctor' Alf Vickers.

By 1970, the stage had been reset once again, this time with the self-made American businessman from San Francisco, Schell Qvale, in command and Donald Healey as his Chairman. Vickers had done much to streamline the company, increasing production still further and cutting the workforce. Jensen's future looked much brighter, added to which Qvale had plans to introduce a new range of cars: a sports model to replace the big Healey, an Interceptor GT replacement, and — later still — an exciting mid-range car which would encompass the best features of the sports and the GT.

The styling for the new sports car was drawn up by Hugo Poole. His brief was to design a car of simple lines — thereby keeping down tooling costs — and to use Vauxhall running gear and drivetrain. Unfortunately, when Qvale saw the proposal he was less than impressed and brought in another ex-Rootes man, William Towns. Towns developed another, totally different and altogether more pleasing shape but again it was not quite what Qvale had in mind.

By this time the whole project was getting a little out of hand. Qvale's business commitments were keeping him almost permanently in America, so he was not able to watch each stage of development personally. Moreover, time was running out and the Healey's replacement *had* to be launched soon. It was decided to retain the Poole design, although by now the car had become the subject of committee decisions, the Jensen Board making styling suggestions in an effort to improve it. Finally, the car went into production — as the Jensen-Healey — most people liking some of it, but few liking all of it. Kevin Beattie was one person who certainly was not impressed.

Meanwhile, since the Interceptor had been in production some five years, thoughts were being turned to a replacement. Jensen's approach to the new car, code named the F-type, was that it should be further up-market than the Interceptor, with up-to-date styling and featuring better aerodynamics, more sophisticated suspension and improved interior trim. It was to be powered by the same 7·2-litre Chrysler V8 engine with full Californian emission control equipment.

Jensen invited styling proposals from several sources and Bertone, Trevor Fiore, Ital Design and William Towns all tendered suggestions. Eventually, after each one had been scrutinised, it was Towns' ideas which were accepted. Towns says now that he was totally uninfluenced by any other car at the time, although a styling colleague had once pointed out the treatment of the roof line on the Lamborghini Espada (where the curve from the windscreen rearwards maintains an almost constant radius). He admits to having been intrigued by this and included this *theme* in his proposal, as well as a vertical panel of glass in the stern — also a feature from the Espada.

First, Towns produced a 0·4 scale clay model which was approved by Jensen and then crated up and sent by refrigerated aircraft to Italy where Industor (a firm of industrial designers) transposed the model into full-size working drawings using computer-controlled equipment. These drawings were then sent to Coggilla, a company of coachbuilders, who made a full-size plaster replica. Jensen were invited to make comments at this point, and it was decided to alter the nose slightly, which in full-size form looked a little droopy, and also to remove a somewhat unsightly NACA airscoop which had been moulded into the bonnet line to hide the necessity for a bulge to clear the power unit. With the full-size plaster shape finally accepted it was then arranged for Coventry Motor Panels to begin making a set of five prototype bodyshells.

Below, this was William Towns' proposal for the Jensen-Healey. From this angle the model looks rather more attractive than the modified version of it which Jensen boss Schell Qvale, eventually chose. Only a partial success, the launch of the Jensen-Healey coincided with the Lotus decision to drop the Elan on the grounds that the design philosophy behind such a car was by then outdated

Meanwhile, Kevin and his chief development engineer, Brian Spicer, were working on the new suspension system which was to be used on the F. It was to have Girling self-levelling suspension using gas struts with spring assistance and a de Dion axle on the rear, with a conventional wishbone arrangement on the front. To develop and perfect the system, an Interceptor (which came to be known as 'Big Bertha' because of its big wheels and boy racer appearance) was modified, increasing its width by four inches and its length by six inches, to take a prototype suspension.

As for the car's interior, the F-type was to be a full four-seater with at least four inches more room in the rear than in that of the Interceptor. In fact, when the F type was finally cancelled and Towns became involved in styling the Aston Martin Lagonda, many of his ideas for the F were used again. So, while the F would not have had the same futuristic instrumentation (although Jensen were testing some Lucas-made touch switches for the dashboard) it would still have had the same solid state feel about it.

As the F-type programme began to develop, one of the prototype bodyshells was used for side intrusion, roof crush and barrier tests while another was made into a fully-running car. This was taken to Mira where it was clocked at over 140mph at 5500rpm — the car's maximum speed being governed by its axle ratio rather than its power output or aerodynamics. By now it had been given a name, too. It was called *Esporanda* and the name had been registered.

Unfortunately, the F-type was never to reach production. In the early days, Jensen were happy with the Interceptor's sales — running at some 30/35 units per week in the early Seventies. Then came the Middle East war and the turn away from large cars with powerful, greedy engines. However, by the time Jensen collapsed a considerable amount of money had been spent on body tooling and Esporanda was well on the way to production. As it was, all but two bodies were cut up.

Another Jensen prototype, possibly even more interesting than the F, was the G-type. With the early teething troubles of the Vauxhall-based Lotus dohc engine (which was fitted to the Jensen-Healey) almost cured, Qvale began to look seriously at a car more in keeping with the current market trends. What he envisaged was a full four-seater car, but smaller than the F-type, fitted with the J-H power unit clothed in a sporting bodyshell using gull-wing doors. Again, Towns was given the job of producing styling proposals.

Using the same principles as for the F-type, a 0·4 scale clay model was produced and, after agreement with Jensen, taken out (this time in the back of a Vauxhall estate car) to Italy, where Industor transposed the model into full-size drawings. Then, the drawings were sent to Coggilla for a plaster mock-up to be made.

But time was to run out for the G-type and in the end only one prototype bodyshell was ever made. There had not been time to discuss interior trim styles, so all that emerged were general plans. However, of one thing we can be certain. The G-type would have been offered with a 4·0-litre V8 version of Lotus's tohc alloy engine, had one become available.

As for Kevin Beattie, his health began to deteriorate and in March 1974 he became very ill. However, he was determined to keep working and continued until October, when he gave up temporarily. He returned to work in 1975, part-time only, three days per week. Tragically, he died in September that year.

Kevin had seen the good years. Through his efforts the Interceptor and the technically advanced FF had reached the market place, and the F-type had come so close to being a reality. Within eight months of his death Jensen was dead, too.

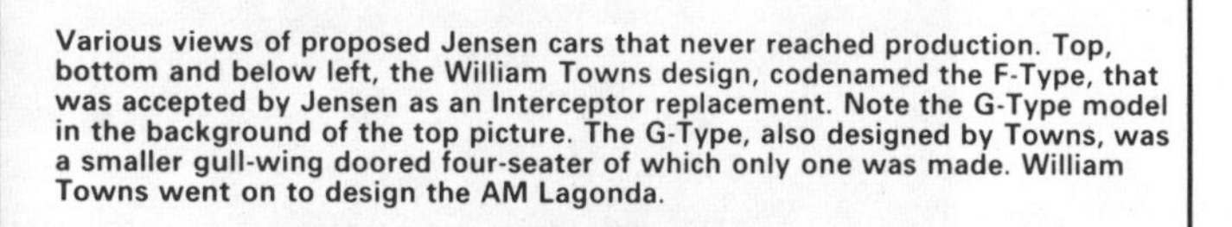

Various views of proposed Jensen cars that never reached production. Top, bottom and below left, the William Towns design, codenamed the F-Type, that was accepted by Jensen as an Interceptor replacement. Note the G-Type model in the background of the top picture. The G-Type, also designed by Towns, was a smaller gull-wing doored four-seater of which only one was made. William Towns went on to design the AM Lagonda.

Looking through history

Jensen FF

Like the two-wheel-drive Interceptor, the FF Series 2 model pictured here was an excellent grand touring car. The entire rear window and shelf lifted up to reveal a capacious boot

WHAT'S NEW about the Audi Quattro? Nearly 20 years ago Jensen decided to produce a fast GT car with four-wheel-drive. The difference between the Jensen and the Audi is that the Quattro is a commercial, and rallying, success, while the FF was really a failure.

The roots of the FF were in two projects – the Jensen CV8 car, with its massively strong platform chassis frame Chrysler V8 engine and gearbox, and the Ferguson four-wheel-drive transmission. Harry Ferguson's small team, based in Coventry, had been developing a completely new concept – transmission, engine, anti-lock braking, and chassis – since the 1950s, but had repeatedly failed to sell it to the sceptical British motor industry. The breakthrough came in 1964, when Jensen agreed to blend the transmission to a car of their own.

The result, seen at the London Motor Show in October 1965, was that Jensen showed an arguably ugly modified CV8, complete with lengthened wheelbase, and 6.3-litre Chrysler engine, to which the FF, or Ferguson Formula, had been mated. Chassis changes were few, except that space had to be found at the front for a differential casing, and there was new front suspension, complete with power-assisted rack rack and pinion steering.

It was the transmission, however, and the Dunlop Maxaret anti-lock braking system which went with it, which delighted the observers. The conventional Jensen engine and automatic transmission, powered by Chrysler, were in place, but behind that there was the unique Ferguson torque-splitting centre differential and transfer box, from which a conventional propeller shaft went rear, and another propeller shaft was fed up the side of the engine to the front differential. The Maxaret braking sensor worked from the transfer box.

There was talk of putting this car into limited production at once, but in the event it waited for an entirely new body style (from Touring of Italy), offered on the Jensen chassis from the end of 1966. The FF then went on limited sale, and sold slowly

Predecessor of the Interceptor-based FF was the CV8 shown here. It was the first car to win the Don Safety Trophy in 1966, but only the prototype, pictured here, was actually built

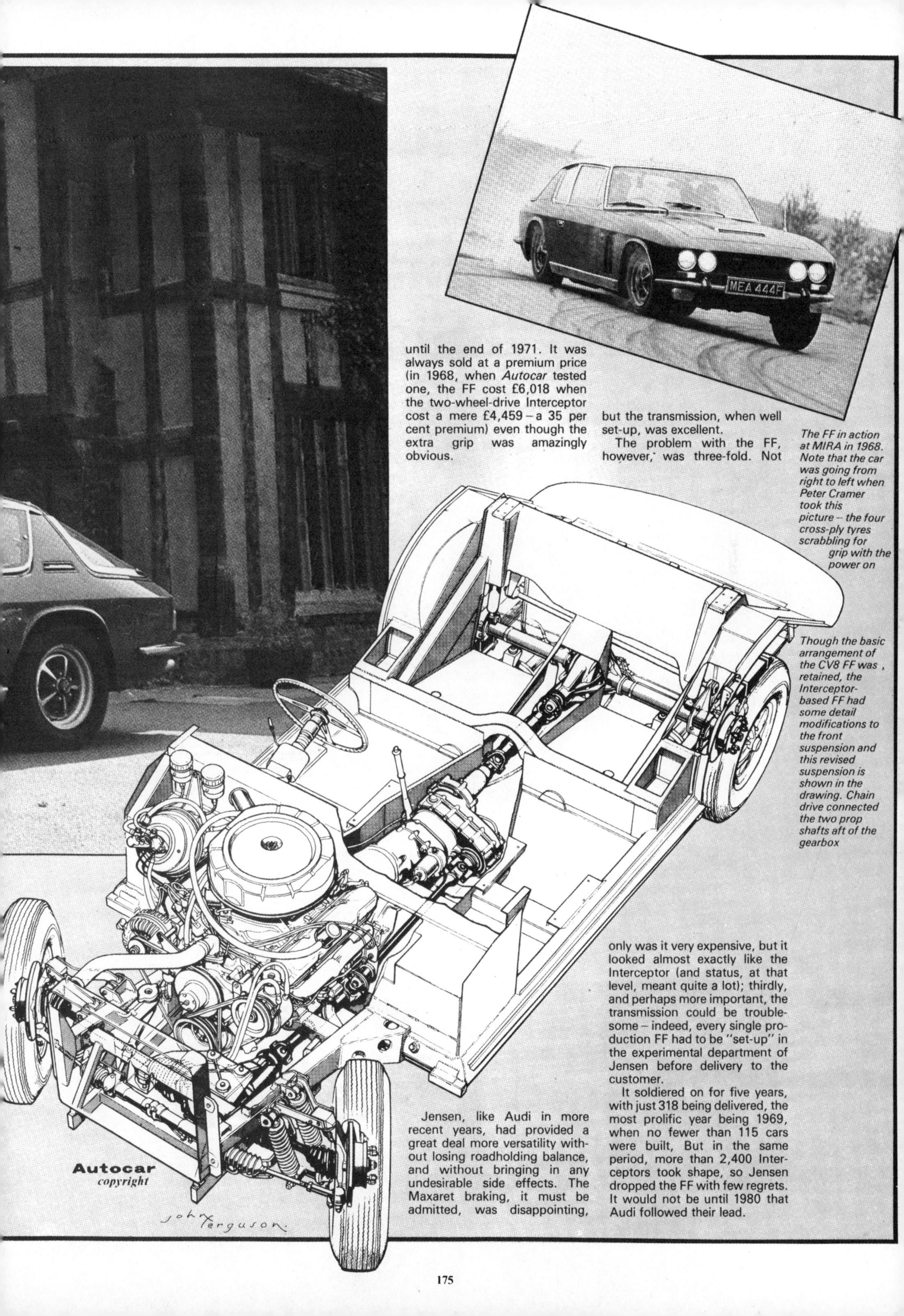

until the end of 1971. It was always sold at a premium price (in 1968, when *Autocar* tested one, the FF cost £6,018 when the two-wheel-drive Interceptor cost a mere £4,459 – a 35 per cent premium) even though the extra grip was amazingly obvious.

Jensen, like Audi in more recent years, had provided a great deal more versatility without losing roadholding balance, and without bringing in any undesirable side effects. The Maxaret braking, it must be admitted, was disappointing, but the transmission, when well set-up, was excellent.

The problem with the FF, however, was three-fold. Not only was it very expensive, but it looked almost exactly like the Interceptor (and status, at that level, meant quite a lot); thirdly, and perhaps more important, the transmission could be troublesome – indeed, every single production FF had to be "set-up" in the experimental department of Jensen before delivery to the customer.

It soldiered on for five years, with just 318 being delivered, the most prolific year being 1969, when no fewer than 115 cars were built, But in the same period, more than 2,400 Interceptors took shape, so Jensen dropped the FF with few regrets. It would not be until 1980 that Audi followed their lead.

The FF in action at MIRA in 1968. Note that the car was going from right to left when Peter Cramer took this picture – the four cross-ply tyres scrabbling for grip with the power on

Though the basic arrangement of the CV8 FF was retained, the Interceptor-based FF had some detail modifications to the front suspension and this revised suspension is shown in the drawing. Chain drive connected the two prop shafts aft of the gearbox

RISE OF THE

Close to a decade after its demis
Roger Bell went t

PHOENIX

ensen's mighty Interceptor is back in production.
est Bromwich to drive it

Ian Orford (left) — the man behind the Jensen revival. His insistence on building in the grand manner shows in the quality of the interior (right). Power is by a 5.9 litre Chrysler V8, and the distinctive greenhouse rear is retained (far right)

THE RECARO'S hugging backrest reclines a few degrees more under electric power. A twist on the steering column collar and the thick-rimmed wheel eases out. The driving position is now perfect, the view a striking one. Ahead, a great gleaming bonnet, perforated with louvres, stretches imposingly towards the invisible snout. A rich smell of leather pervades the airy cabin, cream trimmed to match the deep-lustre walnut veneer. This is opulent Olde English decor at its best, yet there are concessions to modernity too. The mirror adjusts electrically, digital tell-tales are flashed on a panel between the speedo and tacho, refrigerated air streams from the facia outlets.

The big 5.9-litre Chrysler V8 burbles smoothly. It sounds lazy, classy; yet there's an underlying sense of muscle. It is not false. Pressure on the smooth throttle unleashes an urgent surge of acceleration. The roar is muted, discreet. A half-octave drop in the gruff waffle betrays an oily-smooth gearchange, then another. It's as good as ever, the Torqueflite auto transmission. The surge continues, not so much violently as strongly and fluidly.

At speed, the car runs arrow straight, rock stable, reassuringly settled. Its big 70-series 215 Dunlops are not edged off course by cambers and ridges. Nor do they thud or crash loudly over broken surfaces. The chassis imparts a feeling of immense integrity, of Benz-like solidity. Yes, and of craftsmanship too. And why not? The car was lovingly assembled by people steeped in the Jensen tradition, by people who evidently take a pride in their work. This is no "bitsa" Interceptor, nor even a cheap copy. Far from that, at £40,000! It's an honest reincarnation of the real thing, faithfully reproduced in broad outline, updated only in detail to make good a decade's lost development.

The Jensen Interceptor 4 is the brainchild of Ian Orford, owner and managing director of the newly formed Jensen Cars Ltd, until recently Jensen Parts and Service Ltd — one of two companies (the other was Jensen Special Products) formed by the Receiver when the original Jensen operation went into liquidation in 1976. Had the Labour government of the day put a higher priority on Jensen's jobs (2000 of them), the company might never have gone to the wall. Despite union representations, pleas for a £2 million rescue plan were rejected. Later on, under both Labour and Tory Governments, De Lorean got £77 million of taxpayers' money — misguidedly, as it turned out — to create employment in Northern Ireland. Little wonder there is a lingering feeling of bitterness in West Bromwich.

What went wrong? Let's recap, as a little history is relevant to this story. Although the fuel scare certainly threatened Jensen, as it did every manufacturer dependent on the sale of thirsty performance cars, it was not the successful Interceptor that brought the company to its knees so much as the Jensen-Healey sports car.

Jensen's American chief, Kjell Ovale, had seen the hybrid two-seater as spiritual successor, and mighty dollar earner, to the Austin-Healey he had once sold in the States. It might have been just that had chronic trouble with the car's under-developed Lotus engine not caused crippling warranty claims, which were Jensen's loss, not those of Lotus. For the odd car to need a replacement engine is one thing. For many to need several is quite another. By the time the crank-breathing problems had been resolved, it was too late. That engine sucked funds from the company almost as quickly as it could disgorge sump oil through its carbs.

Orford, who joined Jensen in 1968, was then parts manager of the service operation, across the way from the main factory, since sub-divided into industrial units. With Jensen's demise, he was appointed general manager of Parts and Service. Soon after, fresh business was generated through advertising.

"No-one knew we were here," he recalls. "After promotion, we were suddenly packed out with work." Later on, Orford raised the necessary funds to buy the company; since 1982 he has run his own show.

The mainline business was (and still is) to provide Jensen owners worldwide with a decent parts, maintenance and restoration service.

"With credit-card 'phone orders, we can offer same-day despatch," says Orford, who reckons to be able to provide practically any Jensen spare part. During our visit, the large workshop was crowded with customer cars, some undergoing ground-up rebuilds, others lesser repair and refurbishments.

"These two were sent over by owners in California." Orford points out a couple of pristine Interceptors, well preserved by the West Coast weather. "The current exchange rate makes it cheaper to ship them here than to have them done in the US."

Orford's 49-strong workforce, mostly ex-Jensen Motors people, underlines the size of the operation, justified by the large number of potential customers. At their peak, Jensen made 25 Interceptors a week. All told, they produced 6207 of these striking Touring-styled Anglo-Italo-American supercars, the bulk of them "greenhouse" saloons. The rarest variant was the Series 3 Coupé, of which only 54 were made. The coveted convertible, 267 — and the FF, 320 — are pretty scarce too. Before that, there were 494 CV8s (the chassis of which was the basis of the Kevin Beattie-inspired Interceptor) and 849 541s, not to mention 10,453 Jensen-Healeys. Plenty of after-sales work, then, for an enterprising service workshop staffed by men who once built the cars they now tend. Although body rust has taken its toll, the massive twin-tube chassis beneath is practically indestructible according to

Show car: the purposeful S4 (left) ready for the NEC. Older Jensens undergo renovation (above), while new ones are hand built (below) — a painstaking 3000 man-hours task

Orford. Most Interceptors, he believes, still survive, the bulk of them abroad.

By the mid-Seventies, Jensen had an exciting new-model programme in the pipeline, but no money to see it through. In the wings were a Healey update, a 3-litre gullwing and an Interceptor replacement, styled by Williams Towns. Later on, Towns was to incorporate some of the stillborn Interceptor's ideas into the current Lagonda — with less satisfactory results, judging by photos of its precursor. The prototype body, which still exists in private hands, was one of many cherished items Orford and the P and S team would have liked to acquire but couldn't afford at the liquidation auction in August 1976. The master jigs were broken up for scrap and what components Parts and Service *did* manage to salvage were exhausted ages ago.

Orford got the idea to build a "new" Jensen while he was still general manager. He was going to have it assembled secretly and then spring it on his bosses like a rabbit from a hat — "There, what do you think?" Actually, building a new car was not so very different from a ground-up restoration of an old Series 1, most of which (chassis excepted) was replaced with new parts. However, between conception and execution, Orford became his own boss and Jensen's new master.

Now he could do as he wished. Assembly went ahead not, as is widely believed, using old parts dusted off the shelf. There were none. Practically everything was brand new. The car was finished in mid '84 and exhibited last October at the NEC Show, where it attracted a lot of attention — perhaps more, then, as curio than as a serious commercial exercise, which is how Orford saw it.

Folletts of Cricklewood Broadway, who had handled Jensen sales before, took it seriously too. They got the sole distributorship for the first 10 cars — nearly half-a-million pounds' worth, most of them £46,000 convertibles, most of them still to be delivered. It takes 3000 man-hours spread over nine months to handbuild each one. Type Approval (for Britain only) caused inevitable delays. Not for Orford the kit-car ruse that would have side-stepped TA problems.

"A Jensen must be made in the grand manner or not at all," he asserts. Quite so. Fortunately, a video of the original Interceptor's successful crash test programme was accepted by the authorities, thus avoiding a costly repeat.

Orford believes that his Jensen 4 is a better car than the '76 Series 3 it effectively succeeds. "We know what the old car's weaknesses were, so it was easy to eliminate them during assembly." To look at, the metallic blue saloon you see here (the NEC show car) is indistinguishable to untrained eyes from the original. However, Orford reckons there are perhaps 500 detail changes, mostly as a result of replacing old components, that are no longer available, with new ones.

The biggest difference is under the bonnet. The first Series 4 was powered by an obsolete 7.2 litre detoxed engine like that used in the Series 3 cars and high-performance SP. Subsequent ones, including the car we drove, have Chrysler's current 5.9 litre V8, said to give a top speed of 140 mph. That's probably optimistic judging by our 1975 7.2 litre S3 test car which clocked 7.7 seconds for the 0-60 mph yardstick dash, and was rev limited to 129 mph. Earlier on, the 6.8 litre S1 clocked 7.3 seconds and 138 mph. Not that such figures are of any great consequence. The S4 is, I suspect, adequately fast for the sort of nostalgia-loving buyer it will attract. They're unlikely to be young tearaways.

The chassis is made by Jensen on a new jig they built themselves, and the sheet metal comes from Motor Panels of Coventry, who still hold the original dies. Orford has resisted the temptation to modernise the car too much — to equip it with spoilers and low-profile tyres, for instance — though he doesn't discount the possibility of aerodynamic aids on some future high-performance variant. Inside and under the skin there are many changes, among them those German Recaros which I rather liked, though they might be a tight fit for broad-beamed tycoons. The heating and ventilation, now regulated by little linear motors rather than vacuum servos, has also been improved. It would certainly pump out lots of cold air — too much, perhaps, judging by the vapour trails from the facia vents, and the icelets that formed inside them.

Anti-corrosion measures are more thorough (undersealing used to be an optional extra!) and the spring and damper rates have been changed to suit the lighter engine, weighing 180 lb less than the old ones. Suspension of 'Sixties vintage — coils and wishbones up front and a live, leaf-spring axle behind, additionally located by a Panhard rod — doesn't feel as crude as it looks on paper. There's a sort of steamroller quality to the ride, as well as respectable grip and composure. Ian Orford asserts that the car's 50/50 weight distribution gives it better balance than any of its nose-heavy predecessors. I wouldn't dispute that. What I didn't like was the feeble self-centring of the lifeless power steering. More castor, perhaps?

Orford have no plans to revive the 4wd Jensen, though Tony Rolt's FF Developments have expressed an interest in doing a modern S4 4×4, using hardware, including limited-slip viscous couplings, developed after the demise of the original all-drive Maxaret-braked Jensen FF. The future? Orford won't commit himself. Nor can he at this juncture. Time will tell whether Jensen Cars Ltd becomes a latter-day Morgan, trading on nostalgia with a contemporary classic.

ROLLS-ROYCE

ROLLS-ROYCE SILVER CLOUD 1955-1965

The development of the Silver Cloud is traced through some 33 articles drawn from the US, Australia, Ireland and the UK. They include 9 road tests, a consumer analysis, a used car test, plus articles on buying secondhand, touring, history and list full specifications. Models covered include SCI, SCII, SCIII, the Drophead and LWB and reference is made to all the 'S' Series Bentleys.

100 Large Pages.

ROLLS-ROYCE SILVER SHADOW 1965-1980

The 24 articles that lead us through the Silver Shadow story from its announcement in 1965 are drawn from the leading motoring journals of Australia, Ireland, the U.S.A. as well as Britain. They are made up of ten road tests, a comparison test vs. Mercedes Benz, new model introductions, factory visits plus advice on acquiring a used vehicle. Models covered include the MkI and MkII, plus the long wheel based cars and reference is also made to the Bentley T2s.

100 Large Pages.

These soft-bound volumes in the 'Brooklands Books' series consist of reprints of original road test reports and other stories that appeared in leading motoring journals during the periods concerned. Fully illustrated with photographs and cut-away drawings, the articles contain road impressions, performance figures, specifications, etc. NONE OF THE ARTICLES APPEARS IN MORE THAN ONE BOOK. Sources include Autocar, Autosport, Car, Cars & Car Conversions, Car & Driver, Car Craft, Classic & Sportscar, Modern Motor, Motor, Motor Manual, Motor Racing, Motor Sport, Practical Classics, Road Test, Road & Track, Sports Car Graphic, Sports Car World and Wheels.

From specialist booksellers or, in case of difficulty, direct from the distributors:
BROOKLANDS BOOK DISTRIBUTION, 'HOLMERISE', SEVEN HILLS ROAD, COBHAM, SURREY KT11 1ES, ENGLAND. Telephone: Cobham (09326) 5051
MOTORBOOKS INTERNATIONAL, OSCEOLA, WISCONSIN 54020, USA.
Telephone: 715 294 3345 & 800 826 6600

JENSEN

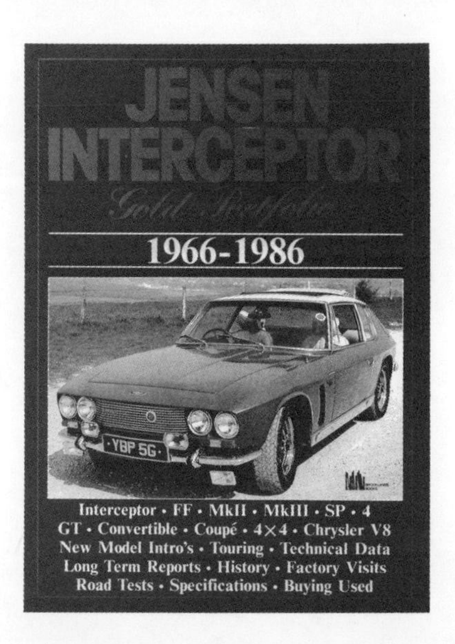

JENSEN INTERCEPTOR GOLD PROFILIO 1966-1986

A total of 53 articles trace the Interceptor story from its introduction in 1966 up to the new series 4. Other models covered are the 4x4 FF, the MkI, MkII, SP and Mk III in GT, Coupé and Convertible configuration. Included are over twenty road tests plus long term reports, details of factory visits, full specifications, a used car test, advice on buying a secondhand vehicle, also articles on touring and a full historical profile.
180 Large Pages.

JENSEN CARS 1946-1967

This book consists of twelve road tests, and 24 other articles which cover new model introductions, modifications, Jensen history, specifications and used car tests. Models dealt with are the 1946 4 litre – 8 cyc. convertible – the 1951 Interceptor Cabriolet – 541 – 541R – 541S – C-V8 5916cc – C-V8 6276cc – C-V8 FF – C-V8 MK 3 – 1965 Interceptor and convertible.
100 Large Pages

JENSEN-HEALEY 1972-1976

The twenty seven articles on the Jensen-Healey cover the model from its inception in early 1972 to it's end in 1976 and all models including the GT are fully reported on. There are 11 road tests, a long term report and test, factory visits, comparison tests against the Austin Healey 3000 and the Alfa Romeo 2000 SV, driving impressions, new model introductions and a comprehensive owner survey.
100 Large Pages.

These soft-bound volumes in the 'Brooklands Books' series consist of reprints of original road test reports and other stories that appeared in leading motoring journals during the periods concerned. Fully illustrated with photographs and cut-away drawings, the articles contain road impressions, performance figures, specifications, etc. NONE OF THE ARTICLES APPEARS IN MORE THAN ONE BOOK. Sources include Autocar, Autosport, Car, Cars & Car Conversions, Car & Driver, Car Craft, Classic & Sportscar, Modern Motor, Motor, Motor Manual, Motor Racing, Motor Sport, Practical Classics, Road Test, Road & Track, Sports Car Graphic, Sports Car World and Wheels.

From specialist booksellers or, in case of difficulty, direct from the distributors: BROOKLANDS BOOK DISTRIBUTION, 'HOLMERISE', SEVEN HILLS ROAD, COBHAM, SURREY KT11 1ES, ENGLAND. Telephone: Cobham (09326) 5051 MOTORBOOKS INTERNATIONAL, OSCEOLA, WISCONSIN 54020, USA. Telephone: 715 294 3345 & 800 826 6600